BUSINESS STUDIES

Fourth Edition

AS Level
AQA

Dave Hall-Rob Jones-Carlo Raffo-Alain Anderton

Edited by Ian Chambers and Dave Gray

CP

Acknowledgements

Dedication
To Elaine, Holly, Caitlin, Amanda Jane, Mandy, Sandra, Georgina, Rebecca, Jan, Natalie, Holly and Nicole for all their love and support in the writing of this book.

Cover design by Tim Button, illustration provided by Shutterstock.
Graphics by Caroline Waring-Collins, Kevin O'Brien and Anneli Jameson.
Photography by Andrew Allen and Dave Gray.
Typing by Annette Birchall
Proof reading by Sheila Evans-Pritchard, Sue Oliver and Heather Doyle.

The publishers would like to thank the following for the use of photographs and copyright material. Other copyright material is acknowledged at source.
Alvey & Towers p 152(c), Corel p 77, DigitalVision pp 149, 152(b), Manganese Bronze Holdings p 222, Philippe Hays/Rex Features p 117, Richard Burns/Reuters/Popperfoto p209, Shutterstock pp 2, 3, 5, 7, 8, 10, 12, 16, 20, 22, 23, 24, 26, 29, 31, 36, 39, 56, 59, 63, 66, 68, 73, 84, 89, 92, 93, 98, 103, 107, 113, 116, 135, 139, 141, 143, 146, 151, 156, 159, 160, 162, 176, 206, 218, 225, 227, 231, Stockbyte pp 61, 87, 101, 123, 129, 142, 152(t), 213.

Office for National Statistics material is Crown Copyright, reproduced here with the permission of Her Majesty's Stationery Office.

Every effort has been made to locate the copyright owners of material used in this book. Any errors and omissions brought to the notice of the publisher are regretted and will be credited in subsequent printings.

British Library Cataloguing in Publication Data
A catalogue record for this book is available from the British Library.

ISBN 978 1 4058 9220 9

Pearson Education
Edinburgh Gate, Harlow, Essex CM20 2JE
Contribution © Dave Hall, Rob Jones, Carlo Raffo, Alain Anderton, Ian Chambers, Dave Gray
1st edition 1993,
2nd edition 1999
3rd edition 2004
4th edition 2008.

Typesetting by Caroline Waring-Collins, Waring Collins Ltd. www.waringcollins.com
Printed and bound in Great Britain at Scotprint, Haddington.

Contents

Preface

Business Studies does not provide a step-by-step guide to how to be 'good at business'. There is no simple set of rules that can be applied at all times which will always be successful. However, by being analytical, rigorous and critical it may be possible to develop skills and approaches which can be useful, at certain times and in certain situations, when making business decisions. It is possible that different approaches will be used by different people in business and there may be disagreement as to which approach to take.

Business Studies is integrated and different areas of business are interdependent. There are links, for example, between:

- what is being produced and the funds available to pay for it (production and finance);
- the selling of the product and ethical considerations (marketing and ethics);
- the type of business and many aspects of its operation.

Being aware of these aspects of business will help us to understand how and why business decisions are made, and how they affect a variety of people, both within and outside the business. The aim of **Business Studies AS level AQA (Fourth Edition)** is to help those studying Business to understand business decisions and to be analytical, rigorous and critical in their business thinking. A number of features are included in the book which we believe will help this task.

Comprehensive course coverage The book contains material that covers the AQA AS level Business Studies specification. It is organised into short units, based on the AS level course:

- AS level 3.1 Unit 1 Planning and financing a business
- AS level 3.2 Unit 2 Managing a business

There is a development in the units contained in each section which reflects progress throughout the course. In addition, there are three units on analysing business data, study skills and assessment at the end.

Flexible unit structure The units in the book follow the AQA AS level specification. However, Business Studies teachers and lecturers often teach different aspects of the course in different orders. So, whilst there is a logical order to the book, following the specification, it has been written on the assumption that teachers or lecturers and students may also piece the units together to suit their own teaching and learning needs and the requirements.

Accessibility The book has been written in a clear and logical style which should make it accessible to all readers. Each unit is divided into short, easily manageable sections.

A workbook The text is interspersed with questions. The questions which appear as part of the units mostly refer to preceding information. Answers in most cases are expected to be relatively short. Questions are based on a variety of case studies, data, articles, photographs, etc. They should allow the student and teacher/lecturer to assess whether the information has been understood. Shorter 'knowledge' questions provide a means of revising each unit. A longer case study appears at the end of each unit. It draws on information contained in the whole unit and answers are expected to reflect this. The questions asked reflect the type which are set in examinations. They help students to develop knowledge, application, analysis and evaluation - the criteria used in examinations to assess responses.

Business Studies A level AQA Teachers' Guide (Fourth Edition) provides suggested answers and mark schemes for the activities and questions that appear in this book. Further case study materials can be downloaded free at www.alevelbus.co.uk

Use of business examples, case studies and data Modern technology has allowed much of the book to proceed from manuscript to book form in a very short period. This has meant that we have been able to use the latest statistics and business examples available. The materials used have been chosen to demonstrate appropriate arguments and theories. They should, therefore, allow students to answer questions which require knowledge of what has happened 'in recent years' or 'over the past decade', as well as questions which deal with current debates.

Skills At the end of the book there is a skills section. The unit on 'Analysing Business Data' allows students to learn and practice the presentation and analysis of business data. The last two units in the book provide guidance on how to study and the methods of assessment used in Business Studies. They are presented in the form of a manual and are designed to be used at various stages throughout the course.

Key terms Many units contain a key terms section. Each section defines new concepts, which appear in capitals in the text of the unit. Taken together, they provide a comprehensive dictionary of business terms.

Presentation Great care has been taken with how the book has been presented. It is hoped that the layout of the book, the use of colour and the use of diagrams will help learning.

Critque At appropriate points in the book there are sections which highlight that the accepted views and theories in an area of Business Studies are not without their critics. Students are encouraged to be aware that there are sometimes alternative opinions and to consider and evaluate alternatives.

Support MyBusSpace.co.uk is an online support resource for use by teachers and students using the book. It includes an online student book, an accurate graphing tool, questions from the student book that can be answered and marked online, links to key websites providing access to latest data and a regular updated news section.

We would like to thank the following for their efforts in the preparation of the three editions of this book: Richard Dunill, for keeping the debate sharp and yet accessible; Ingrid Hamer and Annette Birchall for their long hours of typing; Nigel Lewis; Michael J. Forshaw and Chris Sawyer for bringing a 'real' accountant's view to the book; all staff and students at Bolton Sixth Form College, King George V College, Loreto College, and Manchester University School of Education; Diane Wallace and Steve Robertson for working on the early development of the book; everyone who has proof read earlier editions.

Dave Hall   Rob Jones   Carlo Raffo   Alain Anderton
Ian Chambers   Dave Gray

Small businesses

There are over 60 million people living in the UK today. In 2006, according to official government statistics, there were 4.5 million private business enterprises. This means there was approximately one business for every 13 people in the country. Here are three more statistics about UK business.

- Three quarters of these businesses were small businesses where there was only one person working in the business.
- Almost all other businesses were also small businesses where there were between 2 and 49 people working in the business.
- There were only 33,000 businesses in the UK which were classified as medium or large where there were 50 or more people employed. This can be compared to the 4.27 million small businesses that existed.

A BUSINESS or ENTERPRISE is an organisation whose purpose is to produce goods and services. Of the 4.5 million UK businesses, some extract oil from the North Sea and some produce the carrots you eat on your plate. Others manufacture cars, provide taxi services or are local shops. The word 'business' comes from the word 'busy'. 'Enterprise' also comes from the idea that the organisation has a purpose, providing comes what they want to buy.

Entrepreneurs

Small businesses are run by ENTREPRENEURS. An entrepreneur is someone who:

- **owns** the business and has provided the money to start it up and possibly to expand it;
- **organises** the business, from hiring and buying inputs like raw materials and workers to producing the finished product for sale;
- has to be a **risk taker** because the business could perform poorly or even fail; the entrepreneur can lose money in a business as well as make it.

So the **role** of the entrepreneur is to provide at least some of the finance for the start up, run the business but take the risk of success or failure.

There are some famous entrepreneurs. Richard Branson, for example, has built a business empire from small beginnings publishing a magazine called 'Student' at the age of 15. Today he owns a string of companies from airlines to mobile phone companies to record companies. However, Richard Branson is exceptional. The more typical entrepreneur running one of the 4.27 million small businesses in 2006 is someone who is self employed.

- They are painters and decorators, plumbers or owners of a corner shop. They are farmers, architects or doctors.
- They may run their business full time. Or they may have an ordinary job working for someone else and run their

business on the side, part time.

- They are likely to have started the business themselves but in some industries like farming it is common for the entrepreneur to have inherited the business from parents. Also some entrepreneurs may buy existing mature businesses.
- They may take on a lot of risk in their business or the business may have little risk attached.
- Entrepreneurs may be at the cutting edge of innovation. Or they may be providing traditional services like decorators cutting wallpaper or owners of a hairdressing salon cutting hair.

Risks, rewards and opportunity cost

According to the CBI, approximately 200 000 new businesses are started each year. But 10 per cent of these have ceased trading within 12 months. One third have been closed within three years of starting to trade. Less than half are still trading after five years. Starting up a new business offers the potential for high rewards. Some entrepreneurs, like Richard Branson, have become rich through developing their own businesses. Starting a new business also offers a chance for many people to do something different. If nothing else, it means working for yourself rather than for someone else.

However, being an entrepreneur is risky. The downside of success is business failure. If the business fails, it may leave debts to be paid off. The entrepreneur might have borrowed money to start the business or to finance growth. Getting back into a normal job may also be difficult, especially if the entrepreneur left a well paid job in the first place. The risk of failure is a major motivator for entrepreneurs to carry on and made a success of their enterprise even when the going is tough.

Success and failure have an OPPORTUNITY COST. The opportunity cost of an activity is the benefits lost from the next best alternative. For example, an entrepreneur who has just started up a business might have left a job earning £40,000 a year. Part of the opportunity cost of setting up the business would then be the benefits gained from earning £40,000 a year. They would only be part of the opportunity cost because the job would probably have had other benefits too, including the satisfaction from doing the job. For a successful entrepreneur, the opportunity cost of being an entrepreneur is likely to be lower than the benefits of owning a business. For an unsuccessful entrepreneur, the opportunity cost is likely to be higher. This is why the unsuccessful entrepreneur is likely to close the business and move on to something else.

Characteristics of entrepreneurs

Starting your own business is very common. Hundreds of

Question 1.

John Baker set up his business after working for an airline. As security manager, he was given an office with a box full of foreign coins collected from the on-board duty free sales of products like whisky and cigarettes. He thought that his airline might not be the only organisation which had boxes full of assorted foreign coins. When he left the airline, he set up his own business, Coin Co International, to collect, sort and cash coins.

His most lucrative years were when the euro was introduced and replaced the currencies of 12 different countries. There were a lot of old currency coins which needed to be exchanged for new euros. In 2001, he collected and exchanged more than 3,500 tonnes of cash and employed 110 people with offices in Germany, Canada and Australia. But this bonanza didn't last and within a couple of years, he had cut his workforce in half and sales were tumbling.

Today he is exploring new lines of business. He has already won contracts to collect the drivers' cash boxes on London buses, sort the coins and then bank them. He would like to win contracts to empty parking meters.

Source: adapted from the *Financial Times*, 7.7.2007.

(a) An entrepreneur is someone who owns a business, runs it and takes risks. Explain why John Baker is an entrepreneur.
(b) Suggest what might have been the opportunity cost for John Baker of setting up his own business.
(c) John Baker is thinking of retiring and would like to pass the business on to his two children who already work in the business. (i) Think of ONE possible problem that could occur for the business if he did this. (ii) Compare TWO possible ways round this problem and suggest which would be the best solution to the problem.

thousands of small businesses are started each year. People give up their jobs to work for themselves or they start a new business alongside a normal full-time job. Not everyone is suited to becoming an entrepreneur either because they lack the skills needed or because they don't want to cope with the risk involved in setting up a business. Business Link, the government agency

which encourages business start ups, identifies seven characteristics of successful entrepreneurs.

Self-confidence Successful entrepreneurs are people who believe that they are going to succeed. They think they have a winning formula for their business. They can persuade other people, for example, to buy the product or help finance the business.

Self-determination Successful entrepreneurs are ones who think they can take control of events going on around them. They can influence those events and turn them into something which will benefit their business.

Being a self-starter Many people work best when being told what to do. But to be a successful entrepreneur, you have to be a self-starter. Entrepreneurs are able to work independently and can take decisions. They have their own ideas about how things should be done and they are able to develop those ideas.

Judgment The business environment is changing all the time. A successful entrepreneur is one who is taking in information and listening to advice. At the same time, they are able to see where the business might go in the future and what they want out of the business. This helps them to make judgements and decisions.

Commitment Many people think when starting up a business that it is going to be easier than working for someone else. All the evidence shows that entrepreneurs work longer hours than those with a normal job. Running your own business can sometimes be more stressful because of the risks that are always present. So successful entrepreneurs are ones who are committed to what they do.

Perseverance All businesses have successes and failures. There is always an element of risk that their business could perform poorly or even fail. Therefore, successful entrepreneurs have to show perseverance. They have to be able to get through the bad times and the setbacks.

Initiative Successful entrepreneurs are able to take the initiative in situations. They don't allow events to overwhelm them by doing nothing. They are able to change and be proactive.

Not every successful entrepreneur has all of these characteristics. Few entrepreneurs are strong in every area. But people who run their own businesses tend to show different characteristics from people who work for someone else.

Motives for becoming an entrepreneur

People start their own business for a variety of different reasons.

Financial reward When people work for someone else, there is a limit to what they can expect to get paid. But owning a business gives someone the opportunity to earn much more. In practice, entrepreneurs tend, if anything, to earn less per hour than those in a paid job. Entrepreneurs have to work longer hours to earn their money. But there is always the possibility that you will become the next Richard Branson.

Independence Entrepreneurs tend to enjoy being independent

and in control. They prefer to be in charge of their day to day work affairs rather than having an employer telling them what to do. In practice, this independence is limited. Work has to be done. Taxes have to be paid. Those financing the business, like a bank giving a loan, have to kept satisfied that the business is doing well. But those who own their own business, in general, do have more independence than employees working for someone else.

Building a business Entrepreneurs get satisfaction from having built their own business. Creating a successful business is a deeply satisfying experience and can help people to meet higher level goals in life.

Job satisfaction Many entrepreneurs start a business because they think they will get greater job satisfaction by working for themselves. It could be that they prefer working on their own. Or they might be able to change the sort of work they do compared to a normal job.

The product Many entrepreneurs have an interest in what they sell. They are passionate about brewing beer or selling goth clothes or providing high quality care for the elderly.

Different entrepreneurs are motivated by different factors. Some are highly motivated by financial rewards. Others are highly motivated by the job satisfaction they get from running their own business. Equally for some, also, running a business is little different from working for someone else.

Government support for enterprise and entrepreneurs

The government promotes the creation of small businesses. It knows that small businesses are vital to the success of the economy. Nearly half of all jobs in the private sector are in small businesses and they produce one third of private sector output. Small businesses are essential for the future success of the economy because many of tomorrow's large businesses will come from today's small businesses. They are also linked to new ideas and new products. They provide an essential competitive dynamism in the economy.

To help new small businesses, the government has set up **Business Link**. Controlled by Regional Development Agencies, different areas of the country have their own Business Link organisation. They provide advice and support to business start-ups and to existing small businesses. They aim to provide a single point of contact on a wide variety of issues from finance and sales to tax and employment.

More generally, the government offers grants and subsidised services through a variety of schemes. For example, new start-ups might be eligible for grants if the entrepreneur is unemployed, or setting up in a rural area. More support is likely to be available in areas where unemployment is relatively high or incomes below the national average.

Question 2.

Joshua Roberts has worked for three years as the sales representative for a small print company. It employs ten people and serves the needs of local businesses in a market town and the surrounding rural areas. It prints everything from brochures and posters to invitations, specifications and flyers.

Joshua is ambitious and would like to set up his own business so that he can earn substantially more money. Over the past three years, he has been disappointed with his earnings. He has consistently failed to meet sales targets set for him by the company and so his bonuses have been negligible. In the next market town, there is no print company. By setting up there, he hopes to be able to carve out a profitable market niche.

Joshua's boss couldn't deny that he has enormous self-confidence. He is always talking about what sales he will achieve over the next few weeks and months. When he doesn't win sales contracts, he always picks himself up and gets on with the next job. In his appraisals, however, his boss is constantly pointing out that his timekeeping could improve. He can be late into the office and almost never in the office at closing time. Joshua always says he is seeing a client at that time. A quick check in his diary shows he never makes appointments to see clients outside of office hours. Joshua's boss, Natalie, thinks he tends to only see those clients who he is fairly certain will give him work. Once or twice, she has pointed out that Joshua is not pursuing sufficiently large contracts. He doesn't seem to listen, though, to this constructive criticism.

(a) Do you think Joshua would be successful if he set up his own business? In your answer, consider whether Joshua has the right characteristics to be an entrepreneur.

KEYTERMS

Business or enterprise – an organisation whose principal economic purpose is to produce goods and services.

Entrepreneur – an individual who, typically, sets up and runs a business and takes the risks associated with this.

Opportunity cost – the cost of a decision as measured by the benefits foregone of the next best alternative.

KNOWLEDGE

1. How many businesses are there in the UK?
2. What is the role of an entrepreneur?
3. Why is profit and risk important for a business?
4. What might be the opportunity cost for you of studying Business Studies?
5. Outline two characteristics of successful entrepreneurs.
6. What might motivate someone thinking of starting up their own business?
7. What support does government give to entrepreneurs?

Case Study: Annabel Karmel Group

Annabel Karmel is a highly successful entrepreneur. She started her working life as a professional harpist, performing in concerts, appearing on television and recording CDs. She wrote her first book after the death of her first child from a viral infection. Her second child was not eating well and she decided to write a cookery book for feeding children. 'I didn't know anything about it,' said Annabel Karmel.' I didn't even know how to type. But I thought it would be good therapy.' Two and half years later, the book was finished and she sent it to 15 publishers who all turned it down. Then a friend took it to Europe's biggest book fair in Frankfurt and she finally found a publisher to take it on. The book, The Complete Baby and Toddler Meal Planner, has since sold more than 2 million copies. 'You do need luck', she said. 'But you should never give up.' Since then, she has written another 14 books about feeding children.

After her success, she was approached by Boots, the high street chemist chain, to design a range of cookery equipment which could be used to prepare food for children. When the range was a commercial success, this set her thinking about developing a range of ready-prepared meals. 'I was approached by a lot of very large companies to work with them and I think I lost time by talking to them. Eventually I realised that, to begin with, it would be better to do it by myself because I wanted to be in control of what I was doing.'

In 2007, her new range was launched after an investment of £350,000. It is now stocked by J Sainsbury and Ocado. Total sales from her books, meals and cooking equipment are expected to be £14 million in 2008.

'If you have a vision, you have to trust yourself. Don't let other people put you off. And don't be worried about doing something by yourself', said Annabel. 'I was worried about doing a food range by myself. I though I had to have a big company behind me, but actually it has been okay doing it by myself and very rewarding. Sometimes you

think that everyone else is an expert and you are not, but if you have a passion, then go with it.' Success has come partly by working long hours. 'I regularly stay up until 3 a.m. just to finish something off. I don't sleep much and I usually work the whole weekend. I gave up my social life for several years.'

Source: adapted from *The Sunday Times*, 20.5.2007.

(a) 'Annabel Karmel is a highly successful entrepreneur.' Explain, using Annabel Karmel as an example, what is meant by an 'entrepreneur'. (15 marks)

(b) What might have been the opportunity cost for Annabel Karmel of writing her first book? (5 marks)

(b) Analyse what characteristics are likely to be make an entrepreneur successful. In your answer, use Annabel Karmel as an example. (15 marks)

(c) To what extent do you think Annabel Karmel has been motivated by the financial rewards of running her own business? (15 marks)

Finding an initial idea

Each year, hundreds of thousands of people set themselves up in business. Instead of working for someone else, they become the owner. Or, they move from owning one business to owning another business. If they are successful, they may start to own and set up a string of businesses. But how do most would-be **entrepreneurs**, (those who risk their own capital in setting up and running a business) find a business idea? There are a number of ways.

Business experience For most people starting a small business, the business idea comes from their existing job. A plumber might work for a plumbing company and decides to set up on her own. A marketing consultant working for an advertising agency sets up his own marketing agency. This is likely to be the most risk free way of setting up a business because the would-be entrepreneur already has knowledge of the market.

Personal experience Some people draw on their personal experience outside of work to find a business idea. Some turn a hobby into a job. An amateur cyclist might buy a cycle shop. A keen gardener might set up a nursery. Some use their customer experience to spot a gap in the market. A mother might find it difficult to find a baby product and so sets up up a business to provide it.

Skills Some entrepreneurs draw on their broad skills base to start a business. A person with an administration job might judge that they have good 'people skills' and decide to set up a business in selling. A plumber might judge that in his area electricians can charge more for their work. So he gets training as an electrician and set himself up as a self employed electrician.

Lifestyle choices Some business areas attract people who want to make a lifestyle change. They might want to move to the country and invest in a small holding. They might always have wanted to run a pub and so buy a pub. Or they might be retiring from a full-time job but still want to carry on working on their own. So they invest in a seasonal Bed and Breakfast (B&B) business.

Identifying a product or market niche

For most entrepreneurs, identifying a broad business idea is relatively easy. But it becomes much more difficult to turn a vague idea into a practical reality. What will be the exact product to be made? What will be the market niche to be occupied?

For example, a painter and decorator setting up on his own may have to decide whether to go mainly for domestic work or for contract work with companies. Will he specialise in indoor work or outdoor work? Someone setting up in the B&B business has to decide whether to go upmarket or downmarket. Do they want to convert their own home into a B&B or will they buy new premises? Will the B&B be aimed mainly at holiday makers or people on business?

The process of identifying an exact product or market niche can take a long time. A process might be used where a lot of different ideas are discussed. Then ones which are worth exploring can be selected and worked on further. Sometimes, would-be entrepreneurs start out with an initial idea. As they explore it further, they realise it won't work but something very similar might be better. A whole range of options might be explored as each idea is considered, rejected but opens up a further idea.

Question 1.

Claire Brynteson is an entrepreneur who found the right idea. She was working in a high powered job in the City of London. She noticed that there were plenty of people around her earning very large salaries but worked such long hours that they didn't have the time to organise the ordinary, everyday things in life. So she founded Buy Time, a lifestyle management service for businesses and individuals.

The business gives clients access to a personal assistant. The personal assistant will do everything from organising a parking permit, to getting broadband connected, to buying flowers for a partner, to getting a leaking tap fixed to organising a foreign holiday. The current 300 customers of Buy Time are either individuals or businesses which buy the service on behalf of their top employees. It employs 12 staff.

Claire Brynteson said: 'I could see that people round me were suffering from a lack of time and really needed this service. With women increasingly working the same hours as men, there was nobody at home to take care of anything.'

Source: adapted from *The Sunday Times*, 20.7.2007.

(a) How did Claire Brynteson get the idea for her business?
(b) Business Link sets out a number of criteria for checking against a possible business idea (see top of page 6). How well does Claire Brynteson's idea do when compared to this list of criteria?

Business Link, the government organisation set up to help small businesses, suggests that each business idea needs to be checked out against a number of criteria.

- What can the would-be entrepreneur bring to the business in terms of relevant experience and expertise?
- Is there a market for the product? Does it serve a need and will customers will pay for it?
- How big is the market and how can it be reached?
- What will be the main competitors in the market?
- Is there something special about the idea? Or will it be a similar product to what is already in the market place?
- How will the business be funded?
- What are the risks involved and what can go wrong?

Franchises

Starting up your own business carries a lot of risk. Most new start-ups have ceased to exist after five years of trading. One way of possibly reducing this risk is to buy a FRANCHISE. The **franchisor** is a company which owns the franchise. It has a track record of running a successful business operation. It allows another business, the **franchisee**, to use its business ideas and methods in return for a variety of fees. In the UK, there are a large number of franchise operations including Dairy Crest, Domino's Pizza, Dyno-Rod, McDonald's, Subway and Tumble Tots.

The franchisor provides a variety of services to its franchisees.

- Its gives the franchisee a licence to make a product which is already tried and tested in the market place. This could be a physical product but is far more likely to be a service.
- The franchisor provides a recognised brand name which customers should recognise and trust. This helps generate sales from the moment the franchise starts trading.
- The franchisor will provide a start-up package. This will include help and advice about setting up the business. The franchisor might provide the equipment to start the business. It might help find a bank which will lend money. It will provide training for the new franchisee.
- Many franchises provide materials to use to make the product. A company like McDonald's, for examples, sells food ingredients to its franchisees. If the franchisor doesn't directly sell to the franchisee, it might organise bulk-buy deals with suppliers to cut costs for all its franchise operation.
- It is likely to provide marketing support. For example, it might have national advertising campaigns. It may provide marketing materials like posters to place in business premises or leaflets to circulate to customers.
- There should be ongoing training. This will be linked to issues such as maintaining standards, sales and new products.
- There is likely to be a range of business services available at competitive prices. For example, the franchisor might negotiate good deals on business insurance or vehicle leasing with suppliers.
- Many franchises operate exclusive area contracts. This is where one franchisee is guaranteed that no franchise deal will be signed with another franchisee to operate in a particular geographical area. This prevents competition between franchisees and so helps sales.
- Over time, the brand should be developed by the franchisor. For example, new products should be developed to appeal to customers.

In return for these services, the franchisee has to pay a variety of fees.

- There will be an initial start-up fee. Part of this will cover the costs of the franchisor in giving advice or perhaps providing equipment. Part of it will be a payment to use the franchise name.
- Most franchisors charge a percentage of sales for ongoing management services and the ongoing right to use the brand name.
- Franchisors will also make profit on the supplies they sell directly to their franchisors.
- There may also be one-off fees charged for management services such as training.

The benefits and costs for franchisors and franchisees

There are a variety of benefits and costs to both franchisors and franchisees of the franchise model.

Benefits to franchisees For the franchisee, franchising could be a relatively safe way to start a business. Partly this is because the franchisor has vetted potential franchisees and rejected applications from individuals it thinks will fail. Partly this is because the franchise already has a successful business formula which has succeeded in the past. So the new franchisee only has to copy the performance of others. The cost of setting up the franchise is predictable. Too many start-ups have grossly over-optimistic forecasts of how little they can spend to get the business up and running on a sound financial footing. The franchisor also provides ongoing support and will provide help to franchisees which are underperforming.

Costs to franchisees Franchisees have to pay a variety of fees to the franchisor. These costs vary from franchise to franchise but franchisees are likely to lose at least 10 per cent of their revenues. This can have a significant impact on profit margins. Franchisees are locked into contracts. If they fail to keep to the contract, they can lose the franchise and as a result lose most, if not all, of their investment in the business. In some cases, contracts allow franchisors to take away a franchise without any compensation simply because it is in their commercial interests to do so.

Benefits to franchisors Many businesses are highly successful. But they find it difficult to expand because of finance and control. Finance is a problem because banks are not always prepared to lend for growth. Even if they do, it might be too little money to take the business in the right direction. Control is a problem because employees don't necessarily have the same motivation for success as the entrepreneur who founded the business. A franchise model is one way of getting round these problems. Finance for growth comes from franchisees who pay most of the cost of expanding the business. Franchisees also have the motivation to succeed. The franchisor is harnessing the skills and enthusiasm of another entrepreneur, the franchisee. Another benefit to the franchisor is that it reduces risks from failure. If the franchise proves a failure, much of the cost is borne by the franchisee rather than the franchisor.

Costs to franchisors In successful franchises, some of the profit goes to the franchisee. The franchisor, therefore, might have been better off with a traditional business expansion model rather than turning the business into a franchise operation. Running a franchise can increase costs because franchisees have to be supported in various ways. Franchisees can also be a problem. Some franchisees will fail to work hard enough or show sufficient business skills. Their franchises will underperform or fail and this will hit the profits of the franchisor. Other franchisees will not operate according to the franchise formula. For example, if it is a fast food franchise, some franchisees might cut costs by not cleaning the premises sufficiently and not keep the furniture and decor in good condition. This could tarnish the brand image of the whole chain of franchises.

Franchising associations claim that franchising is a much safer business model for an entrepreneur than opening their own business. They claim the failure rate for franchisees is much lower than for other business start-ups. Some academic research, however, suggests that franchisees, if anything, are more likely to fail than if they set up independently. This is mainly because the cost base of franchisees is higher since they have to pay a percentage of their sales to the franchisor. Successful franchises are ones where being a franchisee generates substantially more sales than if the business were independent.

Trademarks, copyright and patents

Every business has a name which is crucial to its business success. If another business starts using your business name to sell the same goods or services in the same markets, then you may be able to sue them and stop them using your business name. Businesses can further protect their name, or the names of their products, by registering them as a TRADE MARK. In the UK, this is done by registering them with the Intellectual Property Office (UK-IPO). Other businesses are then not allowed in law to use that trademark name. Trade mark protection can also be applied to signs, symbols, logos, words, sounds or music.

Business start-ups should also think about whether they want an Internet domain name (i.e. a web address). Unique domain names can be registered so that no one else can use that address.

For example, no one can use www.tesco.com because it has already been registered by Tesco, the supermarket chain. Common popular names are likely to have been taken already. So a start-up business might have to use a less obvious name for their web address.

A small number of business start-ups are linked to selling a new, innovative product which can be protected through copyright and patents. COPYRIGHT is given for original artistic works such as music, films, photographs, plays and books. PATENTS are given for inventions. Both copyrights and patents have to be registered with the Intellectual Property Office.

Trademarks, copyrights and patents aren't just there to

KEYTERMS

Copyright – legal ownership of material such as books, music and films which prevents these being copied by others.

Franchise – an agreement where a business (the franchisor) sells the rights to other businesses (the francisees) allowing them to sell their products or use the company name.

Patents – right of ownership of an invention or process granted by government for a fixed period of time to the individual or business which registers the original invention or process.

Trade mark – signs, symbols, logos, words, sounds or music that distinguish the products and services of one business from those of competitors.

protect a business from others copying their ideas. They can be used to generate income by **licensing** them to other businesses.

KNOWLEDGE

1. How might would-be entrepreneurs find a business idea?
2. What criteria might an entrepreneur use to judge whether an idea can be turned into a successful business?
3. Explain what a franchisee and a franchisor might gain from a franchising arrangement.
4. Explain what a franchisee and a franchisor might lose from a franchising arrangement.
5. What is the difference between a trade mark, copyright and a patent?

These other businesses then pay **royalties** to copy the idea legally. Businesses can also generate income from their intellectual property by selling it. So the rights to a song, for example, can be sold by one record company to another record company. The patent on a new drug can be sold by one pharmaceutical company to another pharmaceutical company.

Case Study: Business ideas

The Rolla Washa

A Wolverhampton firm, Washa Ltd, has developed a revolutionary new device for cleaning paint rollers. The Rolla Washa is 'designed to save users time, effort and water' according to Brett Smart, Wash's managing director. Rollers, rather than paint brushes, are used by painters and decorators for walls and ceilings. But rollers take time to clean properly and normal cleaning takes a lot of water. The Rolla Washa is a plastic container into which rollers are put for cleaning. Water mains pressure cleans dirty rollers quickly and easily. Far less water is used making it environmentally friendly.

The Rolla Wash is a now it its final stage of development and a patent has been applied for. It is currently on trial with two of Europe's leading paint manufacturers for their endorsement.

Business advisors have put a potential value on Washa Ltd of £2.5 million assuming the invention takes off.

Source: adapted from the *Express & Star*, 18.6.2007.

Red Star Natural Liquid Soaps

A Staffordshire couple, who started their business in their kitchen, are looking to sell their products globally. After two years of formulating and selling handmade soap in their spare time, Tim and Elaine Woodley launched their business product in 2004. Red Star soaps are made using cruelty and animal product free soaps. 'We're determined to make soaps from scratch using the original, constituent natural ingredients that contain no animal products and involve no animal testing,' said Tim.

The Red Star range includes liquid soap products for people, dogs and most recently, horses. 'The jewel in our crown is the new Red Star Pony Polish,' said Tim. 'It's the only horse shampoo on the market that's both natural and free from animal products and we worked with horse owners around the country to make sure it's right.'

The soaps are mainly sold online direct to customers, but the business is steadily building a distributor network both in the UK and overseas with products regularly exported to Europe and the Americas. They are even talking to the camel racing community in Arabic countries to develop a specialist shampoo for camels.

Business Link West Midlands, the government agency, have helped Tim and Elaine to develop their business model. It has ensured that steps were taken to protect intellectual property, including the business name and logo.

Source: adapted from the *Express & Star*, 18.6.2007.

(a) What is distinctive about the products described in the data which might make them stand out against competing products? (5 marks)

(b) Explain how the developers of each idea might have checked that their innovate product could be turned into a successful business. (10 marks)

(c) What is meant by 'intellectual property'? (10 marks)

(d) To what extent was it important for both businesses to protect their intellectual property? (15 marks)

3 Transforming resources

Inputs

From an economic viewpoint, the function of a business is to transform inputs into outputs. There are a variety of inputs to the production process which a business might use.

- There are raw materials such as oil and gas.
- They might use semi-manufactured and finished manufactured goods. For example, a car manufacturer might use steel, a semi-manufactured product, to make body panels. It might use pencils and pens, a manufactured good, in its offices.
- Capital equipment such as machines and buildings are likely to be part of the production process.
- Workers are an essential input.

Sometimes, inputs are classified into four different FACTORS OF PRODUCTION. These are **land** (all raw materials including land itself), **labour** (workers), **capital** (capital equipment) and **entrepreneurship**. Entrepreneurs are individuals who combine the other factors of production to create outputs.

Outputs

Outputs are what is produced by a business. Outputs might be **goods**, such as coal or cars, or **services** such as haircuts, holidays or management consultancy. In the private sector of the economy, outputs are sold by businesses either to other businesses or to consumers. For example, a gas company might sell gas to a hotel chain. It might also sell gas to a domestic consumer. A machine manufacturer might sell lathes to a car manufacturer. A car manufacturer might sell cars to consumers.

Sometimes the economy is split up into three sectors to show what types of good or service is produced.

The primary sector In the primary sector, raw materials are produced, grown or extracted. These include fuels such as coal or crude oil, and forestry, agriculture and fishing.

The secondary or manufacturing sector Manufactured goods are produced in the secondary sector of the economy. This includes all goods such as processed food, steel, car components, textiles and aeroplanes.

The tertiary or service sector The tertiary sector is where services are produced.

In an advanced economy like the UK, the primary sector is relatively small. It accounts for only a few per cent both of total output and total employment. The secondary sector accounts for less than 20 per cent of output and employment. Around 80 per cent of output and employment is accounted for by the tertiary or service sector. So most businesses make services rather than goods and most workers are employed in the tertiary sector.

In less advanced economies, the primary and secondary sectors are more important. In very poor countries, up to 50 per cent of the workforce can still be employed in agriculture. In rapidly developing countries like China, the manufacturing sector is growing fast at the expense of agriculture. But over time, it will start to shrink again as a percentage of the total as

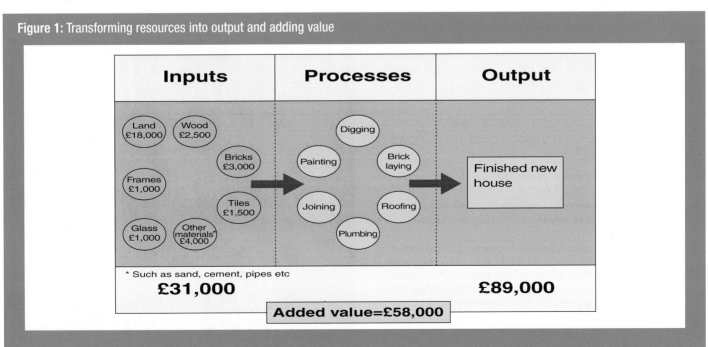

Figure 1: Transforming resources into output and adding value

Inputs	Processes	Output
Land £18,000; Wood £2,500; Bricks £3,000; Frames £1,000; Tiles £1,500; Glass £1,000; Other materials* £4,000	Digging; Painting; Brick laying; Joining; Roofing; Plumbing	Finished new house

* Such as sand, cement, pipes etc

£31,000   **£89,000**

Added value=£58,000

services become more important.

Adding value

Businesses **add value** as goods and services pass down the **chain of production**. Take the example of a haircut.

The chain of production for a haircut can stretch right back to a gas field in the North Sea where natural gas is being extracted by a company. It is then sold to a gas distributor company. This pays for the gas to pass through the pipelines owned by another company to arrive at the hairdressing salon. Here it is used to heat the premises.

The haidressing salon adds value by selling its services for more than the combined total of the inputs its pays from other businesses. If it sold £10,000 worth of hair cuts and heating bills of £1,000 were its only paid input, then the added value of the salon would be £9,000. This £9,000 will have been used mainly to pay wages and salaries for staff but it will also include the taxes the business has to pay as well as profit for the owners.

Sales and value added can be very different. The value of sales of the supermarket chain, Tesco, in 2007, was over

£50 billion. But its value added was only a fraction of this because most of the £50 billion was used to pay other businesses for all the items sold on Tesco shelves.

KNOWLEDGE

1. What are the four factors of production?
2. Explain the difference between inputs to and outputs from a business.
3. What are the differences between the primary, secondary and tertiary sectors of the economy?
4. How does a business add value?

Case Study: Recycling

The two friends who set up Recycled UK, Paul Green and Paul Cotton, have seen it expand beyond their wildest dreams in just 12 months. First year turnover rocketed past £250,000, which was 20 per cent up on expectations.

The company specialises in waste management and the recycling of plastic. With the cost of taking waste to landfill sites going up and new government regulations and targets coming in, recycling is big business today. The company collects plastic waste from companies and local authorities in its own collection vehicles. It brings them back to its large storage yard in Cosely in the Black Country. The plastic is processed using a state-of-the-art granulating system which cost the company £100,000. 'All plastics are recyclable and we can handle scrap mouldings, scrap packing, post industrial rejects, components, video cassettes, bottles, shrink wrap and even crisp wrappers,' said Paul Green. 'We are collecting from all sorts of industries, including automotive, aerospace and food processing.'

The company currently employs six workers but plans to take on four more staff within the next six months as demand for its services increases.

Source: adapted from the *Express & Star*, 14.5.2007.

(a) What inputs are being used by Recycled UK? In your answer, classify these inputs into the four factors of production. (10 marks)
(b) 'Recycled UK provides a service to businesses because it removes their plastic waste for them. It is also produces a good because it manufactures plastic pellets which can be reused to make new plastic products.' Explain, using the example of Recycled UK, the difference between a good and a service. (8 marks)
(c) How does Recycled UK add value in the chain of production? (7 marks)

(d) Recycled UK has expanded fast in its first twelve months of operation. Evaluate the factors which will determine whether it continues to grow and be successful in the future.

4 Business plans

Why write a business plan?

Research shows that start-up businesses which have prepared a BUSINESS PLAN are more likely to survive than ones which have not. The business plan is a plan of how the business will develop over a period of time, like one or two years. Writing a business plan is important for a potential start-up business for three main reasons.

- Writing the plan forces the would-be entrepreneur to look at every key aspect of the future business. It is easy to concentrate on some aspects of running a business, like the product to be sold or its location. Most start-ups have some idea about what might give the business a **competitive advantage** against other businesses But other aspects are often not thought out well, such as finance or tax. The business plan forces the entrepreneur to consider every aspect equally.
- If the business is to borrow money from a bank, it will expect there to be a business plan. It uses the business plan to judge whether the business is likely to be creditworthy.
- The plan is useful once the business has started to trade. The actual operation of the business can be compared to the forecasts contained in the plans. This will highlight problems that are occurring. The business owner can then take steps to overcome the problem.

The contents of a business plan

The outline of a business plan can be obtained from any of the major banks in leaflets they produce on starting up a business. They give a very detailed list of points which must be addressed in the plan. These include the following.

An executive summary – this is an overview of the business start-up. It describes briefly the business opportunity to be exploited, the marketing and sales strategy, operations and then finance. According to the government organisation, Business Link, many lenders and investors make judgements about the business on this section alone.

The business and its objectives – the name of the business, its address, its legal structure and is aims and objectives.

The business opportunity – a description of the product or range of products to be made, the quantity to be sold and the estimated price;

The market – the size of the potential market and a description of the potential customers, the nature of the competition, marketing priorities, all backed up with evidence from market research.

Personnel – who will run the business, how many employees if any there will be, the skills, qualifications and experience of those in the business.

Buying and production – where the business will buy its supplies, production methods to be used, the cost of production.

Premises and equipment – the premises to be used, equipment which needs to be obtained and financed.

Financial forecasts – a variety of financial forecasts need to be included. They include a **sales forecast** showing how the value of sales will change over time; a **cash flow forecast** which shows how money will move into and out of the business on a week to week or month to month basis; a **profit and loss forecast**, showing when the business might move from making a loss to making a profit and how big a profit; and a **break-even analysis**, showing at what level of sales the business will make

---

Question 1.

Robert Crampton is a journalist who had a great idea for a business. He called it the Bobstacle: a soft play area, a cross between an obstacle course and an assault course with slides, trapezes and nets. It would aimed not just at children but at teenagers and adults too.

He took his idea to the television cult show, Dragons' Den. On this show, five multimillionaires who have already successfully run their own businesses, act as a panel. Would-be entrepreneurs have to 'pitch' their ideas. If any one of the multimillionaires likes the idea, then they say they are prepared to put their own money into the start-up and help it become established.

The panel of multimillionaires quickly punched huge holes in Robert Crampton's business plan. Robert hadn't thought through his future sales or costs. He found it difficult to state accurately how any money put into the business at the start would be spent. He hadn't thought through how many staff he would need, let alone what qualities he would be looked for in them. He also hadn't thought through what would be his competitive advantage.

By the end of the interview, Robert was thinking to himself that he still liked the idea of the Bobstacle. The adventure and the risk were attractive as would be the profits. But he wouldn't want to work there himself. At that point, he gave up on any dream of becoming an entrepreneur. Perhaps a career in journalism was attractive after all.

Source: with information from *The Times*, 3.2.2007.

(a) What is the advantage for a would-be entrepreneur, like Robert Crampton, to write a business plan? Use the passage to help you write your answer.

(b) Is it a waste of time of time to write a business plan when afterwards you decide not to go ahead with the business idea?

Question 2.

Tahira Hussein wants to open her own beauty salon which would offer a range of beauty treatments. She is in the process of drawing up a business plan and has just written down her objectives. These are as follows.

Objectives

1. By the third month of opening, to have sales of £25 000 per month offering 20 treatments per day.
2. By the sixth month of opening, to have sales of £40 000 per month offering 32 treatments per day.
3. By the end of 12 months, to have sales of £50 000 per month offering 40 treatments per day.
4. At the end of 12 months, to have 80 per cent of clients as repeat clients and 20 per cent as new clients.
5. By the end of 12 months, to be making a profit before tax of £1 000 per month.
6. By the end of 3 years to be in a position to open a second beauty salon.

(a) List six other items that might be found in a business plan apart from objectives.
(b) Suggest why it might be important to list business objectives in a business plan for a start-up company.

zero profits or losses.

Finance – where the finance to start-up and run the business will come from, including savings of owners and borrowing.

Sources of information and guidance

Entrepreneurs setting up a business can turn to a wide variety of sources of help.

Friends, family and work colleagues Initially, would-be entrepreneurs are likely to talk about their ideas to friends, family and work colleagues. They may just provide common sense advice. But some could have specialist business knowledge. They might have started up a business themselves in the past. They might be running a successful business now. Networking, talking to a wide variety of individuals or organisations, will generate ideas and identify obstacles to be overcome.

Bank managers All the major banks offer banking services to start-up businesses including loans. They have specialist teams of advisors who assess applications for loans from those wanting to start a new business. They will give advice about preparing a business plan and identify strengths and weaknesses in the plan. Their aim is to lend to a start-up which will be strong enough financially to repay any loans taken out.

Accountants There are many accountancy firms which specialise in preparing the accounts for small and medium sized businesses. They will sell advice to start-up businesses. They will be particularly good at providing advice on the finance side of the business.

Small business advisors Would-be entrepreneurs can buy advice from a wide range of small business advisors. They will help with everything from writing a business plan, to market research to recruiting workers.

Business Link The government provides help and advice to small businesses through Business Link. Each region in the UK has its own Business Link organisation. They provide a wide range of written resources, including a website. They also have business advisors who will provide help on a one-to-one basis. They run seminars and courses for would-be entrepreneurs. They also provide advice as the business grows. For the most part, these services are free.

Local Enterprise Agencies These are non-for-profit companies whose primary objective is to help new and growing businesses. Like Business Link, they provide a wide variety of resources and help to business start-ups including consultancy and training. Their funds come mainly from local authorities and other bodies.

The Prince's Trust and Shell LiveWIRE The Prince's Trust and Shell LiveWIRE are two organisations which provide help to young people starting up in business. They will not only provide advice, but they will also give limited financial support for new businesses.

KEY TERMS

Business plan – a plan for the development of a business, giving details such as the products to be made and sold and forecasts such as costs and cash flow.

KNOWLEDGE

1. 'Writing a business plan helps identify the problems with a business idea.' Explain what this means.
2. What might be contained in the part of a business plan which deals with personnel for a start-up (a) restaurant; (b) local grocery store; (c) biological research company?
3. Where could a would-be entrepreneur find advice in writing a business plan which (a) would be free of charge; (b) would have to be paid for.

Case Study: AKC Home Support

Darren Jones launched his care business, AKC Home Support Services, in 1991 with his wife Sharron. One of the first things they did was to write a business plan. But they saw it more as just one more form to fill in. 'When we started the firm, I knew we needed a business plan but saw it more as a document for everyone else than something to help us.'

They got help to write the business plan from their local enterprise centre. 'We looked at examples from other businesses and a template from the bank. We mixed and matched bits from these sources because not everything applied to us. For example, because we were going into a new market, we couldn't write about our competitors but needed a lot of information about the market for care services.'

The business plan contained their financial and strategic goals - what they wanted to achieve with the business. This helped them early on when they were offered work in another county. Looking at their business plan, they realised that they could get into short-term financial difficulties if they took on too much work. This was because they would have to pay out costs like wages months before they themselves might get paid by the client.

They regularly update their business plan. This helped them four years ago when they wanted a loan from the bank to buy a residential unit care home. Carefully working out how the loan could be repaid from the extra revenues coming into the business impressed the bank.

Their business plans also helped them get support from Shell LiveWIRE. They were awarded prizes twice which brought into both publicity for the business and extra money. Their business plan essential because you have to have a business plan to enter the competition.

Their advice when drawing up a business plan is to get as much help and advice as possible. 'Show the plan to an independent third party - such as friends or family who have run their own businesses - who will be able to point out if anything is missing. It's much better to make mistakes on a practice run than when it really matters.'

Source: adapted from www.businesslink.gov.uk.

(a) Explain, using AKC Home Support Services as an example, what might be contained in a business plan. (15 marks)
(b) How might outside organisations help a would-be entrepreneur write a business plan? (10 marks)
(c) 'Writing a business plan is a waste of time. You are better off starting your business as quickly as possible.' To what extent do you think this is correct? Use AKC Home Support Services as an example in your discussion. (15 marks)

5 | Market research

What is market research?

Business activity will only be successful if the output produced can satisfy people's wants and needs. Information about the things people want and need will help businesses to decide what to produce. This information is often found through MARKET RESEARCH.

Market research can be defined as the collection, collation and analysis of data relating to the marketing and consumption of goods and services. For example, a business might gather information about the likely consumers of a new product and use the data to help in its decision-making process. The data gathered by this research might include:

- whether or not consumers would want such a product;
- what type of promotion will be effective;
- the functions or facilities it should have;
- what style, shape, colour or form it should take;
- the price people would be prepared to pay for it;
- where people would wish to purchase it;
- information about consumers themselves - their ages, their likes, attitudes, interests and lifestyles;
- what consumers buy at present.

Some, mainly smaller or local, businesses have just a few customers who are well known to them. For these businesses, information about their markets can be relatively easy to find. This may be through personal and social contact with their customers. Such businesses, however, must be careful that they do not misread their customers' views and actions. Other businesses, both small and large, have a more distant relationship with their customers. This may be because they have a large number of customers, operate in a range of different markets or market their products in international as well as national markets. For these businesses, market information may be less easy to come by. Such businesses often find that in order to gather marketing information they need to use sophisticated marketing research methods.

The terms **market research** and **marketing research** are usually used interchangeably in business books and in the media. This is the approach taken in this book. Some have suggested a distinction between the two terms. Market research, they argue, is about researching consumers' preferences and tastes. Marketing research is a wider term, which also includes the analysis of marketing strategies, for example the effect of promotions such as advertising.

The uses of market research

A market is anywhere that buyers and sellers come together to exchange goods and services. Markets are in a constant state of change. As a result, a business is likely to use market research on a regular basis for a number of reasons.

Descriptive reasons A business may wish to identify what is happening in its market. For example, a brewery may want to find trends in its sales of various types of beer over a certain period, or to find out which types of customer are buying a particular beer.

Predictive reasons A business may wish to predict what is likely to happen in the future. For example, a travel company will want to discover possible changes in the types of holiday that people might want to take over the next two to five years. This will place it in a better position to design new holiday packages that will sell.

Explanatory reasons A business may want to explain a variety of matters related to its marketing. This may include sales in a particular part of the country. A bus company, for example, might wish to research why there has been a fall in the number of passengers on a specific route.

Table 1: The scope of market research

Area of research	Possible elements to be considered
The market	Identifying market trends Discovering the potential size of the market Identifying market segments Building up a profile of potential/actual consumers Forecasting sales levels
Competition	Analysing the strengths and weaknesses of competitors Identifying relative market shares Identifying trends in competitors' sales Finding information on competitors' prices
Promotion	Analysing the effectiveness of promotional materials Deciding upon choice of media for promotions
The product	Testing different product alternatives Identifying consumer wants Developing new product ideas Assessing consumer reaction to a newly launched product
Distributing the product	Identifying suitable retail outlets Exploring attitudes of distributors towards products
Pricing the product	Discovering the value consumers place on the product Identifying the sensitivity of the demand for the product to changes in its price

Exploratory reasons These are concerned with a business investigating new possibilities in a market. For example, a soft drinks manufacturer could trial a new canned drink in a small geographical area to test customer reaction before committing itself to marketing the product nationally.

Once a business has decided how it wishes to use market research data, the next stage is to identify the aspects or areas that it wants to concentrate on. Table 1 shows the different areas that could be researched and some possible elements that might be considered in each.

Secondary research

SECONDARY or DESK RESEARCH involves the collection of SECONDARY DATA. This is information which **already exists** in some form. It can be internal data, from records within the business or external data, from sources outside the business.

Internal data This may be collected from existing business documents or other publications, including the following.
- Existing market research reports.
- Sales figures. The more sophisticated these are the better. For example, sales figures which have been broken down according to market segments can be particularly useful.
- Reports from members of the sales force resulting from direct contact with customers.
- Annual Report and Accounts published by businesses.
- Businesses increasingly make use of company intranets to provide up-to-date information. These are restricted to company employees. But some information may be available on the Internet on company websites.
- Stock movements. These can often provide the most up-to-date information on patterns of demand in the market. This is because they are often recorded instantly, as opposed to sales figures, which tend to be collected at a later date.

External data Secondary data will also be available from sources outside the business. Individuals or other organisations will have collected data for their own reasons. A business might be able to use this for its own market research. Examples are given below.
- Information from competitors. This may be, for example, in the form of promotional materials, product specifications or price lists.
- Government publications. There are many government publications that businesses can use. These include general statistical publications such as *Social Trends*, the *Census of Population* and the *Annual Abstract of Statistics*. Many are now online.
- Data from customer services on complaints which have been received about a product.
- The European Union. The EU now provides a wide range of secondary data which can be highly valuable to businesses operating within EU countries. Such publications include *Eurostatistics*, which is published by

Table 2: Advantages and disadvantages of secondary or desk research

Advantages
- It is relatively easy, quick and cheap to collect, especially if the sources that exist are known. This makes it very useful for smaller businesses.
- Several sources may be used. This allows the data to be checked and verified.
- Historical data may be used which can show a trend over time.
- It can be used before carrying out secondary research, which helps to establish the most useful questions to be asked in questionnaires.

Disadvantages
- Data is not always in a form that a particular business would want because it has been collected for another purpose. Adapting it may take time and become expensive.
- Data may be out of date and not relevant, especially in fast changing markets.
- Researchers must be aware of bias. For example, company reports and accounts may show figures in the best possible light to satisfy shareholders.
- There may have been problems with the research. For example, the footnotes to research may state that the sample used was too small and that the results may be inaccurate as a result.

Eurostat (the Statistical Office of the European Union).
- International publications. There is a huge amount of information about overseas marketing published each year by organisations such as the World Bank and the International Monetary Fund.
- Commercial publications. A number of organisations exist to gather data about particular markets. This information is often highly detailed and specialised. Mintel, Dun & Bradstreet and Verdict are examples of such organisations.
- Retail audits. The widespread use of Epos (electronic point of sale) has meant that it is now much easier to collect detailed and up-to-the-minute data on sales in retail outlets such as supermarkets and other retail chains. Retail audits provide manageable data by monitoring and recording sales in a sample of retail outlets. Businesses find these audits especially helpful because of the way in which they provide a continuous monitoring of their performance in the market. A well known example is data on the best selling records or CDs which make up weekly music charts. This information is collected from retail outlets in the UK.

- General publications. A business may use a range of publications widely available to members of the public for its market research. These include newspaper and magazine articles and publications such as the *Yellow Pages*.
- Internet website pages. Increasingly businesses make use of the Internet to search for secondary data outside of their own organisations. Many of the sources of secondary information above (including, for example, government publications) can now be found on the Internet.

Primary research

PRIMARY or FIELD RESEARCH involves collecting PRIMARY DATA. This is information which did not exist before the research began. In other words, it has to be collected by the researcher. It can either be carried out by a business itself or by a **market research agency**. Because of the high costs of using the services of a market research agency many small businesses choose to conduct market research themselves.

Most primary information is gathered by asking consumers questions or by monitoring their behaviour. The most accurate way to do this would be to question or observe all consumers of a particular product (known as the population). However, in all but a few instances this would be either impractical to carry out or expensive. It is usual to carry out a SURVEY of a SAMPLE of people who are thought to be representative of the total market. Methods of choosing samples are dealt with in the next unit.

Methods of primary research

There is a number of different field research methods a business can use. Many of these methods make use of QUESTIONNAIRES. A questionnaire is a series of questions designed to find out the views and opinions of a respondent. It must be designed to meet the needs of the business carrying out the survey. A poorly designed questionnaire may not obtain the results the business is looking for. There are certain features of questionnaires which are important in their design.

- The balance between **closed** and **open** questions. Closed questions, such as 'How many products have you bought in the last month?', only allow the interviewee a limited range of responses. Open questions, however, allow interviewees considerable scope in the responses which they are able to offer. Open questions allow certain issues to be investigated in great detail, but they do require a high degree of expertise from the interviewer. For example, an open question might be 'Suggest how the product could be improved'.
- The clarity of questions. The questions used must be clear and unambiguous so that they do not confuse or mislead the interviewee. 'Technical' language should be avoided if possible.
- The use of leading questions. Leading questions are those which encourage a particular answer. For example, a small shop wanting to find out about its consumer preferences for Coke and Pepsi should avoid the question: 'Do you

Question 1.

The local gym could be the new place for match making. A survey by Mintel found that around 19 per cent (1 in 5) of members have met good friends or partners there. Around 25 per cent (1 in 4) see it as a place to meet people with similar interests. 'Health and fitness clubs are now so much more than just somewhere to exercise and get fit.... . Clubs could look to organise more networking and evening socials for their members, while major dating agencies might like to consider acquiring a strategic stake in health and fitness clubs as a base for their activities,' said Mark Brechin, senior leisure analyst at MINTEL.

After a number of years of facing rising costs and competition MINTEL predicted a 9 per cent rise in revenue in 2006, compared with around 5 per cent in the recent past. The size of the market for leisure services was predicted to reach £2.5 billion, with more than 5 million visitors, and one in ten as club members. Most revenue (76 per cent) was from membership fees, but a growing amount comes from bars and personal treatments. This grew 32 per cent between 2002 and 2006. MINTEL's research also showed that among those adults who have never been to a health and fitness club, 8 per cent would be interested in using one. MINTEL also forecast impressive growth. The market value was predicted to reach £3.4 billion by 2012, increasing almost 40 per cent over the next five years, with the number of members set to reach 7.6 million. ' Competitive pressures and energy prices have eased off from their peak at the end of 2005 and the start of 2006. Meanwhile, consolidation within the industry has removed a lot of the discounting on membership and joining fees among the leading club chains,' explained Mark Brechin.

Source: adapted from www.mintel.com.

(a) If a health club seeking to research its market found the above report on the Internet would this be an example of primary or secondary research? Explain your answer.
(b) Explain, using examples from the article, how a health and fitness club might use the research conducted by Mintel for: (i) descriptive reasons; (ii) predictive reasons; (iii) explanatory reasons.

think that Diet Pepsi is better than Diet Coke?' A better question would be: 'Which brand of diet cola do you prefer - Pepsi or Coke?'

- The questionnaire can provide **quantifiable** information. For example, it might tell a business that 75 per cent of its sales are to people below the age of 25 and only 25 per cent are to over-25s. It may be able to use this information to make decisions.
- Whether it is to be completed by the person carrying out the survey or completed by the respondent.

Personal interviews These involve an interviewer obtaining information from one person face-to-face. The interviewer rather than the interviewee fills out the responses to questions on a questionnaire, which contains mainly 'open' questions. The main advantage of interviews is that they allow the chance for interviewees to give detailed responses to questions that concern them. Long or difficult questions can also be explained by the interviewer and the percentage of responses that can be used is likely to be high. If needed, there is time and scope for answers to be followed up in more detail. Interviews, however, can be time consuming and tend to rely on the skill of the interviewer. For example, a poorly trained interviewer asking questions on a product she did not like may influence the responses of the interviewees by appearing negative.

IT-based research Advances in IT have led to the development of new ways in which businesses can carry out field research.

- Businesses are increasingly making use of Internet and email surveys, where customers can provide data on a business website or email directly to businesses' email addresses.
- Retail audits consist of information collected by retailers about consumers, usually at the point at which a purchase is made. Epos (electronic point of sale) data can be used, for example, to analyse patterns and trends in sales. Data gathered from retail audits is also valuable for identifying the types of consumers purchasing particular products.
- In the UK many shopping centres have devices installed which record where customers shop. Recorders have been developed which 'count' the number of customers entering a shop and some even differentiate between adults, children and pushchairs. The technology provides information which allows shops to see which areas of the centre attract most shoppers. It can also be used to compare shopping centres.
- Interactive methods can also be used to gather information. Consumers may be able to express their views via Internet websites or digital television. Information can be collected when orders are placed directly via the Internet or a digital television link.
- Spending patterns may be analysed from the use of credit cards and store loyalty cards. Loyalty cards allow customers to obtain a certain amount of benefits and discounts with each purchase they make within a shop or supermarket.

Question 2.

Vegran is a company that has developed a healthy lunch bar made from carob and oats. Initially, it has decided to sell the bar in the South West for a trial period, before launching the product throughout the country. Before this, however, it wants to collect views of consumers on the taste and appearance of the bar. It is particularly interested to find out whether consumers would notice a difference in taste between chocolate and carob and their views on the bar's size and packaging. Vegran is only a small company with a limited budget for its marketing projects.

(a) What potential advantages might test marketing have for Vegran?
(b) How useful might:
  (i) postal surveys; (ii) consumer panels;
  (iii) personal interviews; (iv) Internet surveys;
  be to the business?

Telephone interviews This method allows the interview to be held over the telephone. It has the advantage of being cheaper than personal interviewing and allows a wide geographical area to be covered. However, it is often distrusted by the public and it is only possible to ask short questions.

Postal surveys These involve the use of questionnaires sent to consumers through the post. It is a relatively cheap method of conducting field research. It also has the advantage that there is no interviewer bias and a wide geographical area can easily be covered. Unfortunately, the response rate to postal questionnaires can be poor and responses can take as long as six weeks. In addition, questions must be short, so detailed questioning may not be possible. Questionnaires must also be well designed and easy to understand if they are to work.

Observation Observation is often used by retail firms 'watching' consumers in their stores. Observers look out for the amount of time consumers spend making decisions and how readily they notice a particular display. Its advantage is that a tremendous number of consumers can be surveyed in a relatively short space of time. However, observation alone can leave many questions unanswered. For example, it may reveal that a particular display at a supermarket is unpopular, but provide no clues as to why this is the case.

Focus groups These involve a group of customers being brought together on one or a number of occasions. They are asked to answer and discuss questions prepared by market researchers. The groups contain a range of individuals who are thought to be representative of the customers of the business or of a particular segment of customers. Because they only involve a small number of customers, focus groups are a relatively cheap and easy way of gathering marketing research information. A problem is that the views of a fairly small number of customers may not reflect the views of the market or the market segment in which the business is interested.

Consumer panels These involve a group of consumers being consulted on their reactions to a product over a period of time. Consumer panels are widely used by TV companies to judge the reactions of viewers to new and existing programmes. Their main advantage is that they can be used to consider how consumer reaction changes over time. Firms can then build up a picture of consumer trends. Their disadvantage is that it is both difficult and expensive to choose and keep a panel available for research over a long period.

Test marketing Test marketing involves selling a product in a restricted section of the market in order to assess consumer reaction to it. Test marketing usually takes place by making a product available within a particular geographical area. For example, before the Wispa chocolate bar was marketed nationally, it was test marketed in the North East of England.

The benefits of market research

A business may benefit in a number of ways from carrying out market research.

An aid to decision making Perhaps the main benefit of market research is that it allows a business to make more informed decisions. This is especially important in fast-changing markets. Businesses operating in such markets constantly need to adjust

their marketing activities.

Reducing risk While the reliability of market research information cannot be guaranteed, it does reduce risk for a business. Without market research, a business might spend large sums developing and launching a new product, which could prove to be unsuccessful. Businesses are less likely to waste resources on failed activities if careful marketing research is carried out.

Providing a link with the outside world Without market research might businesses operate in a vacuum. They would have little or no way of finding out the views of their actual and potential customers. They would also find it difficult to identify future trends in their existing markets and the markets in which they plan to operate in future.

Estimating the size of markets As markets become ever larger and as new markets open up, market research becomes ever more important. As markets get larger it becomes more difficult for businesses to operate without detailed information about the needs of their customers. This is because of differences in their tastes.

Public relations Carrying out market research may be good for the image of a business. Consumers may feel that their views are being considered. They may also think that the business is concerned that its customers are happy. This may lead to 'corporate' brand loyalty.

The problems of market research

If market research was totally dependable, businesses could use it when introducing or changing products and be completely confident about how consumers would respond to them. This would mean that all new products launched onto the market, which had been researched in advance, would be a success. Similarly, no products would flop because businesses would receive advance warning from their research and take any necessary measures.

In reality, things can be different. It has been estimated that 90 per cent of all products fail after they have been initially launched. Some of this may be put down to a lack of, or inadequate, market research. However, a number of businesses that have conducted extensive research among consumers before committing a product to the market place have launched products which have failed. Given estimates which suggest that the minimum cost of launching a new product nationally is £1 million, this is a risky business. Famous examples of thoroughly researched products which have turned out to be flops include the Sinclair C5, a cheap vehicle with more stability than a moped and lower costs than a car. In research, consumers enthused over this vehicle. In reality, it was almost impossible to sell. Similarly, when Coca-Cola launched 'New Coke' with a new formula flavour onto the market, research suggested it would be a huge success. In practice, 'New Coke' was quickly withdrawn from the shops.

Table 3: Advantages and disadvantages of primary or field research

Advantages

- Data can be collected that directly applies to the issue being researched. Secondary data will be data collected for another purpose.
- The business which initially collects the data will be the only organization with access to it. It can be used to gain marketing advantages over rival firms.
- Secondary data may be unavailable in a certain area.

Disadvantages

- It can be expensive to collect and may take longer than desk research
- The sample taken may not represent the views of all the population.
- If the research method is flawed, the findings will also be flawed. For example, a badly worded questionnaire may not provide the data a business requires.

Businesses want to be sure that the data they collect is reliable. One way of checking the reliability of data is to pose the question, 'If this information was collected again would the same or broadly similar results be obtained?' Businesses acting upon research data need to be sure that they can depend upon it. There is a great deal of debate among researchers about the reliability of different research methods. There is a number of reasons why **primary research** does not always provide reliable information for businesses.

- **Human behaviour.** Much marketing research depends upon the responses of consumers who participate in the collection of primary data. While the responses of consumers may be honest and truthful at the time, it does not mean that they will necessarily respond in the same manner in future. This is because all human behaviour, including the act of consuming and purchasing goods, is to some extent unpredictable.
- **Sampling and bias.** When carrying out market research, it is usual to base the research upon a sample of the total population. This is because it would be impossible and costly to include every person when dealing with a large population. It is possible, however, that results from the sample may be different from those that would have been obtained if the whole population had been questioned. This is known as a sampling discrepancy. The greater the sampling discrepancy, the less reliable will be the data obtained.
- As mentioned earlier, questionnaires need to be carefully constructed to avoid the problem of encouraging particular responses from consumers through the use of leading questions. Similarly, the behaviour of interviewers can affect the outcome of interviews.

Businesses must also be careful when using **secondary data**. For example, businesses may use a government publication to estimate the size of markets in which they might wish to operate. However, these market sizes may not always accurately match the product market being researched.

Quantitative and qualitative research

Data collected through desk and field research can be either quantitative or qualitative in nature. QUALITATIVE RESEARCH involves the collection of data about attitudes, beliefs and intentions. Focus groups and interviews are common methods used to collect qualitative data. An example of qualitative research could be face-to-face interviews with 100 purchasers of new Land Rover Discoveries to find out why they prefer this product to similar four wheel drives sold by other car manufacturers. The information collected through qualitative research is usually regarded as being open to a high degree of interpretation. This means that there are often disagreements within businesses about the significance and importance of qualitative research data.

QUANTITATIVE RESEARCH involves the collection of data that can be measured. In practice this usually means the collection of statistical data such as sales figures and market

share. Surveys and the use of government publications are common methods of collecting quantitative research data. An example of quantitative research would be a survey of four wheel drive owners in West Derbyshire to establish their places of residence, ages, occupations, incomes and gender. The information collected through quantitative research is usually regarded as being open to less interpretation than that collected through qualitative research.

KEYTERMS

Confidence level – a statistical calculation which allows a business to gauge the extent of its confidence in the results of research.
Market or marketing research – the collection, collation and analysis of data relating to the marketing and consumption of goods and services.
Primary data – information which does not already exist and is collected through the use of field research.
Primary or field research – the gathering of 'new' data which has not been collected before.
Qualitative research – the collection of data about attitudes, beliefs and intentions.
Quantitative research – the collection of data that can be quantified.
Questionnaire – a series of questions designed to find out the views and opinions of a respondent.
Sample – a selection of part of the population, which must be representative of the population to be effective.
Secondary data – data which is already in existence. It is normally used for a purpose other than that for which it was collected.
Secondary or desk research – the collection of data that has already been collected for another purpose.
Survey – where respondents provide information to researchers about their actions, habits, attitudes and perceptions.

KNOWLEDGE

1. Why is market research important to businesses?
2. Explain the difference between:
   (a) descriptive research;
   (b) predictive research;
   (c) explanatory research.
3. State five areas that market research could concentrate on.
4. What is meant by desk research?
5. What is meant by field research?
6. Why might field research be of benefit to a business?
7. In what circumstances might:
   (a) postal surveys;
   (b) questionnaires;
   (c) observation;
      be useful?
8. Suggest three benefits of market research to a business
9. What is the difference between qualitative and quantitative market research?

Case Study: Beer sales plunge as Britons stay at home

Sales of beer dropped to their lowest level since the 1930s, according to figures released today. The British Beer and Pub Association (BBPA), which represents the brewing and pub industry, revealed that 14 million fewer pints are being sold daily in pubs today - a slump of 49 per cent since the peak in 1979. Part of the long-term trend has been the move towards drinking at home. In the late 70s, 90 per cent of beer was drunk in pubs, but the figure now stands at 58 per cent. While the biggest casualties of Britain's increasing preference for wine and spirits have been the pubs, they are, however, not alone: overall beer sales have plunged by 22 per cent from the peak 1979 level.

The BBPA says the situation is exacerbated by rising production costs as the prices of barley, malt, glass, aluminium and energy increase. It also feels that taxes on beer in the form of a duty imposed by the Treasury is making matters worse. Since 1997, beer duty has risen by 27 per cent while consumption has fallen by 11 per cent. Wine duty, meanwhile, has increased by just 16 per cent, while wine-drinking has gone up by 46 per cent. It's a similar story with spirits. Although consumption has risen by 20 per cent over the last decade, duty has increased by only 3 per cent.

Major British brewers saw their profits tumble by 78 per cent between 2004 and 2006. Last week, two major brewers - Scottish & Newcastle UK and Carlsberg UK - warned pubs that rising costs and a poor summer meant that big rises in wholesale beer prices were likely.

A senior executive at S&NUK told the pub trade paper *The Morning Advertiser* that prices would probably increase 'way above the rate of inflation' during the first part of next year. He said that rising cereal, crude oil and aluminium prices meant that brewers would be forced to charge more to recoup their losses.

Beer is not only falling victim to the growing fondness for wine among Britons. Its popularity is also suffering because of a cultural shift to drinking at home. In 2005, 60 per cent of all the wine sold in the UK was bought in supermarkets. And the wine and champagne market, which is now worth more than £10.2 billion, increased by 26 per cent between 2002 and 2006. Over the same period, sales of spirits and liqueurs went up by 16 per cent. However, some sections of the brewing industry are performing well, and real ale has enjoyed a quiet revival over recent years as consumers develop a taste for more authentic, natural and traditional products.

'This comes against a backdrop of a slump across the whole beer market,' said Owen Morris, a spokesman for the Campaign for Real Ale, a pressure group seeking to promote sales of traditionally brewed beers. 'But we've seen a 7.5 per cent year-on-year growth in sales of regional beers. People are enjoying regional beer more, even though the large breweries are forgetting about traditional beers and pushing lagers.' Mr Morris also referred to the threat posed by the supermarkets, which use cheap beer as a loss leader.

Table 4: The UK beer market

1930s The last time the volume of beer sold through pubs was this low
22 per cent The amount by which the total beer market has fallen since its peak in 1979
49 per cent The amount by which pub beer sales have fallen since 1979, equivalent to 14 million fewer pints every day
78 per cent The fall between 2004 and last year in the profits enjoyed by the major British brewers

Source: adapted from the *Guardian*, 20.11. 2007.

Consider the research above from the perspective of the owner of an independent pub.

(a) Is the research referred to in the article primary or secondary research? Explain your answer. (4 marks)

(b) Outline the reasons why a pub owner may find the research in the above article useful. (6 marks)

(c) Explain the various ways in which a pub owner might seek to collect primary data to complement the data provided in the article above. (10 marks)

(d) Analyse the potential usefulness of the data provided in the article for a pub owner. (10 marks)

6 Sampling

What is a sample?

Sometimes a business or market research organisation may be able to carry out market research by means of a **survey** of all its target POPULATION. The **target population** is those people whose views it wants to find out. For example, a business making components might only supply five companies with parts. So it should be fairly easy to survey all of its customers. But in most cases it is impractical to survey the whole population. It would take too long and would be too costly to gather and process the information.

Instead, researchers take a sample of the population. Samples should be REPRESENTATIVE. They should have the same characteristics as the whole population. If they don't, results from the sample which are generalised to the whole population may be inaccurate. For example, a survey may be carried out by

Question 1.

A pharmaceutical (drugs) company wanted to commission a study on male health worldwide. The results would be used to make major marketing decisions. A market research agency was commissioned to carry out the study. It set about conducting a two phase research project using survey techniques. In the first phase, 20,000 interviews were completed with target respondents in eight countries. A combination of phone and web interviewing was used. In the second phase, a random selection of about 5 per cent of the initial respondents for participation in a second interview were identified. These interviews were conducted on the Internet for those with access or through the use of a paper questionnaire.

The research methods used meant that the same questions were put to all respondents and answers collated in the same manner.

(a) Explain the type of sampling method used by the business.
(b) The market research agency interviewed 20,000 males in eight countries. Suggest why it interviewed (i) males only; (ii) respondents in eight countries rather than one country only and (iii) 20,000 people rather than 1,000 or 500,000.
(c) How much statistical bias would you expect to see in the findings from this research?

a food company to find out how many people would buy a new, up-market product. If it only asked pensioners on low incomes, it would almost certainly find that the survey predicted fewer sales than would actually be the case. This is because the sample chosen did not accurately reflect the whole population. In this case SAMPLING BIAS is present. **Questionnaires** are often used to gather data from a sample.

Size of sample

The SAMPLE SIZE will influence how representative the sample is of the population. Larger samples tend to be more representative. For example, say that the target population is 10,000 customers. If the sample were the same size as the target population, 10,000, it would be totally representative. A sample of 9,000 people is more likely to reflect the characteristics of the target population than 10 people surveyed on the street. So decisions based on the results of the larger sample are more likely to be accurate. There is a number of ways in which a sample can be chosen.

Type of sample

There are different types of sample and sampling methods that can be used by a business carrying out primary research.

Random sampling RANDOM SAMPLING gives each member of a group an equal chance of being chosen. In other words, the sample is selected at random, rather like picking numbers out of a hat. Today computers can be used to produce a random list of numbers, which are then used as the basis for selecting a sample. The main advantage of random sampling is that bias cannot be introduced when choosing the sample. However, it assumes that all members of the group are the same (homogeneous), which is not always the case. A small sample chosen in this way may not have the characteristics of the population, so a very large sample would have to be taken to make sure it was representative. It would be very costly and time consuming for firms to draw up a list of the whole population and then contact and interview them.

Systematic sampling One method sometimes used to reduce the time taken to locate a random sample is to choose every tenth or twentieth name on a list. This is known as SYSTEMATIC SAMPLING. It is, however, less random.

Stratified random sampling This method of sampling is also random. However, unlike the types of random sampling described above, STRATFIED RANDOM SAMPLING is where the sample is divided into **segments** or **strata** based on previous knowledge about how the population is divided up. For example, a business may be interested in how employment status affected the demand for a food product. It might divide the population up into different income groups, such as higher managerial and professional occupations, small employers and 'own account' workers etc. A random sample could then be chosen from each of these groups, making sure that there were the same proportions of the sample in each category as in the population as a whole. Therefore, if the population had 10 per cent upper class males, so would the sample. Stratified sampling is often preferred by researchers as it makes the sample more representative of the whole group and is less likely to privilege particular sub-groups than random sampling.

Quota sampling QUOTA SAMPLING involves the population being segmented into a number of groups which share specific characteristics. These may be based on the age and sex of the population. Interviewers are then given targets for the number of people out of each segment who they must interview. For example, an interviewer may be asked to interview 10 males between the ages of 18 and 25, or 15 females between the ages of 45 and 60. Once the target is reached, no more people are interviewed from that group. The advantage of this sampling method is that it can be cheaper to operate than many of the others. It is also useful where the proportions of different groups within the population are known. However, results from quota sampling are not statistically representative of the population and are not randomly chosen.

Snowballing SNOWBALLING is a highly specialised method of sampling. It involves starting the process of sampling with one individual or group and then using these contacts to develop more, hence the 'snowball' effect. This is only used when other sampling methods are not possible, due to the fact that samples built up by snowballing cannot be representative. Businesses operating in highly secretive markets, such as the arms trade, may use this method of sampling. Similarly, firms engaged in producing highly specialised and expensive one-off products for a very limited range of customers may need to rely upon snowballing when engaged in marketing research. Examples might include firms engaged in the nuclear and power generating industries.

Cluster sampling CLUSTER SAMPLING involves separating the population into 'clusters', usually in different geographical areas. A random sample is then taken from the clusters, which are assumed to be representative of the population. This method is often used when survey results need to be found quickly, such as in opinion polls.

Multi-stage sampling This involves selecting one sample from another sample. So, for example, a market researcher might choose a county at random and then a district of that county may be selected. Similarly, a street within a city may be chosen and then a particular household within a street.

Factors affecting the sampling method and size of sample

Businesses will take account of a number of key factors when making their choice as to which sampling method to deploy:

Finance available For some small businesses this means that random sampling can be beyond their means. Larger businesses, however, may have the resources to undertake market research methods that give more random results and use larger sample sizes.

The nature of the product The nature of a product produced by a business can affect the sampling method chosen during market research. This relates, in particular, to whether a product is the same for all consumers (uniform) or carefully adapted to meet the needs of individual consumers or very small groups of consumers (bespoke). For products that are uniform, a business will need to ensure that all of the population are properly represented in a sample and will need to ensure that little or no statistical bias is introduced in the sample. This is likely to mean a relatively large sample size. For products that are 'one-offs', bespoke or made to order, the population is likely to be very small or confined to just one person or business. In this case sampling is likely to be very straightforward and rely upon a relatively small sample, without the accompanying need for

Question 2.

Graham Hunter is a farmer in Cambridgeshire, producing a range of vegetables. All of his supplies go to three large supermarket chains and he and his farm have been featured on the packaging at one of these supermarkets. In making decisions about what vegetables to grow in the forthcoming year, Graham has decided to undertake some market research. His research will be based upon speaking to the Head Buyer at each of these supermarkets and asking their opinions.

(a) **Explain why Graham Hunter can be said to have used a sample.**

(b) **Explain TWO factors that may have influence Graham's choice of sample.**

(c) **How reliable do you think the results of his research might be?**

Question 3.

DPX is a market research company. In 2003, it completed a report for a manufacturer of building materials and fittings which had seen an unexpected fall in sales over the previous 12 months. The manufacturer wanted to find out how its immediate customers, DIY chains such as B&Q and Wickes, and the larger number of builders' and plumbers' merchants, viewed its products. For example, it wanted to find out whether customers saw its products as giving value for money compared to those of competitors, whether the fittings were reliable and whether the range of products was large enough. It also wanted information about sales and profits of rival businesses to see if they had experienced a similar downturn.

DPX devised a telephone questionnaire for customers. In its sample, it interviewed all the large DIY chains. But it only conducted 30 interviews with smaller builders' and plumbers' merchants. The sample of 30 was judged to be representative of all smaller builders' and plumbers' merchants and a 95 per cent confidence level was given for the responses.

The research showed that a major rival company had completely updated its range over the previous 24 months. The products of the manufacturing company commissioning the research had lost competitiveness as a result. For example, they were said by respondents to be giving less good value for money than before.

(a) Explain what is meant by 'a 95 per cent confidence level was given for the responses' from the smaller plumbers' and builders' merchants.

(b) How might the business reduce the chance that its results did not reflect the views of all small builders and plumbers' merchants?

(c) Discuss ONE strategy the manufacturing company might develop to reverse the decline in its sales.

sophisticated sampling techniques such as those described above.

The risk involved The greater a risk a business is taking, the more reliable it would like its results to be. Thus a business taking a large risks for example financially, or in terms of the business's future survival, would want to use the most reliable and sophisticated sampling method available to it. This would for many businesses mean a relatively larger sample size. It would reduce the risk of statistical bias and increase the reliability of the findings from the sample. By way of contrast, a business taking a small risk might be prepared to go ahead with less reliable and, possibly, informal sampling methods such as talking to a few customers. A small ice cream business that has one shop, for example, might introduce a new flavour of ice cream after asking the views of, or in response to requests from, just a few customers. If the new flavour doesn't prove popular with customers, it could be rapidly withdrawn and replaced by another. Little would be lost by the business. A large ice cream manufacturer, on the other hand, selling products to millions of customers, would be unlikely to change its production processes on the basis of such a small sample. This is because the risk associated with a wrong decision would be so great.

The target market The nature of a product's target market will influence the sampling undertaken as part of market research. For example, if there is a small target market for a product, then the sample chosen will be smaller. Similarly, if the characteristics of a products' target market are similar or the same and they are in a particular market segment, then this will influence the sampling method. In such cases businesses may use cluster or quota sampling. For products aimed at mass markets with a range of consumers, the sampling methods chosen will need to reflect this diversity and this is likely to mean a larger sample size.

Sample results and statistical significance

The only way to get an accurate picture of a population is to have all relevant data about that population. But this takes time and is expensive. So researchers take a sample and the results obtained from the sample are then applied to the whole population. But how confident can a business be about the results of such a survey? When analysing data from a sample, researchers are interested in certain statistics.

- The mean. This is the average result For example, the average amount spent on a Monday by a shopper may be £10. On Saturday it may be £20.
- The STANDARD DEVIATION. This tells researchers about the spread of results. Standard deviation measures the average difference (deviation) of each item of data from the mean. For example, the standard deviation from the average amount spent may be £2 on Monday and £5 on Saturday. Comparing the means shows that shoppers spent

Figure 1: A normal distribution

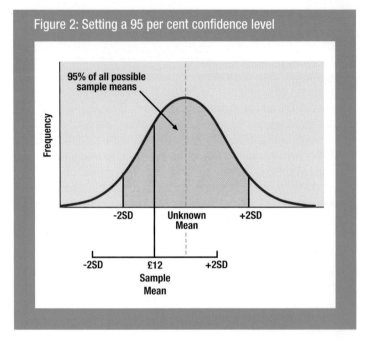

Figure 2: Setting a 95 per cent confidence level

twice as much on Saturday than on Monday. The standard deviations show that the spread of amounts spent was greater on Saturday than on Monday. So, on Monday, the amounts spent by shoppers varied less and were generally closer to the mean.

- Researchers also make use of a NORMAL DISTRIBUTION curve. This is a 'bell shaped' frequency distribution. It shows the results that can be usually be expected when the whole population is surveyed.

There is a relationship between the normal distribution, the mean and the standard deviation. The mean is in the centre. Most results cluster around the mean, with a few high and low values away from the mean. The data is symmetrically distributed around the mean, so that 50 per cent of results lie either side of the mean, as in Figure 1. In a normal distribution:

- about 68 per cent of values lie within 1 standard deviation of the mean on either side;

- about 95 per cent of values lie within 2 standard deviations of the mean on either side;
- about 99.8 per cent of values lie within 3 standard deviations of the mean on either side.

Look at Figure 2. What if a business did not know the mean (average) spending, but a sample found that it was £12? How would it know whether this was an accurate reflection of the population? To do this a range of values must be taken either side of £12, which will hopefully include the unknown mean spending. A 95 per cent CONFIDENCE LEVEL could be set, where values of 2 standards deviations either side of the mean are included. The business would then know that in 95 out of

KEYTERMS

Cluster sampling – where respondents are chosen for interview in a few locations, to reduce the cost of research, rather than being spread evenly across the population.

Confidence level – expresses as percentages an indication of how likely results obtained from a sample can be applied to the population. A 95 per cent confidence level, for example, indicates that the results will be representative 95 times out of 100.

Normal distribution – a naturally occurring frequency distribution where many of the values cluster around the mean, and where there are few high and low values away from the mean.

Population – the total number of consumers in a given group.

Questionnaire – a list of questions, given to a number of respondents to answer, which provide data.

Quota sampling – where respondents are selected for interview in a non-random manner in the same proportion as they exist in the whole population.

Random sampling – where respondents are selected for interview at random.

Representative (sample) – a sample which has the same characteristics as the population.

Sampling bias – where the sample chosen is not representative of the population studied.

Sample size – the number of people chosen for the sample from the whole population.

Snowballing – a non-random method of market research, where a small number of selected respondents are asked to nominate further potential respondents for interview and so on.

Standard deviation – a measure of the average difference (deviation) of each result from the mean.

Stratified random sampling – a method of quota sampling where respondents are chosen at random.

Systematic sampling – a non-random method of sampling, where a researcher chooses respondents by taking every nth name on a list.

100 (19÷20) cases the unknown mean would fall within the range either side of the £12 sample mean. If it wanted to reduce the margin of error, it could set a confidence level of 99 per cent. This would involve a larger range of results. So the business could be more certain that the sample reflected the population.

Researchers often use 95 per cent and 99 per cent confidence levels. For a normal distribution, a 95 per cent confidence level spans 2 standard deviations either side of the population mean. A 99 per cent confidence level spans just under 3 standard deviations either side of the mean.

What about sample size? In terms of time and cost, the smaller the sample, the better. But to give meaningful results from random or stratified samples, researchers argue that the size of the sample should be over 30. As the sample gets larger, the variance of results decreases. So there is less chance that

there would be a 'distorted sample', which would give an inaccurate picture of the population.

KNOWLEDGE

1   Why do most surveys involve a sample of a population rather than all the population?
2   What is the difference between a random sample and a systematic sample?
3   What is the difference between stratified random sampling and cluster sampling?
4   What does standard deviation show?
5   Explain the meaning of 'confidence levels'.

Case Study: Public transport in South West England

In 2006 Synovate Ltd, a market research company, published a report that it carried out on behalf of the Competition Commission. The report was based upon an investigation into the attitudes of the public towards transport links in the South West of England. They focused upon rail and bus services and the customers of the two main companies operating in the area at the time of the research: Wessex Rail and First Group buses. They wanted to know why people chose particular transport services and to establish whether they considered other possible services as realistic transport alternatives.

The research was based upon questionnaires. The questionnaires were conducted by researchers who boarded trains and buses between 7.00 a.m. and 7.45 p.m. Reply paid envelopes were provided where passengers did not have sufficient time to complete the survey during their journey. The sample size was 10,111 with 482 FirstGroup

passengers and 529 Wessex passengers.

Some of the key findings of the research were as follows.

- Over a third of Wessex passengers are heading to work (36%) compared to just 17% of FirstGroup passengers.
- 31% of FirstGroup passengers travel on the bus route three or more times a week compared to 41% of Wessex Trains passengers.
- The factors of most importance to passengers of FirstGroup are 'stops at convenient station/stop', 'frequency of service' and 'cost of ticket', which are identified as the top three factors of importance.
- Wessex Trains passengers identify the 'short journey time', 'departure time' and 'stops at convenient station/stop' as most important.
- 'Space for luggage' is of least importance to passengers on both FirstGroup buses and Wessex Trains. In terms of how easy it would be to permanently change their mode of transport, no more than half of the FirstGroup or Wessex passengers identify any alternatives as quite or very easy to change to.
- FirstGroup passengers would find it easiest to change to 'train' (48% saying it would be quite or very easy) and Wessex Trains passengers would find it easiest to change to using a 'car as a driver' (48% saying quite or very easy).

Source: adapted from www.competition-commission.org.uk.

1   Explain what is meant by the terms:
    (a) 'sample size'; (3 marks)
    (b) 'questionnaire'. (3 marks).
2   Explain TWO reasons why the research was commissioned. (6 marks)
3   Explain the sampling method used by Synovate Ltd. (8 marks)
4   How useful might the owner of a taxi business in the South West of England find the research? (10 marks)

Table 1: Respondent Profile

		FirstGroup	Wessex Trains
		Base: 482	Base: 529
Age (Q26)	16-34	48%	50%
Excludes 'not answered'	35-54	23%	35%
	55-64	13%	9%
	65+	14%	4%
Gender (Q25)	Male	33%	49%
Excludes 'not answered'	Female	65%	50%
Employment (Q28)	Employed (FT/PT/self)	58%	78%
Excludes 'not answered'	Retired	17%	5%
	Other	24%	16%
Number of Adults in Group (Q27)	One	72%	75%
	Two	15%	14%
Excludes 'not answered'	Three +	6%	4%

The nature of markets

A MARKET is anywhere that buyers and sellers communicate to exchange goods or services. They can range from street markets, to markets for cars in many countries around the world, to goods and services bought over the Internet. Sometimes markets are actual places, such as the fruit and vegetable markets or the shopping centres and high streets found in towns and cities. At other times markets are virtual and cannot be seen. For example, the market for many second-hand goods operates through the Internet on websites such as eBay and through newspapers such as *Loot*.

Types of market

Markets might be classified in a number of ways.

Geographical Markets might be **local**, **national** or **international**. A market held every Saturday in a small town is an example of a local market, as products are sold in the local area. National markets in the UK might be newspapers sold around the UK, such as *The Guardian* or the *Financial Times*. Some products are sold in many countries, in international markets, such as Coca-Cola and Pepsi, whereas some are sold only in areas such as Europe or Asia.

Electronic and physical Markets that are **electronic** are those where the buyer and seller do not come into contact. In electronic markets business is mainly conducted over the Internet or through other computer-based networks. Electronic markets are also sometimes referred to as virtual markets. For example, a consumer buying a book from amazon.com never meets an actual bookseller in the transaction. Instead, the transaction is conducted entirely electronically. On the other hand, a consumer buying a book from a bookshop will **physically** enter the bookshop and make a transaction. Thus physical markets are those where the buyer and seller physically come into contact.

Buyer Here markets are classified according to who the buyer is. Goods such as ice cream and services such as DVD rental are bought by consumers in **consumer markets**. But sometimes products, such as machinery, are bought from a business by another business in **industrial** or **producer markets**.

Industry Markets might be classified according to whether they involve PRIMARY INDUSTRY, such as oil extraction or fishing, SECONDARY INDUSTRY involving manufacturing, or TERTIARY INDUSTRY involving services. Sometimes markets are classified according to individual industries or products. So, for example, the motor car industry and the computer industry

Question 1.

(a) Using different market classifications, describe each of the markets shown in the photographs.

make up different markets within the manufacturing sector.

Size Markets might be **mass markets**, where products are sold to many people in many countries who have similar needs, such as market for washing up liquid. Or they might be **niche markets** for specialist products sold to consumers with particular tastes and needs, such as the market for vegan food products.

Products are likely to fit into different categories. For example, a computer business such as Apple is a manufacturer in secondary industry, selling computer products in international markets, to both businesses and consumers. A hair salon might sell niche market hair products and beautician tertiary services to consumers in local markets.

The importance of demand

Businesses operate in markets where they produce and sell, or supply, products that consumers want and are able to buy, or demand. There is a number of factors that can affect the demand for an individual business's products.

The price of the product For most products:
- as the price goes up, the quantity demanded goes down;
- as the price goes down, the quantity demanded goes up.

For example, a bicycle shop selling a particular brand of bike at £175 each might sell on average ten of these bikes per week. If this bicycle shop lowered the price to £99 it might sell 25 in a week. On the other hand, if the bicycle shop raised the price of this bike to £240 it might sell as few as two or three bikes per week on average. This illustrates the inverse relationship between the price of a business' products and the demand for the product.

However, there are some products where this relationship is different over particular price ranges. 'Prestige' products such as luxury perfumes are designed to appeal to consumers' sense of exclusivity and feeling special. A low price might put off consumers of such a product, as there is an association made between a higher price and high quality. This means that the quantity demanded over lower price ranges may increase as the price rises for such a product. Speculative goods can also act in this way. As prices rise people buy more of them, hoping to sell them for a profit at a later date. For example, as the prices of houses rose in the UK between 2000-2005 the demand for houses also rose as house buyers anticipated prices rising even further.

Consumer incomes The incomes of the consumers of a product will affect demand. The consumers at whom a product is aimed may experience an increase in income. If this happens a business may be able to sell more of the product at a given price or charge a higher price. So, the bicycle shop owner is likely to experience an increase in demand from target customers if their incomes rise. On the other hand, if consumer incomes fall, the demand for products is also likely to fall on average. So, the bicycle shop owner may experience a fall in demand for bicycles if the target customers' incomes fall.

Competitor actions There are two main ways in which the action of a competitor may affect the demand for a business' products. First, the price of a rival's goods may change. If a rival's price goes up, customers may be more willing to buy more of this product. If a rival's prices fall, customers may reduce demand for this product. For example, the bicycle shop described above may be competing with a larger retailer of bicycles such as Decathlon. If Decathlon lowers the prices of its equivalent bicycles, then the bicycle shop may find that the demand for its bikes falls. Second, a competitor business may have a successful marketing campaign. For example, were Decathlon to run a popular and successful marketing campaign that was successful in attracting large numbers of new customers, then this would be likely to have a negative effect upon the demand for the bicycle shop's products.

Success of a business' marketing A business may run a successful marketing campaign that attracts new customers and increases demand. So, for example, the bicycle shop may sponsor a series of popular local bike races. This may lead to an increase in the number of customers visiting the shop.

Changes in tastes and fashion Changes in consumer tastes and fashions can have major effects upon the demand for particular products. For example, there have been many changes in the type of bicycles favoured by consumers over the past 30 years. These have ranged from 'choppers' in the 1970s through to BMX bikes and mountain bikes in the 1990s. These changes in tastes have had an effect upon the demand for particular types of bikes.

Changes in population Demographic changes can affect the demand for a product. For example, the increase in the number of specialist 'Polish shops' in UK towns and cities reflects the increase in the number of Polish people who have moved to the UK. Similarly, the increase in the number of up-market furniture stores in regional cities such as Manchester, Birmingham and Leeds reflects the movement into these cities of large numbers of young, affluent consumers.

Seasonal factors Many businesses experience large changes in the demand for their products between different seasons. For example, many isolated Cornish beaches have cafes that are very busy in the summer season due to a high demand for consumers. Yet these same cafes may close or offer only a limited service during other seasons due to a lack of consumer demand.

Government legislation and regulation Government legislation and regulation can affect demand. Pubs, for example, may experience a fall in demand as a result of an increase in the legal age of people buying alcohol or as a result of the ban on smoking indoors.

Case Study: *Marple Road Garage*

Marple Road Garage is a thriving Cheshire based family business that offers a range of garage-based services, such as repairs and MOTs to local car drivers. As well as providing these more general garage services, it also sells second hand vehicles with a particular specialism in Land Rover Defenders.

Tim Hill, one of the partners in the business, has been responsible for Land Rover sales and has overseen the expansion of this part of the business over recent years. Tim described the success of his business in the following terms: 'One of the key factors in driving our business has been an increase in the general popularity of four wheel drive vehicles. The Land Rover Defender has remained popular among consumers such as land owners and farmers wanting a sturdy, practical and 'down to earth' vehicle, but it has also attracted new customers, particularly well off business people and professionals, who use their Defenders mainly at weekends'. One of Tim's principal marketing innovations was the establishment of a website (www.marpleroadgarage.co.uk) that enabled him to trade in Land Rovers to customers nationally and, in some cases, throughout the world. Reflecting upon this Tim reported: 'Before we created our website we mainly sold to local customers in Cheshire and Greater Manchester. In those days our business used to be much more regionally based, with very few sales outside of our immediate region. Now we have customers all over the UK and 90 per cent of our Land Rover sales are internet led. Recently we sold four Defenders to a game park in Africa and we now have Reuters, the international news agency, as an established customer'. Looking to the future, Tim expects demand for second-hand Defenders to remain strong, but he does have some concerns about the state of the economy and is worried that a fall in income among consumers in his target groups will reduce demand.

Source: adapted from www.marpleroadgarage.co.uk.

(a) Identify THREE different markets in which Marple Road Garage operates. (3 marks)
(b) Using evidence from the article, outline factors influencing the demand for second-hand Land Rover Defenders (6 marks)
(c) Explain how the creation of a website has enabled Marple Road Garage to increase sales of second-hand vehicles. (8 marks)
(d) Analyse the possible threats to Marple Road Garage's future sales of second-hand Defenders. (8 marks)

8 Market segmentation

Market segments

Market research provides a variety of information about the people who may be interested in buying a business's products. For example, it might tell a business that a new car will mainly be bought by women aged 18-35. It might indicate that older people have bought more copies of a magazine than younger people in the last year. Producers may use this information to identify people with similar needs. Breaking down a market into sub-groups with similar characteristics is known as MARKET SEGMENTATION. A business can then target these groups and develop products and services for each of them.

Health clubs in the UK make use of segmentation. For example, daytime users tend to be younger mothers with children and older retired people. Clubs often provide facilities such as crèches for such members. Members who visit in the evening tend to be people who work in the day and want to exercise at night.

The benefits of market segmentation

There is a number of benefits of market segmentation that lead businesses to attempt to identify different market segments.
- Successful market segmentation should allow a business to sell more products overall and perhaps increase its profit.
- By identifying different MARKET SEGMENTS, a business should understand its consumers better. Greater knowledge about its customers will allow a business to vary its products to suit their needs better.
- It might enable a business to target particular groups with particular products.
- It can help to prevent products being promoted to the wrong people. This would be wasteful of resources and might possibly lead to losses.
- It might allow a business to market a wider range of differentiated products.
- Customers may feel that their needs are being better targeted and develop loyalty to the business.

Types of market segmentation

There are four main ways in which consumers tend to be segmented:
- geographically – by where they live;
- demographically – by their gender, social class, age, income, ethnicity or religion;
- psychographically – by their lifestyle and personality;
- behaviourally – by how they act, for example whether they make repeat purchases, buy on impulse or want high quality products.

Question 1.

One of the most commonly targeted groups for advertisers are ABC1s. In the past commercial radio was not seen as a useful way of reaching such audiences. However, recently there has been a growth in the number of 'medium' ABC1s which are part of the listenership. During a typical week, 65 per cent of ABC1s tune in or listen to commercial radio. Over a month its reach rises to 83 per cent. ABC1s tend to listen for extended periods of time, around 12 hours a week. They also have high loyalty levels to their favourite stations. On average they tune in to 2.6 different stations a week. Even younger ABC1s, who might be more experimental, tend to stay loyal to one or two stations. This information is particularly useful for advertisers using a mixed media to promote products. ABC1s often avoid TV advertising.

Main listening periods tend to take place in the morning. In a typical week 61 per cent of ABC1 adults tune in to commercial radio. nineteen per cent listen on Saturdays and 15 per cent on Sundays. Around a fifth of time spent listening to commercial radio by ABC1s is in the car. Most is done at breakfast and when going home.

Source: adapted from www.rab.co.uk.

Figure 1: ABC1 profiles

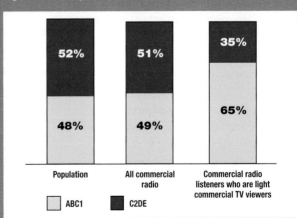

52%	51%	35%
48%	49%	65%
Population	All commercial radio	Commercial radio listeners who are light commercial TV viewers

☐ ABC1   ■ C2DE

(a) Examine the reasons why commercial radio might be a useful promotional medium for small and medium sized businesses aiming at ABC1s.

(b) Suggest how a small to medium sized business might appeal to ABC1s most effectively using this medium.

Geographic segmentation

This might include considering the region of a country where consumers live and the nature of the region, e.g. rural, urban, semi-rural or suburban. It may also consider the type of house, road or area of a city that people live in. This method can be especially useful in large or highly culturally diverse markets, where buying patterns are influenced by region. Businesses selling into the EU are likely to break this area down into more manageable segments. Many large businesses selling into global markets have different products for different countries or areas. For example, Nestlé has sold refrigerated profiteroles in France and a fortified drink called Milo with a malted taste in Japan. The Maggi and Crosse & Blackwell soups are adapted to suit different tastes, by varying the ingredients from one country to another. It may also be possible for a company to price goods differently in different markets. For example, car manufacturers sell the same cars at different prices in different countries in the European Union. The prices will depend, in part, on what they think customers are prepared to pay.

A drawback of geographic segmentation is the evidence that consumer tastes are becoming more uniform across geographic boundaries. This can mean that regional boundaries and national boundaries become less important in determining tastes. For example, 30 years ago the vast majority of supporters of Manchester United or Liverpool FC could be found within a 30 mile radius of the clubs. Today supporters of these clubs and consumers of their products can be found in large numbers in other locations such as the South East of England, Asia or Southern Africa.

Demographic segmentation

DEMOGRAPHY is the study of population. Demographic segmentation splits people up into different groups according to different characteristics.

Age Many businesses pay attention to the age of their customers. For example, the over-65s could be seen as one segment, while teenagers aged 14-18 could be seen as another. R&B CDs might be marketed to teenagers, whilst a 'Hits of the 1960s' CD may be more likely to be attractive to older buyers. The over-60s are of particular interest to business as this segment is

Table 1: Socio-economic groups – IPA classification

Social grade	Social status	Head of household's occupation
A	Upper middle class	Higher managerial, administrative or professional such as doctors, lawyers and company directors
B	Middle class	Intermediate managerial, administrative or professional such as teachers, nurses and managers
C1	Lower middle class	Supervisory or clerical and junior managerial, administrative or professional such as shop assistants, clerks and police constables
C2	Skilled working class	Skilled manual workers such as carpenters, cooks and train drivers
D	Working class	Semi-skilled and unskilled manual workers such as fitters and store keepers
E	The poorest in society	State pensioners or widows, casual or lower grade workers, or long-term unemployed

Table 2: Socio-economic groups – Registrar General's classification

Class 1	Higher managerial and professional occupations **1.1** Employers in large organisations (*eg corporate manager*) **1.2** Higher professionals (*eg doctor or barrister*)
Class 2	Lower managerial and professional occupations (*eg journalist, actor, nurse*)
Class 3	Intermediate occupations (*eg secretary, driving instructor*)
Class 4	Small employers and own account workers (*eg publican, taxi driver*)
Class 5	Lower supervisory, craft and related occupations (*eg plumber, butcher, train driver*)
Class 6	Semi routine occupations (*eg shop assistant, traffic warden*)
Class 7	Routine occupations (*eg waiter, road sweeper*)
Class 8	Never worked/long-term unemployed

Table 3: Financial Services and ABC1s

- More than one-third of ABs and more than three in ten C1s borrow more than they save. Those with children are nearly twice as likely as those without to owe more than they have saved.
- ABs and C2s find saving easier than C1s, Ds and Es.
- Just over two-thirds of ABs, and almost two-thirds of C1s, expect to fund their children out of savings and investments.
- Around one-third of ABs and one-fifth of C1s have bought savings plans, investments or insurance over the telephone. Only three ABs and two C1s in 100 have bought them over the Internet.
- Only one AB in eight, and one C1 in 16, sets aside more than £200 a month to save for a retirement pension, in addition to National Insurance contributions.
- Almost one in five ABs, and nearly one in four C1s, puts less than £50 a month into a pension.
- ABs are less worried than other social groups about the accessibility of bank or building society branches, and so are less worried about branch closures.

Source: adapted from www.researchmarkets.com.

growing as a proportion of the total population. The marketing of financial services for older people has become popular in recent years. So has a number of other products and service areas, ranging from specialist holidays to the development of retirement housing.

Gender Businesses may target either males or females. This is because men and women often have different spending patterns. Some car producers, for example, have targeted women in their promotional campaigns for smaller hatchbacks. Manufacturers of perfumes and related products have realised the growing market for personal care products among men. Major brand names such as Armani and Yves Saint Laurent, as well as sports companies, have produced a range of products geared towards

males. Mobile phone manufacturers target a growing number of females buying the latest 'technological gadgets', by designing accessories to suit their requirements.

Social class Markets are often divided by social class. Tables 1 and 2 show two measures of social class used in the UK. For the 2001 population census, the Registrar General divided social class into eight areas. Classes are based on employment status and conditions. This division is usually used in government reports and surveys. The Institute of Practitioners in Advertising (IPA) divides social class into six categories. These are used to decide which group to target for promoting a product. Because of regular changes in the pay and status of different occupations, these categories are revised from time to time. For example, the

Question 2.

(a) Using information in the Table, advise a medium sized manufacturer of sporting equipment on segments of the market it might target.

Table 4: Participation in selected sports during the past four weeks by sex and age, 2005/06

England										Percentages
	Men					**Women**				
	16-24	25-44	45-64	65 and over	All aged 16 and over	16-24	25-44	45-64	65 and over	All aged 16 and over
Indoor swimming or diving	16	18	10	5	13	23	24	16	6	18
Health, fitness, gym or conditioning activities	22	18	9	4	13	19	16	13	3	13
Recreational cycling	16	16	11	4	12	8	9	6	1	6
Snooker, pool, billiards	34	13	7	4	13	12	3	1	-	3
Keep fit, aerobics, dance exercise	4	4	4	3	4	13	12	10	5	10
Outdoor football	43	14	3	-	12	5	1	1	-	1
Golf, pitch and putt, putting	10	9	9	9	9	1	1	2	1	1
Jogging, cross-country, road running	11	10	4	-	7	6	5	2	-	3
Tenpin bowling	9	4	3	1	4	8	4	2	-	3
Darts	16	6	3	1	6	4	2	1	1	2

Source: *Taking Part: The National Survey of Culture, Leisure and Sport*, Department for Culture, Media and Sports.

Registrar General's classification previously had only five classes.

Research often breaks these categories down even further. For example, AB, C1, C2, D and E are sometimes used to highlight the differences between levels of management, and skilled and unskilled manual workers. The media often refers to ABC1s. It is suggested that some businesses are particularly interested in people who might fall into this category as they tend to have higher incomes and levels of spending. Table 3 shows information from a study about the attitudes of people in the ABC1 group to financial services. This could be used by banks, insurance or pension companies to decide which customers to target.

Income Although linked to some extent to the 'social classes' described above, income groups can be different. For example, a self-employed skilled manual worker, such as an electrician, may receive the same income as a middle manager. Similarly, a self-employed builder may receive the same income as or more than a professional. However, because of his or her occupation the two people will be in different social classes.

The population can be split up into income groups and targeted accordingly. So a Cartier watch, for example, is likely to be marketed at the highest income groups.

Religion Businesses may divide markets by religious groups. Food producers, for example, may specialise in producing Kosher food for Jewish people. Digital television has seen the growth of American style Christian television channels in the UK.

Ethnic grouping Markets can sometimes be segmented by country of origin or ethnic grouping. Radio stations have been geared towards African-Caribbean groups. Some products, such as clothing or hair accessories, are also geared towards this grouping.

A drawback of demographic segmentation is that consumers try to defy consumption patterns associated with their demographic groups. For example, young people from lower income groups may seek out expensive high status products, such as certain brands of designer clothes, that were initially marketed at high income groups.

Psychographic segmentation

Geographic and demographic segmentation have limitations. For example, there is a wide variety of spending patterns among females aged 16-18 living in Manchester. Yet people in this consumer group share the same gender, age and location. An alternative way of grouping customers is through psychographic segmentation. This groups customers according to their attitudes, opinions and lifestyles.
- Sports products may be aimed at those who are interested in 'extreme' sports such as skiboarding.
- Chocolate manufacturers have identified two categories of

chocolate eaters. 'Depressive' chocolate lovers eat chocolate to unwind predominantly during the evening. 'Energetic' chocolate eaters eat chocolate as a fast food and live life at a fast pace.
- People's attitudes to life may also be used to segment the market. Some pension funds are geared towards those who only want investments in 'ethical' businesses.
- Clothes may be geared at those who are interested in 'retro' fashions from earlier decades.
- Mobile phones provide services such as Internet access for business travellers.
- Travel companies target holidays at families with younger children.
- Certain newspapers are geared towards Labour voters, while others are geared towards Conservative voters.

One of the drawbacks of psychographic segmentation is that it can be difficult for businesses to collect data about the beliefs, attitudes and lifestyles of consumers. In order to do this they may require the help of specialist businesses.

Behavioural segmentation

Behavioural segmentation attempts to segment markets according to how consumers relate to a product. There is a number of different methods of behavioural segmentation:

Usage rate This is when consumers are categorised according to the quantity and frequency of their purchases. One example of this is British Airways, which established an 'Executive Club' to encourage and develop the custom of regular business travellers.

Loyalty Consumers can be categorized according to their product loyalty. The Tesco Clubcard, for example, which offers discounts to regular customers of Tesco supermarkets seeks to reward and encourage loyalty to Tesco and its products.

Time and date of consumption Consumers often consume particular products at particular times and dates. Businesses can take advantage of this in order to improve their marketing. So, for example, manufacturers of breakfast cereals, while recognising that their product will be primarily consumed in the morning, encourage consumers also to consume their products in the evening. Similarly, many bars and clubs seek to encourage different groups of consumers according to the night of the week. For example, Thursday nights are often for older singles and Friday nights for younger consumers in many such establishments.

Like other segmentation methods, a drawback of behavioural segmentation is that on its own it may fail to adequately capture a target market for a business. For this reason, in many cases a business might employ a **variety** of the segmentation methods explained above. So, for example, a manufacturer of luxury apartments may be interested in segments that included single men or women with no children, in the 30-40 age range, with high incomes that fall into social class AB. Because of the likely one-off nature of such a purchase, behavioural segmentation would be less important in this instance.

KEYTERMS

Demography – the study of population, its composition and how it is changing over time.

Market segment – part of a whole segment which contains a group of buyers with similar characteristics, such as age, income, social class or attitudes.

Market segmentation – breaking down a market into sub-groups which share similar characteristics.

KNOWLEDGE

1. How can a market be segmented geographically?
2. Explain three ways in which the spending patterns of females aged 25-35 with children who are in paid employment might differ from those of males aged 55-65 who have taken early retirement and whose children have left home.
3. (a) What is meant by 'social class'?
   (b) Give two ways in which the spending of social class A households might differ from that of social class D.
4. How might understanding the personalities of different groups of consumers help in the marketing of a product?
5. Briefly explain five ways in which consumers might be segmented on a behavioural basis.

Case Study: The power of the Muslim pound

Marian Salzman is one of the world's foremost trend-spotters. She can see something coming before others have even raised their heads to look and the next big thing in marketing she argues is the 'Muslim pound'. According to Mintel, a market research company, the estimated spending power of Muslim people in the UK is £20.5 billion. There are more than 5,000 Muslim millionaires in the UK, with combined assets worth more than £3.6 billion.

'It's a unique market with a unique set of needs, for example in the banking area,' says Salzman, the executive vice president and chief marketing officer of consultancy JWT. 'Under sharia law (which governs how Muslims can borrow money), different kinds of mortgages need to be written in order for someone who is Muslim to acquire a home. And there's halal law (which is concerned with the way in which animal are slaughtered) which affects consumption of food, beauty and healthcare products.'

This trend may provide demographic segmentation opportunities for business. There has been a huge surge in marketing to Muslims this year, according to Salzman. 'I think it is a recognition of the size of the market,' she says. 'Another thing I believe has been driving it is all the coverage of whether Turkey will be part of the EU, which has also raised the visibility of the question about the sheer percentage of the European population that is Muslim.' Muslims are also more sensitive about the moral attributes of brands and the way in which they are marketed according to research. Fifty-nine per cent agreed that there was too much suggestiveness or immodesty in most advertising compared to 28 per cent of the general sample.

Their buying behaviour is also heavily influenced by expert endorsement and opinion. In the survey, almost two-thirds agreed with the statement, 'I feel reassured if a product has been endorsed by an expert' – almost twice as many as the general sample. Muslims also have a higher level of trust in expert opinions and reviews than non-Muslims: 75 per cent compared to 56 per cent.

Source: adapted from *The Independent*, 9.7. 2007.

(a) What is meant by (i) market segmentation (3 marks) and (ii) demographic segmentation in the article? (3 marks)
(b) Explain why a small business offering financial services might benefit from market segmentation. (8 marks)
(c) Examine how targeting Muslim customers might affect a business marketing financial services. (6 marks)
(d) Discuss the extent to which selling to one market segment, such as people of a particular religion, is likely to be a successful marketing strategy for a small business offering financial services. (10 marks)

Market size

The size of a market can be estimated or calculated by the total sales of all businesses in the market. Market size is usually estimated in a number of ways.

Value This is the total amount spent by customers buying products. For example, it was estimated that fast food products in the UK accounted for sales worth £8.38 billion in 2004. This included branded fast food chains and independent outlets selling hot or cold eat-in food without table service, or takeaway food.

Volume This is the physical quantity of products which are produced and sold. For example, global crude steel production was over 1.1 billion tonnes in 2005, the highest ever. The UK produced around 12 million tonnes. Some estimates of volume are based on the number or percentage of users, subscribers or viewers. This is often the case in markets for services, such as the number of mobile phone users, the number of television viewers or the percentage of households with digital television.

Different markets are likely to differ in size. For example, sales of chilled desserts like cream cakes, cheesecakes and trifles were £390 million in 2006. On the other hand over £1.9 billion was spent by British consumers on increasingly popular holiday cruises.

Market growth

Markets can grow either rapidly or slowly, or they might contract and get smaller. Take the example of the market for sandwiches in the UK. Between 2002 and 2006 average year on year growth in sandwich sales was 3.5 per cent, but from 2006-2007 growth was 9 per cent, almost three times that of previous years. Similarly, the value of the UK budget hotel market increased by 38 per cent between 2002 and 2006, to reach £1 billion. This growth was three times that of the overall UK hotel market (worth £11.2 billion), which increased by just 12 per cent over the same four year period. On the other hand the market for sales of ties fell from £158 million in 1999 to just £154 million by 2004. It was suggested that the fall was due to the growing trend amongst men for dressing down at work.

What factors are likely to influence whether a market gets bigger or becomes smaller and the rate of growth or decline?

- **Economic changes.** An increase in income, for example, can affect different markets. Rising incomes might help the growth of the market for high class restaurants or specialist furniture makers.
- **Social changes.** Changes in society can lead to a growth or a decline in markets. The decline in the number of marriages, an increase in the proportion of working

Question 1.

Ormskirk is a town in Lancashire. It has a market on Thursdays and Saturdays every week which attracts customers from both the town and local counties. Traditionally it has had local teashops and a few restaurants. But over the period 2000-2007 the market for shops providing food has increased. There are now retailers selling ready made sandwiches and meals. There are takeaways. There are Chinese, Indian, Italian, French and Tapas restaurants. There are wine bars selling food in the daytime as well as the traditional teashops. There are regular rail and bus Links to Liverpool and Preston. In 2005 after 120 years of providing education, Edge Hill was granted university status. In 2007, the university had 17,000 students. It planned to spend £220 million from its own coffers to provide extra student accommodation, new teaching buildings and facilities. A study to assess its impact on the area found that it contributed £77 million a year to the North West of England's economy. This figure was predicted to rise to £172 million by 2022. The study also showed that the number of jobs supported by the university is anticipated to rise from its current level of 2,650 to 4,850. In 2007 a planned bypass was being proposed, linking the M58 to the Ormskirk to Southport main road.

Source: adapted in part from http://info.edgehill.ac.uk, http://news.bbc.co.uk.

(a) Suggest factors that might affect the size and growth of the market in which an Ormskirk restaurant operates.
(b) Discuss whether this market will grow in future.

Question 2.

Commercial radio stations have found it difficult to match the listener numbers of BBC. In 2007 the BBC attracted 54.5 per cent of listening, up 0.3 percentage points on 2006 Commercial radio was 0.3 percentage points down to 43.3 per cent. Radio 1 gained listeners, partly due to the stability of the weekday DJ line-up and the extension of Chris Moyles' breakfast show to start half an hour earlier at 6.30a.m. Radio 2's audience was up by a quarter of a million people and market share was up from 15.5 per rcent to 15.8 per cent, attracted by long-standing, popular programmes such as Terry Wogan's breakfast show.

Johnny Vaughan, at Capital Radio, made a strong gain in number of listeners, adding 246,000 with market share holding steady. The worry for Capital is that its new listeners can easily change to other stations. Capital must build on its gains if the station is to catch up with Heart and Magic. Both have opened up and sustained a sizeable lead in London. Radio 1 and Radio 2 have also both increased their listener base in the capital in

the past 12 months.

The decline in total listening to local commercial stations has been the trend for two years. This continues, with a drop in the past year from 32.6 per cent to 31.7 per cent of total listening. Stations such as Radio City in Liverpool, Clyde 2 in Glasgow and Smooth Radio in North-West England were among those to lose audience. But not all stations lost out. Choice FM in London gained 111,000 new listeners, taking the station to a new record of 611,000 listeners. Xfm Manchester increased its weekly audience by 33 per cent, lifting its market share by a third.

Source: adapted from the *Guardian*, 29.10.2007.

(a) Outline the changes in the share of the market of (i) Radio 2, (ii) national commercial and non-commercial radio stations and (iii) local commercial radio stations.
(b) Explain two factors that may influence the share of the market of radio stations.

women and the growth in the number of one parent families is linked to a growth in the market for child care and other child support services, and for housing.
- **Technological changes.** Changes in technology can cause a rapid growth in certain markets and a decline in others. The DVD market has expanded rapidly in recent years at the expense of the video market. The growth in iPods and other MP3 players and the downloading of music from the Internet are associated with a decline in CD sales.
- **Demographic changes.** Changes in the age structure of the population can affect markets. The ageing of the UK population has led to a growth in products aimed at people aged over 50, such as specialist holidays, mobility aids and insurance products.

- **Changes in legislation.** Changes in the law governing the use of radio frequencies has enabled a large growth in the number of commercial radio stations.

Market share

MARKET SHARE or MARKET PENETRATION is the term used to describe the proportion of a particular market that is held by a business, a product, a brand or a number of businesses or products. Market share is shown as a percentage. The market share of a business can be calculated as:

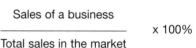

$$\frac{\text{Sales of a business}}{\text{Total sales in the market}} \times 100\%$$

Why might the measurement of market share be important? It might indicate a business that is a market leader. This could influence other companies to follow the leader or influence the leader to maintain its position. It might influence the **strategy** or **objectives** of a business. A business that has a small market share may set a target of increasing its share by 5 per cent over a period of time. It may also be an indication of the success or failure of a business or its strategy.

Figure 1 shows the market shares of supermarkets in the UK in June 2007. It shows, for example, that the market leader was Tesco and that three quarters of the market sales were accounted for by the 'big five' supermarket chains. However, care must be taken when interpreting the market share of businesses.
- The share of the market can be measured in different ways. Market share is calculated as the sales of a business as a percentage of total market sales. Sales can be calculated in a number of ways. They might be the value of sales, such as £100 million a year. Or they might be calculated by the number or volume of sales, for example, 6 million products sold each year or 10 million visitors to attractions owned by a theme park company.

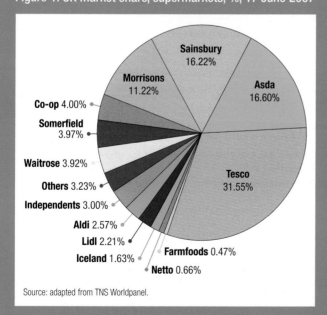

Figure 1: UK market share, supermarkets, %, 17 June 2007

Sainsbury 16.22%
Morrisons 11.22%
Co-op 4.00%
Somerfield 3.97%
Waitrose 3.92%
Others 3.23%
Independents 3.00%
Aldi 2.57%
Lidl 2.21%
Iceland 1.63%
Farmfoods 0.47%
Netto 0.66%
Asda 16.60%
Tesco 31.55%

Source: adapted from TNS Worldpanel.

- The market and the time period chosen can affect the results. For example, in 2004 Safeway was taken over by Morrisons. This significantly increased Morrison's market share from below 10% to over 11% as shown in Figure 1.
- The type of product and business included might also affect the results. For example, in 2007 it was reported that Scottish and Newcastle plc had 26 per cent of the beer market. However, in the UK drinks market, beer made up only 35 per cent of drinks spending. So the market share of the UK drinks market of Scottish and Newcastle plc would be less than 26 per cent because the drinks market would include the sales of other drinks manufacturers such as Coca-Cola (carbonated soft drinks) and Tetley GB Ltd (tea).

KEYTERMS

Market share or market penetration – the proportion of total sales in a particular market for which one or more businesses or brands are responsible. It is expressed as a percentage and can be calculated by value or volume.

KNOWLEDGE

1. Explain two ways in which the size of a market can be calculated.
2. What is meant by a market that is (a) growing and (b) declining?
3. Give four factors that might influence market growth.
4. What is the formula used to calculate market share?
5. Give three examples of the problems of measuring market share.

Case Study: British cheese

When it comes to cheese, continental varieties such as Brie and Emmental were once the height of sophistication. Research from Mintel has found that cheese buyers are increasingly opting for British regional cheeses, such as Lancashire, Cheshire and Red Leicester. Sales of specialist British cheese increased by as much as 16 per cent between 2004 and 2006, to reach £220 million. Growth has outpaced the likes of soft and continental cheese.

'With growing interest in environmental and ethical concerns we are becoming increasingly interested in the origin of our food. As a result we are seeing a growing trend towards "buying British", which has provided a huge boost for sales of British regional cheese,' comments David Bird, Senior Consumer Analyst. 'Many varieties of regional British cheese have extended their ranges by adding fruits, liqueurs and even curry. This has really caught the imagination of cheese customers and has lead to the rise in sales of locally produced cheese,' he adds.

Although sales by volume of continental cheese have continued to rise, the value of sales has not. Market value fell 7 per cent between 2004 and 2006 to £340 million. 'Continental cheese such as Brie used to be seen as a luxury for special occasions. But today many continental varieties are now more an everyday staple than an occasional treat. This has inevitably brought prices down and as a result market value has declined, despite rising volume sales,' explains David Bird.

Specialist British regional cheese has seen the greatest growth. But cheddars, which are not classified as specialist cheeses, from the UK and abroad accounted for over half (52 per cent) of all cheese sales in the UK last year, having grown 7 per cent between 2004 and 2006 to reach £985 million. What is more, this year sales of the humble block of cheddar will hit the £1 billion mark for the first time ever. 'Cheddars have clearly stood the test of time and are now still very much a British staple. The market has done well to see growth despite heavy

discounting and many buy-one-get-one-free offers in the supermarkets,' comments David Bird.

The British cheese market was worth £1.9 billion in 2006, having increased 4 per cent between 2004 and 2006. Sales are set to rise to £1.93 billion this year. This is no mean feat considering the trend towards healthy eating.

Source: adapted from www.mintel.com.

(a) Outline the features of the market for cheeses in the UK. (4 marks)

(b) (i) Calculate the size of the market for British cheese in 2004. (4 marks)
(ii) Calculate the value of the decline in sales of continental cheeses between 2004 and 2006. (4 marks)

(c) How would you explain the increase in sales volume of specialist and regional British cheeses? (8 marks)

(d) How would you explain why the value of the sales of continental cheeses has fallen while the volume of sales has increased over the period 2004-2006? (8 marks)

(e) Examine the factors that may affect the size of the market for Cheddar cheeses in the UK in future. (8 marks)

10 Legal structure - sole traders and partnerships

What is a business organisation?

Businesses are often referred to as organisations. An ORGANISATION is a body that is set up to meet needs. For example, the St. John's Ambulance organisation was originally set up by volunteers to train the public in life saving measures.

Business organisations satisfy needs by providing people with goods and services. All organisations will:

- try to achieve objectives;
- use resources;
- need to be directed;
- have to be accountable;
- have to meet legal requirements;
- have a formal structure.

Private sector business organisations

One method of classifying businesses is by **sector**. The PRIVATE SECTOR includes all those businesses which are set up by individuals or groups of individuals. Most business activity is undertaken in the private sector. The types of business in the private sector can vary considerably. Some are small retailers with a single owner. Others are large multinational companies such as Cadbury Schweppes. Businesses will vary according to the legal form they take and their ownership.

- **Unincorporated businesses.** These are businesses where there is no legal difference between the owners and the business. Everything is carried out in the name of the owner or owners. These firms tend to be small, owned by either one person or a few partners.
- **Incorporated businesses.** An incorporated body is one which has a separate legal identity from its owners. In other words, the business can be sued, can be taken over

and can be liquidated.

Figure 1 shows the different types of business organisation in the private sector, their legal status and their ownership. These are examined in the rest of this unit.

Sole traders

The simplest and most common form of private sector business is a SOLE TRADER or SOLE PROPRIETOR. This type of business is owned by just one person. The owner runs the business and may employ any number of people to help.

Sole traders can be found in different types of production. In the primary sector many farmers and fishermen operate like this. In the secondary sector there are small scale manufacturers, builders and construction firms. The tertiary sector has large numbers of sole traders. They supply a wide range of services, such as hairdressing, retailing, restaurants, gardening and other household services. Many sole traders exist in retailing and construction, where a very large number of shops and small construction companies are each owned by one person. Although there are many more sole traders than any other type of business, the amount they contribute to total output in the UK is relatively small.

Setting up as a sole trader is straightforward. There are no legal formalities needed.

However, sole traders or self-employed entrepreneurs do have some legal responsibilities once they become established. In addition, some types of business need to obtain special permission before trading.

- Once turnover reaches a certain level sole traders must register for VAT.
- They must pay income tax and National Insurance contributions.

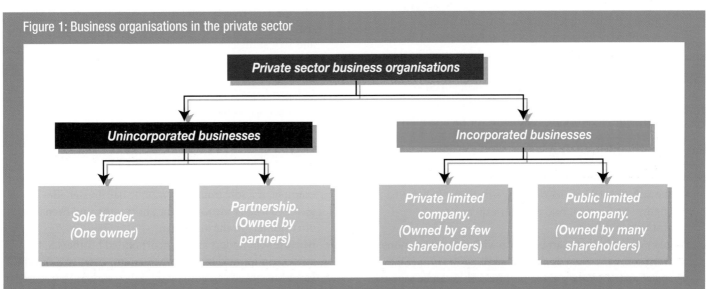

Figure 1: Business organisations in the private sector

- Private sector business organisations
  - Unincorporated businesses
    - Sole trader. (One owner)
    - Partnership. (Owned by partners)
  - Incorporated businesses
    - Private limited company. (Owned by a few shareholders)
    - Public limited company. (Owned by many shareholders)

Question 1.

Joanna Carter owns Joanna Carter Contemporary Flowers in Wallingford. She attracts customers in three areas - weddings, corporate work for local business and flowers for private homes. Despite only setting up in July last year, demand has soared thanks to Joanna's growing reputation for creative arrangements. She set up as a sole trader after leaving her job to raise a family. 'After leaving my personnel job to have my children, now aged nine and six, I had time to think about where I really wanted to go in my career. I was keen to develop my passion for flowers with proper training and so I took a two-year part-time course at Abingdon and Witney College'. She also gained work experience working one day a week in a florists' shop in Wallingford. When she graduated, she had already received a number of offers from people wanting her to do private arrangements for them. So she left the shop to run her own business from home.

Joanna approached the local Business Link, a free and impartial guide to business advice, resources and information shortly after setting up the business. 'I've been able to book a place on an advanced bridal skills course with highly respected London florist Jane Packer in May. The course costs £900 and half of the cost will be paid for through the Skills Development Team at Business Link. I am also looking into a broadband grant so I can provide a slide show of my work for potential corporate customers and wedding bookings.   I'm in the process of applying for an Enterprising Woman grant run by Surrey University which will give me £350-worth of funding'.

Source: adapted from www.businesslink.gov.uk.

(a)   As a sole trader Joanna Carter has unlimited liability. What does this mean?

(b)   Explain two advantages to Joanna Carter of operating as a sole trader.

(c)   How did Business Link help Joanna Carter in running her small business?

- Some types of business activity need a licence, such as the sale of alcohol or supplying a taxi service or public transport.
- Sometimes planning permission is needed in certain locations. For example, a person may have to apply to the local authority for planning permission to run a fish and chip shop in premises which had not been used for this activity before.
- Sole traders must comply with legislation aimed at business practice. For example, legally they must provide healthy and safe working conditions for their employees.

Advantages of sole traders

Sole traders have a number of advantages.
- The lack of legal restrictions. The sole trader will not face a lengthy setting up period or incur expensive administration costs.
- Sole proprietorships can be set up with little or no money in the business. They don't cost anything to set up. So the capital cost of creating a sole proprietorship can be minimal.
- Any profit made after tax is kept by the owner.

- The owner is in complete control and is free to make decisions without interference. For many sole traders independence is one of the main reasons why they choose to set up in business.
- The owner has flexibility to choose the hours of work he or she wants and to take holidays. Customers may also benefit. Sole traders can take individual customers' needs into account, stocking a particular brand of a good or making changes to a standard design, for example.
- Because of their small size, sole traders can offer a personal service to their customers. Some people prefer to deal directly with the owner and are prepared to pay a higher price for doing so.
- Such businesses may be entitled to government support.

Disadvantages of sole traders

However, there are also disadvantages of sole traders.
- Sole traders have UNLIMITED LIABILITY. This means that if the business has debts, the owner is personally liable. A sole trader may be forced to sell personal possessions or use personal savings to meet these debts.
- Sole proprietorships can be risky for their owners. If the business is unsuccessful, sole traders can end up working for nothing or even subsidising the business out of their own private resources. Also, because the business is the sole trader, long term illness can have a devastating effect on it. Becoming an employee is less risky and is one reason why workers may not want to work for themselves.
- Sole proprietorships face continuity problems. Will the business survive if the sole trader dies, takes retirement or decides to do something different? Some sole traders run family businesses where parents tend to pass on their business to their children. Farming is an example. However, many sole traders will not pass their businesses on to family members. So these businesses will disappear.
- The money used to set up the business is often the owner's savings. It may also come from a bank loan. Sole traders may find it difficult to raise money. They tend to be small and lack sufficient **collateral**, such as property or land, on which to raise finance. This means money for expansion must come from profits or savings.
- Independence is an advantage, but it can also be a disadvantage. A sole trader might prefer to share decision making, for example. Many sole traders work very long hours, without holidays, and may have to learn new skills.
- In cases where the owner is the only person in the business, illness can stop business activity taking place. For example, if a sole trader is a mobile hairdresser, illness will lead to a loss of income in the short term, and even a loss of customers in the long term.
- Because sole traders are unincorporated businesses, the owner can be sued by customers in the event of a dispute.
- Large businesses can employ specialist workers. A sole trader often has to be purchaser, driver, accountant, lawyer and

labourer to run the business. Allowing workers to specialise can lead to lower costs of production per unit. So sole traders can be at a disadvantage competitively which they are forced to make up for by paying themselves lower wages.

- Sole proprietorships are usually small businesses. So they are unable to gain reductions in unit costs of production as the volume of output rises, known as **economies of scale**. Sole traders tend to be concentrated in industries such as farming, where economies of scale are limited.

Partnerships

A PARTNERSHIP is defined in **The Partnership Act, 1890** as the 'relation which subsists between persons carrying on business with common view to profit'. Put simply, a partnership has more than one owner. The 'joint' owners will share responsibility for running the business and also share the profits. Partnerships are often found in professions such as accountants, doctors, estate agents, solicitors and veterinary surgeons. After sole traders, partnerships are the most common type of business organisation. It is usual for partners to specialise. A firm of chartered accountants with five partners might be organised so that each partner specialises in one aspect of finance, such as tax

Question 2.

Sarah Otaka, Gillian Peters and Maria Ampat run a dental practice in Scunthorpe. They operate as a partnership. They undertake work for the NHS, but an increasing amount of their income comes from private work. The partnership was established in 2003. The three dentists each contributed £20,000 to provide start-up capital. A further £20,000 was borrowed from a bank. The money was used to convert a property into dental surgeries and buy equipment. The business employs four other staff – three dental assistants and a receptionist.

After three successful years in business together a problem arose. Gillian wanted to attract more private clients, particularly those requiring cosmetic work which is usually very lucrative. Sarah and Maria were more committed to NHS work. They were not in it just for the money. After a period of disagreement, where communications deteriorated, a partners' meeting was held to find a solution. Gillian, however, felt that the only way forward was for her to break away from the partnership.

(a) At the end of the third year a profit of £180,000 was made by the practice. How much is each partner likely to get if there is no deed of partnership?

(b) Explain two advantages to the dentists of operating as a partnership.

(c) How does this case illustrate one of the main disadvantages of partnerships?

law, investments or VAT returns.

There are no legal formalities to complete when a partnership is formed. However, partners may draw up a DEED OF PARTNERSHIP. This is a legal document which states partners' rights in the event of a dispute. It covers issues such as:

- how much capital each partner will contribute;
- how profits (and losses) will be shared amongst the partners;
- the procedure for ending the partnership;
- how much control each partner has;
- rules for taking on new partners.

If no deed of partnership is drawn up the arrangements between partners will be subject to the Partnership Act. For example, if there is a dispute regarding the share of profits, the Act states that profits are shared equally among the partners.

Advantages of partnerships

Partnerships have a number of advantages.

- There are no legal formalities to complete when setting up the business.
- Like a sole proprietorship, an ordinary partnership does not need to publish any accounts which may be seen by the public. Only the tax authorities must have access to the accounts of a partnership. In contrast, the accounts of a company are available to anyone who asks to see them via Companies House. The accounts of a limited liability partnership are open to inspection by the public, but in a less detailed format than those of a company.
- Each partner can specialise. This may improve the running of the business, as partners can carry out the tasks they do best.
- Since there is more than one owner, more finance can be raised than if the firm was a sole trader.
- Partners can share the work. They will be able to cover each other for holidays and illness. They can exchange ideas when making key decisions. Also, the success of the business will not depend upon the ability of one person, as is the case with a sole trader.
- Since this type of business tends to be larger than the sole trader, it is in a stronger position to raise more money from outside the business.

Disadvantages of partnerships

- The individual partners have unlimited liability. Under the Partnership Act, each partner is equally liable for debts.
- Profits have to be shared among more owners.
- Partners may disagree. For example, they might differ in their views on whether to hire a new employee or about the amount of profit to retain for investment.
- The size of a partnership is limited to a maximum of 20 partners. This limits the amount of money that can be introduced from owners.
- The partnership ends when one of the partners dies.
- The partnership must be wound up so that the partner's family can retrieve money invested in the business. It is

normal for the remaining partners to form a new partnership quickly afterwards.

- Any decision made by one partner on behalf of the company is legally binding on all other partners. For example, if one partner agreed to buy four new company cars for the business, all partners must honour this.
- Partnerships have unincorporated status, so partners can be sued by customers.

Limited partnerships

The Limited Partnerships Act 1907 allows a business to become a LIMITED PARTNERSHIP, although this is rare. This is where some partners provide capital but take no part in the management of the business. Such a partner will have LIMITED LIABILITY - the partner can only lose the original amount of money invested. A partner with limited liabillity cannot be made to sell personal possessions to meet any other business debts. This type of partner is called a **sleeping partner**. Even with a

limited partnership there must always be at least one partner with **unlimited liability**. The Act also allows this type of partnership to have more than 20 partners.

The Limited Liability Partnership Act, 2000 allows the setting up of a LIMITED LIABILITY PARTNERSHIP. All partners in this type of partnership have limited liability. To set up as a limited liability partnership, the business has to agree to comply with a number of regulations, such as filing annual reports with the Registrar of Companies.

KEYTERMS

Deed of Partnership – a binding legal document which states the formal rights of partners.
Limited liability – where a business owner is only liable for the original amount of money invested in the business.
Limited Liability partnership – a partnership where all partners have limited liability.
Limited partnership – a partnership where some members contribute capital and enjoy a share of profit, but do not participate in the running of the business. At least one partner must have unlimited liability.
Organisation – a body set up to meet a need.
Partnership – a business organisation which is usually owned by between 2-20 people.
Private sector – businesses that are owned by individuals or groups of individuals.
Sole trader or sole proprietor – a business organisation which has a single owner.
Unlimited liability - where the owner of a business is personally liable for all business debts.

KNOWLEDGE

1. What is the difference between a corporate body and an unincorporated body?
2. State three advantages and three disadvantages of being a sole trader.
3. What is the advantage of a deed of partnership?
4. State three advantages and three disadvantages of partnerships.
5. What is meant by a sleeping partner?

Case Study: Oxford Vintage cars

Hristo Petrov runs a small business buying and selling vintage cars. He buys cars at auctions and from dealers and currently sells them on Ebay. At the moment Hristo does not undertake any renovation work on the cars. He just buys them and sells them on. Last year he made a profit of £37,000. However, Hristo is ambitious.and wants to set up his own website and operate from a car showroom in Oxford. A lot of the cars he sells are MGBs and MGAs. These cars were originally made in Oxford and Hristo likes the idea of locating a showroom in their home city. He also wants to employ a team of mechanics to renovate them. He knows that premium prices are paid for well restored vintage cars.

Unfortunately Hristo can only raise £50,000 of the £100,000 needed to develop the business. He has approached several banks but has not been able to secure funding as he has a poor credit rating after having his house repossessed. A friend of his, however, is keen to get involved in the business. Mark Watkins bought a car from Hristo three years ago and the two have remained in touch ever since. Mark is happy to provide the other £50,000 if he can become an equal partner.

Hristo has eventually accepted Mark's offer and the new showroom is due to open very shortly. The partnership, called Oxford Vintage Cars,

has a smart website which contains details of all the cars in stock and other useful information for enthusiasts.

After a deed of partnership was drawn up Hristo said 'At first I did not want to go into partnership, but now I think it will work. Mark is as committed as me and has come up with some good ideas. For example, he reckons we can rent out some of the cars in stock for special occasions such as weddings. I hadn't even though of that. He will also be good on the restoration side and he will be able to supervise the mechanics more effectively than me. I will concentrate on the buying and selling, that's what I'm good at'.

(a) Using this case as an example, explain what is meant by a partnership. (4 marks)
(b) Oxford Vintage Cars is an unincorporated business. What does this mean? (6 marks)
(c) How does this case highlight one of the problems of operating as a sole trader? (6 marks)
(d) Why do you think Hristo did not want to enter a business partnership? (8 marks)
(e) To what extent will the partners be able to specialise in the business? (12 marks)

Legal structure - limited companies

Companies

There are many examples of LIMITED COMPANIES in the UK. They range from Garrick Engineering, a small family business, to British Airways which has many thousands of shareholders. One feature is that they all have a separate legal identity from their owners. This means that they can own assets, form contracts, employ people, sue and be sued in their own right. Another feature is that the owners all have **limited liability**. If a limited company has debts, the owners can only lose the money they have invested in the firm. They cannot be forced to use their own money, like sole traders and partners, to pay business debts.

The **capital** of a limited company is divided into **shares**. Each member or **shareholder** owns a number of these shares. They are the joint owners of the company and can vote and take a share of the profit. Those with more shares will have more control and can take more profit.

Limited companies are run by **directors** who are appointed by the shareholders. The board of directors, headed by a **chairperson**, is accountable to shareholders and should run the company as the shareholders wish. If the company's performance does not live up to shareholders' expectations, directors can be 'voted out' at an **Annual General Meeting** (AGM).

Whereas sole traders and partnerships pay income tax on profits, companies pay corporation tax.

Forming a limited company

How do shareholders set up a limited company? Limited companies must submit some important information to the Registrar of Companies.

Memorandum of Association The Memorandum sets out the constitution and gives details about the company. The Companies Act 1985 states that the following details must be included.
- The name of the company.
- The name and address of the company's registered office.
- The objectives of the company, and the scope of its activities.
- The liability of its members.
- The amount of capital to be raised and the number of shares to be issued.

A limited company must have a minimum of two members, but there is no upper limit.

Articles of Association The Articles of Association deal with the internal running of the company. They include details such as:
- the rights of shareholders depending on the type of share they hold;
- the procedures for appointing directors and the scope of their powers;
- the length of time directors should serve before re-election;
- the timing and frequency of company meetings;
- the arrangements for auditing company accounts.

Form 10 This form gives details of the first directors, secretary and the address of the registered office. Directors must give their names and addresses, dates of birth, occupations and details of other directorships they have held within the last five years.

Form 12 This form is a statutory declaration of compliance with all the legal requirements relating to the incorporation of the company. It must be signed by a solicitor who is forming the company, a director or the company secretary.

These documents will be sent to the **Registrar** at **Companies House**. If they are acceptable, the company's application will be successful. It will be awarded a **Certificate of Incorporation** which allows it to trade. The Registrar keeps these documents on file and they can be inspected at any time by the general public for a fee. A limited company must also submit a copy of its **Annual Report and Accounts** to the Registrar each year. The accounts will include information such as the balance sheet and income statement or profit and loss accounts of the business. Finally, the shareholders have a legal right to attend the AGM and should be told of the date and venue in writing well in advance.

Question 1.

MD Chris Lay re-mortgaged his house to launch Gigasat Limited in 2000. The business was incorporated on 16.10.2000 and the registered address is 12 Rylands Mews, Lake Street, Leighton Buzzard, Bedfordshire. The company's registration number is 04090608. The company develops satellite communications equipment, such as lightweight, carbon-fibre antennas, and vehicles installed with satellite systems. Clients include the news channels CNN and Al Jazeera. They use Gigasat technology for live television coverage. The equipment has also been adopted by the government and the military for secure satellite transmissions. For example, its equipment allows troops posted abroad to access the Internet and talk to loved ones. Sales have grown 67 per cent a year from £2 million in 2003 to £5.7 million in 2005.

Source: adapted from Tech Track 100 and information from Companies House.

(a) What evidence is there in the case to suggest that Gigasat is a private limited company?
(b) What legal obligations will Gigasat Limited have to: (i) shareholders and (ii) the Registrar of Companies each year?
(c) Discuss two advantages to the owners of Gigasat Limited of operating as a private limited company.

41

Private limited companies

Private limited companies are one type of limited company. They tend to be relatively smaller businesses, although certain well known companies, such as Reebok and Littlewoods, are private limited companies. Their business name ends in **Limited** or **Ltd**. Shares can only be transferred 'privately' and all shareholders must agree on the transfer. They cannot be advertised for general sale. Private limited companies are often family businesses owned by members of the family or close friends. The directors of these firms tend to be shareholders and are involved in the running of the business. Many manufacturing firms are private limited companies rather than sole traders or partnerships.

Advantages of private limited companies

There are certain advantages in setting up a business as a private limited company.

- Shareholders have limited liability. As a result more people are prepared to risk their money than in, say, a partnership.
- More capital can be raised as there is no limit on the number of shareholders.
- Control of the company cannot be lost to outsiders. Shares can only be sold to new members if all shareholders agree.
- The business will continue even if one of the owners dies. In this case shares will be transferred to another owner.
- There may be tax advantages for the owners, particularly if owners are currently paying the higher rate of income tax. Profits can be retained by the company and distributed to the owners at a later date, for example when they retire.
- Some businesses may not deal with unlimited businesses or businesses that are not registered for VAT. This is because they think that limited companies registered for VAT are more likely to be run well, since, they have to keep proper accounts and tend to use the professional advice of accountants and solicitors.

Disadvantages of private limited companies

There are some disadvantages in setting up a business as a private limited company.

- Profits have to be shared out among a much larger number of members.
- There is a legal procedure in setting up the business. This takes time and also costs money.
- Firms are not allowed to sell shares to the public. This restricts the amount of capital that can be raised.
- Financial information filed with the Registrar can be inspected by any member of the public. Competitors could use this to their advantage.
- If one shareholder decides to sell shares it may take time to find a buyer.

Public limited companies

The second type of limited company tends to be larger and is

Question 2.

Burton's Foods, famous for its Wagon Wheels and Jammie Dogders biscuits, was bought by the private equity company, Duke Street Capital in 2007. Burton's, the UK's second largest biscuit producer, employs 3,000 people on five sites in the UK. Founded in the 1930s it became part of Associated British Foods in 1949 before being sold to Hicks, Muse, Tate & Furst seven years ago. The deal was said to be worth around £200 million. However, just two months later the new owners announced that biscuit production would cease at its factory in the Wirral, with the loss of 660 jobs. The announcement of the job cuts sparked an angry reaction from unions.

Tony Woodley, joint general secretary of the newly-created Unite union, said: 'We are not going to just roll over and accept this. We will be urgently consulting with our members about a strategy to keep the factory open and will meet management on Monday to hear their rationale for this body-blow to Merseyside manufacturing'.

The factory in Moreton is the biggest employer in the Wirral after Vauxhall cars. Mr Woodley said the job losses would 'devastate the community'. The company is to stop making biscuits, at the site but will continue to manufacture chocolate and assemble seasonal assortments at the factory. It is thought 330 jobs will remain on the site. Paul Kitchener, chief executive of Burton's Foods, said that while the company 'sincerely' regretted the loss of jobs, the changes were needed because of overcapacity in the biscuit market.

Source: adapted from *The Guardian*, 19.3.2007.

(a) **Using this case as an example, explain what is meant by a private equity company.**
(b) **What evidence is there in the case to suggest that the private equity company is pursuing ruthless efficiency gains?**

called a **public limited company**. This company name ends in plc. There were around 1.85 million registered limited companies in the UK in 2006. Only around 1 per cent were public limited companies. However, they contributed far more to national output and employed far more people than private limited companies. The shares of these companies can be bought and sold by the public on the stock exchange.

When 'going public' a company is likely to publish a **Prospectus**. This is a document which advertises the company to potential investors and invites them to buy shares before a FLOTATION. An example of a company floated on the stock exchange in 2006 is Styles & Wood. It supplies property services to retailers such as Waitrose and B&Q. 'Going public' can be expensive because:

- the company needs lawyers to ensure that the prospectus is 'legally' correct;
- a large number of 'glossy' publications have to be made available;
- the company may use a financial institution to process share applications;
- the share issue has to be underwritten (which means that the company must insure against the possibility of some shares remaining unsold) and a fee is paid to an underwriter who must buy any unsold shares;
- the company will have advertising and administrative expenses;
- it must have a minimum of £50,000 share capital.

A public limited company cannot begin trading until it has completed these tasks and has received at least a 25 per cent payment for the value of shares. It will then receive a **trading certificate** and can begin operating, and the shares will be quoted on the **Stock Exchange** or the **Alternative Investment Market** (AIM).

A stock exchange is a market where second hand shares are bought and sold. A full stock exchange listing means that the company must comply with the rules and regulations laid down by the stock exchange. Many of these rules are to protect shareholders from fraud. The AIM is designed for companies which want to avoid some of the high costs of a full listing. However, shareholders with shares quoted on the AIM do not have the same protection as those with 'fully' quoted shares.

Advantages of public limited companies

Some of the advantages are the same as those of private limited companies. For example, all members have limited liability, the firm continues to trade if one of the owners dies and more power is enjoyed due to their larger size. Others are as follows.

- Huge amounts of money can be raised from the sale of shares to the public.
- Production costs may be lower as firms may gain economies of scale.
- Because of their size, plcs can often dominate the market.
- It becomes easier to raise finance as financial institutions are more willing to lend to plcs.

- Pressures from the financial media and financial analysts, as well as the danger that the plc might be taken over by another company, encourage executives and managers to perform well and make profits. These pressures do not exist for private limited companies.

Disadvantages of public limited companies

There are also disadvantages in setting up a public limited company.

- The setting up costs can be very expensive - running into millions of pounds in some cases.
- Since anyone can buy their shares, it is possible for an outside interest to take control of the company.
- All of the company's accounts can be inspected by members of the public. Competitors may be able to use some of this information to their advantage. They have to publish more information than private limited companies.
- Because of their size they are less able to deal with their customers at a personal level.
- The way they operate is controlled by various Company Acts which aim to protect shareholders.
- There may be a divorce of ownership and control which might lead to the interests of the owners being ignored to some extent.
- It is argued that many of these companies are inflexible due to their size. For example, they can find change difficult to cope with.

Some public limited companies are large and have millions of shareholders and a wide variety of business interests all over the world. They are known as **multinationals**, which means that they have operations in a number of different countries. For example, Kellogg's is an American based multinational company with a production plant and head office situated in Battle Creek, USA. It has also had factories in Manchester, Wrexham, Bremen, Barcelona and Brescia.

Exiting the stock market

Sometimes a business operating as a public limited company is taken back into private ownership. This may be called 'exiting the stock market'. Why does it happen?

- The people responsible for running the business might no longer be willing to tolerate interference from the external shareholders. For example, shareholders such as financial institutions may demand higher dividends when the senior managers would prefer to reinvest profits to generate more growth.
- Sometimes businesses lose favour with the stock market. This may happen when city analysts publish unhelpful or negative reports about companies failing to reach profit targets for example. Such publicity often has the effect of lowering the share price very sharply.
- A business currently operating as a plc may be bought

CRITIQUE

Private equity companies have been criticised for a number of reasons. It is argued that they are often too ruthless when pursuing efficiency gains and that job losses nearly always follow an acquisition by a private equity company. Private equity investors pay very little tax on the profits of their sales. Businesses bought by private equity companies are often saddled with huge debts and some private equity companies have been accused of asset stripping. However, many of the businesses bought by private equity companies are badly managed and in need of change. Some are also undervalued by the stock market and it is suggested that the owners are not getting value for their investment. It is also argued that being taken into private ownership removes unnecessary costs such as compliance and accountancy. Finally, under private ownership the business can focus on the longer term.

outright by a private individual. For example, Philip Green, bought Bhs, the high street clothes retailer, from Storehouse in 2000. He also bought Arcadia in 2002 for a reported £770 million. Both of these companies were part of a plc organisation until purchased.

Private equity companies

An increasing number of businesses are owned by PRIVATE EQUITY COMPANIES. These are organisations that borrow money from banks, add a little of their own, and then use the cash to buy a business. Usually, the businesses they buy are public limited companies, although not always. This often means that public limited companies are taken into private ownership. Three key features of the way in which private equity companies operate are:

- they tend to put the debt used to buy the business into the company. This usually means the company will now have more debt than before it was purchased;
- since they stand to gain all of the profit made by the business, they aim to make ruthless efficiency gains;
- they tend to sell the business after about three years.

How does a private equity deal work? Assume a private equity company borrows £90 million to buy a company worth £100 million, and puts up £10 million of its own money. Its investment is heavily geared. If it can create a 5 per cent increase in the value of the company, it adds £5 million to it. But, because it keeps the whole increase in value for itself, the initial £10 million investment has not risen by 5 per cent, but by 50 per cent - a fantastic return. Some examples of private equity companies include Bain Capital, Apollo Management, Terra Firma, Blackstone Group and Apax Partners. One example of a deal involving a private equity company was the purchase of Alliance Boots, the owner of the 158-year-old high street

chemists chain. Boots was bought by Stefano Pessina and his backers, Kohlberg Kravis Roberts (KKR), for £11 billion.

Holding companies

Some public limited companies operate as HOLDING COMPANIES. This means that they are not only companies in their own right, but also have enough shares in numerous other public limited companies to exert control. This type of company tends to have a very diversified range of business activities. For example, in the UK the TTP Group plc is a holding company for a number of technology businesses. These include TTP LabTech, which supplies products to the healthcare and pharmaceutical sectors, and Acumen Bioscience, which develops and provides screening instruments for the drug discovery industry.

The main advantage of this type of company is that it tends to have a diverse range of business activities. This helps protect it when one of its markets fails. Also, because it is so large, it can often gain financial economies of scale. The main disadvantage is that the holding company may see the businesses it owns only as a financial asset. It may have no long-term interest in the businesses or its development.

KNOWLEDGE

1. What is the role of directors in limited companies?
2. What is the difference between the Memorandum of Association and the Articles of Association?
3. What is a Certificate of Incorporation?
4. Describe the advantages and disadvantages of private limited companies.
5. What are the main legal differences between private and public limited companies?
6. State four financial costs incurred when forming a public limited company
7. What is meant by a statutory declaration?
8. Describe the advantages and disadvantages of plcs.
9. How is a company prospectus used?
10. State one advantage and one disadvantage of a holding company.

KEYTERMS

Flotation – the process of a company 'going public'.
Holding companies – public limited companies which owns enough shares in a number of other companies to exert control over them.
Limited company – a business organisation which has a separate legal entity from that of of its owners.
Private equity company – a business usually owned by private individuals backed by financial institutions.

Case Study: *ImmuPharma plc*

ImmuPharma plc, a drug discovery and development company, floated on the Alternative Investment Market (AIM) at the beginning of 2006. The main purpose of the float was to raise money to finance initial clinical trials on ImmuPharma's drugs for severe pain and MRSA-related infections. At the forefront of ImmuPharma's drug pipeline is a product that targets Lupus, a disease for which there is currently no cure or specific treatment. By 2010 there will be an estimated 1.4 million patients diagnosed with Lupus in the seven key markets. The proceeds of the flotation, together with certain grants, are expected to fund the Phase I trial and a Phase II study for the Lupus product. The flotation involved placing 67.8 million shares with institutional and private investors at the price of 42.5p a share.

Lupus is a chronic, potentially life-threatening autoimmune disease. An estimated one million people worldwide have been diagnosed with this inflammatory disease, which attacks multiple organs such as the skin, joints, kidneys, blood cells, heart and lungs. There is currently no cure or specific treatment and Immupharma's drug, IPP-201101, has a mechanism of action aimed at modulating the body's immune system so it does not attack healthy cells without causing adverse side effects. It has the potential to halt the progression of the disease in a substantial proportion of patients.

According to a Datamonitor report, the currently unique ImmuPharma drug, IPP-201101, has an 'achievable' peak market share of 50 per cent. The report also suggests that the drug could sell at a similar cost to interferon, the multiple sclerosis treatment - around $10,000 a year per patient. Immupharma have stated that due to the nature of the disease and lack of treatments, the US Food and Drug Administration may permit a fast track development and approval process for Phase III once the Phase II study is finished in the first quarter of 2007. If approved, the drug could be available on the market as early as 2010.

Source: adapted from www.drugresearcher.com and ImmuPharma, *Annual Report and Accounts 2006.*

Table 1: Financial Information for ImmuPharma

	2006*	2005**
Turnover	£44,818	£25,409
Loss	(£1,860,038)	(£2,482,778)

*1/4/06 – 31/12/06.
**13/1/05 – 31/3/06.

(a) Why do you think ImmuPharma has decided to become a public limited company? (6 marks)

(b) What is the main advantage of floating on the Alternative Investment Market? (4 marks)

(c) Calculate how much money the flotation will raise for ImmuPharma. (6 marks)

(d) What might be the disadvantages to ImmuPharma of operating as a public limited company? (10 marks)

(e) Evaluate the potential for the success of ImmuPharma in the future. (14 marks)

Not-for-profit organisations

A number of organisations are run according to business principles, but do not aim to make a profit. They are known as NOT-FOR-PROFIT ORGANISATIONS. Their proceeds or surpluses from trading may be shared with employees and customers or passed on to a third party. Such organisations may be involved in a range of business activities. They may also employ staff, raise finance, buy resources, sell goods or services, market themselves, have a formal structure and be required to meet the needs of different stakeholders. They have to operate within the law and may also be faced with competition. Not-for-profit organisations include the following:

- public sector organisations;
- co-operatives;
- mutual organisations;
- charities;
- pressure groups.

Public sector organisations

The PUBLIC SECTOR is made up of organisations which are owned or controlled by central or local government. They may be funded from taxation or generate their own revenue by selling services and in some cases both. Some have unique financing arrangements. For example, the BBC raises money from the sale of television licences. Public sector organisations often exist because the private sector does not make adequate provision for certain services, like health care and education, or because the government wants to keep control of certain services, to protect the public's interest.

The nature of public sector organisations can vary significantly depending on their roles and the types of services they supply. For example, some, like the Post Office, resemble private sector businesses in the way they operate. Others, like The Treasury, are large government departments. Some cater for local needs. For example, libraries, sports halls and parks are provided by local authority organisations. Finally, organisations called executive agencies now provide some services that were previously the responsibility of government departments. For example, Jobcentre Plus, which employs around 100,000 people, is an executive agency responsible for supporting people of working age from welfare into work and for helping employers to fill their vacancies.

Co-operatives

The origins of Co-operatives The UK Co-operative Movement grew from the activities of 28 workers in Rochdale, Lancashire. In 1844 they set up a retail co-operative society - The Rochdale Equitable Pioneers Society. With capital of just £28 they bought

Figure 1: The Co-operative's business activities

Food The largest community food retailer in the UK with more than 2,200 stores, over 52,000 employees.

Healthcare Has more than 700 outlets and 5,000 employees. It is the third largest pharmacy business in the UK.

Travel The UK's most diverse retail travel business, with more than 450 high street branches, strong internet, call centre and home working businesses as well as significant cruise, franchise and business travel operations.

Funeralcare The UK's largest funeral business with over 800 funeral branches and in excess of 3,500 employees.

End of Life Planning A newly established End of Life Planning business which aims to grow its stake in the funeral planning market.

Sunwin Motors One of the top 25 motor businesses in the UK, with a turnover of £250million and 22 dealerships in Yorkshire, Lancashire and the East Midlands.

Cash in Transit Provides services for over half of The Co-operative Bank's ATM estate.

E-Store Operates several e-commerce sites and provides electrical buying, warehousing and distribution services for the Co-operative Movement.

The Co-operative Legal Services Offers free advice and legal help for members of The Co-operative Group on everything from buying or selling a property to will writing.

Property Responsible for property assets including an investment portfolio which is largely invested in the retail and commercial property sectors.

The Co-operative Farms The largest farmer in the UK with over 70,000 acres of farmland in England and Scotland. They supply products such as soft fruit, cider, potatoes and packet flour to The Co-operative food stores.

Shoefayre A leading footwear and accessories retailer with over 1,700 employees and 240 stores throughout the UK.

Mandate A leading designer, manufacturer and distributor of corporate clothing.

Co-operative Financial Services (CFS) An Industrial and Provident Society, which brings together Co-operative Insurance (CIS), The Co-operative Bank and the internet bank Smile under common leadership.

The Co-operative Bank A bank famous for its ethical stance and high standards of customer service.

CIS/Co-operative Insurance A major life assurance and general insurance business with over four and a half million customers.

Smile An award-winning full-service internet bank.

Source: adapted from www.co-operative.co.uk.

food from wholesalers and opened a shop, selling 'wholesome food at reasonable prices'. The surplus (or profit) made was returned to members of the society in the form of a 'dividend'. The dividend was in proportion to how much each member had spent. The principles of the society were:

- voluntary and open membership;
- democratic ownership - one member, one vote;
- the surplus allocated according to spending (the dividend);
- educational facilities for members and workers.

Modern co-operatives Most modern co-operatives operate as CONSUMER or RETAIL CO-OPERATIVES. They are owned and controlled by their members. Members can purchase shares which entitles them to a vote at Annual General Meetings. The members elect a board of directors to make overall business decisions and appoint managers to run day to day business. Co-operatives are run in the interests of their members. Any surplus made by the co-operative is distributed to members as a dividend according to levels of spending. Shares are not sold on a stock exchange, which limits the amount of money that can be raised.

On Sunday 29 July 2007, the two main arms of the Co-op, The Co-operative Group and United Co-operatives, merged The new society, called 'The Co-operative', is the world's largest consumer co-operative with a turnover of more than £9 billion, 4.5 million members and 87,500 employees. The new organisation operates over 4,500 trading outlets throughout the UK. Figure 1 gives a summary of The Co-operatives' business activities.

Worker co-operatives

Another form of co-operation in the UK with common ownership is a WORKER CO-OPERATIVE. This is where a business is jointly owned by its employees. A worker co-operative is an example of a producer co-operative where people work together to produce a good or service. Examples might be a wine growing co-operative or a co-operative of farmers producing milk.

In a worker co-operative employees are likely to:
- contribute to production;
- be involved in decision making;
- share in the profit (usually on an equal basis);
- provide some capital when buying a share in the business.

In 2006 there were less than 400 worker owned and controlled co-operatives in the UK according to Co-operatives UK. One example is the Edinburgh Bicycle Co-operative, a cycle retailer. One advantage of a worker co-operative is that all employees, as owners of the business, are likely to be motivated. Conflict will also tend to be reduced as the objectives of shareholders and employees will be the same. Worker co-operatives can involve the local community, either by giving donations to local bodies or even having them as members of the co-operative. However, there may be problems when operating as a worker co-operative.
- It is often difficult to persuade other workers to join a worker co-operative because it is much easier to set up a partnership.
- Some workers, new ones for example, may not want to join. They may not be able to afford the share.

- Successful worker co-operatives often get sold to companies and the workers are happy to 'sell out' due to the lucrative offers made.
- Fresh capital cannot be raised by recruiting new shareholders. This often limits growth.
- Difficulties might be encountered when trying to recruit highly skilled and qualified staff. They may want more money then the equal wages being paid to existing members.

Building and friendly societies

Most building societies and friendly societies in the UK are MUTUAL ORGANISATIONS. They are owned by their customers, or members as they are known, rather than shareholders. Profits go straight back to members in the form of better and cheaper products. Friendly societies began in the 18th and 19th centuries to support the working classes. Today friendly societies offer a wide range of 'affordable' financial services. These include savings schemes, insurance plans and protection against the loss of income or death. They also provide benefits such as free legal aid, sheltered housing or educational grants to help young people through university. These extra benefits are distributed free of charge, paid for by trading surpluses. The government gives friendly societies special tax treatment, which reduces the amount of tax that members pay.

Building societies used to specialise in mortgages and savings accounts. Savers and borrowers got better interest rates than those offered by banks. This was possible because building societies were non-profit making. In the 1980s building societies began to diversify and compete with banks. In the late 1990s a number of building societies, such as Halifax, Alliance and Leicester, and Northern Rock, became public limited companies.

The main reason for this was that mutual organisations are restricted by law from raising large amounts of capital which might be used to invest in new business ventures. This demutualisation process involved societies giving members 'windfall' payments, usually in the form of shares, to compensate them for their loss of membership.

Charities

Charities are organisations with very specialised aims. They exist to raise money for 'good' causes and draw attention to the needs of disadvantaged groups in society. For example, Age Concern is a charity which raises money on behalf of senior citizens. They also raise awareness and pass comment on issues, such as cold weather payments, which relate to the elderly. Other examples of national charities include Cancer Research Campaign, British Red Cross, Save the Children Fund and Mencap.

Charities rely on donations for their revenue. They also organise fund raising events such as fetes, jumble sales, sponsored activities and raffles. A number of charities run business ventures. For example, Oxfam has a chain of charity shops which sells second hand goods donated by the public.

Charities are generally run according to business principles. They aim to minimise costs, market themselves and employ staff. Most staff are volunteers, but some of the larger charities employ professionals. In the larger charities a lot of administration is necessary to deal with huge quantities of correspondence and to handle charity funds. Provided charities are registered, they are not required to pay tax. In addition, businesses can offset any charitable donations they make against tax. This helps charities when raising funds.

Pressure groups

PRESSURE GROUPS are groups of people that attempt to influence decision makers in politics, business and society. There is a wide variety of pressure groups since they can differ significantly in their aims, objectives and size. For example, a very small pressure group might be made up of residents in a small locality that are campaigning for traffic-calming measures in a particular street to be taken by the council. Such a group would then disband if the council did take acceptable measures. Some groups are quite large and operate as registered charities. Examples include Greenpeace and Friends of the Earth – big environmental pressure groups. Such groups may have formal structures, operate from central offices, employ staff, use large quantities of resources (for example, Greenpeace own a large boat) and promote themselves actively. Some generate large amounts of revenue through donations, fund-raising activities and other sources. Some pressure groups even represent businesses. For example, The Confederation of British Industry (CBI) represents the interests of a wide variety of British companies.

Factors affecting the choice of organisation

Age Many businesses change their legal status as they become older. Most businesses when they start out are relatively small and operate as sole traders. Over time, as needs change, a sole trader may take on a partner and form a partnership. Alternatively, a sole trader may invite new owners to participate in the business, issue shares and form a private limited company. Public limited companies are often formed from established private limited companies that have been trading for many years.

The need for finance A change in legal status may be forced on a business. Often, small businesses want to grow but do not have the funds. Additional finance can only be raised if the business changes status. Furthermore, many private limited companies 'go public' because they need to raise large amounts for expansion.

Size The size of a business operation is likely to affect its legal status. A great number of small businesses are usually sole traders or partnerships. Public limited companies tend to be large organisations with thousands of employees and a turnover of millions or billions of pounds. It could be argued that a very large business could only be run if it were a limited company. For example, certain types of business activity, such as oil processing and chemical manufacturing, require large scale production methods and could not be managed effectively as sole traders or partnerships.

Limited liability Owners can protect their own personal financial position if the business is a limited company. Sole traders and partners have unlimited liability. They may, therefore, be placed in a position where they have to use their own money to meet business debts. Some partnerships dealing with customers' money, such as solicitors, have to have unlimited liability in order to retain the confidence of their clients.

Degree of control Owners may consider retaining control of their business to be important. This is why many owners choose to remain as sole traders. Once new partners or shareholders become a part of the business, the degree of control starts to diminish because it is shared with the new owners. It is possible to keep some control of a limited company by holding the majority of shares. However, even if one person holds 51 per cent of shares in a limited company, the wishes of the other 49 per cent cannot be ignored.

The nature of the business The type of business activity may influence the choice of legal status. For example, household services such as plumbing, decorating and gardening tend to be provided by sole traders. Professional services such as accountancy, legal advice and surveying are usually offered by partnerships. Relatively small manufacturing and family businesses tend to be private limited companies. Large manufacturers and producers of consumer durables, such as cookers, computers and cars, are usually plcs. The reason that these activities choose a particular type of legal status is because of the benefits they gain as a result. However, there are many exceptions to these general examples.

KEYTERMS

Consumer co-operative – a business organisation which is run and owned jointly by the members, who have equal voting rights.

Mutual organisation – businesses owned by members who are customers, rather than shareholders.

Not-for-profit organisation – organisations that are run according to business principles, but that do not aim to make a profit.

Pressure groups – groups of people that attempt to influence decision makers in politics, business and society.

Public sector – business organisations owned and controlled by central or local government.

Worker co-operative – a business organisation owned by employees who contribute to production and share in profit.

KNOWLEDGE

1. What is meant by a not-for-profit organisation?
2. How might a trading surplus' be used by a not-for-profit organisation?
3. State three features of a consumer co-operative.
4. Why do charities promote themselves?
5. Who are the owners of a mutual organisation?

Case Study: Claire House

Claire House is a registered charity. It cares for children aged between 0-18 years with life threatening or life limiting conditions and their families from Merseyside, Cheshire, North Wales and the Isle of Man. Claire House runs a children's hospice on the Wirral which is dedicated to enhancing the quality of life, providing specialist respite, palliative, terminal and bereavement care. The hospice facilities include a multi-sensory room, jacuzzi, hydrotherapy pool, teenage room, art and craft area and physiotherapy/complementary therapy. There is also a multi purpose room where they provide music therapy, group activities or quiet reflection.

The charity has demanding financial needs. Claire House has to raise £120,000 every month to keep the doors of the hospice open. For example, £2,500 is needed each month to pay for a nurse, £1,750 for physiotherapy, £1,500 for medical cover, £550 for family and bereavement support, £400 for pharmacy and sundry expenses and so on. A further £2 million is also needed to build, equip and run the new teenager wing for 12 months.

Claire House has a number of income sources. It relies heavily on donations from the public. For example, it has a web site where donations can be made online. A proportion of income is generated by organising special fundraising events. Examples for 2007 include a beer festival, a golf tournament, a sponsored parachute jump, a comedy night, a garden party, a charity ball and sponsored treks to Brazil and Nepal. It also runs around 20 charity shops in the region. It sells a range of second-hand items, such as unwanted clothes, books, toys, DVDs/videos and ornaments, that have been donated by the general public. It can also take suitable items of furniture for resale at a shop in Mold. Finally, like many charities, Claire House enjoys the support of a number of celebrities. The comedian and actor Norman Wisdom, the actress Patricia Routledge, the Tranmere Rovers goalkeeper Eric Nixon, 60s pop legend Gerry Marsden and the entertainer Claire Sweeney are just a few of the region's celebrities that support Claire House.

Source: adapted from www.claire-house.org.uk.

(a) 'Charities have specialised aims'. Explain what this means using the case as an example. (6 marks)
(b) Describe how Claire House finances its activities. (6 marks)
(c) Examine the role that the celebrities mentioned in the case play in the running of Claire House. (8 marks)
(d) Explain how Claire House faces competition. (8 marks)
(e) Analyse the ways in which Claire House resembles a profit-making organisation. (12 marks)

The need for funds

Firms need money to get started, i.e. to buy equipment, raw materials and obtain premises. Once this initial expenditure has been met, the business can get under way. If successful, it will earn money from sales. However, business is a continuous activity and money flowing in will be used to buy more raw materials and settle other trading debts.

If the owner wants to expand, extra money will be needed over and above that from sales. Expansion may mean larger premises, more equipment and extra workers. Throughout the life of a business there will almost certainly be times when money has to be raised from outside.

The items of expenditure above fall into two categories – CAPITAL EXPENDITURE or REVENUE EXPENDITURE. Capital expenditure is spending on items which may be used over and over again. A company vehicle, a cutting machine and a new factory all fall into this category. Capital expenditure will be shown in a firm's balance sheet because it includes the purchase of fixed assets. It also includes the maintenance and repair of buildings and machines.

Revenue expenditure refers to payments for goods and services which have either already been consumed or will be very soon. Wages, raw materials and fuel are all examples. It also includes the maintenance and repair of buildings and machines. Revenue expenditure will be shown in a firm's profit and loss account or income statement because it represents business costs or expenses.

Internal sources of finance

Figure 1 shows how sources of finance are either internal or external. Internal sources can only be used when a business is established because money cannot be taken out of a business until revenue has been generated by trading activities. Although most of this unit focuses on external sources of finance, internal sources are very important. This is because internal sources are cheap. A business does not have to pay interest, for example, if it uses its own money to fund activities.

There are three important internal sources of finance.

Profit Retained profit is profit after tax that has not been returned to the owners. It is the single most important source of finance for a business. Around 65 per cent of all business funding comes from retained profit. It is the cheapest source of finance, with no financial charges such as interest, dividends and administration. However, there is an opportunity cost. If retained profit is used by the business it cannot be returned to the owners. This may lead to conflict if the shareholders of a public limited company, for example, see that dividend payments have been frozen because the directors have used the profit in the business.

Working capital It may be possible to 'squeeze' working capital to provide extra finance for the business. One way of doing this is to operate a 'tighter' credit policy. For example, a business might reduce the trade credit period, so that money is received

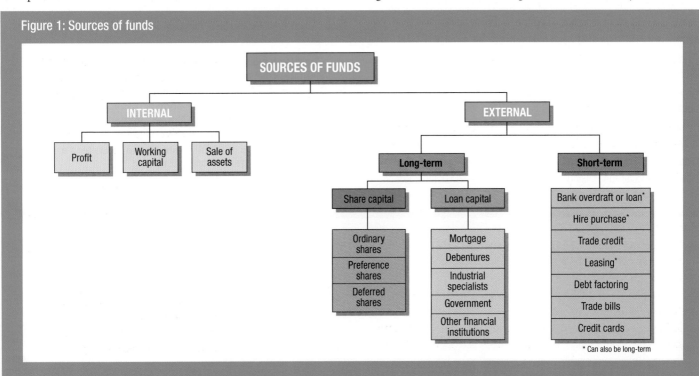

Figure 1: Sources of funds

Question 1.

Godwin's Ice Cream is located in Weston-on-the-Green, Oxfordshire. The business has an ice cream factory and shop attached to a working farm. The business's activities include ice cream manufacture from the farm's own milk, sale of ice cream on-site and sale through a limited number of shops and restaurants. The aim of the business was to replace lost income from falling product prices, through adding value to the existing product. Before setting up the owners wrote a business plan and made an application for a Rural Enterprise Scheme (RES) grant. There were initial problems with the grant due to different interpretations by DEFRA staff of which aspects of the business were eligible for the RES grant. However, it was felt this was probably a teething problem with the scheme as they were one of the first applicants and the forms and guidance are now clearer. The grant was eventually awarded to Godwin's. The other main source of finance for the business is a bank overdraft.

Source: adapted from www.southeast-ra.gov.uk.

(a) What is the advantage to Godwin's Ice Cream of obtaining a grant to help fund the business?
(b) Why do you think it is important to write a business plan when applying for funds?
(c) One of Godwin's main sources of finance is a bank overdraft. Explain (i) why this is an external source of finance and (ii) why this will be a flexible source of finance to Godwin's.

from customers more quickly. Or a business might collect long-standing debts by applying more pressure to customers. Both these options might result in a loss of orders and damage customer relations. Another approach is to reduce stock holding. Money tied up in stocks is unproductive. If a business can reduce stock, money is released and can be used for more productive activities. But having too little stock can be a problem. For example, a business might find it difficult to cope with a surge in demand if stocks are too low.

Sale of assets An established business may be able to sell some unwanted assets to raise finance. For example, machinery, land and buildings that are no longer required could be sold off. Large companies can sell parts of their organisation to raise finance. Another option is to raise money through a SALE AND LEASEBACK. This involves selling an asset, such as property or machinery, that the business still wants to use. The sale is made to a specialist company that leases the asset back to the seller. This is an increasingly popular source of finance. For example, in 2007, HSBC agreed the sale and leaseback of its head office building in Canary Wharf, London for £1.09 billion. A wholly-owned subsidiary of Metrovacesa, S.A., one of Europe's most respected property companies, and HSBC exchanged contracts on the deal which sees the bank retain full control of occupancy while Metrovacesa takes a 998-year lease. HSBC has leased the building back for 20 years at an annual rent of £43.5 million with an option to extend for a further five years.

External long-term sources of finance

External long-term capital can be in the form of share capital or loan capital.

Share capital For a limited company SHARE CAPITAL is likely to be the most important source of finance. The sale of shares can raise very large amounts of money. ISSUED SHARE CAPITAL is the money raised from the sale of shares. AUTHORISED SHARE CAPITAL is the maximum amount shareholders want to raise. Share capital is often referred to as PERMANENT CAPITAL. This is because it is not normally redeemed, i.e. it is not repaid by the business. Once the share has been sold, the buyer is entitled to a share in the profit of the

Table 1: Summary and explanation of the ways in which new shares can be made available to investors on the stock exchange	
INITIAL PUBLIC OFFERING (IPO)	
Public issue	Potential investors might apply to an ISSUING HOUSE, such as a merchant bank, after reading the company prospectus. This is an expensive method, but suits big issues.
Offer for sale	Shares are issued to an issuing house, which then sells them at a fixed price. This is also expensive but suits small issues.
Sale by tender	The company states a minimum price which it will accept from investors and then allocates shares to the highest bidders.
PLACING	
Private placing	Unquoted companies (who do not sell on the Stock Exchange) or those with small share sales approach issuing houses to place the shares privately with investors.
Stock exchange placing	Less popular issues can be placed by the stock exchange with institutional investors, for example. This is relatively inexpensive.
AN INTRODUCTION	Existing shareholders get permission from the Stock Exchange to sell shares by attracting new shareholders to the firm. No new capital is raised.
RIGHTS ISSUE	Existing shareholders are given the 'right' to buy new shares at a discounted price. This is cheap and simple, and creates free publicity. Issues can be based on current holdings. A one for five issue means that 1 new share is issued for every five currently held.
BONUS ISSUE	New shares are issued to existing shareholders to capitalise on reserves which have built up over the years. No new capital is raised and shareholders end up with more shares, but at lower prices.

company, i.e. a dividend. Dividends are not always declared. Sometimes a business makes a loss or needs to retain profit to help fund future business activities. A shareholder can make a CAPITAL GAIN by selling the share at a higher price than it was originally bought for. Shares are not normally sold back to the business. The shares of public limited companies are sold in a special share market called the STOCK MARKET or STOCK EXCHANGE, dealt with later in this unit. Shares in private limited companies are transferred privately. Shareholders, because they are part owners of the business, are entitled to a vote. One vote is allowed for each share owned. Voting takes place annually and shareholders vote either to re-elect the existing board of directors or replace them. Different types of shares can be issued.

- **Ordinary shares.** These are also called EQUITIES and are the most common type of share issued. They are also the riskiest type of share since there is no guaranteed dividend. The size of the dividend depends on how much profit is made and how much the directors decide to retain in the business. All ordinary shareholders have voting rights. When a share is first sold it has a nominal value shown on it - its original value. Share prices will change as they are bought and sold again and again.
- **Preference shares.** The owners of these shares receive a fixed rate of return when a dividend is declared. They carry less risk because shareholders are entitled to their dividend before the holders of ordinary shares. Preference shareholders are not strictly owners of the company. If the company is sold, their rights to dividends and capital repayments are limited to fixed amounts. Some preference shares are cumulative, entitling the holder to dividend arrears from years when dividends were not declared. Some are also redeemable, which means that they can be bought back by the company.
- **Deferred shares.** These are not used often. They are usually held by the founders of the company. Deferred shareholders only receive a dividend after the ordinary shareholders have been paid a minimum amount.

When a company issues shares there is a variety of ways in which they can be made available to potential investors as shown in Table 1.

Loan capital Loan capital may come from a number of sources.
- **Debentures.** The holder of a debenture is a creditor of the company, not an owner. This means that holders are entitled to an agreed fixed rate of return, but have no voting rights. The amount borrowed must be repaid by the expiry date.
- **Mortgages.** Only limited companies can raise money from the sale of shares and debentures. Smaller enterprises often need long-term funding, to buy premises for example. They may choose to take out a mortgage. A mortgage is usually a long-term loan, from, say, a bank or other financial institution. The lender must use land or property as security on the loan.

Figure 2: A hire purchase agreement and the parties involved in the three way transaction

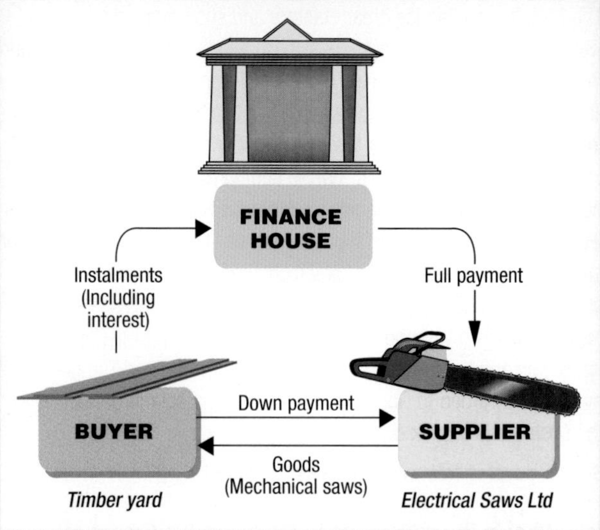

- **Industrial loan specialists.** A number of organisations provide funds especially for business and commercial uses. These specialists tend to cater for businesses which have difficulty in raising funds from conventional sources. In recent years there has been a significant growth in the number of VENTURE CAPITALISTS. These provide funds for small and medium sized companies that appear to have some potential, but are considered too risky by other investors. Venture capitalists often use their own funds, but also attract money from financial institutions and 'Business Angels'. Business Angels are individuals who invest between £10,000 and £100,000, often in exchange for an equity stake. A typical Angel might make one or two investments in a three year period, either individually or together with a small group of friends, relatives or business associates. Most investments are in start-ups or early stage expansions. There are several reasons why people become Business Angels. Many like the excitement of the gamble involved, or being part of a new or developing business. Others are attracted by the tax relief offered by the government. Some are looking for investment opportunities for their unused income, such as retired business people.
- **Government assistance.** Both central and local government have been involved in providing finance for business. Business start up schemes can provide a small amount of income for those starting new businesses for a limited period of time, providing they meet certain criteria. Financial help is usually selective. Smaller businesses tend to benefit, as do those setting up in regions which suffer from heavy unemployment.
- **Other financial institutions.** Banks, for example might under certain conditions give a business a long-term loan

which will be repaid over a number of years. The bank may require some form of collateral on the loan, and a business may need to present a business plan to secure the loan.

External short-term sources of finance

Bank overdraft This is probably the most important source of finance for a very large number of businesses. Bank overdrafts are flexible. The amount by which a business goes overdrawn depends on its needs at the time. Interest is only paid by the business when its account is overdrawn.

Bank loan A loan requires a rigid agreement between the borrower and the bank. The amount borrowed must be repaid over a clearly stated time period, in regular instalments. Most bank loans are short or medium term. Banks dislike long term lending because of their need for security and liquidity. Sometimes, banks change persistent overdrafts into loans, so that firms are forced to repay at regular intervals.

Hire purchase This is often used by small businesses to buy plant and machinery. Sometimes, a hire purchase agreement requires a down payment by the borrower, who agrees to repay the remainder in instalments over a period of time. FINANCE HOUSES specialise in providing funds for such agreements. Figure 2 illustrates the working of an agreement and the parties involved. The buyer may place a down payment on a machine with the supplier and receives delivery. The finance house pays the supplier the amount outstanding and collects instalments (including interest) from the buyer. The goods bought do not legally belong to the buyer until the very last instalment has been paid to the finance house. If the buyer falls behind with the repayments the finance house can legally repossess the item. Finance houses are less selective than banks when granting loans. Hence their interest rates are higher. They add a servicing charge for paying in instalments which also leads to higher rates. Hire purchase agreements can sometimes be for longer periods.

Trade credit It is common for businesses to buy raw materials, components and fuel and pay for them at a later date, usually within 30-90 days. Paying for goods and services using trade credit seems to be an interest free way of raising finance. It is particularly profitable during periods of inflation. However, many companies encourage early payment by offering discounts. The cost of goods is often higher if the firm does not pay early. Delaying the payment of bills can also result in poor business relations with suppliers.

Leasing A LEASE is a contract in which a business acquires the use of resources such as, property, machinery or equipment, in return for regular payments. In this type of finance, the ownership never passes to the business that is using the resource. With a finance lease, the arrangement is often for three years or longer and, at the end of the period, the business is

---

Question 2.

A mobile phone-based information service, 82Ask, launched by one of Britain's top rising female entrepreneurs, is aiming to float on the stock market early next year after raising £1.3 million in funds. The company, which is changing its name to Texperts, is led by Sarah McVittie, a former UBS investment banker. Texperts allows users to text a question to a team of research experts who promise to provide an answer within five minutes. Users are charged £1 per question only if the inquiry is fully completed. The service, which has close to 400,000 users, has a network of 220 experts answering questions on anything from trivia and entertainment to recommending restaurants, providing travel information and sending maps to people's mobile phones.

Odey Asset Management (an industrial loan specialist), is understood to have provided most of the new funding and now has a stake of around 14 per cent in Texperts. McVittie and co-founder Thomas Roberts, each have about a 15 per cent stake. Over the past four years, Texperts has raised £2.5 million, mainly from wealthy individuals in three fundraising rounds. About £1 million of the £1.3 million from the latest round of fund raising is earmarked for advertising and marketing. This is well above the £200,000 spent to date.

Source: adapted from the *Sunday Times*, 19.8.2007.

(a) Why is Texperts raising finance?
(b) How much of the business is owned by the original founders?
(c) Describe the two key sources of finance used by Texperts?
(d) Discuss the drawback to the founders of Texperts of using this type of finance.

---

given the option of then buying the resource. In accounting, the payments are treated as capital expenditure. With an operating lease, the arrangement is generally for a shorter period of time, and the payments are treated as revenue expenditure.

There are some advantages of leasing.
- No large sums of money are needed to buy the use of equipment.
- Maintenance and repair costs are not the responsibility of the user.
- Hire companies can offer the most up to date equipment.
- Leasing is useful when equipment is only required occasionally.
- A leasing agreement is generally easier for a new company to obtain than other forms of loan finance. This is because the assets remain the property of the leasing company.

However:
- over a long period of time leasing is more expensive than the outright purchase of plant and machinery;
- loans cannot be secured on assets which are leased.

Factoring When companies sell their products they send invoices stating the amount due. The invoice provides evidence

Table 2: Advantages and disadvantages of being high geared and low geared

	Advantages	Disadvantages
Low geared	The burden of loan repayments is reduced. The need for regular interest payments is reduced. Volatile interest rates are less of a threat.	Dividend payments have to be met indefinitely. Ownership of the company will be diluted. Dividends are paid after tax.
High geared	The interest on loans can be offset against tax. Ownership is not diluted. Once loans have been repaid the company's debt is much reduced.	Interest payments must be met. Interest rates can change, which causes uncertainty. Loans must be repaid and may be a burden, increasing the risk of insolvency.

of the sale and the money owed to the company. Debt factoring involves a specialist company (the factor) providing finance against these unpaid invoices. A common arrangement is for a factor to pay 80 per cent of the value of invoices when they are issued. The balance of 20 per cent is paid by the 'factor' when the customer settles the bill. An administrative and service fee will be charged.

Trade bills This is not a common source of finance, but can play an important role, particularly in overseas trade and commodity markets. The purchaser of traded goods may sign a **bill of exchange** agreeing to pay for the goods at a specified later date. Ninety days is a common period. The seller of the goods will hold the bill until payment is due. However, the holder can sell it at a discount before the maturity date to a specialist financial institution. There is a well developed market for these bills and all holders will receive payment at the end of the period from the debtor.

Credit cards Businesses of all sizes have uses for credit cards. They can be used by executives to meet expenses such as hotel bills, petrol and meals when travelling on company business. They might also be used to purchase materials from suppliers who accept credit cards. Credit cards are popular because they are convenient, flexible, secure and avoid interest charges if monthly accounts are settled within the credit period. However, they tend to have a credit limit. This may make them unsuitable for certain purchases.

The choice of the source of finance

A number of factors are important when choosing between alternative sources of finance.

Cost Businesses obviously prefer sources which are less expensive, both in terms of interest payments and administration costs. For example, share issues can carry high administration costs while the interest payments on bank overdrafts tend to be relatively low.

Use of funds When a company undertakes heavy capital expenditure, it is usually funded by a long-term source of finance. For example, the building of a new plant may be financed by a share issue or a mortgage. Revenue expenditure tends to be financed by short-term sources. For example, the purchase of a large amount of raw materials may be funded by trade credit or a bank overdraft.

Status and size Sole traders, which tend to be small, are limited in their choices of finance. For example, long-term sources may be mortgages and perhaps the introduction of some personal capital. Public and private limited companies can usually obtain finance from many different sources. In addition, due to their size and added security, they can often demand lower interest rates from lenders. There are significant economies of scale in raising finance.

Financial situation The financial situation of businesses is constantly changing. When a business is in a poor financial situation, it finds that lenders are more reluctant to offer finance. At the same time, the cost of borrowing rises. Financial institutions are more willing to lend to secure businesses which have **collateral** (assets which provide security for loans). Third World countries which are desperate to borrow money to fund development are often forced to pay very high rates indeed.

Gearing GEARING is the relationship between the loan capital and share capital of a business. A company is said to be **high geared** if it has a large proportion of loan capital to share capital. A **low geared** company has a relatively small amount of loan capital. For example, two companies may each have total capital of £45 million. If the first has loan capital of £40 million and share capital of only £5 million it is high geared. The other company may have share capital of £30 million and loan capital of £15 million. It is relatively low geared.

The gearing of a company might influence its finance. If a business is high geared, it may be reluctant to raise even more finance by borrowing. It may choose to issue more shares instead, rather than increasing the interest to be paid on loans.

Table 2 shows the advantages and disadvantages of being low or high geared.

KEYTERMS

Authorised share capital – the maximum amount which can be legally raised.

Capital expenditure – spending on business resources which can be used repeatedly over a period of time.

Capital gain – the profit made from selling a share for more than it was bought.

Equities – another name for an ordinary share.

Finance houses - specialist institutions which provide funds for hire purchase agreements.

Gearing – the relationship between funds raised from loans and from issuing shares.

Issuing house – any institution that deals with the sale of new shares.

Issued share capital – amount of current share capital arising from the sale of shares.

Lease – a contract to acquire the use of resources such as property or equipment.

Permanent capital – share capital which is never repaid by the company.

Revenue expenditure – spending on business resources that have already been consumed or will be very shortly.

Sale and leaseback – the practice of selling assets, such as property or machinery, and leasing them back from the buyer.

Share capital – money introduced into the business through the sale of shares.

Stock market or stock exchange - a market where second-hand shares are bought and sold.

Venture capitalists – providers of funds for small or medium sized companies that may be considered too risky for other investors.

KNOWLEDGE

1. Why do businesses need to raise finance?
2. State the internal sources of finance.
3. State the main advantage of using internal finance.
4. What is the difference between ordinary, preference and deferred shares?
5. Why would someone want to become an Business Angel?
6. State the advantages to a business of a bank overdraft compared with a bank loan.
7. What is trade credit likely to be used for?
8. Which is likely to be more expensive, a bank loan or HP?
9. What is the difference between a finance lease and an operating lease?
10. What factors affect the choice of source of finance?

Case Study: Gamingking

Gamingking plc was established in 1993 and floated on the Alternative Investment Market (a market for shares) in 1996. In May 2005 Gamingking acquired its largest competitor, Kelly's Eye (No. 1) Ltd. In doing so the Group became the leader in the provision of lotteries and game play products and services to the registered members' club marketplace. The Group now has a client base of around 5,000 clubs in the UK. The Group comprises three main wholly-owned trading subsidiaries:

Kelly's Eye No. (1) Kelly's Eye, based in Hemel Hempstead, is responsible for all sales and marketing activities related to lottery and game play products. The Kelly's Eye salesforce operates nationwide and is able to supply the wide-ranging product portfolio into clubs quickly and efficiently.

Lotteryking Ltd. Lotteryking was the original business providing vending machines; pull-tab lottery tickets and online lottery solutions to the private members' clubs.

Following the acquisition of Kelly's Eye, Lotteryking is now focused on the provision of technical support services, manufacturing, R&D, and purchasing.

Logoking Ltd. This division supplies logo-embroidered leisure and workwear to a wide market including the substantial staff and sports needs of the private members' clubs.

In 2006, Gamingking made a profit of £51,000 and retained the entire sum. It did the same in 2005 when profit was £38,000. At 30 April Gamingking had a loan facility of £800,000 from Barclays Bank much of which was used to buy Kelly's Eye (No.1) Ltd. This loan was due to mature on 15th April 2010. Also, at 30th April 2006, Gamingking had authorised share capital of £5 million and issued share capital of £2.907 million. Other sources of finance used by Gamingking include trade credit and hire purchase.

Source: adapted from www.gamingking.co.uk.

(a) **Explain the difference between authorised and issued share capital. (6 marks)**

(b) **How will floating on the Alternative Investment Market (a stock market) affect GamingKing's ability to raise finance? (8 marks)**

(c) **(i) Why did Gamingking borrow £800,000 from Barclay's Bank? (4 marks)**

  (ii) How will this loan affect the gearing of the company? (8 marks)

(d) **Discuss the advantages and disadvantages to Gamingking of retaining all of its profit in 2005 and 2006. (14 marks)**

Making location decisions

Choosing a suitable place to locate a business is an important decision for a business when setting up. This is because it is a long-term decision. Once a business has been set up in a particular location, it is likely to stay there for a period of time. Relocation can be expensive. So a business must find the best possible location when setting up. Business owners may, however, review their location decision from time to time to see if relocation is needed.

Business owners may choose a location near to where they live. But other factors have to be taken into account. Location decisions are likely to be based on the costs and benefits of specific locations. For example, an owner looking to open a restaurant will consider the cost of rent and refurbishment, as well as the proximity to customers and the image a particular location might present. The costs and benefits affecting a location decision may be **quantitative**. This means that they can be measured in monetary terms. An example would be the cost of transporting goods to customers. Other costs and benefits may be **qualitative**. This means that they cannot be measured in monetary terms. An example would be the distance staff have to travel to work.

An increasing number of businesses are being set up at home. This may be because it is cheap and convenient for the owners. Many new businesses are also web-based and can be located anywhere. For example, a business offering educational services over the Internet could be based anywhere in the world.

Technology

Developments in technology have had an impact on business location in recent years. Most businesses now require fast telecommunication links that have the capacity to send and receive voices, text, documents and other images instantly. This usually means that they require access to broadband connections. Developments in technology mean that such links are available almost anywhere and therefore businesses have a wider choice of locations when setting up. Red Gate is a software designer in Cambridgeshire that helps users to run, update and compare databases more efficiently. It delivers its software from its website. Its 200,000 users can download its software and so avoid packaging and shipping costs. Modern telecommunication links might also mean that businesses can set up with less space, as an increasing number of people can work from home.

Many new businesses set up in recent years have produced technological products or offered technology services. Yorkshire-based Sarian Systems, for example, designs and manufactures routers used to process and send data from lottery terminals and cash machines. These companies may operate from **Science Parks**. A Science Park is a business support and technology transfer initiative that:

- encourages and supports the start-up, incubation and growth of innovation-led, high-growth, knowledge-based businesses;
- provides an environment where larger international businesses can develop relations with a particular centre of knowledge creation for their mutual benefit;
- has links with centres of knowledge creation such as universities, higher education institutes and research organisations.

An example of a science park is Aston Science Park based in Aston, Birmingham. Some of the companies located there operate in fields such as software, pharmaceuticals, IT Solutions, E-commerce, multimedia, environmental services and computer hardware.

Location costs

When choosing a suitable location to start a new business, the most important factor is likely to be cost. This is because new businesses are often short of cash and need to minimise location costs. Location costs fall into two categories.

Fixed location costs When setting up a business some 'one-off' costs will be incurred in relation to location. These are fixed costs because they do not vary with output. They might include

Question 1.

Clevon Guillaume is starting up a business to supply high quality desserts to restaurants and hotels. He was encouraged to do so after winning first prize in a local cooking competition. The awards ceremony was covered in the local press and afterwards Clevon was overwhelmed by the enquiries he got from a range of businesses in the catering industry. One of the tasks he is currently faced with is finding a suitable location. Ideally, he wants to rent a factory unit which can be converted into a working kitchen. He has spoke to a number of estate agents and been in touch with the local Chamber of Commerce.

(a) Identify two (i) qualitative and (ii) quantitative factors that Clevon might take into account when choosing a location.
(b) Which of the above factors do you think might be the most important to Clevon?

the following.

- **Search costs.** Finding a suitable location may take time and cost money. These are search costs. They might include the cost of travelling to different sites, fees paid to surveyors for advice or legal searches carried out by solicitors.
- **Planning permission.** It may be necessary to get planning permission when converting premises for business use. This is particularly the case when a property is used for business purposes for the very first time. Obtaining planning permission may incur legal and administration costs.
- **Refurbishment.** Unless new business premises are purpose-built, it will be necessary to pay refurbishment costs. Examples might include painting and decorating, refitting, renovation or wholesale conversion.
- **Purchase cost.** In a minority of cases an entrepreneur might buy a shop, factory, office or other form of premises. This would be a very high cost and because of this many new business owners prefer to start by renting or leasing premises.
- **Government help.** In some cases a new business may choose a location because the government offers to meet some of the costs. The government may offer grants if businesses locate on specific sites – where unemployment is high for example. Grants help to reduce the fixed cost of location.

Other fixed costs relating to location might be ongoing. They do not vary with output but have to be incurred on a regular basis, such as monthly or yearly.

- **Rent or leasing charges.** Rent or leasing charges have to be paid every month and businesses are often tied to long-term agreements that can last five years, for example. Rents can vary significantly. For example, office space in London is more expensive than office space in Glasgow. The rent for a high street shop will be higher than for a side street shop. Business owners will tend to search for premises with lower rents or leasing charges, but the position of premises will also have to be taken into account.
- **Business rates.** Businesses have to pay rates to the local council to pay for amenities such as refuse collection, policing and the fire service. These may vary in different parts of the country. Business rates are usually paid in instalments.
- **Labour.** Some labour costs may be fixed. A certain number and type of staff have to be employed whatever the level of output. Wage rates do vary around the country. For example, wages tend to be higher in London and other parts of the south east.

Variable location costs Variable location costs are those that increase as output rises. Only a minority of location costs are variable.

- **Labour costs.** When businesses expand and sell more, they are likely to need more labour. Businesses that need a large and increasing number of workers might have to consider labour costs carefully. They may decide to locate in regions

---

Question 2.

Founded by managing director Anthony Cook when he was only 21, Mobile Fun has capitalised on the mobile-phone craze by selling accessories and ringtones online. Launched in 2000 with virtually no set-up costs, it now offers 5,000 accessories and 100,000 mobile downloads from its headquarters in Birmingham. Goods are despatched to customers using the services outlined below.

- Royal Mail First Class Delivery (UK) - £2.50 per order.
  Safe & secure shipping. Usually next working day. Please allow up to 5 working days.
- Royal Mail Special Delivery (UK) - £5.95 per order.
  Guaranteed next working day by 1pm for orders received before 6pm. *(Except Scottish Highlands).
- Royal Mail Saturday Special Delivery (UK) - £7.50 per order.
  Guaranteed Saturday delivery for 'In stock' items ordered on Thursday evenings & Fridays until 6pm. *(Except Scottish Highlands).
- First Class International Recorded Post (EU) - £10.00 per order.
  Usually takes 2-5 working days, although varies on customer's local postal service.

Source: adapted from www.fasttrack.co.uk and www.mobilefun.co.uk.

(a) Mobile Fun could be described as footloose. Explain what this means.
(b) (i) Explain why transport is a variable location cost.
    (ii) To what extent is Mobile Fun's location influenced by transport costs?

---

where labour costs are lower. Some businesses have decided to locate overseas for this reason.

- **Transport costs.** Businesses that use bulky or heavy raw materials may need to locate near to their suppliers. This will help to minimise transport costs. For example, oil refineries are usually located on the coast to avoid the high cost of transport crude oil across land. Businesses that produce bulky or heavy products may need to locate near to their customers. Today this is true, for example, for suppliers to just-in-time manufacturers. In the car industry, some suppliers have chosen to locate close to assembly plants in order to reduce transport costs. The main reason for this is because just-in-time manufacturers require multiple deliveries of small quantities. Transport costs would be considerably higher if suppliers were located some distance away.

Infrastructure

When setting up a business will need the support of a sound infrastructure. The quality and proximity of roads, railways, airports, hospitals and schools, for example, can play an important part in the success of a business. Consequently the quality of the infrastructure in different locations will affect the location decision. The following examples help to illustrate the role played by the infrastructure.

- A business that needs to distribute goods quickly to customers on a frequent basis will require access to the motorway network – a business selling goods from the Internet for example.

- A business which plans to export to France might choose to locate near to the Channel Tunnel.
- A business setting up in London might choose to locate near to a Tube station to make it easier for staff to get to work.
- A business trying to attract experienced executives might need to be located close to a good school and an attractive living environment with lots of modern facilities.

A business location that is not supported by a sound infrastructure is likely to incur higher costs and suffer a degree of inconvenience. The image of the business might also suffer.

The market

With some types of business, location near to customers is very important. New businesses are set up to provide financial, domestic, personal, leisure and health services for example. In many cases it is essential that these types of businesses are close to heavily populated areas. People will generally not wish to travel more than a few miles to visit a restaurant or health centre. Also, businesses that offer services in people's homes will not wish to travel long distances when serving a number of customers in the same day.

For some products the market may not be important. An increasing amount of business is done using the Internet. For example, retailers are finding that more and more people are not bothering to go to shops but purchase products online. Enterprises that are set up to provide business services such as advertising, PR and software design do not need to be located near to their customers. Such services can be delivered electronically and effective communications with customers can be maintained in the same way.

Qualitative factors

Qualitative factors are factors which cannot be measured using numbers. There is a variety of qualitative factors which a business might take into consideration when deciding where to set up.

Laws and regulations Any location decision will have legal and regulatory aspects. In many cases, laws and regulations will determine what type of business can occupy what type of premises in what areas. Getting planning permission will be necessary if a business is building new premises. Also, when setting up a new business it may be prudent to get professional advice when in doubt about laws relating to location.

Social, environmental and ethical considerations Many new businesses take social, environmental and ethical considerations into account. For example, a business setting up a market garden to produce organic food may need a plot of land that has been free from pesticides and fertilizers for a period of time. A business setting up a new manufacturing venture may decide to locate a factory in an area where there is high unemployment. It could be argued that the new, younger generation of

entrepreneurs, is more likely to take social, environmental and ethical considerations into account because they are more aware of such issues.

Quality of life Evidence suggests that the interests of those making a location decision are very important. Many new businesses, for example, tend to be located where their owner managers live. Small to medium sized businesses, when considering relocating, will typically relocate within a few miles of the present location. Owner managers don't want to move house or locality even if cheaper premises could be found just 50 miles away. The quality of people's living environments is considered to be very important.

Quality of the workforce The quality of the local workforce is important. A business is unlikely to locate to a place where it is unable to recruit the right quality of local labour. In the UK, London and the South East continue to attract new companies because, despite relatively high wages, there is a large pool of highly educated workers from which to draw.

The importance of location

When setting up a business the importance of location is likely to vary. For some businesses location is not a crucial issue. Businesses that are run from home, web-based businesses and businesses that supply national markets, for example, are FOOTLOOSE. This means that they can locate anywhere. They are not tied by any particular location factor.

However, in other cases, finding the right location is vital. A business that needs large areas of land, such as a new golf course, may have to choose a site where land is cheap. A new guest house hoping to attract visitors to an historic city would clearly benefit from a central location in the city. Businesses that export goods would prefer to be located near to ports. A new fast food outlet hoping to attract shoppers and workers would benefit from a prominent position on the high street. These examples show that the importance of location, and the relative importance of different location factors, all depend on the type of business that is being set up.

KEYTERMS

Footloose businesses – businesses that are not tied to a particular location.

KNOWLEDGE

1. Explain the difference between qualitative and quantitative location factors.
2. State two fixed costs of location.
3. Why is transport a variable cost in relation to location?
4. Why are restaurants likely to be located close to their market?
5. How important is location to a taxi driver?

Case Study: Locating a campsite

Gordon Powell left his job at the age of 55 but was not ready for retirement. He wanted to run a business. Gordon enjoyed camping, particularly in the Scottish Highlands and Islands. He planned to move from his home in Doncaster and set up a camp site on the Isle of Skye. Gordon spent eight months planning his business venture. One important issue was the location of the site. He spent four weeks in Skye searching for 'the perfect location'. He thought location would be important because people are more likely to return to the site if the location is attractive. He wanted a site with scenic views close to the sea or a loch. At the end of his four week search Gordon had identified two suitable locations.

- **Dunvegan**. The pretty village of Dunvegan lies on the east side of the head of Loch Dunvegan, which bites deeply into the Isle of Skye from the north west. It is the largest village on Skye that doesn't stand on the island's east coast. On the village main street is the Giant Angus MacAskill Museum, dedicated to the tallest Scotsman that ever lived. There is also a castle, coral beaches nearby and the views from the village are dominated by the loch and Healabhal Mhòr, a table mountain. The site found by Gordon is about one acre in size, enough for 25 tents and 15 caravans. It also has a derelict farm building which would be suitable for conversion into a toilet block and wash room. However, it would need to be connected to a water supply and the mains electricity.

- **Portree**. Gordon's second site is three miles from Portree, the largest town on the island. Portree has a harbour, fringed by cliffs, with a pier. Attractions in the town include the Aros Centre and the An Tuireann Arts Centre, both of which celebrate the island's Gaelic heritage. The site is on a cliff top with views across the sea to the island of Raasay. There is a derelict croft which has a water supply and could be converted into a toilet block and washroom. There would also be enough room for a small café. The site is over an acre and could accommodate 34 tents and 20 caravans. However, one problem with this site is the prevalence of the Highland Midge, a biting insect. Midges are particularly bad on Skye and on this side of the island.

Some cost information relating to the proposed locations for the

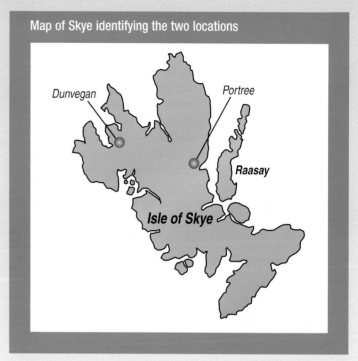

Map of Skye identifying the two locations

camp site is shown in Table 1.

(a) Explain why location is likely to be an important issue for the business in this case. (4 marks)

(b) Do you think Gordon will need to obtain planning permission at all? Explain your answer. (4 marks)

(c) Describe three search costs that Gordon may have incurred when choosing a suitable location for his camp site. (6 marks)

(d) Using this case as an example, explain the difference between 'one-off' fixed costs and 'ongoing' fixed costs, in relation to location. (10 marks)

(e) After a discussion with his accountant, Gordon decided to set up his camp site at Portree. Evaluate whether Gordon should have chosen the Dunvegan site instead. (16 marks)

Table 1: Cost information for the proposed camp site locations

	Dunvegan	Portree
Rent per month	£1,000	£1,200
Toilet block conversion costs	£13,000	£8,000
Other 'one-off' location costs	£2,500	£1,000
Business rates pa*	£2,000	£2,200

* Estimated

15 | Employing people

Types of people needed by small businesses

Whatever businesses entrepreneurs set up, they need to think about the type of employees that are required. In small businesses, a large amount of work may be done by the entrepreneur, such as in a window cleaning business. But many entrepreneurs will need help and employ other people. Entrepreneurs need to think about the reasons, drawbacks and difficulties of employing staff. They also need to consider when it might be more beneficial to use consultants and advisors or contract out work, instead of recruiting employees.

Employees and self-employment

If a business provides and controls work, supplies equipment and pays tax and National Insurance contributions for a worker, then the worker is an EMPLOYEE. An employee will work under the conditions of the contract of employment agreed with the business.

However, if workers make their own decisions about accepting work and conditions of work, and pay their own tax and National Insurance contributions, they are likely to be SELF-EMPLOYED. Working at home does not necessarily mean a worker is self-employed. To be self-employed, a worker must be in business on his or her own account. Businesses sometimes 'contract out' work to self-employed people to save on the costs of extra employees. For example, businesses may employ cleaning contractors rather than employing staff, even though regular cleaning may be needed.

Permanent and temporary employment

PERMANENT workers are employed by a business for an indefinite period of time. For example, an alternative therapy clinic may employ a full-time reflexologist to cover that particular type of treatment in the clinic. He will work for the business until he leaves, either by choice, because he is forced to by the business or when he retires. Employing a worker permanently might help to motivate the employee. It might also help the business to plan in future, knowing it has staff with skills to carry out work.

TEMPORARY workers are employed for a limited period. The clinic may employ a temporary reflexologist for short periods to cover busy periods, for example. Small businesses needing casual work at busy times employ temporary workers. A shop might need to employ retail assistants at Christmas for a fixed period. One advantage of temporary workers is that they no longer have to be employed once demand falls off. They can also be hired when required, to cover staff on maternity leave or for 'one-off' tasks. Costs may be lower because temporary workers do not receive the benefits of permanent workers. Some businesses use temporary jobs to try out workers who may later become permanent. One problem with temporary workers, businesses argue, is that they are less reliable than permanent staff.

Full-time and part-time employment

Workers may be employed full-time or part-time by a business. The Central Office of Information, which communicates government information, says that a part-time worker is someone who works less hours than a full-time worker. It suggests that there is no specific number of hours that makes someone full-time or part-time, but a full-time worker will usually work 35 hours or more a week.

Full-time workers may be taken on by businesses when orders or work are guaranteed on a regular basis. If this is not the case then there may be times when employees are being paid and there is no work for them. A business may also employ a skilled full-time worker to motivate them and retain their services. An advantage of part-time workers is the flexibility they provide. For example, part-time workers may be employed at times of peak trade, such as in public houses at the weekend. They may be employed to allow supermarkets to stay open later in the evening.

Homeworkers and teleworkers

For some businesses setting up, homeworkers may be an ideal solution. Homeworkers can include telesales and computer operators. They may be employed by a business to work at home or they may be self-employed. They may be full-time or part-time. Teleworker homeworkers are people who work from their own home, or use it as base, and who could not do so without a telephone or computer.

For a small business, the use of homeworkers has a number of advantages. As these workers are not based at the place of employment, the cost of equipment is reduced and less space is needed. There are also fewer problems with absenteeism and transport delays, such as people arriving late to work or who are unable to get to work because of bad weather. People with children are able to work more easily, at times when they want. However, there may be communication problems if staff cannot be contacted. Also, it is far more difficult to monitor and control the work of employees.

Using flexible working arrangements

Businesses may decide that they want to organise staff as flexibly as possible and have flexible working arrangements. There are many different types of flexibility open to businesses. Employees may have flexible working hours, working a number of hours in the day or week, but able to choose what hours to work. Or they might work a reduced number of days but longer hours each day.

Job sharing is becoming more popular as people seek part-time work. This is where the tasks involved in a job description are divided between two people, for example. They often work at different times. Examples could be a legal secretary's job, part of which is carried out by one person from 9 a.m. to 12 a.m. and another person from 12 a.m. to 5 p.m. A growing number of businesses are taking advantage of the use of flexible arrangements. It provides them with the chance to change work patterns to fit in with production and demand.

Consultants and advisors

One way a business can take advantage of extra skills and labour without taking on many of the responsibilities of an employer is to use advisors or outside consultants. These are workers who are self-employed or belong to separate outside companies. For example, a business might use an outside IT contractor to build a business's web pages, or hire a freelance PR consultant when it wants a promotional push. An advantage of using consultants or advisors is that in many cases they look after all their own income tax affairs and National Insurance contributions. People who are genuinely self-employed may not be entitled to the same rights afforded to employees. However, depending on the contract under which they are providing services, they may qualify as workers. Under these circumstances they would be entitled to workers' rights such as holiday pay. Quite often independent consultants can be expensive and a business will need to ensure that the services it receives from consultants are deemed to be value for money.

Drawbacks of employing staff

In setting up a business, entrepreneurs must be aware of legal rights that protect employees and that may act as drawbacks and difficulties in employing staff. These rights may lead to constraints on how people are used in the business.

The contract of employment Once a business appoints an employee that employee is entitled to a CONTRACT OF EMPLOYMENT. This is an agreement between the employer and the employee under which each has certain obligations. It is 'binding' to both parties in the agreement, the employer and the employee. This means that it is unlawful to break the terms and conditions in the contract without the other party agreeing. As soon as an employee starts work, and therefore demonstrates that she accepts the terms offered by the employer, the contract comes into existence. It is sometimes a written contract, although a verbal agreement or an 'implied' agreement are also contracts of employment. Employees taken on for one month or more receive a written statement within two months of appointment. This written statement sets out the terms and conditions in the contract.

Employment law Employees that are appointed by a business are covered by certain employment protection rights. Government legislation makes it a duty of employers to

Question 1.

Micah Lampkin recently set up Picks, a guitar and musical instrument workshop in Glasgow. The business wants to offer a variety of services to its customers, including cleaning, setting up and refretting. It also offers more specialist services, including bodywork repair. Micah currently employs one full-time worker, Carla. She deals with most of the professional clients of the business, including regular work on guitars for touring bands that often need work done immediately which requires technical expertise. His other worker is part time. Kevin works in the afternoons. He helps Micah to set up guitars and takes orders that come in.

Recently more orders have come in that need to be worked on during the mornings. Micah is considering employing Ged a young school leaver who wants to learn more about the business. He will work at different times of the day to Kevin. Micah is wondering whether to employ him on a temporary contract or as a permanent part-time employee.

(a) Explain the difference between a full-time and part-time employee.
(b) Why does Micah employ Carla full-time?
(c) Explain TWO factors that might affect Micah's decision about whether to employ Ged as a temporary or permanent part-time worker.

safeguard the rights of individuals at work. These are individual labour laws, as opposed to collective labour laws which affect all employees). They fall into a number of areas.

- **Discrimination.** Employees cannot be discriminated against on grounds of gender, race or disability. So, for example, a business cannot refuse to appoint a candidate for a job only because that person is female.
- **Equality of treatment and pay.** Employees must be paid the same rate as other employees doing the same job, a similar job or a job with equal demands. They also have the right to itemised pay statements and not to have pay deducted for unlawful reasons. Temporary and part-time employees cannot be treated less favourably than similar permanent staff in most cases. Equal treatment also applies to redundancies, training and access to pensions schemes.
- **Absences.** Employees have a right to maternity leave, paternity leave, time off for union or public duties and time off to look for training or work at times of redundancy. They also have a right to guaranteed payments during a period of lay-off or medical suspension. Employees have a right to return to work after maternity leave.
- **Dismissal.** Employees have the right not to be dismissed or face disciplinary action for trade union activity or on health and safety grounds. They also have a right to notice of dismissal. Employers have the right to terminate contracts of employment under certain circumstances, such as misconduct.
- **Health and safety.** Businesses have duties to provide a safe and healthy environment in which employees can work. Many UK and EU regulations exist and are being constantly introduced to raise standards of safety at work.
- **Vicarious liability.** In certain circumstance legislation forces business to have VICARIOUS LIABILITY. This is where a business must accept responsibility for the actions of its employees. Employers are liable for the wrongful acts of employees providing these happen during the course of their employment and are connected with it. So, for example, a construction business may be liable if its workers cause damage to an adjoining building while carrying out repairs to a client's building. Businesses found to be vicariously liable might incur fines or other penalties.
- **Conditions of work and service.** The written statement of the contract of employment will contain information about the conditions of work and service agreed by the employer and employee.

- **The number of hours worked.** A contract of employment will show the hours to be worked per week or over a period such as a year. The number of hours must conform to legislation. Details of the start and finish times may also be included, along with any meal or rest breaks. If an employee is expected to work 'shifts', this should be stated. Shift work is where an employee may work, for example, from 9 a.m.-5 p.m. in the day for a week and then from 9 p.m.-5 a.m. at night the following week. Employees can request flexible working.

KNOWLEDGE

1. Explain three differences between an employee and a person who is self-employed.
2. Why might a business employ temporary workers?
3. What is meant by job sharing?
4. What is meant by a homeworker?
5. Suggest three advantages of homeworkers for a business.
6. What are the advantages and disadvantages of hiring consultants or advisors?
7. Suggest four obligations that businesses have to employees that may be viewed as drawbacks.

KEYTERMS

Contract of employment – an agreement between an employer and an employee in which each has certain obligations.
Employee – a worker for whom an employer provides and controls work, supplies equipment and pays tax and National Insurance contributions.
Permanent employment – employment for an indefinite period of time.
Self-employed – a worker who makes his or her own decisions about accepting work and conditions of work, and pays his or her own tax and National Insurance contributions.
Temporary employment – employment for a limited or finite period of time.
Vicarious liability – when employers are liable for the wrongful actions of their employees.

Case Study: Benefits of a virtual workforce

Small business owners may find it tough to find a balance between giving enough time to ensure success and not running themselves into the ground. They often say that the first few years are the hardest, putting a strain on life outside work. They often find it necessary to get help. But employing additional, permanent staff brings with it extra headaches. Permanent recruitment can be time-consuming. There are costs in advertising the position and time taken on interviews. A small start-up business doing this may lose valuable time making sales or winning new business. There are also training costs and time and effort spent to stay in line with employment legislation. Also there are other fixed costs like tax and National Insurance contributions.

To ease this, many businesses are outsourcing support functions, freeing up time. Virtual personal assistants (PAs), off-site staff who can work on small or large projects for a fixed fee, are an example. Xenios Thrasyvoulou, founder and chief executive of Peopleperhour.com says, 'Small companies are increasingly looking for flexible labour and need a platform on which to do that. Forums, like Peopleperhour.com, help people find skilled freelance professionals to undertake support tasks or functions on a 'per project' basis … It functions like an online marketplace where professionals can put up their profile and companies or 'buyers' can list their requirements. Buyers then receive bids from professionals willing to carry out the work and can choose the most suitable one. We take a 10 per cent commission from the freelancers, which works out less than you'd see from an agency and it remains completely free for the buyers … Remote support can really help small businesses and busy individuals to get projects done in an easy, cost-effective and transparent way, without the hassle and costs associated with employing someone full-time to carry out these tasks.'

A forum, he argues, cuts out intermediaries in the recruitment process. Some employees, like freelancers, are hard to find. So small businesses use a recruitment agency. But recruitment agencies often want to place people in a permanent position because they get better commission. This means they can be quite pricey.

Outsourcing is not new, but until recently it was seen as the privilege of larger companies. Small businesses didn't have the resources to outsource on the large scale needed for it to be worthwhile. Through forums, off-site staff or freelance workers could offer small companies a viable alternative to permanent recruitment.

Source: adapted from http://www.smallbusiness.co.uk/5.6/human-resources/guides/256602/the-benefits-of-a-virtual-workforce.thtml.

(a) Identify the problems of employing permanent staff. (4 marks)

(b) What does outsourcing mean? Give two examples. (4 marks)

(c) Explain how the various services of Peopleperhour.com might help a small business. (8 marks)

(d) Evaluate the potential effectiveness of using outsourcing services such as Peopleperhour.com. (12 marks)

16 Costs, revenue and profit

The costs of production

A business needs accurate and reliable cost information to make decisions. A firm that is aiming to expand production to meet rising demand must know how much that extra production will cost. Without this information it will have no way of knowing whether or not it will make a profit. You will be familiar with your own costs. These are the expenses you have, such as travel costs to school or college. Similarly, businesses have expenses. These might include wages, raw materials, insurance and rent.

Economists usually think of costs as opportunity costs. The **opportunity cost** is the value that could have been earned if a resource was employed in its next best use. For example, if a business spends £40,000 on an advertising campaign, the opportunity cost might be the interest earned from depositing the money in a bank account. A business is also concerned, however, with ACCOUNTING COSTS. An accounting cost is the value of a resource used up in production. This is shown in the business accounts as an asset or an expense. For example, if a firm buys some fuel costing £5,500, this is shown as an expense in the accounts.

It is also important to understand how a firm's costs change in the SHORT RUN and the LONG RUN.

- The short run is the period of time when at least one factor of production is **fixed**. For example, in the short run, a firm might want to expand production in its factory. It can acquire more labour and buy more raw materials, but it has a fixed amount of space in the factory and a limited number of machines.
- In the long run, all factors can vary. The firm can buy another factory and add to the number of machines. This will increase **capacity** (the maximum amount that can be produced and begin another short run period.

Fixed costs

Costs which stay the same at all levels of output in the short run are called FIXED COSTS. Examples might be rent, insurance, heating bills, depreciation and business rates, as well as **capital costs** such as factories and machinery. These costs remain the same whether a business produces nothing or is working at full capacity. For example, rent must still be paid even if a factory is shut for a two week holiday when nothing is produced. Importantly, 'fixed' here means costs do not change as a result of a change in **output** in the short run. But they may increase due to, say, inflation. Figure 1 shows what happens to fixed costs as a firm increases production. The line on the graph is horizontal which shows that fixed costs are £400,000 no matter how much is produced.

What happens over a longer period? Figure 2 illustrates

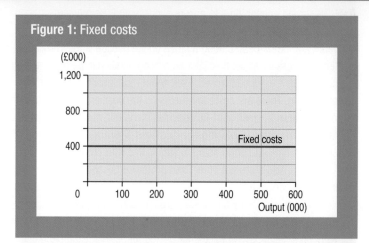

Figure 1: Fixed costs

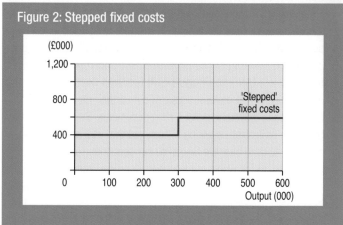

Figure 2: Stepped fixed costs

'stepped' fixed costs. If a firm is at full capacity, but needs to raise production, it might decide to invest in more equipment. The new machines raise overall fixed costs as well as capacity. The rise in fixed costs is shown by a 'step' in the graph. This illustrates how fixed costs can change in the long run.

Variable and semi-variable costs

Costs of production which increase directly as output rises are called VARIABLE COSTS. For example, a baker will require more flour if more loaves are to be produced. Raw materials are just one example of variable costs. Others might include fuel, packaging and wages. If the firm does not produce anything then variable costs will be zero.

Figure 3 shows a firm's variable costs. Assume that the firm buying new machinery in Figure 1 produces dolls and that variable costs are £2 per doll. If the firm produces 100,000 dolls it will have variable costs of £200,000 (£2 x 100,000). Producing 600,000 dolls it will incur variable costs of £1,200,000 (£2 x 600,000). Joining these points together shows the firm's variable costs at any level of output. As output increases, so do variable costs. Notice that the graph is **linear**. This means that it is a straight line.

Figure 3: Variable costs of a doll manufacturer

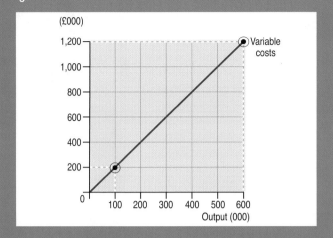

Figure 4: Total costs of a doll manufacturer

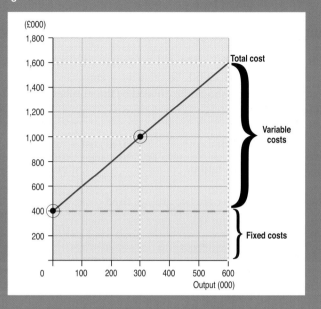

Some production costs do not fit neatly into our definitions of fixed and variable costs. This is because they are not entirely fixed or variable costs. Labour is a good example. If a firm employs a member of staff on a permanent basis, no matter what level of output, then this is a fixed cost. If this member of staff is asked to work overtime at nights and weekends to cope with extra production levels, then the extra cost is variable. Such labour costs are said to be SEMI-VARIABLE COSTS. Another example could be the cost of telephone charges. This often consists of a fixed or 'standing charge' plus an extra rate which varies according to the number of calls made.

Total costs

If fixed and variable costs are added together they show the TOTAL COST of a business. The total cost of production is the cost of producing any given level of output. As output increases total costs will rise. This is shown in Figure 4, which again shows the production of dolls. We can say:

$$\text{Total cost (TC)} = \text{fixed cost (FC)} + \text{variable cost (VC)}$$

The business has fixed costs of £400,000 and variable costs of £2 per doll. When output is 0 total costs are £400,000. When output has risen to 300,000 dolls, total costs are £1,000,000, made up of fixed costs of £400,000 and variable costs of £600,000 (£2 x 300,000). When output is 600,000, total costs are

Table 1: Summary of cost information for the doll manufacturer

000			£000
Output	Fixed cost	Variable cost	Total cost
0	400	0	400
300	400	600	1,000
600	400	1,200	1,600

£1,600,00 made up of fixed costs of £400,000 and variable costs of £1,200,000 (£2 x 600,000). This information is summarised in Table 1. Figure 4 shows the way that total costs increase as output increases. Notice that as output increases fixed costs become a smaller proportion of total costs.

Direct and indirect costs

Costs can also be divided into direct and indirect costs. DIRECT COSTS are costs which can be identified with a particular product or process. Examples of direct costs are raw materials, packaging, and direct labour. INDIRECT COSTS or OVERHEADS result from the whole business. It is not possible to associate these costs directly with particular products or processes. Examples are rent, insurance, the salaries of office staff and audit fees. Indirect costs are usually fixed costs and

Question 1.

Dale Roberts runs EdMedia, an education and training services company based in Stevenage, Hertfordshire. EdMedia produces online and video information films about workplace issues, from disability discrimination to bullying and harassment. Orders have soared as new employment laws create demand for staff training. Large contracts with high profile clients have helped to boost sales from £1.1 million in 2005 to £3.9 million in 2007. In 2006, Dale had to hire a new photocopier. The monthly hire rate was £100. Other costs associated with the photocopier were toner, paper and electricity. These costs amounted to £1 per 100 copies.

(a) Using the photocopier as an example, explain the difference between fixed and variable costs.
(b) Calculate the total annual cost of the photocopier if 68,000 copies were made during the year.
(c) Explain why the total cost of the photocopier is an indirect cost for EdMedia.

direct costs variable costs, although in theory both direct and indirect costs can be fixed or variable.

Average and marginal costs

The AVERAGE COST is the cost per unit of production, also known as the UNIT COST. To calculate average cost the total cost of production should be divided by the number of units produced.

$$\text{Average cost} = \frac{\text{Total cost}}{\text{Output}} \quad \text{or} \quad \frac{\text{Fixed cost + variable cost}}{\text{Output}}$$

It is also possible to calculate average fixed costs:

$$\text{Average fixed cost} = \frac{\text{Total fixed cost}}{\text{Output}}$$

and average variable costs:

$$\text{Average variable cost} = \frac{\text{Total variable cost}}{\text{Output}}$$

Take the earlier example of the doll manufacturer with fixed costs of £400,000 and variable costs of £2 per unit. If output was 100,000 units:

$$\text{Average fixed cost} = \frac{£400,000}{100,000} = £4$$

$$\text{Average variable cost} = \frac{£2 \times 100,000}{100,000} = £2$$

$$\text{Average total cost} = \frac{£400,000 + (£2 \times 100,000)}{100,000}$$

$$= \frac{£600,000}{100,000} = £6$$

MARGINAL COST is the cost of increasing total output by one more unit. It can be calculated by:

$$\text{Marginal cost} = \frac{\text{change in total cost}}{\text{change in output}}$$

For example, if the total cost of manufacturing 100,000 dolls is £600,000 and the total cost of producing 100,001 dolls is £600,002, then the marginal cost of producing the last unit is:

$$\text{Marginal cost} = \frac{£600,002 - £600,000}{100,001 - 100,000} = \frac{£2}{1} = £2$$

Question 2.

Carefabric is a home-based business run by Margaret Parry. She makes a small range of towelling and other products for children. The products are advertised on her website and she distributes about 50 per cent of output to retailers in the southwest on a sale or return basis. Recently she has concentrated more on design and has employed someone full time to do most of the manufacturing - although Margaret still helps out when the orders pile up. One of the new products Margaret has recently added to her line is a skin-friendly suit for small children. Made from natural materials, the costs for each suit are given below.

Fabric	£5.60 per unit
Other materials	£2.40 per unit
Packaging	£1.00 per unit
Machining	£11.00 per unit
Fixed overheads	£50 per month

When setting the price for her products Margaret just adds on 50% of costs. This method has generated good sales and profits in the past and she has no reason to change a successful strategy. Margaret plans to produce 400 suits in the next trading year.

(a) Calculate: (i) total fixed cost; (ii) total variable cost; (iii) total costs (iv) average cost; (v) price.
(b) During the year Margaret managed to sell just 250 suits. Calculate the total revenue.

The problems of classifying costs

There is a number of possible ways in which costs can be classified.

- By type. This involves analysing business costs and deciding whether they are **direct** or **indirect**.
- By behaviour. Economists favour this method. They classify costs according to the effect that a change in the level of output has on a particular cost. **Fixed**, **variable**, **semi-variable**, **average and marginal costs** all fall into this category.
- By function. It is possible to classify costs according to the business function they are associated with. For example, costs could be listed as **production**, **selling**, **administrative** or **personnel**.
- By nature of resource. This involves classifying costs according to the resources which were acquired by a business, for example, **materials**, **labour** or **expenses**.
- By **product**, **job**, **customer** or **contract**. A multi-product manufacturer, such as Heinz for example, might classify costs according to the product line (beans, soups,

Figure 5: Total revenue

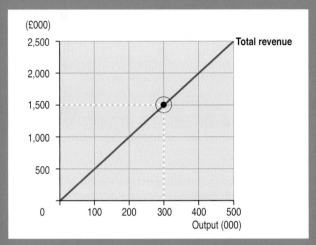

puddings) they are associated with. Solicitors might classify costs by identifying them with particular clients.

The classification of costs is not always straightforward. In some cases the same business cost can be classified in several ways. For example, the earnings of a full-time administrative assistant may be classified as a fixed cost, if they do not vary with output, and an indirect cost, if they are not associated with a particular product. The costs of a worker earning piece rates might be a direct cost if they can be associated with a particular product and a variable cost if they rise as the output of the worker increases.

Another problem relating to costs concerns the allocation of indirect costs. When calculating the cost of producing particular products it is necessary to allocate indirect costs to each of the different products a business manufactures. In practice this may be difficult.

The way in which costs are classified will depend on the purposes for which the classification is being undertaken and the views of the management team.

Long-run costs

Most of the costs discussed so far in this unit have been short-run costs, ie the time period where at least one factor of production is fixed. In the long run, all factors of production are likely to be variable.

Total revenue

The amount of money which a firm receives from selling its product can be referred to as TOTAL REVENUE. Total revenue is calculated by multiplying the number of units sold by the price of each unit:

$$\text{Total revenue} = \text{quantity sold} \times \text{price}$$

For example, if the doll producer mentioned earlier sells 300,000 dolls at a price of £5 each:

$$\text{Total revenue} = 300,000 \times £5 = £1,500,000$$

Figure 5 shows what happens to total revenue as output rises. Notice that the graph is linear.

Profit and loss

One of the main reasons why firms calculate their costs and revenue is to enable them to work out their **profit** or **loss**. Profit is the difference between revenue and costs.

$$\text{Profit} = \text{total revenue} - \text{total costs}$$

For example, if the doll manufacturer in the earlier example produces and sells 300,000 dolls, they sell for £5, fixed costs are £400,000 and variable costs are £2 per unit, then:

$$
\begin{aligned}
\text{Profit} &= £5 \times 300,000 - (£400,000 + [£2 \times 300,000]) \\
&= £1,500,000 - (£400,000 + [£600,000]) \\
&= £1,500,000 - £1,000,000 \\
&= £500,000
\end{aligned}
$$

It is possible to calculate the profit for a business at any level of output using this method.

KEYTERMS

Accounting cost – the value of an economic resource used up in production.

Average cost or unit cost – the cost of producing one unit, calculated by dividing the total cost by output.

Direct cost – a cost which can be clearly identified with a particular unit of output.

Fixed cost – a cost which does not change as a result of a change in output in the short run.

Indirect cost or overhead – a cost which cannot be identified with a particular unit of output. It is incurred by the whole organisation or department.

Long run – the time period where all factors of production are variable.

Marginal cost – the cost of increasing output by one more unit.

Semi-variable cost – a cost which consists of both fixed and variable elements.

Short run – the time period where at least one factor of production is fixed.

Total cost – the entire cost of producing a given level of output.

Total revenue – the amount of money the business receives from selling output.

Variable cost – a cost which rises as output rises.

But if the variable costs were £4 per unit, the business would make a loss.

Loss = £5 x 300,000 - (£400,000 + [£4 x 300,000])

     = £1,500,000 – (£400,000 + £1,200,000)

     = £1,500,000 – £1,600,000

     = - £100,000

KNOWLEDGE

1. What is the difference between opportunity costs and accounting costs?
2. How do you account for a 'stepped' fixed cost function?
3. Why are some costs said to be semi-variable?
4. What happens to variable costs as a proportion of total costs when output rises?
5. Explain the difference between direct and indirect costs.
6. How is: (a) average fixed cost; (b) average variable cost; calculated?
7. How is total revenue calculated?
8. What information is required to calculate a firm's profit?
9. What problems might there be when classifying costs.

Case Study: Wilkins

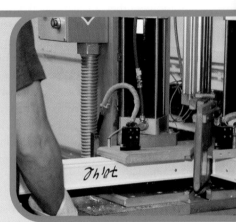

Wilkins manufactures and supplies a range of PVC products such as windows, doors, door canopies, conservatories, garage doors and porches. It is a north eastern company and operate from a factory in Gateshead. The company is committed to high quality standards and as a result gets regular work from large building contractors. Wilkins uses a number of control procedures which are outlined briefly below.

- **The Environmental Test Chamber** uses computer technology to reproduce the conditions of a warm living room and more extreme weather conditions.
- **Weather Cycle Tests** are carried out using data from studies undertaken with the Met Office over the last 30 years, and subjecting our samples to similar patterns.
- **Weld Testing Equipment** is used to check the quality of welds, and a Salt Spray Cabinet ensures that the metal fittings are of the highest quality.
- **Security Test Rig** simulates the damage that a burglar might inflict and the results are assessed to ensure high standards of security in our products.

Wilkins' management system is registered to BS EN ISO 9001-2000 and all products are covered by British and European Standards.

Wilkins is about to start work on a large contract in Newcastle. The contract is to supply 100 standard conservatories on a new housing development. The variable costs for manufacturing and supplying the conservatories are £4,000 each. The fixed costs for the contract are £20,000. An incomplete cost schedule is shown in Figure 6. Wilkins will receive £6,000 for each conservatory.

(a) Give two examples of variable costs that Wilkins is likely to incur when manufacturing and supplying the conservatories. (4 marks)
(b) Complete the cost schedule in Figure 6. (10 marks)
(c) Plot the: (i) fixed cost; (ii) variable cost; (iii) total cost functions on a graph. (12 marks)
(d) Calculate the profit that Wilkins will make on the contract. (8 marks)
(e) How will this profit be affected if fixed costs rise to £35,000? (6 marks)

Figure 6: Cost information for Wilkins

	0	10	20	30	40	50	60	70	80	90	100
Fixed cost	£20,000										
Variable cost											
Total cost											

17 | Contribution

What is contribution?

Craig Eckert sells second-hand cars. His last sale was £990 for a Golf GTI. He bought the Golf at a car auction for £890. The difference between what he paid for the car and the price he sold it for is £100 (£990 - £890). This difference is called the CONTRIBUTION. It is not profit because Craig has fixed costs to pay such as rent, insurance and administration expenses. Contribution is the difference between selling price and variable costs. In this case the selling price was £990 and the variable cost was £890. The £100 will **contribute** to the **total fixed costs** of the business and the profit.

Contribution per unit and total contribution

A business might calculate the contribution on the sale of a single unit, or the sale of a larger quantity, such as a whole year's output.

Unit contribution In the above example the unit contribution was calculated. It was the contribution on the sale of one unit, a single car. The formula for calculating the unit contribution is:

Contribution per unit = selling price - variable cost
= £990 - £890
= £100

Total contribution When more than one unit is sold the total contribution can be calculated. For example, a textile company receives an order for 1,000 pairs of trousers. The variable costs are £7.50 a pair and they will be sold for £9.00 a pair. The total contribution made by the order is:

Total contribution = total revenue - total variable cost
= (£9.00 x 1,000) - (£7.50 x 1,000)
= £9,000 - £7,500
= £1,500

The £1,500 in this example will contribute to the textile company's fixed costs and profit. The total contribution can also be calculated by multiplying the unit contribution by the number of units sold.

Total contribution = unit contribution x number of units sold
= (£9.00 - £7.50) x 1,000
= £1.50 x 1,000
= £1,500

Contribution and profit

Contribution can be used to calculate profit. Take the example again of Craig Eckert the car salesperson. He wants to calculate the profit his business makes in January. Table 1 shows the variable cost and selling price of cars in January.

The fixed costs of the business in the same month are also shown in Table 2.

The total contribution from car sales in January was £3,160. This is calculated by subtracting the total variable costs, ie the cost of purchasing the cars, from the total revenue (£21,760 - £18,600). Total revenue is the amount of money received from the sale of the 10 cars during January. The profit for January 2007 is:

Profit = total contribution - fixed costs
= £3,160 - £1,160
= £2,000

So the business made £2,000 profit in January.

Profit can be calculated by subtracting total costs from total revenue. If this method is used here, the profit made by Craig Eckert's business in January is:

Profit = total revenue - total cost
= total revenue - (fixed cost + variable cost)
= £21,760 - (£1,160 + £18,600)
= £21,760 - £19,760
= £2,000

Table 1: Variable cost and selling price of cars in January

			(£)
Description	Variable cost	Selling price	Contribution
Nissan Micra	900	1,100	200
VW Polo	1,100	1,450	350
Fiat Tipo	780	900	120
Volvo 740 SE	1,400	1,700	300
Seat Ibiza	670	700	30
Astra Auto	2,300	2,700	400
Nissan Primera	3,100	3,600	500
BMW 318i	6,900	8,000	1,100
Escort estate	560	620	60
Golf GTI	890	990	100
Total	**18,600**	**21,760**	**3,160**

Table 2: Monthly fixed costs for Craig Eckert

Description	(£)
Office rent	700
Insurance	60
Telephone	100
Administrative expenses	300
	1,160

Unit 17
Contribution

Figure 1: The relationship between fixed costs, variable costs, profit and contribution for Craig Eckert's business in January

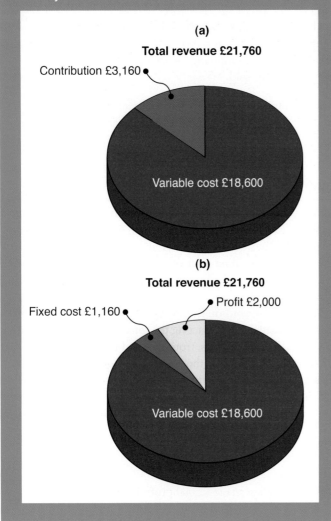

(a)
Total revenue £21,760

Contribution £3,160

Variable cost £18,600

(b)
Total revenue £21,760

Profit £2,000

Fixed cost £1,160

Variable cost £18,600

The answer is the same as before, £2,000. However, the contribution method can often be quicker than this method because there is slightly less calculation.

Fixed costs, variable costs, contribution and profit

The relationship between fixed costs, variable costs, profit and contribution is shown in Figure 1. The pie charts show information from Craig Eckert's business in January.

Figure 1(a) shows how the total revenue of £21,760 is divided between the variable cost (£18,600) and contribution (£3,160). Figure 1(b) shows how total revenue of £21,760 is divided between variable cost (£18,600), fixed costs (£1,160) and profit (£2,000). Note that the value of contribution (£3,160) is equal to the value of fixed cost (£1,160) and profit (£2,000) added together.

Contribution costing

How can a business make use of contribution calculations? Calculating the contribution to fixed costs and profit that a product makes might help a business in decision making. This is known as contribution costing. For example, say that a design business has limited time and resources. It has been approached by two clients who want a new corporate logo and image designing this week. The prices and variable costs and contribution are shown below.

- Design 1 - Price £3,000, variable costs £2,500, contribution per unit £500 (£3,000 - £2,500)
- Design 2 - Price £3,000, variable costs £800, contribution per unit £2,200 (£3,000 - £800)

So the business might choose the second design as it contributes more to fixed costs and profit.

Contribution pricing

Some businesses use contribution when setting their price. This approach involves setting a price for orders or individual products which exceeds the variable cost. This means that a particular order or product will always make a contribution when sold. This approach ignores fixed costs since a single order or product may not generate enough contribution to cover fixed cost. This approach needs to be used with caution. Obviously, to make a profit fixed costs have to be covered. Contribution pricing is most likely to be used when fixed costs are low or when a business knows through experience that fixed costs will be covered.

Table 4 shows some financial information for R G Edwards, an engineering company, that receives four big orders in a particular month. The table shows the price charged, the variable cost and contribution for each order. The total contribution is £35,500. Through experience R G Edwards knows that these prices will cover fixed costs. Fixed costs are £10,000 per month. Therefore the profit for the month is £25,500 (£35,500 - £10,000).

Contribution can also be used to calculate the break-even output of a business. This is covered in the next unit.

Question 1.

AblePrint Ltd is a medium-sized printing company based in Worcester. It offers professional quality-controlled printing with a clear and competitive pricing policy. Examples of its servcies include the printing of business cards, compliment slips, brochures and price lists. AblePrint Ltd has received an order from a local tour operator. It wants 1,000 brochures printed to supply travel agents. The business has agreed a price of £540 for the job.

(a) Calculate the total contribution for the job.
(b) Calculate the profit from the job.

Table 3: Print costs

Fixed costs	£100
Variable costs	
Paper	15p per brochure
Ink	10p per brochure
Other variable costs	10p per brochure

Table 4: Financial information for R G Edwards

	Price	Variable cost	Contribution (£)
Order 1	45,000	32,000	13,000
Order 2	23,000	21,000	2,000
Order 3	49,000	39,500	9,500
Order 4	58,000	47,000	11,000
Total	175,000	139,500	35,500

KEYTERMS

Contribution – the amount of money left over after variable costs have been subtracted from revenue. The money contributes towards fixed costs and profit.

KNOWLEDGE

1. A product sells for £10 and the variable costs are £8.50. What is the contribution per unit?
2. A clothes retailer buys 240 jumpers for £27. The jumpers are sold for £39 each. What is the total contribution made by the jumpers?
3. What is the formula for calculating profit using contribution?
4. If the total contribution is £120,000 and fixed costs are £96,000, what is the profit?
5. If the total variable costs are £450,000 and contribution is £225,000, what is the total revenue?
6. State three ways in which contribution can be used by a business to help make decisions.

Question 2.

Laura Wooding runs a catering company. She provides dinner parties for people in their own homes. Laura has built up an excellent reputation in her local town and only has to work four nights a week to make a very comfortable living. Most of her costs are variable. These include the cost of food, wine, dining accessories such as table decorations and napkins and the hire of glassware and eating utensils if necessary. Laura uses her client's kitchen and cooking utensils when working. The fixed costs of the company are only £100 per week. Laura uses contribution pricing. The price is influenced by the number of diners and the choice of food. Table 5 shows some financial information for a typical week.

(a) What is meant by contribution pricing?
(b) Calculate the week's profit made by Laura's company using the information in Table 5.
(c) Why should contribution pricing be used with caution?

Table 5: Financial information for Laura's company

	Price	Variable cost	Contribution (£)
Party 1	240	155	85
Party 2	140	70	70
Party 2	320	180	140
Party 3	200	60	140

Case Study: Timmings Ltd

Timmings Ltd is a family business set up in 2001 when Frank Timmings, a plastics factory manager, decided that he no longer wanted to work for someone else. Frank set up a small production facility to manufacture transparent plastic containers for storage of documents. He was surprised by the demand because he thought that most documents were stored electronically now. His main customers are office suppliers and large businesses.

Sales have grown from £1.1 million in 2003 to £3.64 million in 2006. Timmings Ltd is operating at almost full capacity. At the moment Frank has no plans to expand and is content with current profit levels. But Frank does have to turn work down. When faced with a choice of orders he only accepts those which make the largest contribution. One week in February 2007 he received the four orders outlined in Table 6. The factory can only meet the demands of two.

(a) State three possible fixed costs for Timmings Ltd. (3 marks)
(b) Using the Butlers order as an example, explain the difference between unit contribution and total contribution. (6 marks)
(c) Calculate the total contribution made by each of the four orders. (8 marks)
(d) (i) Which two orders should Timmings accept? (2 marks)
(ii) Calculate the profit made by the two orders. (6 marks)
(e) What might be the long-term effect on Timmings Ltd of selecting orders in this way? (8 marks)

Table 6: Details of four orders for Timmings Ltd

	Butlers	A & P Ltd	VC Singh	VWD plc (£)
Number of units	20,000	30,000	25,000	20,000
Contract price per unit	£8.00	£8.50	£7.00	£10.50
Material costs per unit	£2.20	£2.00	£2.40	£3.00
Labour costs per unit	£3.40	£4.20	£2.10	£3.80
Other variable costs per unit	£1.00	£1.40	£1.20	£1.30
Fixed costs	£5,000	£5,000	£5,000	£5,000

18 Break-even analysis

The break-even output

Businesses, particularly those that are just starting up, often like to know how much they need to produce or sell to BREAK-EVEN. If a business has information about fixed costs and variable costs and knows what price it is going to charge, it can calculate how many units it needs to sell to cover all of its costs. The point where **total costs** are exactly the same as **total revenue** is called the BREAK-EVEN POINT. The level of output a business needs to produce so that **total costs** are exactly the same as **total revenue** is called the BREAK-EVEN OUTPUT.

For example, if a business produces 100 units at a total cost of £5,000, and sells them for £50 each, total revenue will also be £5,000 (£50 x 100). The business will break-even at this level of output. So the break-even output is 100 units. It makes neither a profit nor a loss.

Calculating break-even using contribution

It is possible to calculate the break-even output if a firm knows the value of its fixed costs, variable costs and the price it will charge. Take an example of a small producer, Jack Cadwallader, who has just set up a business making wrought iron park benches. His fixed costs (FC) are £60,000 and variable costs (VC) £40 per bench. He sells the benches to local authorities across the country for £100 each.

The simplest way to calculate the break-even output is to use **contribution**. Contribution is the amount of money left over after the variable cost per unit is taken away from the selling price. For Jack's park benches, the contribution is:

Contribution	=	selling price - variable cost
Contribution	=	£100 - £40
Contribution	=	£60

To calculate the number of benches Jack needs to sell to break-even, the following formula can be used:

$$\text{Break-even output} = \frac{\text{Fixed costs}}{\text{Contribution}}$$

$$= \frac{£60,000}{£60}$$

$$= 1,000 \text{ benches}$$

Jack Cadwallader's business will break-even when 1,000 park benches are sold.

Calculating break-even using revenue and costs

Another way of calculating the break-even output is to use the total cost and total revenue figures. In the case of Jack Cadwallader:

Total cost	=	fixed cost + variable cost
or TC	=	£60,000 + £40Q
and Total revenue	=	price x quantity sold
or TR	=	£100Q

where Q is the quantity produced and sold, ie the number of park benches. A firm will break-even where total cost is equal to total revenue. Therefore we can write:

TC	=	TR
£60,000 + £40Q	=	£100Q

To find Q we can calculate:

60,000	=	100Q - 40Q
60,000	=	60Q
$\dfrac{60,000}{60}$	=	Q
1,000	=	Q

It is possible to check if this answer is correct by calculating total cost and total revenue when 1,000 benches are produced. If the answers are the same, the break-even output is correct.

TC = £60,000 + (£40 x 1,000) = £60,000 + £40,000 = £100,000
TR = £100 x 1,000 = £100,000

Both TC and TR are equal to £100,000, so the break-even output is 1,000 benches. This also confirms that the answer using the contribution method was correct.

Total cost and total revenue figures can be used to calculate the amount of profit or loss the firm will make at particular levels of output.

- At any level of output below the break-even output the firm will make a **loss**.
- Output produced above the break-even level will make a **profit**. If the bench manufacturer were to produce 1,200 benches, profit would be:

Profit	=	TR - TC
	=	(£100 x 1,200) - (£60,000 + [£40 x 1,200])
	=	£120,000 - (£60,000 + £48,000)
	=	£120,000 - £108,000
Profit	=	£12,000

Figure 1: Break-even chart for Jack Cadwallader

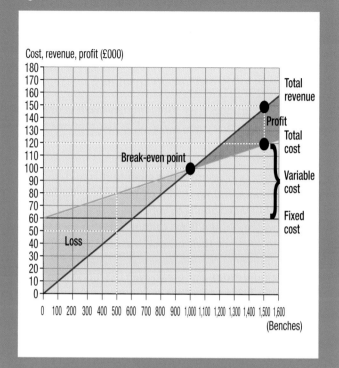

Calculating break-even using break-even charts

The use of graphs is often helpful in break-even analysis. It is possible to identify the break-even point and break-even output by plotting the total cost and total revenue equations on a graph. This graph is called a BREAK-EVEN CHART. Figure 1 shows the break-even chart for Jack Cadwallader's business.

Output is measured on the horizontal axis and revenue, costs and profit are measured on the vertical axis. What does the break-even chart show?

- The value of total cost over a range of output. For example, when Jack produces 1,500 benches total costs are £120,000.
- The value of total revenue over a range of output. For example, when Jack produces 1,500 benches total revenue is £150,000.
- Break-even charts can show the level of fixed costs over a range of output. For example, the fixed costs for Jack's business are £60,000.
- The level of output needed to break-even. The break-even point is where total costs equal total revenue of £100,000. This is when 1,000 benches are produced. So the break-even output is 1,000 benches.
- At levels of output below the break-even output, losses are made. This is because total costs exceed total revenue. At an output of 500 a £30,000 loss is made.
- At levels of output above the break-even output, a profit is made. This profit gets larger as output rises. At an output of 1,500 a profit of £30,000 is made.
- The relationship between fixed costs and variable costs as output rises. At low levels of output fixed costs represent a large proportion of total costs. As output rises, fixed costs become a smaller proportion of total costs.
- The profit at a particular level of output. If Jack produces 1,500 benches, profit is shown by the vertical gap between the total cost and total revenue equations. It is £30,000.

The margin of safety

What if a business is producing more than the break-even output? It might be useful to know by how much sales could fall before a loss is made. This is called the MARGIN OF SAFETY. It refers to the range of output over which a profit can be made. The margin of safety can be identified on the break-even chart by measuring the distance between the break-even level of output and the current (profitable) level output. For example, Figure 2 shows the break-even chart for Jack Cadwallader. If Jack produces 1,200 benches the margin of safety is 200 benches. This means that output can fall by 200 before a loss is made. If Jack sells 1,200 benches the chart shows that total revenue is £120,000, total cost is £108,000 and profit is £12,000.

Businesses prefer to operate with a large margin of safety. This means that if sales drop they still might make some profit. With a small margin of safety there is a risk that the business is more likely to make losses if sales fall.

Question 1.

Jun Shan produces Chinese rugs using traditional techniques and sells them online. The rugs are high in quality and made from natural materials. The rugs sell for £105 and variable costs are £65 per rug. Jun Shan's fixed costs are £2,000 pa.

(a) Calculate how many rugs Jun Shan needs to produce and sell to break-even.

(b) How much profit will Jun Shan make if 500 rugs are sold during a year?

(c) How many rugs will Jun Shan need to sell to break-even if the price is increased to £115?

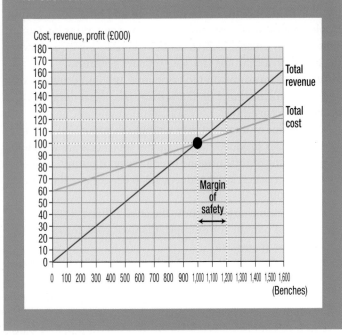

Figure 2: Break-even chart showing the margin of safety for Jack Cadwallader's business

Using break-even analysis

Break-even analysis is used in business as a tool to make decisions about the future. It helps answer 'what if' questions. For instance:

- if price went up, what would happen to the break-even point?
- if the business introduced a new product line, how many would the new product have to sell to at least break-even?
- if the business is just starting up, what has to be the level of output to prevent a loss being incurred?
- what will happen to the break-even point if costs are forecast to rise?
- would the break-even point be lower if components were bought in from outside suppliers rather than being made

in-house?

Break-even analysis is also found in business plans. Banks often ask for business plans when deciding whether or not to give a loan. So break-even analysis can be vital in gaining finance, especially when starting up a business.

Weaknesses of break-even analysis

Break-even analysis does have some limitations. It is often regarded as too simplistic and some of its assumptions are unrealistic.

Output and stocks It assumes that all output is sold, so that output equals sales, and no stocks are held. Many businesses hold stocks of finished goods to cope with changes in demand. There are also times when firms cannot sell what they produce and choose to stockpile their output to avoid laying off staff.

Unchanging conditions The break-even chart is drawn for a given set of conditions. It cannot cope with a sudden increase in wages and prices or changes in technology.

Accuracy of data The effectiveness of break-even analysis depends on the quality and accuracy of the data used to construct cost and revenue functions. If the data is poor and inaccurate, the conclusions drawn on the basis of the data are flawed. For example, if fixed costs are underestimated, the level of output required to break-even will be higher than suggested by the break-even chart.

Non-linear relationships It is assumed that the total revenue and total cost lines are linear or straight. This may not always be the case. For example, a business may have to offer discounts on large orders, so total revenues fall at high outputs. In this case the total revenue line would rise and then fall, and be curved. A business can lower costs by buying in bulk. So costs may fall at high outputs and the costs function will be curved.

Multi-product businesses Many businesses produce more than one single product. It is likely that each product will have different variable costs and different prices. The problem is how to allocate the fixed costs of the multi-product business to each individual product. There is a number of ways, but none is perfect. Therefore, if the fixed costs incurred by each product is inaccurate, break-even analysis is less useful.

Stepped fixed costs Some fixed costs are stepped. For example, a manufacturer, in order to increase output, may need to acquire more capacity. This may result in rent increases and thus fixed costs will rise sharply. Under these circumstances it is difficult to use break-even analysis.

KEYTERMS

Break-even – where a business sells just enough to cover its costs.
Break-even chart – a graph containing the total cost and total revenue lines, illustrating the break-even output.
Break-even output – the output a business needs to produce so that its total revenue and total costs are the same.
Break-even point – where total revenue and total costs are the same.
Margin of safety – the range of output between the break-even level and the current level of output, over which a profit is made.

KNOWLEDGE

1. How can the contribution be used to calculate the break-even level of output?
2. How can the break-even level of output calculation be checked?
3. State five things which a break-even chart can show.
4. What effect will a price increase have on the margin of safety?
5. What effect will a fall in fixed costs have on the margin of safety?
6. State three uses of break-even analysis.
7. State three weaknesses of break-even analysis.

Question 2.

Paul Roberts makes Spanish guitars from a rented room in a rural business park. Figure 3 shows a break-even chart for his business.

(a) What is the total revenue of the business at an output and sales level of (i) 0 (ii) 20 guitars?
(b) What are the fixed costs of the business?
(c) (i) What is the break-even level of output? (ii) What are the revenue and costs at this level?
(d) What is the margin of safety if the business sells (i) 12 guitars; (ii) 20 guitars?
(e) If the business produces and sells 15 guitars, what would be the: (i) total revenue; (ii) total costs; (iii) profit or loss (iiii) total variable costs; (v) variable cost of each guitar?

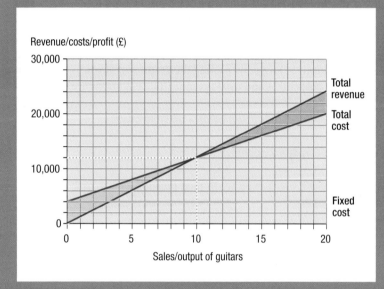

Figure 3: A break-even chart for Paul Roberts' business

Case Study: Carl Hurst Balti Pies

After following his football team to an away fixture at Villa Park last year, Carl Hurst discovered Balti pies on sale at half-time at the ground. These are pies, filled with chicken balti, a curry dish for which Birmingham is famous. Carl decided that Balti pies could provide him with a new and successful opportunity. He thought he could make the pies himself and sell them in the north-west.

Carl did some research and found that there were few outlets in the north-west where Balti pies were sold. He made some pies at home and took them to various retailers, pubs and clubs to see whether they would be interested. People who liked curry (an overwhelming majority) loved them. Those that had no taste for curry were uninterested.

But Carl was sure he had a winner. He found a disused kitchen unit in Wigan, previously used for pie-making. A week before he signed a 12 month lease for the unit, Carl put some figures together to help him assess the possible profitability of the venture. Carl planned to produce pies in batches of 100 and sell pies for 50p each. He also prepared a business plan to help in the setting-up process. Some financial information is shown below.

Fixed costs

Lease	£2,500 per year
Other fixed costs	£500 per year

Variable costs

Food ingredients	£14 per batch
Fuel	£2 per batch
Other variable costs	£4 per batch

(a) Calculate the contribution per batch of pies. (4 marks)
(b) How many batches would Carl need to produce in his first year of trading to break-even? (6 marks)
(c) How much profit would Carl make if he sold 55,000 pies in his first year? (6 marks)
(d) In the second year of trading the landlord raised the lease for the kitchen unit to £4,500 per year. Carl responded to this by raising the price of his pies to 70p each. What effect would this have on the break-even level of output? (6 marks)
(e) To what extent will break-even analysis be useful to Carl Hurst? (18 marks)

19 | Break-even and changes in prices and costs

Constructing break-even charts

A break-even chart can be constructed by plotting the total cost and total revenue lines on a graph. The graph should measure output on the horizontal axis and costs, revenue and profit on the vertical axis. Consider Reidle Bros, a small canoe manufacturer. It incurs fixed costs of £20,000 per annum and variable costs of £75 per canoe. The canoes are sold for £125 to agents and wholesalers. The following steps can be used to construct a break-even chart.

Calculating the break-even output It is helpful to calculate the break-even output before constructing the graph. For Reidle Bros the total costs (TC) and total revenue (TR) equations are:

TC = £20,000 + £75Q (fixed costs + variable costs)

TR = £125Q (price x quantity)

Reidle Bros will break-even when total revenue equals total costs. This is where:

$$£20,000 + £75Q = £125Q$$
$$£20,000 = £125Q - £75Q$$
$$£20,000 = £50Q$$
$$\frac{£20,000}{£50} = Q$$
$$400 = Q$$

Therefore, Reidle Bros will break-even when it manufactures 400 canoes.

Calculating revenue and total cost Both the total cost and total revenue lines are linear or straight. Therefore the lines can be drawn by joining two points which lie on each function. To plot total revenue choose two levels of output and calculate the total revenue at each level. Any two levels of output could be chosen but 0 is often chosen as one of the points. Chose a second value which is twice that of the break-even point, such as 800 (2 x 400) in the case of the canoe manufacturers. This will ensure that the break-even point is in the centre of the chart, improving

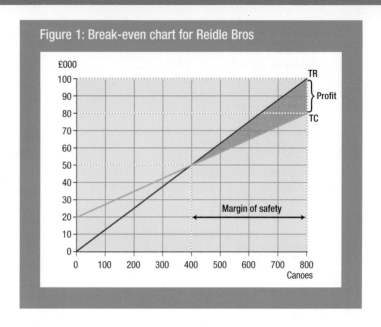

Figure 1: Break-even chart for Reidle Bros

presentation. The value of total revenue at each of these output levels is shown in Table1. This is based on fixed costs of £20,000, variable costs of £75 per canoe and a sale price of £125.

Plotting total revenue Total revenue (TR) can now be plotted on the graph. The output axis should run from 0 to 800 canoes and the other axis from 0 to £100,000. Using the information in Table 1, the two points, or coordinates, on the total revenue line are (0, 0) and (800, £100,000). If these are plotted on the graph and joined up the total revenue will appear as shown in Figure 1.

Plotting total costs To plot total costs, calculate the total cost at two levels of output. It is useful to use the same values as those used for total revenue, ie 0 and 800. From Table1 the two points which lie on the total cost line are (0, £20,000) and (800, £80,000). If these are plotted on the graph and joined up the total cost line will appear as shown in Figure 3. Total costs do not start at coordinates 0,0. At an output of zero, the business still has fixed costs of £20,000.

Analysis from the diagram The break-even chart is now complete. An analysis of certain points on the diagram can be made.

The break-even output can be identified and plotted. It is usual to draw lines to show the number of canoes Reidle Bros

Table 1: Values of TR and TC at two levels of output for Reidle Bros					
Output (£)	Fixed costs (£)	Variable costs (£)	Total costs (£)	Total revenue (£)	Profit /loss (£)
0	20,000	0	20,000	0	-20,000
800	20,000	60,000 (800 x £75)	80,000	100,000 (800 x £125)	+20,000

Figure 2: Break-even chart – an increase in price

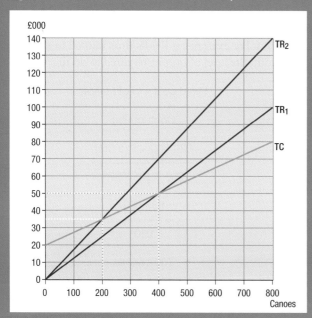

must sell to break-even (400), and the value of TR and TC at this level of output (£50,000). The break-even output should coincide with the calculation made in the first step, ie 400 canoes.

- The profit at certain levels of output may be indicated. For example, at an output of 800 canoes, the profit is £100,000 - £80,000 = £20,000.
- The margin of safety can be indicated. This is the difference between the current output of the business and the break-even point. At an output of 800 canoes it is 800 - 400 = 400 canoes.

Figure 3: Break-even chart – an increase in fixed costs

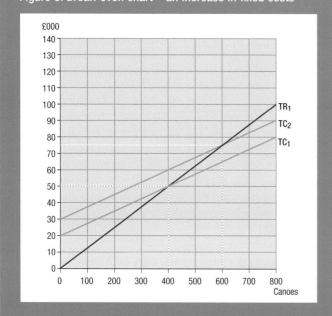

Question 1.

Ryestairs is a Benedictine monastery which earns part of its living by running The Haven, a guest house and retreat centre. It charges £80 per day for full board and overnight stay per person. The variable costs of items such as food and laundry cleaning come to £30 per day per visitor. The fixed costs of running the business venture are £50 000 per year.

(a) Draw a break-even diagram for The Haven. The horizontal axis will be the 'number of overnight stays per year'. Label the axis up to 1,500 overnight stays per year. Mark on it the break-even level of output.

(b) The management of The Haven decide to raise the price to £110 per day. (a) Draw a new total revenue function on your diagram for question 1. (b) Show on the diagram what has happened to the break-even level of output.

(c) If prices remained at £80 per day and variable costs are still £30, but The Haven cut its fixed costs to £40,000 per year, what would happen to the break-even level of output? Illustrate your answer by drawing a new diagram.

(d) Prices remain at £80 per day and fixed costs remain at £50,000, but The Haven manages to reduce its variable costs to £20. Explain, using a diagram, the effects of this on: (a) the break-even point, (b) the margin of safety assuming the number of overnight stays is 1,200 a year.

Changes in variables

Break-even charts provide a visual means of analysing the effect of changes in output on total cost, total revenue, profit and the margin of safety. The effects of changes in fixed costs, variable cost and price on profit and the margin of safety can also be shown. These will help a new or existing business to make decisions.

Changes in price Figure 2 shows the effect of an increase in price from £125 to £175 for Reidle Bros. This causes the total revenue line to become steeper, shifting from TR_1 to TR_2. This shows that total sales revenue has increased at all levels of

Figure 4: Break-even chart – an increase in variable costs

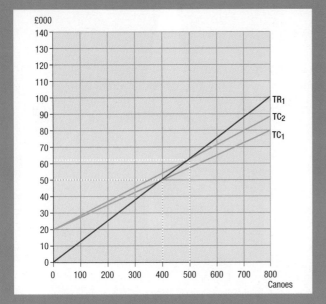

output. The higher price means that the business will break-even at a lower level of output. This is 200 canoes. It will also mean higher levels of profit (or lower losses) at every level of output. The margin of safety will also increase assuming an output of 800 canoes is produced. This is not shown in Figure 2.

For a price reduction, the total revenue line would become flatter. This would raise the break-even level of output and reduce the margin of safety. At a lower price more canoes would have to be sold to break-even.

Changes in fixed costs Figure 3 shows the effect of an increase in fixed costs from £20,000 to £30,000 for Reidle Bros. The total cost function makes a parallel shift upwards from TC_1 to TC_2. This occurs because a rise in fixed costs causes total cost to increase by the same amount at every level of output. As a result the break-even level of output rises to 600 canoes. At all levels of output profit falls (or losses rise). The margin of safety has also fallen assuming production remains at 800 canoes. This is not shown in Figure 3.

If fixed costs fell, the total cost function would make a parallel shift downwards. This would lower the break-even level of output and raise the margin of safety. Fewer canoes would need to be sold to break-even.

Changes in variable costs An increase in variable costs will increase the gradient of the total cost function. This is illustrated in Figure 4 by a shift from TC_1 to TC_2 when variable costs rise from £75 to £85 per canoe. The break-even level of output for Reidle Bros rises to 500 canoes. Assuming that production remains at 800 canoes, the margin of safety will fall.

If variable costs fell the total cost function would become flatter. This would lower the break-even level of output and raise the margin of safety. With lower variable costs, fewer canoes need to be sold to break-even.

Other uses of break-even charts

Target rate of profit Break-even analysis can be used to calculate the amount of output needed to generate a certain level of profit. For example, if Reidle Bros wanted to make £15,000 profit, the level of output required to do this would be:

$$\frac{\text{Fixed cost} + \text{profit target}}{\text{Contribution}}$$

$$= \frac{£20,000 + £15,000}{£50 (£125 - £75)}$$

$$= \frac{£35,000}{£50}$$

$$= 700 \text{ canoes}$$

Thus, when Reidle Bros produces and sells 700 canoes profit is:

Profit = total revenue - total costs

= £125 x 700 - (£20,000 + [£75 x 700])

= £87,500 - (£20,000 + £52,500)

= £87,500 - £72,500

= £15,000

Break-even price Sometimes a business may want to know how much to charge for its product to break-even. In these circumstances a business must know how much it is going to produce and sell. For example, assume Reidle Bros aimed to sell 500 canoes and its objective was to break-even at that level of output. The price it should charge to break-even would be:

Question 2.

Julia Robinson owns a large farm and supplies apples to cider producers. Apple production is only part of the farm's output. Most of the profit is generated from milk production. Julia is happy if apple production breaks-even each year. The orchard was inherited from her grandfather and Julia does not wish to cease apple production for sentimental reasons, even though it is generally unprofitable. Whether she achieves her aim depends on how many apples she harvests and the going market price. At the end of the season Julia had picked 60,000 kilos. The fixed costs associated with apple production were £6,000 for the year. Variable costs were 40p per kilo.

(a) Calculate the price per kilo Julia would need to receive in order for apple production to break-even.
(b) Calculate the profit Julia would make from apple production if the market price was: (i) 48p per kilo; (ii) 51p per kilo.

Break-even price $=$ $\dfrac{\text{Total cost}}{\text{Output}}$

$$= \dfrac{£20,000 + (500 \times £75)}{500}$$

$$= \dfrac{£20,000 + £37,500}{500}$$

$$= \dfrac{£57,500}{500}$$

$$= £115$$

Thus, if output was 500, Reidle Bros must charge £115 per canoe to break-even.

Price needed to reach a target rate of profit A business may want to determine the price it needs to charge in order to reach a target rate of profit. For example, if Reidle Bros wanted to make a profit of £40,000, and its production capacity was 1,000 canoes, the price it would need to charge to reach this target rate of profit would be:

Price $=$ $\dfrac{\text{Profit target + total cost}}{\text{Output}}$

$$= \dfrac{£40,000 + (£20,000 + 1,000 \times £75)}{1,000}$$

$$= \dfrac{£40,000 + £95,000}{1,000}$$

$$= \dfrac{£135,000}{1,000}$$

$$= £135$$

Thus, Reidle Bros would have to charge £135 for each canoe in order to make £40,000 profit if it produced and sold 1,000.

KNOWLEDGE

1 When constructing a break-even chart, why is zero always used as one of the levels of output?
2 What does the vertical distance show between TC and TR on a break-even chart?
3 What happens to the break-even level of output if price is increased?
4 What effect will a fall in variable costs have on the break-even level of output?
5 What happens to the margin of safety if fixed costs fall?
6 What happens to the margin of safety if price is cut?
7 How is break-even price calculated?

Case Study: Organic Hampers

Amelia Hume and Julia Nuttall worked in a food factory, but wanted to start their own business. They had seen adverts for organic hampers. Having bought one, they found it was 'all show and presentation' as Amelia put it. The food was unimaginative and inadequate for a large family. The hamper was also expensive at £120. Amelia and Julia both felt they could improve easily on this and exploit the current trend in organic food. They decided to set up a business selling organic picnic hampers from a website.

After estimating demand and finding suppliers to use they were able to come up with some costs. These are outlined below. The fixed costs included items like website design, advertising, insurance and a variety of setting-up costs. These fixed costs were for the first year of trading. They were expected to fall in future years. Examples of the food they planned to include in the hampers were French cheese, antipasta, pickles, pasta salad, rice salad, pitta breads, olives, fresh fruit salad, a bottle of organic wine and fruit juice.

Amelia and Julia decided they would sell the hampers for £80. This was lower than many of their competitors. At this price it was felt that 400 hampers could be sold in the first year of trading. Before making the final decision to launch the business, Amelia insisted that they work out how many hampers they would need to sell to break-even. Amelia and Julia also agreed that they should not give up their jobs at the factory until the business was established.

Fixed costs = £4,000	
Wicker hamper	£12
Food	£39
Utensils	£2
Delivery	£3
Other variable costs	£4

(a) Using this case as an example, explain what is meant by break-even. (4 marks)
(b) (i) Construct a break-even chart for Organic Hampers. (10 marks)
(ii) How many hampers need to be sold to break-even in the first year? (2 marks)
(c) (i) Show the margin of safety if annual sales meet the 400 sales target. (2 marks)
(ii) How much profit is made at this level of sales? (2 marks)
(d) In the second year, it was expected that fixed costs would only be £2,000.
(i) Why are fixed costs likely to fall in the second year of trading? (4 marks)
(ii) Show the new break-even output on the chart. (2 marks)
(iii) If 500 hampers were sold in the second year, could Amelia and Julia leave their factory jobs? (Show any necessary calculations). (6 marks)
(e) What measures could be taken to lower the break-even output in this case? (8 marks)

20 Cash flow forecasting

The importance of cash

Cash is the most LIQUID of all business assets. A business's cash is the notes and coins it keeps on the premises and any money it has in the bank, for example. Cash is part of, but not the same as, working capital. Working capital contains other assets, such as money owed by debtors, which are not immediately available if a business needs to pay bills, for example.

Why is cash so important to a business? Without cash, it would cease to exist. There is a number of reasons why firms fail. The most common tend to be:

- lack of sales;
- inadequate profit margins;
- poor choice of location;
- reliance on too small a customer base;
- poor management of working capital;
- poor cash flow.

According to a Confederation of British Industry (CBI) survey, 21 per cent of business failures are due to poor cash flow or a lack of working capital. Even when trading conditions are good, businesses can fail. Many of these businesses may offer good products for which there was some demand. They have the potential to be profitable and yet still went into RECEIVERSHIP. Probably the most likely cause of this is that they ran out of cash.

The role of cash in a business is shown in Figure 1. It shows a

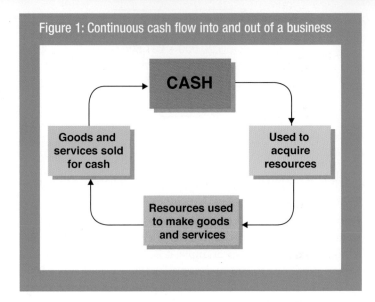

Figure 1: Continuous cash flow into and out of a business

simple CASH FLOW cycle. Cash flow is the continuous movement of cash into and out of a business. Initially, cash is used to buy or hire resources. These resources are converted into goods or services which are then sold to customers in exchange for cash. Some of the money from sales will be used to finance further production. In a successful business, this flow of cash is endless. If this flow of cash ceases at some stage then the business will be unlikely to continue.

Table 1: Cash flow forecast for Fishan's Ltd

												(£000s)
	Jan	Feb	Mar	Apr	May	Jun	Jul	Aug	Sep	Oct	Nov	Dec
Receipts												
Cash sales	451	360	399	410	490	464	452	340	450	390	480	680
Capital introduced									300			
Total receipts	451	360	399	410	490	464	452	340	750	390	480	680
Payments												
Goods for resale	150	180	150	180	150	180	150	180	150	180	220	250
Leasing charges	20	20	20	20	20	20	20	20	20	20	20	20
Motor expenses	40	40	40	40	40	40	40	40	40	40	40	40
Wages	100	100	100	100	100	100	100	105	105	105	125	125
VAT			126			189			187			198
Loan repayments	35	35	35	35	35	35	35	35	35	35	35	35
Telephone		11				12			12			14
Miscellaneous	20	20	20	20	20	20	20	20	20	20	20	20
Total payments	365	406	491	395	377	584	365	412	557	400	474	688
Net cash flow	86	(46)	(92)	15	113	(120)	87	(72)	193	(10)	6	(8)
Opening balance	11	97	51	(41)	(26)	87	(33)	54	(18)	175	165	171
Closing balance	97	51	(41)	(26)	87	(33)	54	(18)	175	165	171	163

Brackets show minus figures.

Controlling cash flow

It is important that a business continually monitors and controls its cash flow. It must ensure that it has enough cash for its immediate spending. However, it should avoid holding too much cash because cash is an unproductive asset. Holding cash means that the business might lose out on the profit from investing the cash. A business will have more effective control over its cash flow if it:

- keeps up to date business records;
- always plans ahead, for example by producing accurate cash flow forecasts;
- operates an efficient credit control system which prevents slow or late payment.

The need to keep up to date records of business transactions is very important. The quality of decision making is better if accurate information is available when choosing between different courses of action. Problems can arise if decisions are based on inadequate or inaccurate information. For example, say a business fails to record that a £20,000 payment has been made to a supplier. A manager may go ahead with the purchase of a new machine costing £30,000 believing that the firm's cash position is better than it actually is. The business may not have enough money in the bank to cover a cheque given in payment.

Advances in information technology have enabled businesses to keep more up to date records and access information very quickly. However, mistakes can still occur if computer operators fail to input information correctly.

Cash flow forecasts

Most businesses produce a regular CASH FLOW FORECAST. This lists all the likely receipts (**cash inflows**) and payments (**cash outflows**) over a future period of time. All the entries in the forecast are estimated because they have not occurred yet. The forecast shows the planned cash flow of the business month by month. Table 1 shows a twelve month cash flow forecast statement for Fishan's Ltd, a grocery wholesaler located in Ipswich.

What is predicted to happen to cash flow at Fishan's over the twelve month period?

January The company will have an opening cash balance of £11,000 in January. In January receipts are expected to be £451,000 and payments £365,000. This means that an extra £86,000 (£451,000 - £365,000) will be added in this month - a positive NET CASH FLOW. The closing balance should be £97,000 (£11,000 +£86,000).

February In February expected payments (£406,000) are greater than expected receipts (£360,000). This means that there will be a negative net cash flow of £46,000 in February. However, the opening balance of £97,000 will cover this and the business will not have a cash flow problem. It ends the month with a positive closing balance of £51,000 (£97,000 - £46,000).

March In March payments again will be greater than receipts,

The **receipts** of the business are the monthly inflows of cash. For Fishan's, cash sales result from the sale of groceries to local retailers and other customers. The sales figures are probably based on the previous year's. In September the owners have introduced £300,000 of fresh capital to the business. The total amount of cash a business expects to receive each month is shown as total receipts. Some businesses sell goods on credit. If this is the case, the figures in the statement should show cash actually received in that month and not the value of goods sold.

Payments are the outflows from the business. Some payments are for the same regular amounts, such as leasing charges (£20,000) and loan repayments (£35,000). Other payments vary, such as purchases of goods for resale. Some payments such as telephone charges are made on a quarterly basis. It is also possible for payments to be annual such as accountancy fees. These do not appear for Fishan's, perhaps because they employ their own accountant. The total amount of cash a business expects to pay out each month is shown as total payments. If a business buys goods on credit, cash payments made to suppliers are included when they occur and not the value of goods received in a particular month.

Net cash flow for a month is found by subtracting total payments from total receipts. If receipts are greater than payments, net cash flow is positive. If payments are greater than receipts, net cash flow is negative - shown by brackets around a figure.

- The **opening balance** in January will be the value of December's closing balance in the previous year.
- The **closing balance** for a month is found by adding or subtracting the net cash flow for the month from the opening balance.
- The closing balance of one month becomes the opening balance of the next month. It can be a positive or negative figure.

giving a negative net cash flow of £92,000. However, this is now greater than the opening balance of £51,000. This means that the business faces a negative closing balance of £41,000 and will have a cash flow problem. It would have to find some way to finance this, perhaps by borrowing from a bank.

March to May The business will have cash flow problems in March and April, when it faces negative closing balances, even though in April receipts are greater than payments (a positive net cash flow). In May, however, the negative opening balance of £26,000 is outweighed by the positive net cash flow of £113,000. The business will have a positive closing balance of £87,000 and no cash flow problem.

June to December In June and August, but not July, the business would have cash flow problems. From September onwards, when there will be positive closing balances every month, there appear to be no cash flow problems. This is because the owners plan to introduce £300,000 into the business in September.

Why do businesses prepare cash flow forecasts?

Businesses draw up cash flow forecast statements to help control and monitor cash flow in the business. There are certain advantages in using statements to control cash flow.

Identifying the timing of cash shortages and surpluses A forecast can help to identify in advance when a business might wish to borrow cash. At the bottom of the statement the monthly closing balances are shown clearly. This will help the reader to identify when a bank overdraft will be needed. For example, Table 2 showed that Fishan's would need to borrow money in March, April, June and August. In addition, if a large cash surplus is identified in a particular month, this might provide an opportunity to buy some new equipment, for example. A business should try to avoid being overdrawn at the bank because interest is charged. If certain payments can be delayed until cash is available, this will avoid unnecessary borrowing.

Supporting applications for funding When trying to raise finance, lenders often insist that businesses support their applications with documents showing business performance, outlook and solvency. A cash flow forecast will help to indicate the future outlook for the business. It is also common practice to produce a cash flow forecast statement in the planning stages of setting up a business.

Enhancing the planning process Careful planning in business is vital. It helps to clarify aims and improve performance. Producing a cash flow forecast is a key part of the planning process because it is a document concerned with the future.

Monitoring cash flow During and at the end of the financial year a business should make comparisons between the predicted figures in the cash flow forecast and those which actually occur. By doing this it can find out where problems have occurred. It

Question 1.

Norfolk-based Longacre Farm is owned by the Durrant family. The farm has a shop and one weekend a number of customers asked Janet Durrant if they sold homemade soup. This set Janet thinking. She approached her father with the idea of a new business activity - making soup and selling it in the farm shop. She explained that vegetables produced on the farm could be used. Janet produced a business plan with a cash flow forecast. Her father said he would lend Janet £1,000 if she could match the amount to provide start-up capital for Janet's new business venture, Longacre Farm Homemade Soups. A copy of the nine month forecast is shown in Table 2.

Table 2: Cash flow forecast for Longacre Farm Homemade Soups

		May	Jun	Jul	Aug	Sep	Oct	Nov	Dec	(£) Jan
Receipts										
Loan from Mr Durrant		1,000								
Own capital		1,000								
Cash		200	400	500	400	500	600	900	800	1,200
Total receipts		2,200	400	500	400	500	600	900	800	1,200
Payments										
Cooking equipment		900								
Other setting up costs		700								
Vegetables		50	100	125	100	125	150	225	200	300
Other food ingredients		60	80	90	80	90	100	150	130	180
Packaging		50	100	125	100	125	150	225	200	300
Overheads		100	100	100	100	100	100	100	100	100
Total payments		1,860	380	440	380	440	500	700	630	880
Net cash flow		140	20	60	20	60	100	200	170	320
Opening balance		0	140	160	220	240	300	400	600	770
Closing balance		140	160	220	240	300	400	600	770	1,090

(a) Using examples from the month of June, explain how Janet would calculate:
    (i) total payments;
    (ii) net cash flow;
    (iii) closing balance.

(b) Why is the opening balance in May zero?
(c) Explain what is happening to the cash balance resulting from Janet's soup venture.

Question 2.

Kieran Venkat runs an off-licence in the Manchester suburb of Rusholme. He has recently extended his premises into the property next door and is looking to acquire a wider range of stock. The cost of the extension has completely exhausted the business of its cash reserves and Kieran needs to borrow some money to buy stock. He needs to borrow £5,000 for nine months. In order to support his application for a bank loan he drew up the nine month cash flow forecast shown in Table 3. The forecast assumes that the loan has been granted and repayments are included.

(a) Calculate the following figures for Kieran's cash flow forecast.
   (i) Cash sales and total receipts for October.
   (ii) Total payments for August.
   (iii) Closing balance for November.
   (iv) Opening balance for January.

Table 3: Cash flow forecast statement for Kieran Venkat

									(£)
	Jul	Aug	Sep	Oct	Nov	Dec	Jan	Feb	Mar
Receipts									
Cash sales	3,800	4,000	5,000	?	6,000	9,000	7,000	3,000	3,500
Bank loan	5,000								
Total receipts	8,800	4,000	5,000	?	6,000	9,000	7,000	3,000	3,500
Payments									
Stock	7,000	3,000	3,400	3,400	4,000	6,100	4,800	2,000	2,400
Loan repayments	620	620	620	620	620	620	620	620	620
Casual labour	200	200	200	200	200	400	200	200	200
Miscellaneous costs	100	100	100	100	100	100	100	100	100
Drawings	500	500	500	500	500	500	500	500	500
Insurance				450					
Advertising	370								
Telephone			170			200			210
Total payments	8,790	?	4,990	5,270	5,420	7,920	6,220	3,420	4,030
Net cash flow	10	(420)	10	(270)	580	1,080	780	(420)	(530)
Opening balance	(90)	(80)	(500)	(490)	(760)	(180)	?	1,680	1,260
Closing balance	(80)	(500)	(490)	(760)	?	900	1,680	1,260	730

(b) As well as supporting his application for a bank loan, how else might this cash flow forecast help Kieran in running his business?
(c) On the basis of this cash flow forecast alone, discuss whether a bank would grant Kieran a loan.

could then try to identify possible reasons for any significant differences between the two sets of figures. For example, it might be that an overpayment was made. Constant monitoring in this way should allow a business to control its cash flow effectively.

Improving forecasts

Cash flow forecasts may not be helpful if they are inaccurate. Very inaccurate forecasts could lead to businesses getting into trouble and running out of cash. How can a business improve the accuracy of its cash flow forecasts?

Accurate data A cash flow forecast is based on anticipated flows of cash into and out of the business. Some of these flows will be known for certain. For example, a business usually knows what some of its overheads will be next year, such as rent, rates and insurance. Other costs such as wages may have been negotiated for the next year. Variable costs such as raw materials are may be more difficult to predict. This is because output might fluctuate unexpectedly or suppliers may change their prices.

Generally, cash outflows are easier to predict than cash inflows. Most of the cash coming into the business is from sales. It can sometimes be difficult to estimate what sales will be exactly in future. Some businesses have advanced orders, such as firms in the holiday industry, which will help to improve accuracy. Others do market research, while many rely on projections based on the previous year's figures. When cash

inflows and outflows are unknown it is better to overestimate costs and underestimate revenues. New businesses have particular problems when producing forecasts. This is because they have no past data on which to base projections. They also tend to underestimate costs and over-estimate revenues.

Biased forecasts Businesses sometimes manipulate cash flow forecasts. For example, a business may overestimate cash inflows to improve the strength of the business on paper. It might do this if it was borrowing money from a bank. A manager may overestimate costs and underestimate sales so that credit can be taken when the real figures are better. If forecasts are biased they are not likely to be accurate.

Coping with external factors Cash flow forecasts could be improved if business managers could predict future events such as changes in interest rates, the weather and the behaviour of competitors. One way to allow for unforeseen events is to have **contingency funds** built into the cash flow forecast. For example, a business may make a monthly allowance for unexpected costs, including it as a cash outflow. Another approach could be to make regular adjustments to cash flow forecasts during the trading period. If forecasts are updated regularly, predictions may be more accurate. It is also possible to produce a series of forecasts. For example, a business might produce three, a 'worst case', a 'best case' and one in the 'middle'. This could show the business what is likely to happen to its cash position in different situations.

KNOWLEDGE

1. Explain the operation of the cash flow cycle.
2. Why is it important that a business: (i) does not hold too much cash; (ii) holds sufficient cash?
3. Briefly explain what a cash flow forecast includes.
4. How does a cash flow forecast indicate whether a business faces cash flow problems in future?
5. Explain why a business prepares a cash flow forecast.
6. What are the advantages of businesses preparing cash flow statements?
7. How is it possible for a profitable business to collapse?

KEYTERMS

Cash flow – the continuous movement of cash in and out of the business.
Cash flow forecast – the prediction of all expected receipts and expenses of a business over a future time period which shows the expected cash balance at the end of each month.
Liquid asset – an asset which is easily changed into cash.
Net cash flow – cash inflows minus cash onflows over a period of time.
Receivership – the liquidation (selling) of a firm's assets by an independent body following its collapse.

Case Study: Kay Jones Garden Designs

Having completed a HND in Landscape Construction and Garden Design, Kay Jones wanted to run her own garden design business. The design process would involve Kay meeting with a client to discuss their needs and carrying out a survey. A second meeting would establish a more precise brief and a budget. Kay would then put together a 3D masterplan, showing drawings and materials. In addition to design, Kay also planned to do all the construction work. She felt that people might spend between £500 and £5,000 on a new garden design in her local area.

Kay did not have very much capital of her own, so she needed a bank loan. To obtain a loan she would have to draw up a business plan, including an accurate and realistic cash flow forecast. Kay knew that she would stand a better chance of a loan if she had some orders. She decided to get a job and save, develop some orders in her spare time and then launch the business in April. She lived at home and thought she could save £2,000 before the launch.

By February Kay had 5 definite orders for garden designs. She was sure that once she got started people would see her work and orders would follow. However, she did plan to market the business and applied for a listing in *Yellow Pages*. Table 4 shows the predicted revenue for the first nine months of her business. The following financial information was also gathered.

- A bank loan of £3,000 would be needed.
- Kay would contribute £2,000 of her own savings as capital in April.
- A van for £2,000 would be purchased in April.
- Tools and equipment for £3,400 would be purchased in April.
- A laptop computer with specialist design software for £600 would be purchased in April.
- A *Yellow Pages* listing will cost £100 in May.

- General overheads would be £400 per month.
- Advertising will be £100 in alternate months starting in May.
- Kay would take out £800 per month starting in June.
- Loan repayments will be £200 per month.

(a) Explain the meaning of the term 'cash flow forecast'. (4 marks)
(b) Draw up a nine month cash flow forecast for Kay Jones Garden Designs. (12 marks)
(c) (i) Comment on the cash position of the business during the nine month period. (4 marks)
(ii) What would you expect to happen to the cash position of the business in early 2008? Explain your answer. (4 marks)
(d) Once Kay was 'up and running' she had some bad news at the end of April. The van she bought needed some urgent repairs to the value of £1,200. A client with a firm £1,300 order in June cancelled. Produce an amended cash flow forecast. (6 marks)
(e) Do you think the bank would grant a loan based on the amended forecast? (10 marks)

Table 4: Predicted revenue for Kay Jones Garden Designs (first nine months)

	Apr	May	Jun	Jul	Aug	Sep	Oct	Nov	(£) Dec
Predicted revenue	2,000	2,100	2,000	2,500	2,500	2,000	1,000	500	0

NB The predicted revenue is net of the cost of plants and other materials used in the construction of the gardens.

21 | Setting budgets

What is a budget?

The control of a business becomes more difficult the larger it is. A new, small business setting up may be run informally. The owner is the manager, who will know everyone, be aware of what is going on and will make all decisions. In medium sized and larger firms, work and responsibility are delegated, which makes informal control impractical. To improve control, budgeting has been developed. This forces others to be accountable for their decisions.

A BUDGET is a plan which is agreed in advance. It must be a plan and not a forecast. A forecast is a prediction of what might happen in the future, whereas a budget is a planned outcome which the firm hopes to achieve. A budget will show the money needed for spending and how this might be financed. Budgets are based on the objectives of businesses. They force managers to think ahead and improve co-ordination. Most budgets are set for twelve months to coincide with the accounting period, but there are exceptions. Research and Development budgets, for example, may cover several years.

Information contained in a budget may include revenue, sales, expenses, profit, personnel, cash and capital expenditure. In fact, budgets can include any business variable (known as a budget factor) which can be given a value. One well known budget is 'The Budget'. The Chancellor of the Exchequer prepares a budget for a particular period. It will take into account the government's spending plans and how these plans will be financed by taxes and other sources of funds.

The reasons for setting budgets

There is a number of reasons why a business sets budgets.

Control and monitoring Budgeting helps control a business. It does this by setting objectives and targets. These are then translated into budgets for, say, the coming year. Success by the business and the workforce in achieving those targets can be found by comparing the actual results with the budget. The reasons for failing to achieve the budget can then be analysed and appropriate action taken.

Planning Budgeting forces businesses to think ahead. Without budgeting, people might work on a day-to-day basis, only dealing with opportunities and problems as they arise. Budgeting, however, plans for the future. It anticipates problems and their solutions.

Co-ordination As a business grows in size its organisation becomes more complicated. There may be different departments or different production and administrative sites. A multinational company will have workers spread across the world. Budgeting is one way of co-ordinating the activities of areas of the business.

Communication Planning allows the objectives of the business to be communicated to its employees. By keeping to a budget, employees have a clear framework within which to operate. So budgeting removes an element of uncertainty within decision making throughout the business.

Efficiency In medium sized or larger businesses it may be difficult for one person to make every decision. Budgeting gives financial control to those workers who are best able to make decisions in the business.

Motivation Budgeting should act as a motivator to employees. It provides workers with targets and standards. Improving on the budget position is an indication of success. Fear of failing to reach budgeted targets may make workers work harder.

The preparation of budgets

The way in which a budget might be prepared is shown in Figure 1. It is a step-by-step process.

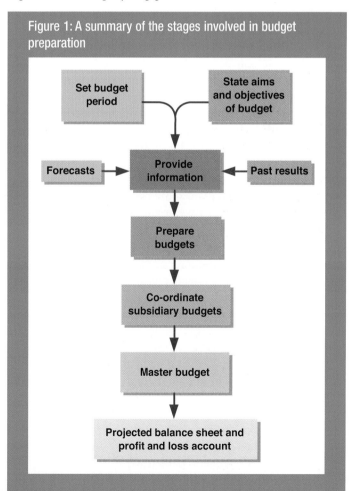

Figure 1: A summary of the stages involved in budget preparation

Table 1: Planned sales figures for Emerald Artwork

	Feb	Mar	Apr	May
AD23	100	100	100	100
AD24	50	80	80	100
AE12	40	50	40	50
AE13	30	30	50	50

- Decide on a budget period and state the objectives and targets which are to be achieved. The budget period may vary according to the type of budget. One month or one year is usual. Targets for performance, market share, quality (provided it can be quantified) and productivity are all examples.
- Obtain information upon which to base the budget. A new business setting up will not be able to base its budgets on its own historical information. So it will need to estimate future figures. It may do this from market research. Some business variables are easier to estimate than others. It may be easier to quantify future costs than future sales, for example. This is because sales levels are subject to so many external factors. Once the business has traded for a period, budgets can be based on past figures.
- Prepare budgets. Two important budgets are the sales budget and the production budget. These budgets are related and affect all other budgets. For example, sales targets can only be met if there is productive capacity. Also, a firm would be unlikely to continue production if it could not sell its products. The sales budget will contain monthly sales estimates, expressed in terms of quantities per product, perhaps, and the price charged. From the sales budget, and with knowledge of stock levels, the production budget can be determined. This will show the required raw materials, labour hours and machine hours. At this stage the business should know whether or not it has the capacity to meet the sales targets. If it is not possible, then it may be necessary to adjust the sales budget.
- Draw up subsidiary operating budgets. These are detailed budgets usually prepared by medium sized and larger businesses. Budgets can be broken down, so that each person in the hierarchy can be given some responsibility for a section of the budget.
- The MASTER BUDGET is a summary statement of all budgets. For example, it shows the estimated income, anticipated expenditure, and, thus, the budgeted profit for the period. The cash budget can be prepared when all other budgets are complete. This budget is particularly useful since it shows the monthly flows of cash into and out of the business. It will help to show

whether future cash flow problems might occur.
- Prepare the projected balance sheet and profit and loss of the business. These show the financial position that will result from the firm's budgets.

Income or sales revenue budget

An INCOME or SALES REVENUE BUDGET shows the planned income or revenue for a period of time. Emerald Artwork produces four products, AD23, AD24, AE12 and AE13. They sell for £12, £20, £25 and £30 respectively. The planned sales levels for a four month period are shown in Table 1.

The budget is prepared by showing the planned income or sales revenue in each month. This is calculated by multiplying the predicted sales levels by the prices. The sales revenue budget is shown in Table 2.

Table 2: A sales revenue (income) budget for Emerald Artwork

	Feb	Mar	Apr	May
				(£)
AD23	1,200 (12 x 100)	1,200 (12 x 100)	1,200 (12 x 100)	1,200 (12 x 100)
AD24	1,000 (20 x 50)	1,600 (20 x 80)	1,600 (20 x 80)	2,000 (20 x 100)
AE12	1,000 (25 x 40)	1,250 (25 x 50)	1,000 (25 x 40)	1,250 (25 x 50)
AE13	900 (30 x 30)	900 (30 x 30)	1,500 (30 x 50)	1,500 (30 x 50)
Total	4,100	4,950	5,300	5,950

Table 3: A production budget for Emerald Artwork covering production of all 4 products

	FEB	MAR	APR	MAY
				(£)
Cost of materials	660	780	810	900
(£3 per unit)	(3 x 220)	(3 x 260)	(3 x 270)	(3 x 300)
Direct labour costs	880	1,040	1,080	1,200
(£4 per unit)	(4 x 220)	(4 x 260)	(4 x 270)	(4 x 300)
Indirect labour costs	440	520	540	600
(£2 per unit)	(2 x 220)	(2 x 260)	(2 x 270)	(2 x 300)
Production Overheads				
(10% of direct &	1,320 x 10%	1,560 x 10%	1,620 x 10%	1,800 x 10%
indirect costs)	= 132	= 156	= 162	= 180
Total	2,112	2,496	2,592	2,880

Table 4: An expenditure budget for Emerald Artwork

	Feb	Mar	Apr	May (£)
Materials	660	780	810	900
Direct labour	880	1,040	1,080	1,200
Indirect labour	440	520	540	600
Production overheads	132	156	162	180
General overheads	300	600	200	700
Capital expenditure	2,000	0	200	1,700
Total expenditure	4,412	3,096	2,992	5,280

Table 5: Profit budget for Emerald Artwork

	Feb	Mar	Apr	May (£)
Income (sales revenue)	4,100	4,950	5,300	5,950
Expenditure	2,412	3,096	2,792	3,580
Profit	1,688	1,854	2,508	2,370

Production budget

Once Emerald Artwork has produced a sales budget, it is possible to calculate its production budget. The example in Table 3

assumes stock levels stay the same throughout the four month period. The figures are based on expected sales in Table 1.

Expenditure budget

An EXPENDITURE or TOTAL COST BUDGET shows how much money a business is expected to spend for a period of time. It is based on the production budget. Expenditure might include raw materials, labour, production overheads, general overheads and capital expenditure such as new machinery. An expenditure budget is shown for Emerald Artwork in Table 4. It is based on the production budget but includes all other business expenditure for the four month period.

Profit budget

A PROFIT BUDGET shows the amount of profit a business is expected to make over a period. It contains information on all income generated by the business and all expenditure. However, the profit budget would not include capital expenditure. A profit budget for Emerald Artwork is shown in Table 5. Note that capital expenditure has been excluded. In the profit budget, expenditure is subtracted from income to get the monthly profit.

Problems of setting budgets

Businesses may sometimes find that there are problems when setting budgets.

Question 1.

Hannah Ngilo and David Saunders run Penzance Motor Services. The business generates revenue in a number of ways. It sells petrol, a limited range of grocery and confectionery items, car accessories and a few second-hand cars. The garage also carries out servicing, motor repairs and MOT testing. An income budget for a six month period is shown in Table 6.

(a) Complete the income budget for Penzance Motor Services by calculating the total monthly income.
(b) Hannah and David set sales targets for each source of income. What role will setting budgets play when setting such targets?
(c) Explain how the information in this budget might be used in a profit budget.

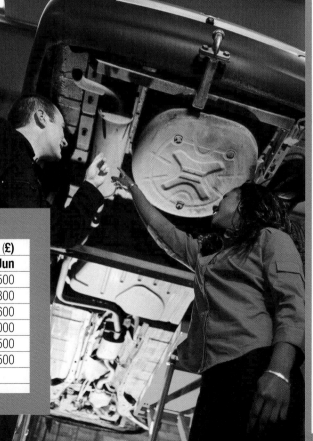

Table 6: Income budget for Penzance Motor Services

	Jan	Feb	Mar	Apr	May	Jun (£)
Petrol sales	3,400	3,500	3,400	3,600	4,000	4,500
Grocery sales	650	650	700	700	750	800
Car accessories	450	500	500	550	550	600
Car sales	1,000	1,500	2,000	4,000	5,000	6,000
Servicing and repairs	4,300	4,800	5,000	4,500	4,000	3,500
MOTs	400	500	450	550	600	500
Total income						

Question 2.

Melanie Croft runs the Motherwell Leisure Centre, a private leisure facility for residents in the Motherwell and Hamilton areas of Scotland. The centre has about 900 members and offers a range of facilities. In order to keep control of costs Melanie sets expenditure budgets every six months for the various departments within the complex. An expenditure budget for the first six months of 2007 is shown in Table 7.

(a) Complete the expenditure budget shown in Table 7 and calculate the total expenditure for the sixth month period.
(b) What might account for the pattern of expenditure for the café bar over the time period?
(c) Explain how using an expenditure budget could help Melanie control costs in the business.

Table 7: Expenditure budget for the Motherwell Leisure Centre – January to June 2007

	Jan	Feb	Mar	Apr	May	Jun (£)
Sports Hall	1,400	1,600	1,700	1,700	1,500	1,300
Swimming pool	2,300	2,400	2,400	2,500	3,000	3,500
Games room	600	700	600	500	400	200
Fitness centre	3,200	3,500	3,600	3,600	3,400	3,200
Outdoor activities	500	400	500	600	800	1,000
Massage & beauty treatments	5,300	5,300	6,000	6,000	7,000	7,000
Administration	2,000	2,000	2,000	2,000	2,000	2,000
Café bar	3,200	3,500	3,700	4,000	5,000	7,000
Total expenditure						

Using planned figures Problems tend to arise because figures in budgets are not actual figures. Planned figures may be inaccurate. The most important data in the preparation of nearly all budgets is sales data. If sales data are inaccurate, many of the firm's budgets will be inexact. The accuracy of sales data might be improved if market research is used. However, it may be difficult to estimate sales of new products for a future period.

Collecting information The setting of budgets in some businesses may require a great deal of co-ordination. This is because different parts of the business may provide information for budgets. Some medium sized and larger businesses appoint a budget officer. This person is responsible for collecting data and opinions, keeping managers to the budget timetable and carrying out budgetary administration.

Conflict The setting of budgets may lead to conflict between staff. For example, a business may only have limited funds. One person may want to spend this on marketing, but another may feel that new machinery is needed.

Cost The time spent setting budgets could have been spent on other tasks. This is very important for a small, new business with limited resources.

Over-ambitious objectives Sometimes businesses set over-ambitious objectives. When this happens, the budgeting process is pointless because budgets are being drawn up for targets which are unachievable. The budget then ceases to become a benchmark with which to compare the outcome.

External influences In some industries, it is difficult to plan ahead because of large and unpredictable changes in the external environment. In farming, for instance, there can be variations in price from year to year and the weather can have large effects on output. This doesn't mean that businesses in such industries should not draw up budgets. However, it can be difficult to analyse outcomes against the budget. It may be unclear if external influences or the way in which a business is run have affected whether a budget is achieved or not.

KNOWLEDGE

1. How might a budget improve employee accountability?
2. Why is the sales budget such an important budget?
3. How might budgets motivate staff?
4. State examples of three types of budget.
5. Why might a business manipulate a budget?
6. What costs are incurred when setting budgets?

KEYTERMS

Budget – a quantitative economic plan prepared and agreed in advance.
Income or sales revenue budget – shows the planned income or revenue for a period of time.
Expenditure or total cost budget – shows how much money a business is expected to spend for a period of time
Profit budget – shows the amount of profit a business is expected to make over a period.
Master budget – a summary statement which brings together information from budgets.

Case Study: Agarka Mini Market

A garka Mini Market is a small supermarket serving residents in the Poole area of Dorset. The store is divided into a number of sections.

- Dairy – maintains refrigerated products such as milk, cheese, other dairy products, smoothies and fruit juices.
- Delicatessen – serves cold meats, olives, fresh pickles, dips and other delicatessen products.
- Fresh produce – is responsible for all fruit and vegetables.
- Grocery – is the largest department and is responsible for all food products in cans and packets, household goods such as cleaning materials, drinks, confectionery and products which do not fall neatly into other departments.
- Meat – stocks pre-packaged refrigerated meat products for customers and prepares many of these packages for sale. Also cuts meat to order for customers.
- Liquor – this is a new department since a liquor licence was only granted in 2006. However, it is expected to grow rapidly. A wide range of wines, beers and spirits are offered.

Six members of the Agarka family work in the store and a further nine people are employed part-time. In order to monitor the progress of different parts of the business profit budgets are set for every department. The head of each department is paid a six month bonus of 5 per cent of profit if the profit targets are reached. The income and expenditure budgets are shown in Tables 8 and 9.

(a) Explain what is meant by the term budget. (2 marks)

(b) Produce separate profit budgets for each of the sections at the Agarka Mini Market. (18 marks)

(c) (i) Which section has the poorest profit record over the time period? (4 marks)
(ii) How might you account for the poor profit record of the section identified in (i)? (4 marks)

(d) (i) How will profit budgets serve to motivate staff in the store? (6 marks)
(ii) Calculate the six month bonus due to the person responsible for the Grocery department. (4 marks)

(e) Discuss three problems which might be encountered by the Agarka family when setting budgets for their Mini Market. (12 marks)

Table 8: Income budget for Agarka Mini Market

						(£)
	Jul	**Aug**	**Sep**	**Oct**	**Nov**	**Dec**
Dairy	7,500	7,500	8,000	8,000	8,000	9,000
Delicatessen	9,000	9,000	9,500	9,500	9,500	12,000
Fresh produce	5,700	6,000	6,000	6,500	6,000	8,000
Grocery	27,000	28,000	29,000	29,000	30,000	34,000
Meat	8,000	8,000	8,500	8,500	9,000	12,000
Liquor	3,000	4,000	5,000	6,000	8,000	17,000

Table 9: Expenditure budget for Agarka Mini Market

						(£)
	Jul	**Aug**	**Sep**	**Oct**	**Nov**	**Dec**
Dairy						
Goods for resale	5,000	5,000	5,200	5,300	5,300	6,100
Wages and other costs	1,300	1,200	1,600	1,600	1,500	1,700
Delicatessen						
Goods for resale	6,000	6,000	6,100	6,200	6,000	7,500
Wages and other costs	2,000	2,000	2,100	2,100	2,200	3,000
Fresh produce						
Goods for resale	4,300	4,400	4,700	5,300	5,200	6,300
Wages and other costs	1,000	1,000	1,000	1,000	1,000	1,300
Grocery						
Goods for resale	19,000	19,500	20,000	20,500	20,600	21,200
Wages and other costs	4,200	4,200	4,300	4,300	4,500	6,000
Meat						
Goods for resale	5,100	5,000	5,100	5,300	5,400	7,100
Wages and other costs	1,400	1,400	1,400	1,600	1,600	2,100
Liquor						
Goods for resale	1,800	2,200	3,000	3,500	5,200	10,000
Wages and other costs	500	500	700	700	900	1,200

Assessing start-ups

Business start-ups may succeed or they may fail. Most new businesses have ceased to operate within five years of their starting. So how is it possible to judge the strengths and weaknesses of a business start-up? The place to start is to consider the **objectives** of the start-up and assess the risks involved in the business activity. The business plan should give an indication about whether the objectives are realistic and whether **risks** have been assessed. If the business plan has been poorly thought through, or there is no business plan at all, the chance of failure is much higher.

Objectives of business start-ups

The business plan for a start-up should contain a number of financial objectives. These are likely to include the following.

Sales objectives The plan will almost certainly contain sales objectives. Monthly projections of sales revenue will be given in the cash flow forecast. But there may 'headline' objectives elsewhere in the business plan. For example, the plan may set out objectives for sales in the first month, the sixth month and the twelfth month of operation. There are likely to be two sales figures given. One is the volume of sales. For example, the objective is to sell 20 beds a week, or service 1000 customers a week. The other is the value of sales, the sales revenue or turnover. This is the money generated from sales and is equal to the volume of sales times the average selling price.

Sales objectives might also contain a breakdown of sales. A business plan for a car dealership, for example, might state that first year sales volume will be made up of 40 per cent new cars and 60 per cent second-hand cars. Or a plumber starting up on his own might state that 70 per cent of the work in the first year would be as a contractor for building companies and 30 per cent would be working for private clients.

Profit objectives The plan will almost certainly have profit objectives. One set of profit objectives is likely to relate to the break-even point: at what point in time will the business move from making a loss to making a profit? This may be linked in as well to cash flow forecasting, although profit and cash flow are different. Another set of profit objectives will concern the level of expected profitability on an ongoing basis. For example, the business plan may state that the business will make a profit of £5 000 in its first year and £30,000 in its second year of operation. The plan may also sometimes contain objectives about profit margins: the ratio of profit to sales.

Market share objective Some business plans have market share objectives. For these to be meaningful, the business plan must also contain some research about the size of the market. Market share objectives are helpful to identify what is needed to be competitive against other businesses in the market.

Drawings from the business Some business plans will have objectives about how much the owner will draw from the business over a period of time. Drawings from the business for a start-up one-person business are the equivalent of a wage paid to the owner of the business. It can be different from profit. For example, a person may aim to draw £10,000 from the business in its first year, but another objective might be to make £8,000 operating profit in the first year. The implication is that the owner would have to borrow an extra £2,000 in the first year to finance the drawings. On the other hand, the second year objective might be to draw £20,000 from the business but operating profit will be £30,000. There will then be £10,000 left in the business perhaps to repay loans or to finance expansion of the business.

Cost objectives Most business plans are unlikely to have explicit cost objectives. Sometimes, there is one relating to the start-up costs of the business. For example, for a new restaurant, an objective might be to refurbish premises at a cost £50,000. However, there are always implicit cost objectives if the plan has both profit and sales revenue objectives. This is because cost is equal to profit minus sales revenue.

Question 1.

Expresso Maestro is the name that has been chosen by Retta Feyissa and Emma Hartley for a new coffee and cake shop in Leeds. Their objective is to take £150,000 in sales in the first year. They each need to take £15,000 from the business to live off. With these sales and drawings from the business, they will be breaking even. By the end of the second year, their objective is to take £200,000 in sales and be able to draw £25,000 each from the business which again would see the business break-even. In their business plan, they have stated no further financial objectives.

John Miles is setting up his own recruitment agency. In his business plan, he expects to take on ten staff within the first year and have a sales turnover of £700,000. He has set himself the objective of taking a 10 per cent share of the market in his local area within 12 months, rising to 20 per cent by the end of his third year of operation. At this stage, three years into operation, his objective is to have a business which could be sold to a buyer for £1 million. He needs to raise £150,000 in capital to start the business.

(a) State two differences in the objectives of the two businesses.
(b) Explain which business has the more ambitious objectives.
(c) Evaluate whether these business objectives are in any way linked to the risk of failure of the business start-up.

Raising capital Many business plans for start-ups will contain objectives about the amount of financial capital that needs to be raised. So, for example, an objective may be to raise £70,000 of capital before starting operations and then a further £50,000 in the following 12 months. Raising capital is an important objective in itself because without start-up capital, the business won't be able to start trading. However, it is also placed as an objective because the business plan will be read by anyone thinking of investing in or lending to the business.

The financial objectives of a start-up will differ according to the size of the start-up and the audience for the business plan. The objectives above would be typical for a small business start-up. However, if the business start-up were a multi million pound company with a number of shareholders as owners, then there would be likely to be a more complex mix of financial objectives. For example, there might be an objective about the value of the company in three years' time. Or there might be an objective about when the first dividend, a share of the profit made, would be paid to shareholders.

Financial objectives also cannot be completely separated from other objectives. For an ordinary start-up, the overall aim will be to get the business up-and-running and profitable as quickly as possible. Then growth of the business should see a growth of profits and an increase in the value of the business. However, the main aim of some start-ups is not financial. Some start-ups are **social enterprises**, where providing a service to disadvantage groups is the main aim. These start-ups have to break-even to survive. But other objectives are more important.

Risk

All economic activity has an element of risk. If you get a job today with a company, there is a possibility that tomorrow the company will fail and everyone will lose their jobs. You buy a new car and may be involved in an accident within minutes of driving it off the garage forecourt.

Starting up a business, however, is likely to carry greater risks than working for someone else. There is so much more that could go wrong: sales might be disappointing, costs higher than predicted, the entrepreneur might fall ill at a crucial moment or the bank may refuse to lend more money.

Risks differ from start-up to start-up. For example, a painter and decorator may be working for a company. He works on a lot of jobs where the company is taking on self-employed painters and decorators. He finds out that it is easy to get contracts and gets information about how to do this. Then he quits his job and sets up on his own. He has no problems about getting work from day one. But he also knows that it would be relatively easy to go back to getting a job working for someone else. His costs of setting up on his own are very low whilst his revenues are reasonably assured. The risk of the start-up here is very low.

At the other extreme might be a new biological research company. Its objective is to find a cutting edge new process or product that can be developed into something that can be sold to customers. There is no guarantee at the start that it will find

anything that will be marketable. Millions of pounds could be spent and no revenues generated. Eventually it will run out of start-up money and be forced to close. Science research companies like this are very high risk because there is no assured source of revenues.

Most business start-ups fall between these two extremes. However, the greater the uncertainty about future costs and revenues, the riskier the start-up. To understand more about risk, it is important to consider what can cause a business to fail.

Why businesses fail

Businesses fail from a financial viewpoint for a number of reasons.

Lower than expected revenues Many start-ups don't generate enough sales revenues. Either they don't sell enough or the price they get for what they sell is too low. For example, in its business plan, a hairdressing salon might have predicted that it would have 150 customers a week each paying on average £20. Its sales revenue was therefore predicted at £3,000 per week. By the end of its first year, the salon is only attracting 100 customers a week each paying on average £15. Sales revenue is therefore only £1,500, half of what was predicted. If revenues are too low, the business could make a loss which would lead to its failure. Or it may make insufficient profit for the entrepreneur to want to carry on in business. For example, the owner of the hairdressing salon might make £10,000 a year from the business. But if she could make £20,000 a year working for someone else, there would be a strong financial incentive for her to close her business and go back to an ordinary paid job.

Higher than expected start-up costs The majority of start-ups underestimate the cost of the start-up. For example, for a new restaurant, the cost of fitting out a building is likely to be higher than expected. Or an entrepreneur setting up a recruitment agency might underestimate the amount of time needed to comply with regulations. Some entrepreneurs simply run out of money at this stage and the start-up fails to get off the ground. Most will find extra money often by borrowing more from the bank. But then they have higher than expected loan repayments to make. If their revenues aren't high enough to cover these, the business will fail.

Higher than expected operating costs Many business plans underestimate the day-to-day running costs of the business. Sometimes this is because costs are simply not included in the business plan. More often, it is because actual costs are higher than predicted costs. If costs are too high, profits will be too low or the business might make a loss. In the long term, this is likely to lead to the closure of the business.

Unexpected shocks Some businesses fail because of unexpected shocks. In 1988, for example, the UK was experiencing an economic boom. The government was encouraging people to set up their own businesses. Within two years, the economy was in recession. Unemployment doubled, interest rates doubled and house prices fell. Not surprisingly, many new

Question 2.

Drawing up a business plan is no guarantee of success as Chris Watkins found out. Chris Watkins was the production manager for a firm which produced mainly own label toiletries for some of the big supermarket groups. It was in a competitve market and profit margins were wafer thin. Chris was continually being asked to cut costs at the factory or risk facing redundancy along with the rest of the production staff. He decided that he had had enough and would start his own business manufacturing toiletries. His business idea was that he would go up-market to avoid price competition. He would sell mainly to smaller stores and avoid dealing with the major supermarket chains.

He did some market research, contacting a number of small local stores, and they all said that they would definitely be interested in buying his products. He produced samples and did some costings based on buying some second-hand equipment and renting a unit on an industrial estate. The financial figures looked good and there was a substantial margin between revenues and costs, even in the first year of operation. But he had trouble borrowing the £100,000 he needed as start-up capital. Three banks refused him an ordinary business loan saying that his business plan was weak. In the end, he remortgaged his house for the £100,000 he needed.

He was full of hope when he started operations. He had some small orders for his products but he intended to launch his real marketing campaign once he had sorted out production. The problem was that the marketing campaign was a disaster. He ended up with four weeks of unsold stock and no cash left to continue. He was forced to close the business.

(a) Explain three reasons for the failure of Chris Watkins' business.

(b) 'The most important reason why the business failed was the weak business plan.' To what extent to do you agree with this?

start-ups failed too because they couldn't generate enough sales to survive. Also their cost of borrowing was substantially more than they had expected. Another example of an unexpected shock is flooding. In recent years, a number of areas of the UK have experienced unexpected flooding. Some businesses have failed as a result. They have lost orders and equipment. Some have been uninsured and haven't had the financial capital to be able to restart.

Reliance on a few large customers Small businesses are vulnerable if they rely on just a few customers for most of their orders. For example, a new start-up business may have landed a contract which accounts for 40 per cent of its orders. It borrows a substantial amount of money to buy equipment to fulfil the contract. Then, suddenly, the customers cancels the contract. Forty per cent of sales immediately have gone. But the repayments on the loans for the equipment have to be kept up. In these circumstances, a new business start-up can go from being profitable to being loss making and subsequently fail.

Operational problems Some start-ups fail because of operational problems. For example, a business may suddenly find it very difficult to find supplies. Perhaps an existing supplier discontinues a product and the start-up business then can't find an alternative supplier. Or it takes much longer to do a job than expected.

Cash flow problems Cash flow through a business is the difference between the money coming in and the money going out on a day-to-day, month to month basis. Start-ups can be profitable but fail because of cash flow problems. One reason for this is the system of credit operated by businesses. When a business sells to another business, it typically has to give at least 30 days' credit. So it won't get paid for 30 days after the work has been completed. Even then, many businesses pay late. So it could be 60 days or 90 days before the start-up business is paid. On the other hand, many costs have to be paid now. Rents, loan repayments, cost of supplies and wages have to be paid on a regular basis. A start-up can simply run out of cash and then fail.

Lack of profitability Some start-ups fail because they are loss making. They make a loss on their day-to-day operations and on top of that the entrepreneur will have spent money on starting up the business. Entrepreneurs can lose tens of thousands of pounds if not more on a new business venture. Some have mortgaged their houses to raise the money to start the business and are forced to sell the house to repay the debts. Most start-ups, however, cease trading because they are not sufficiently profitable. Running your own business has many advantages. But most entrepreneurs work much longer hours running their own business than they would if they were in a normal paid job. If then they are getting much less financially from their business than they would as a wage, they are likely to give up their business. Entrepreneurs have to weigh up the **opportunity cost**, the benefits from their next best activity, of running their own business. If the opportunity cost is too high, because they could be earning £30,000 a year in a job but the profits on their business are only £3,000 a year, then they are likely to close down their business.

Strengths and weaknesses of a business plan

Research evidence shows that business planning is crucial to the success or failure of a start-up business. A good business plan is one which has three characteristics.
* It is comprehensive and has been well researched. It covers all aspects of the business and each aspect has been explored thoroughly.
* It is realistic. The objectives of the business must be

realistic. So too must the assumptions built into the plan. One key reason why business start-ups fail is because the would-be entrepreneur is far too optimistic about sales, costs and profits. It is very easy to get carried away with an idea and overestimate sales or underestimate costs.

- It is coherent. So one part of the business plan must fit with another part of the plan. For example, a would-be entrepreneur might develop a business plan for football coaching for 5-11 year olds. If one part of the business plan says that there will be 40 children attending between 10 and 11 o'clock on a Saturday morning, but another part of the business plan states that he will not be employing anyone to help him, then the business plan is not coherent. One person legally cannot look after 40 children.

Weak business plans are over-optimistic, poorly researched and not properly thought through. Many start-ups, particularly when the business is small and is operated on a part-time basis, have never had a business plan. Where the business is very simple, and there are few costs and revenues, this probably won't matter. But effective business planning helps sort out complex issues. It allows the owner to align the goals of the business with its operations. It considerably reduces the risk of failure because potential problems and opportunities have been identified.

KNOWLEDGE

1. Explain the differences between a sales objective, profit objective and market share objective for a business start-up.
2. Why might raising capital be an important objective for a business start-up?
3. Explain two sources of risk for a start-up business.
4. A business can fail because sales are lower than expected or costs are higher than expected. Explain why.
5. Business failure can sometimes occur because of unexpected events. Give two examples of such events and explain why they might force a business to cease trading.

Case Study: RD Servicing and Repairs

Rosie and Dean Spencer have just finished their first year of trading and it has been an unimaginable success. Dean worked for 20 years as a driver and then a mechanic of HGVs (heavy goods vehicles). Rosie had worked in the same garage as a car mechanic. For a long time, they felt that the business they worked for was inefficient. It didn't seem to care about its customers. Prices were high and the quality of workmanship was not always very good. Two years ago, they decided they wanted to set up on their own. Their business idea was to offer a better quality of service at lower prices than other firms in the area.

They spent a year drawing up their business plan. Two of their financial objectives were for sales revenue to be £200,000 in their first year and for the business to break even after Rosie and Dean had been paid a salary of £20,000 each. A third objective was to get an overdraft facility of £10,000 and a bank loan of £50,000 to cover start-up costs.

Having resigned from their jobs where between them they were earning £50 a year, they started operations. The first year of operation was hectic. The first month, Rosie and Dean spent a great deal of time marketing their new HGV maintenance and repairs service to local customers. Then, as the work built up, over the next couple of months, Dean was forced to spend all his time as the mechanic. The business plan anticipated that the company would have to take on two more mechanics at the end of the sixth month of operation. In fact, he had to take on three mechanics. By the end of the twelfth month they were employing thirteen staff, including seven mechanics. By that stage, the first year's sales turnover was £370,000.

However, this growth had not been without its problems. Half way through the year, it became apparent that they were running out of cash. Bills were having to be paid faster than customers were paying their invoices. The £10,000 overdraft was going to be breached. What's more, customers were asking for services which needed equipment the business didn't have. They went back to the bank to ask for £30,000 in loans, but the bank refused them saying they were too risky at this stage. They then turned to a local government funded business development agency which stepped in with the £30,000 loan. The crisis was averted, but only just.

Another major problem occurred when they had to move premises after six months. Because of their unexpected expansion, they found their initial premises on an industrial estate were too small. They arranged to move to larger premises on the same industrial estate. On the Friday night before they were due to move on the Saturday, vandals burnt down the industrial unit they were to occupy. Equipment had been packed and three working days cleared of all appointments. The move had to be put back by two months until another industrial unit became available. Not only was time lost, but customers had to wait longer for an available appointment and it took more time to do the work because of the lack of space.

(a) Briefly explain why drawing up a business plan is important for a business start-up. (10 marks)

(b) Evaluate the risks that Rosie and Dean Spencer took in starting their business. (15 marks)

(c) 'Rosie and Dean's business plan was poor because it failed to identify how quickly the business would grow and the risks that it might face.' To what extent do you agree with this statement? (15 marks)

23 | Using budgets

Managing finance

Once a business is established the owners will generally want to improve its performance. In the early stages of business development the emphasis is often on survival. But once the business is through this stage, other issues become important. Owners will probably want to grow their businesses and improve their effectiveness. One aspect of improving the effectiveness of a business is financial management. This involves managing the financial resources of the business. In most businesses this means:

- making sure that costs are kept down;
- ensuring that there is enough money to buy resources;
- ensuring that customers pay for what they have bought;
- measuring and monitoring financial performance indicators, such as profit and returns on capital.

Businesses have developed a number of systems to help manage financial resources and one of these is budgeting.

Using budgets

BUDGETARY CONTROL or BUDGETING involves a business using budgets to look into the future, stating what it wants to happen, and then deciding how to achieve these aims. The control process is shown in Figure 1.

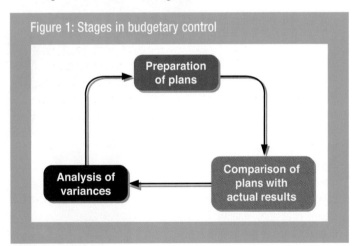

Figure 1: Stages in budgetary control

Preparation of plans → Comparison of plans with actual results → Analysis of variances

Preparation of plans All businesses have objectives. If the sales department increases sales by 10 per cent, how does it know whether or not this is satisfactory? Targets are usually set which allow a business to determine whether its objectives have been met. The results it achieves can then be compared with the targets it sets.

Comparisons of plans with actual results Control will be effective if information is available as quickly as possible. Managers need budgetary data as soon as it is available. Recent developments in information technology have helped to speed up the supply of data. For budgeting purposes the financial year has been divided up into smaller control periods - usually four weeks or one calendar month. It is common to prepare a budget for each control period. At the end of the period the actual results can then be compared with targets set in the budget.

Analysis of variances This is the most important stage in the control process. VARIANCE ANALYSIS involves trying to find reasons for the differences between actual and expected financial outcomes. Variances are explained in the next section. A variance might be the result of some external factor influencing the business. In this case the business may need to change its business plans and adjust the next budget.

Variances

A VARIANCE in budgeting is the difference between the figure that the business has budgeted for and the actual figure. Variances are usually calculated at the end of the budget period, as that is when the actual figure will be known.

Variances can be **favourable** (F) or **adverse** (A). Favourable variances occur when the actual figures are 'better' than the budgeted figures.

- If the sales revenue for a month was budgeted at £25,000, but turned out to be £29,000, there would be a £4,000 favourable variance (£29,000-£25,000) as sales revenue was higher than planned.
- If costs were planned to be £20,000 and turned out to be £18,000, this would also be a favourable variance of £2,000, as actual costs were lower than planned.

Adverse variances are when the actual figures are worse than the budgeted figures. Actual sales revenues may be lower than planned, or actual costs may be higher than planned. Managers will examine variances and try to identify reasons why they have occurred. By doing this they might be able to improve the performance of the business in the future.

Types of variance

Variances can be calculated for a wide range of financial outcomes. Most budgets are set for expenditure (costs) and income (sales revenue). Consequently, variances will also focus on a firm's expenditures and income. This suggests that variance analysis provides a very good way of monitoring business costs. Examples of variances could be wages, materials, overheads and sales revenue. Variances can also be calculated for volumes. For example it is possible to calculate a sales variance or a labour hours variance. One of the most important variances of all is the profit variance. The profit variance is influenced by all other variances. A change in any variance will affect profit. This is because all variances relate to either the costs or the revenue of a business, both of which affect profit levels. The number of

Table 1: Income budget, actual income and income variances for Wishart Ltd

	Jan	Feb	Mar	Apr	May	Jun	Total (£)
Budgeted income	16,500	17,000	17,500	18,000	19,000	20,000	108,000
Actual income	16,600	17,400	17,900	17,700	18,500	20,800	108,900
Variance	**100F**	**400F**	**400F**	**300A**	**500A**	**800F**	**900F**

Table 2: Budgeted expenditure, actual expenditure and expenditure variances for Wishart Ltd

	Jan	Feb	Mar	Apr	May	Jun	Total (£)
Budgeted expenditure	11,400	11,900	12,500	13,000	14,000	15,000	77,800
Actual expenditure	11,500	11,600	12,700	13,500	14,200	15,600	79,100
Expenditure variances	**100A**	**300F**	**200A**	**500A**	**200A**	**600A**	**1,300A**

Table 3: Budgeted profit, actual profit and profit variance for Wishart Ltd

	Jan	Feb	Mar	Apr	May	Jun	Total (£)
Budgeted profit	5,100	5,100	5,000	5,000	5,000	5,000	30,200
Actual profit	5,100	5,800	5,200	4,200	4,300	5,200	29,800
Profit variances	**0**	**700F**	**200F**	**800A**	**700A**	**200F**	**400A**

possible variances is equal to the number of factors which can influence business costs and revenue.

Income or sales revenue variances Table 1 shows the budgeted income, actual income and income variances for Wishart Ltd, a bamboo and wicker furniture manufacturer. Four of the monthly variances are favourable while two are adverse. The biggest variance occurred in June. In this month actual income was £800 greater than the budgeted income. The variance for the whole six month period is also shown. Over the period the total income variance was £900. Wishart Ltd's shareholders are likely to be pleased with this.

Possible causes of the favourable income variance over the six months in this case might be the result of:
- the ability to charge higher prices;
- an increase in demand due to a marketing campaign;
- improvements in the quality of the product;
- an increase in consumer incomes;
- a change in consumer's tastes in favour of bamboo and wicker furniture.

Expenditure or cost variances Table 2 shows the budgeted expenditure, actual expenditure and expenditure or total cost variances for Wishart Ltd over the six month period. Most of the

monthly expenditure variances are adverse over the time period. For example, in April the variance was £500A. This means that costs were £500 higher than planned. Over the whole six month period the expenditure variance was adverse at £1,300. There is a number of possible reasons for such adverse variances.
- Costs might be higher because production was higher.
- Suppliers may have raised prices.
- There may be some inefficiencies in production.
- Wages may have been higher due to wage demands by workers.

Profit variances The most important of all variances is the profit variance. Differences between actual profit and planned profit will be of particular interest to business owners, managers and other stakeholders. The performance of most businesses is often measured by profit. Table 3 shows the budgeted profit, actual profit and profit variance for Wishart Ltd. Some of the monthly variances are favorable while others are unfavourable. In January there was no variance at all. This is because budgeted profit was exactly the same as actual profit. Over the six month period the profit variance was adverse at £400. This means that profit was £400 lower than planned.

The main reason for Wishart's adverse profit variances over the six month period is the adverse cost variance of £1,300. Costs have been higher than planned. Higher costs may have been caused by a number of factors, such as those listed in the examples above.

Using variances for decision making

The final stage in budgetary control is the analysis of variances. It is important to identify the reasons why variances have occurred. If variances are adverse it will be necessary to take action to ensure that adverse variances are avoided in future. If variances are favourable the business can learn from understanding the reasons why this has occurred and can introduce strategies and systems to help sustain performance improvements in the future.

When making decisions about how the business should be run, information about the causes of variances will be very helpful. For example, if a business has an adverse cost variance, it might discover that the cause was higher prices charged by suppliers. The business might then decide to look for new suppliers. A favourable sales revenue variance might be the result of an effective advertising campaign. The business might

Question 1.

FT Office Supplies sells office equipment and computer accessories such as printers, toners, computer cables, port hubs and laptop bags. It used to operate three stores in the south of England, but it recently closed the stores and now conducts all business online. To monitor sales the business sets budgets every six months. Table 4 shows an income (sales revenue) budget for the first six months of 2007. Actual income figures are also shown.

Table 4: Income budget and actual income for FT Office Supplies

	Jan	Feb	Mar	Apr	May	Jun	(£000) Total
Budgeted income	1,200	1,300	1,400	1,400	1,500	1,600	8,400
Actual income	1,140	1,190	1,430	1,400	1,390	1,450	8,000

(a) Calculate the sales revenue variances for each month and the total sales revenue variance for the whole budget period.

(b) Explain the variance in April.

(c) Analyse two possible reasons for the pattern of variances for FT Office Supplies over the six month time period.

decide to make more use of the same or similar campaigns in the future. Variance analysis can help business decision-makers because of the information they provide about financial outcomes and their causes.

Zero-based budgeting

The financial information used in most budgets is based on **historical** data. For example, the cost of materials in this year's production budget may be based on last year's figure, with perhaps an allowance for inflation. Production and manufacturing costs, such as labour, raw materials and overheads, are relatively easy to value and tend to be controlled using methods such as standard costing.

However, in some areas of business it is not so easy to quantify costs. Examples might be certain marketing, administration or computer services costs. Where costs cannot be justified then no money is allocated in the budget for those costs. This is known as ZERO-BASED BUDGETING (ZBB) or ZERO BUDGETING. A manager must show that a particular item of spending generates an adequate amount of benefit in relation to the general objectives of the business in order for money to be allocated in a budget.

This approach is different to the common practice of extrapolating from past costs. It encourages the regular evaluation of costs and helps to minimise unnecessary purchases. The concept of **opportunity cost** is linked to ZBB. Opportunity cost is the cost of the next best alternative. When choices are made, businesses try to minimise the opportunity cost. ZBB also involves a cautious approach to spending, so that costs are minimised. Both approaches include an element of 'value for money'.

The main advantages of ZBB are that:
- the allocation of resources should be improved;

- a questioning attitude is developed which will help to reduce unnecessary costs and eliminate inefficient practices;
- staff motivation might improve because evaluation skills are practised and a greater knowledge of the firm's operations might develop;
- it encourages managers to look for alternatives.

ZBB also has some disadvantages.
- It is time consuming because the budgeting process involves the collection and analysis of quite detailed information so that spending decisions can be made.
- Skilful decision making is required. Such skills may not be available in the organisation. In addition, decisions may be influenced by subjective opinions.
- It threatens the status quo. This might adversely affect motivation.
- Managers may not be prepared to justify spending on certain costs. Money, therefore, may not be allocated to spending which could benefit the business.

To deal with these possible problems, a business might give each department a 'base' budget of, say, 50 per cent. Departments could then be invited to bid for increased expenditure on a ZBB basis.

Benefits of using budgets

Monitoring performance Budgets allow managers to monitor the performance of a business as a whole, as well as different sections. For example, analysing departmental cost variances may allow a business to find out why certain departments are incurring high costs. Alternatively, it allows businesses to identify good practice and discover why some costs are lower.

Identifying factors affecting performance Prompt variance analysis allows managers to assess whether variances are caused by internal or external factors. Once causes have been traced, they can be corrected.

Improved plans in future By identifying variances and their causes managers may be able to produce more accurate budgets in future. This will aid planning and perhaps improve the performance of the business.

Improved accountability Budgetary control in general helps to improve accountability in businesses. It can also be linked to performance-related pay. For example, budget holders may receive a bonus payment at the end of the budget period if they can show favourable variances. Consequently motivation in a business can be improved.

Question 2.

Armstrong Ltd makes components for games machines in arcades. The company operates from an industrial estate in Slough. It has experienced some problems in recent months due to worn out machinery. An expenditure budget and actual expenditure are shown in Table 5.

Table 5: Budgeted costs and actual costs for Armstrong Ltd

							(£000)
	Jan	Feb	Mar	Apr	May	Jun	Total
Budgeted direct costs	2,300	2,500	2,500	2,600	2,600	2,700	15,200
Budgeted overheads	200	200	200	300	300	300	1,500
Budgeted total cost	2,500	2,700	2,700	2,900	2,900	3,000	16,700
Actual direct costs	2,200	2,450	2,400	2,550	2,600	2,600	14,800
Actual overheads	210	220	190	890	750	320	2,580
Actual total cost	2,410	2,670	2,590	3,440	3,350	2,920	17,380

(a) Calculate the following variances: (i) direct cost (ii) overheads and (iii) total cost.
(b) Analyse the variances calculated in (a).

Drawbacks of using budgets

Motivation In some businesses, workers are left out of the planning process. If workers are not consulted about the budget, it will be more difficult to use that budget to motivate them. Budgets which are unrealistic can also fail to motivate staff.

Manipulation Budgets can be manipulated by managers. For example, a departmental manager might have great influence over those people co-ordinating and setting budgets. The manager may be able to arrange a budget which is easy to achieve and makes the department look successful. But the budget may not help the business achieve its objectives.

Rigidity Budgets can sometimes constrain business activities. For instance, departments within a business may have different views about when it is best to replace vehicles. The more often vehicles are replaced, the higher the cost. However, the newer the vehicle, the lower the maintenance cost and the less likely it is to be off the road for repairs. The budget may be set so that older vehicles have to be kept rather than replaced. But this may lead to customer dissatisfaction and lost orders because deliveries are unreliable.

Short-termism Some managers might be too focused on the current budget. They might take actions that undermine the future performance of the business just to meet current budget targets. For example, to keep labour costs down in the current budget period, the manager of a supermarket might reduce staffing on customer service. This might save costs now, but it could lead to customers drifting away over time due to poor service. Consequently the long-term performance of the business would suffer.

KEY TERMS

Budgetary control or Budgeting – a business system which involves making future plans, comparing the actual results with the planned results and then investigating causes of any differences.
Variance – the difference between actual financial outcomes and those which were budgeted.
Variance analysis – the process of calculating variances and attempting to identify their causes.
Zero-based budgeting or zero budgeting – a system of budgeting where no money is allocated for costs or spending unless they can be justified by the fundholder (they are given a zero value).

KNOWLEDGE

1. What is meant by financial management?
2. Describe the three steps in budgetary control.
3. Explain how a variance is calculated.
4. What is meant by an adverse variance?
5. State two possible causes of a favourable sales revenue variance.
6. State two possible causes of an adverse cost variance.
7. State four benefits of using budgets.

Case Study: *Cynplex.com*

Cynplex.com, founded and owned by Josh Howarth, develops software for e-transactions including payments, document distribution and account verification. Cynplex.com, based in Glasgow, has a good proportion of the UK market for electronic funds transfer with over 10,000 business customers. Cynplex.com's software provides a range of integrated e-business solutions for businesses of any type and size. The software is designed to improve efficiency by reducing the time and expense of manual day-to-day business processes. The products include:

- payment solutions – for processing transactions such as payroll and supplier payments;
- electronic data interchange – for streamlined communications between trading partners;
- collections management – for managing multiple Direct Debit and credit card transactions;
- e-document distribution – for fast, efficient distribution of financial documents such as purchase orders and invoices.

Josh has grown the business successfully since it was setup five years ago. He employs an accountant who is responsible for the financial management of the business. He uses variance analysis to monitor income, expenditure and profit. Some financial information is shown in Table 6 for Cynplex.com.

Table 6: Financial information for Cynplex.com

			(£000)
	2007	2006	2005
Budgeted income	4,500	3,800	3,200
Budgeted expenditure	3,900	3,350	2,800
Budgeted profit	600	450	400
	2007	2006	2005
Actual income	4,890	4,010	3,600
Actual expenditure	4,050	3,400	3,100
Actual profit	840	610	500

(a) Using this case as an example, explain what is meant by a favourable variance. (3 marks)
(b) Calculate the income, expenditure and profit variances for Cynplex.com for each year. (9 marks)
(c) Why is the profit variance probably the most important of all? (4 marks)
(d) Analyse the variances calculated in (c). (10 marks)
(e) Josh is hoping to float the company on the stock market in order to raise finance to break into overseas markets. How might the profit variances influence this decision? (10 marks)
(f) Evaluate the drawbacks to Cynplex.com of using budgets as a means of financial management. (14 marks).

24 | Improving cash flow

Cash flow and financial management

One crucial aspect of financial management is making sure that the business has enough cash when it is needed. If a business runs out of cash it will find it difficult, if not impossible, to trade. It will probably have to close down. In 2007, music retailer Fopp closed down after an 'extraordinary stock take'. It revealed that it had run out of cash after the company overreached itself through the purchase of the ailing Music Zone group in February. In July receivers were called in and it was announced that all 105 of its stores would be closed at the expense of 700 jobs.

This example illustrates the importance of careful financial management. Prudent owners and managers may use budgets, cash flow forecasts and credit control systems to manage financial resources effectively. Effective financial management will ensure that the business has enough cash when it is needed.

Causes of cash flow problems

Shortages of cash in a business often result from a number of errors in the control of financial resources.

Overtrading Young and rapidly growing businesses are particularly prone to OVERTRADING. Overtrading occurs when a business is attempting to fund a large volume of production with inadequate cash. Established companies trying to expand can also face this problem.

Investing too much in fixed assets In the initial stages of a business, funds are limited. Spending large amounts quickly on equipment, vehicles and other capital items drains resources. It may be better to lease some of these fixed assets, leaving sufficient cash funds.

Stockpiling Holding stocks of raw materials and finished goods is expensive. Money tied up in stocks is unproductive. Stocks may become obsolete. In addition, stocks of raw materials in particular cannot easily be changed into cash without making a loss. Stock control is an important feature of managing liquid resources. Firms should not buy in bulk if discounts are not enough to compensate for the extra cost of holding stocks.

Allowing too much credit A great deal of business is done on credit. One of the dangers is that businesses allow their customers too long to pay their bills. This means that they are waiting for money and may actually be forced to borrow during this period. Failure to control debtors may also lead to bad debts. Taking early action is the key to the effective control of debtors. At the same time businesses must maintain good relations with customers. Small firms are particularly vulnerable

if they are owed money by much larger companies. Powerful businesses are often accused of endangering smaller companies by delaying payments to them.

Taking too much credit Taking more credit might appear to help a firm's cash position since payments are delayed. However, there are some drawbacks. Taking too much credit might result in higher prices, lost discounts, difficulties in obtaining future supplies and a bad name in the trade. At worst, credit might be withdrawn.

Overborrowing Businesses may borrow to finance growth. As more loans are taken out, interest costs rise. Overborrowing not only threatens a firm's cash position, but also the overall control of the business. It is important to fund growth in a balanced way, for example by raising some capital from share issues. Examples of overborrowing are not uncommon in the mortgage market. Sometimes people 'overstretch' themselves. They take out mortgages to buy houses that they can't really afford. In the worse cases, people are not able to meet interest payments and their houses are repossessed. The same could happen to businesses if they borrow too much. If they are not able to meet interest payments, their businesses could be wound up.

Underestimating inflation Businesses often fail to take inflation into account. Inflation raises costs, which can cause cash shortages. This is often the case if higher costs, such as wages or raw materials, cannot be passed on in higher prices. Inflationary periods are often accompanied by higher interest rates which place further pressure on liquid resources. Inflation is also a problem because it is difficult to predict future rates. Although it can be built into plans, firms often underestimate it. In the last ten years inflation has not been a real problem. However, sharp increase in the price of certain raw materials, such as oil, has put pressure on some businesses, particularly those that rely heavily on oil.

Unforeseen expenditure Businesses are subject to unpredictable external forces. They must make financial provision for any unforeseen expenditure. Equipment breakdowns, tax demands, strikes and bad debts are common examples of this type of emergency expense. In the early stages of business development, owners are often hit by unforeseen expenditure. This might be because they lack experience or have not undertaken sufficient planning.

Unexpected changes in demand Although most businesses try to sustain demand for their products, there may be times when it falls unexpectedly. Unpredicted changes in fashion could lead to a fall in demand. This could lead to a lack of sales and cash

Question 1.

In July 2007, Kwik Save the supermarket chain, collapsed after it ran out of cash. Most of its workers had not been paid for up to six weeks. Kwik Save was founded in 1959 as one shop in Rhyl, north Wales, and floated on the stock exchange in 1970. By the 1990s it had more than 1,000 stores and recently became part of Somerfield. However, it was sold on to a new firm, BTTF, headed by Mr Niklas, in February 2007. Some new cash was injected into the business but it was not enough to save the chain.

The firm collapsed due to a combination of tough competition from the big supermarkets which have slashed prices, foreign low-cost rivals such as Aldi and Lidl, and bad management. In May suppliers halted bread and milk deliveries saying that there were considerable difficulties getting paid by Kwik Save. Just before the company collapsed 81 stores were closed and 700 people lost their jobs. A further 90 stores were closed on the day it collapsed with around 1,100 people being laid off. However, it was hoped that some of the stores would be bought by other retailers and that some people would be kept on. Amanda Higgins, the former deputy manager of a store in Ellesmere Port that has been closed down, heard the news on television, while the company remained silent. 'It's diabolical,' she said. 'I just don't know what to do.'

She phoned the Little Sutton store near her home and was told by staff there that the shop had been shut down. Staff were also told that if they came in and handed over the store in a rational manner they would be paid a week's wages, but Ms Higgins could not believe it.

Source: adapted from *The Guardian*, 6.7.2007 and www.a2mediagroup.com

(a) Using this case as an example, explain the importance of cash when running a business.
(b) Explain how: (i) employees and (ii) the owner will be affected by the collapse of Kwik Save.
(c) Analyse the possible causes of the collapse of Kwik Save.

though, they have to pay expenses without any cash flowing in. This situation requires careful management, although it is possible to predict these changes.

Poor financial management Inexperience in managing cash or a poor understanding of the way cash flows into and out of a business may lead to cash flow problems. For example, if a business plans to spend heavily just before it receives large amounts of cash from customers who have bought on credit, it is likely to face problems. It is not prudent to spend cash when it is not definitely there.

Methods of improving cash flow

Cash flow problems can be prevented by keeping a tight control on financial resources. The use of budgets and cash flow forecasts will improve the financial management of the business. Inevitably, though, there will be occasions when firms run short of cash. When this does happen the firm's main aim will be survival rather than profit. The following measures might be used to either generate cash or save it.

Use of overdraft facilities If a business is not able, or does not wish, to use the options listed above, an obvious option is to borrow money. Most businesses have an overdraft facility with their banks. An overdraft is a type of flexible loan. The borrower can choose to borrow up to a certain sum of money agreed with the bank, called the overdraft limit. But they are free to pay back part of the money borrowed at any time and do not have to be borrowing money to have an overdraft facility. A business can increase its cash by borrowing more money on its overdraft. For example, it might have an overdraft limit of £5,000. It is currently borrowing £3,000. So it could borrow up to £2,000 extra.

There is more of a problem if a business is already borrowing up to its overdraft limit. Then it has to negotiate with its bank to that limit. There is no guarantee that the bank will do this. A business experiencing cash flow problems could well be a business in difficulties. The bank will not want to increase lending to a business which could cease trading in the immediate future. The bank is likely to want to see a cash flow forecast to judge whether or not the business will be able to pay the interest on the overdraft and the overdraft itself in the future.

flowing into a company. Travel companies in the UK have faced this problem in the past. Companies have to 'buy' holidays before they are sold. External factors, including a recession, may have led to many of these holidays remaining unsold as consumers changed their holiday buying patterns. Firms may also have lost revenue if holidays were discounted in an attempt to sell them.

Seasonal factors Sometimes trade fluctuates for seasonal reasons. In the agriculture industry, cereal farmers have a large cash inflow when their harvest is sold. For much of the year,

Negotiate additional short-term or long-term loans A business may be able obtain a short-term loan from a bank to inject some extra cash. If a business feels that extra money will be needed for a longer period of time a long-term loan might be considered. A business could pay back smaller installments over a longer period of time to help cash flow. However, once it is known that a business is short of cash, banks and other money lenders may be reluctant to provide cash for fear of the business collapsing.

Sell off or reduce stocks Sometimes it may be possible to sell stocks of raw materials, components or semi-finished goods for cash. To generate cash quickly they can be sold cheaply in a sale or below cost if necessary. Some stocks may be quite specialised and prove difficult to sell quickly.

A business might simply reduce the amount of stocks it holds. A machine manufacturer may buy in fewer stocks of components to make machines. Stocks cost money to hold. So fewer stocks can increase cash in the business. The danger is that stocks will not be available to make products that are required for sale.

Use a factoring company An alternative to pressurising customers for money is to sell the debts to a specialist **debt factor**. A factor is a business that will provide finance to another business against its debts for a fee. It often pays a certain amount to the business 'up front' and the remainder once debts are collected. Debt factors give businesses cash immediately and take the responsibility for collecting the debt. However, they make a charge for this and the debts must be good.

Sell off unwanted or non-vital fixed assets A business may be able to sell off unwanted or non-vital fixed assets like vehicles, machines and property. Unfortunately, to sell assets like these quickly they are likely to be sold at auctions and they may be sold below their true value.

Use of sale and leaseback Businesses are increasingly using sale and leaseback to raise cash. Assets like property and machinery can be sold to specialists in the market, such as Arnold Clark and Lease Direct. The assets are then leased back to the seller. This means that cash can be raised and the business can

continue to use the assets. However, it may take a while to set up such agreements and can be an expensive way to fund assets in the long term.

Stimulate sales for cash Many businesses, retailers for example, can generate cash by offering large discounts for customers who pay in cash. In the example at the beginning of this unit, Fopp tried to generate cash in this way by selling records, CDs and other stock for cash only. Unfortunately, the measure was not enough to save the business.

Mount a rigorous drive on overdue accounts This involves a business putting pressure on its customers to pay back what they owe more quickly. Allowing customers to receive products and pay for them at a later date is called TRADE CREDIT. The DEBTORS of a business are those customers (individuals or businesses) that owe a business money. However, pressurising customers in this way may mean that they find other suppliers.

Only make essential purchases It obviously makes sense during a cash crisis to postpone or cancel all unnecessary spending. A business should only buy resources for cash when it absolutely has to.

Delaying payments A business may simply delay payments. It then keeps this cash in the business for a longer period of time. It will only make payments when it is put under pressure to do so by CREDITORS – businesses that are owed money.

Extend credit with selected suppliers It will help a business to save cash if it can delay paying suppliers for goods and services that have already been bought. It may be able to extend its credit payment period from 30 to 60 days, for example. However, delaying for too long could mean that suppliers withdraw their credit facilities or refuse to deliver goods in the future.

Reduce personal drawings from the business Owners who regularly take cash from the business for their own personal use could attempt to take less. Obviously some cash might be needed for living expenses, but making a reduction in drawings is a quick way to stop cash leaving the business.

Introduce fresh capital Owners may be able to provide some new capital to improve cash flow. For example, small businesses may be able to use savings or take out loans using personal possessions as security. A small business may be able to persuade friends or relatives to invest in it – new partners might be taken on for example. Larger companies may be able to sell shares to raise fresh capital. However, attracting fresh capital might be very difficult if the business is struggling. It is likely to be up to the current owners to provide more capital.

In all the above cases, action must be taken quickly. If the business survives the cash crisis, it is important to identify the causes and to make sure it does not happen again. It is also

Question 2.

Adrian Talbot owns and runs a small garment manufacturing business. He employs 12 workers, using rented premises in London. Cash flow is always a problem for him. The businesses that buy from him often pay late while the profit margins he earns are wafer thin in an industry notorious for cut throat competition. At least finished stock is never a problem. He makes a sample and wins orders based on that. As soon as an order is complete, it is sent out to the purchaser.

(a) Suggest and explain THREE ways in which Adrian Talbot could possibly improve his cash flow situation.

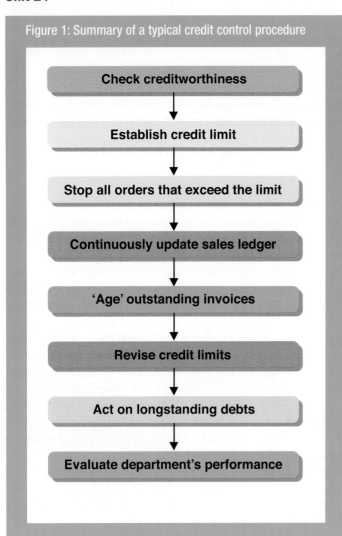

Figure 1: Summary of a typical credit control procedure

- Check creditworthiness
- Establish credit limit
- Stop all orders that exceed the limit
- Continuously update sales ledger
- 'Age' outstanding invoices
- Revise credit limits
- Act on longstanding debts
- Evaluate department's performance

they set targets for the credit control department, such as the maximum value of bad debts or the length of time it takes to collect debts.

Firms have procedures to help credit control. Figure 1 shows an example.

- Many firms will not do business with new customers until their creditworthiness has been checked. This can be done by asking for references from a supplier, a banker's reference or a credit-rating agency's report. From this information the credit controller can set a credit limit based on the risk involved.
- When an order exceeds the credit limit, the credit controller should investigate. This may result in a stop being placed on the order, requesting the customer to pay any outstanding debt or simply allowing the order to go ahead.
- Credit control records, which show customer orders and payments, must be up to date. Every month, outstanding invoices must be 'aged' to identify customers who owe money over 30, 60 and 90 days.
- If there are persistent debts, the credit controller must take action. A statement of the account should be sent, followed by a second one with a letter. Next, a telephone call to the debtor should be followed by a personal visit. Finally, as a last resort, it may be necessary to take legal action to recover the debt.
- Some firms use an independent **debt factor** to assist in credit control. There has been quite a growth in this type of business in recent years. A factor is a business that will provide finance to a business against its debts for a fee. It often pays a certain amount to a business' up front' and the remainder as debts are collected.

evident that measures taken to alleviate a cash crisis are likely to reduce profits. For example, selling goods at a discount to raise cash will reduce profit margins; selling off assets and leasing them back can reduce profit in the long term; borrowing money from banks will incur interest charges; inviting new members to provide capital will dilute ownership.

Credit control

Most businesses have some sort of CREDIT CONTROL system, so that cash that is owed can be collected quickly and easily. A 'tight' or 'easy' credit policy may be adopted. Tight credit terms may be used to improve liquidity, reduce the risk of bad debts, exploit a seller's market or maintain slender profit margins. Easy credit terms may be designed to clear old stocks, enter a new market or perhaps help a regular customer with financial difficulties.

The company accountant and the sales manager often work closely with the credit controller, since credit policy will affect the financial position of the firm and its sales. Between them

KEYTERMS

Creditors – those to whom a business owes money for goods or services delivered but not yet paid for.

Credit control – the process of monitoring and collecting the money owed to a business.

Debtors – those who owe a business money for goods or services delivered but for which they have not yet paid.

Overtrading – a situation where a business does not have enough cash and other liquid resources to support its production and sales.

Trade credit – given when a supplier allows a customer to receive goods or services but pay for them at a later point in time. Typically, trade credit is given for 30 days.

KNOWLEDGE

1. What might happen if a business runs out of cash?
2. What methods might a business use to manage its financial resources effectively?
3. Explain why young and rapidly growing businesses are prone to overtrading.
4. Explain how: (i) stock piling (ii) overborrowing and

(iii) underestimating inflation can cause cash-flow problems.
5. State four ways in which a business can improve cash flow.
6. Why might it be difficult to extend a bank overdraft to generate more cash?
7. What is meant by 'credit control'?

Case Study: *Hotel Condor*

Hotel Condor is a 45 room hotel, with conference facilities, a restaurant and a bar. It is located in north London, about 35 minutes drive from Heathrow Airport. The hotel business, which includes the property, is owned by Asif and Ashraf Hussain. The hotel uses a booking agent in the USA and about 80 per cent of the hotel's guests are American business travellers and tourists. The hotel has many facilities, including coffee makers in the room, room service, safe deposit boxes, televisions with cable and high-speed Internet connection.

The hotel has not performed particularly well in the last couple of years. The flow of American guests has dwindled due to the strength of the pound against the dollar. Occupancy rates have fallen from 82 per cent in 2005 to less than 50 per cent in 2006. To keep the business going, the owners put in £20,000 cash, in the hope that the exchange rate would eventually reverse. £4,000 of the money was spent on obtaining some listings in hotel directories. Although this did generate some more business, it was nowhere near as much as promised. £4,000 was spent relaunching the restaurant, but unfortunately the appointment of a new head chef, and a change in the menu, did not attract many more customers. By the end of 2006, the hotel had £5,600 in the bank and cash flow forecasts showed that more cash would need to be injected in June 2007 unless business picked up significantly.

The hotel was contacted by a British company that was undertaking some work in the north London area. The company wanted to book 25 rooms for three months (May to July) to accommodate their employees. They also wanted to make regular use of the conferencing facilities. A price was agreed, a deposit was received, and it looked as though the hotel was about to get back on an even keel. However, as luck would

have it, the hotel was forced to close for two weeks in April after a visit from health and safety inspectors. Hygiene conditions in the large kitchen, which served both the hotel and the restaurant, were not up to standard. About £15,000 of work needed to be done before it could reopen. There was £9,200 in the bank.

(a) Using this case as an example, explain what is meant by a cash flow problem. (4 marks)
(b) Explain how external factors have contributed to cash flow problems in this case. (12 marks)
(c) Ashraf and Asif have invited a relative of theirs to become a sleeping partner in the business and contribute £50,000 capital. Do you think the relative should accept the invitation? (14 marks)
(d) Evaluate the measures the Hotel Condor might take to resolve its cash crisis. (20 marks)

Measuring profit

Business owners and financial managers will monitor the profitability of a business very carefully. Profit is perhaps the most important performance indicator. This is because, for most businesses, making profit is the main aim.

The actual size of profit is not always a true indicator of performance. In 2007, Next, the high street clothes retailer, made a profit of £478 million and BA, the airline, made a profit of £611 million. In contrast, Wetherspoons, the pub chain, made a profit of just £62 million.

Does this mean that BA was the best performing business out of the three? It may do but not necessarily. A number of other factors have to be taken into account. For example, how much money was invested in the business and how much profit was made in relation to turnover? A closer examination of more financial information would be required before a conclusion could be drawn about which company had performed the best.

Profit margins

One way of measuring profit is to calculate a PROFIT MARGIN. A profit margin expresses profit as a proportion of turnover, usually as a percentage. A profit margin can be used to compare the performance of a business in different periods when turnover changes. It can also be used to compare the performance of different sized businesses. There are two common profit margins.

Gross profit margin GROSS PROFIT is the amount of profit a business makes after direct costs have been subtracted from turnover. It can be calculated using the formula:

$$\text{Gross profit} = \text{turnover} - \text{cost of sales}$$

It is the profit before overheads (indirect costs) are subtracted. For a retailer gross profit would be turnover minus the cost of buying goods for resale. For a manufacturer it would be turnover minus the costs of raw materials, components and direct labour.

The GROSS PROFIT MARGIN or MARK-UP is the gross profit expressed as a percentage of turnover. It is calculated using the formula:

$$\text{Gross profit margin} = \frac{\text{Gross profit}}{\text{Turnover}} \times 100$$

Table 1 shows some financial information for Prior's, a large independent electrical goods store. Figures are shown for 2006 and 2007. The gross profit margins for the two years are calculated as follows.

$$\text{For 2007 Gross profit margin} = \frac{£550,000}{£1,230,000} \times 100 = 44.7\%$$

$$\text{For 2006 Gross profit margin} = \frac{£450,000}{£1,100,000} \times 100 = 40.9\%$$

Higher gross profit margins are preferable to lower ones. However, it is difficult to say what a 'good' margin is likely to be. Gross profit margins will vary in different industries. For example supermarkets, which generally have a fast stock turnover, will have lower gross profit margins than, say, a car dealer, which will operate with a much slower stock turnover. The gross profit margins for Prior's have increased over the two years from 40.9 per cent to 44.7 per cent. This shows that performance has improved. Margins of around 40 per cent for

Table 1: Financial information for Prior's

	2007	(£) 2006
Turnover	1,230,000	1,100,000
Cost of sales	780,000	650,000
Gross profit	550,000	450,000
Overheads	340,000	280,000
Net profit	210,000	170,000

Question 1.

Goodalls is a small chain of butchers operating in Kent. It has a shop in Dover, Ashford and Canterbury. Table 2 shows some financial information for Goodalls for 2007.

Table 2: Financial information for Goodalls

	Dover	Ashford	(£) Canterbury
Turnover	158,000	142,000	197,000
Cost of sales	102,000	101,000	146,000
Gross profit			
Overheads	31,000	29,000	33,000
Net profit			

(a) Complete the table by calculating gross profit and net profit.
(b) Calculate the net profit margins for the three shops.
(c) (i) Which shop has performed the best in 2007?
(ii) How will these figures assist Goodalls in the financial management of the business?

an electrical goods retailer are probably acceptable.

Net profit margin NET PROFIT is the amount of profit after all costs have been subtracted from turnover. It is calculated as:

Net profit = gross profit - overheads

Or

Net profit = turnover – cost of sales - overheads

The NET PROFIT MARGIN is net profit expressed as a percentage of turnover. The net profit margin shows how effectively a business has controlled its overheads and its cost of sales. The net profit margin is calculated by:

$$\text{Net profit margin} = \frac{\text{Net profit}}{\text{Turnover}} \times 100$$

When calculating the net profit margin it is important to use net profit before tax and interest. The net profit margins for Prior's in 2006 and 2007 are calculated as follows.

$$\text{For 2007 Net profit margin} = \frac{£210,000}{£1,230,000} \times 100 = 17.1\%$$

$$\text{For 2006 Net profit margin} = \frac{£170,000}{£1,100,000} \times 100 = 15.5\%$$

Again, higher margins are better than lower ones. The net profit margin for Prior's has improved over the two years from 15.5% to 17.1%. This suggests that the business has been able to control its overheads slightly more effectively in 2007.

Return on capital

Another way to measure the profitability of a business is to calculate the RETURN ON CAPITAL. Capital is the money invested in a business by the owners. The return on capital is the amount of profit expressed as a percentage of the capital invested in a business. Owners can use this measure to see how well their investment in the business is doing. The return on capital is:

$$\text{Return on capital} = \frac{\text{Net profit}}{\text{Capital}} \times 100$$

In 2007, the amount of capital invested in Prior's, the electrical goods retailer in the example above, was £1 million. The same amount was invested in 2006. The return on capital for 2007 and 2006 is shown below.

$$\text{For 2007 Return on capital} = \frac{£210,000}{£1,000,000} \times 100 = 21\%$$

$$\text{For 2006 Return on capital} = \frac{£170,000}{£1,000,000} \times 100 = 17\%$$

Clearly, the return on capital increased over the two-year period. In 2006 the owners of Prior's got a 17 per cent return on their £1,000,000 investment. This rose to 21 per cent in 2007. One way to determine whether 21 per cent is a good return or not, is to make a comparison with another electrical goods retailer. However, it may not be possible to obtain the information required to do this. A 21 per cent return does look good when compared with the return the owner might get if the £1,000,000 was deposited in a bank. This would have been about 6 per cent in 2007 (£60,000). Clearly, the money is generating a much bigger return when it is invested in the business. However, the £1,000,000 invested in the business is at risk and investors would expect a bigger return to compensate for this risk.

Finally, when comparing profit measures between businesses, it is important to compare 'like with like'. The profit margins and returns on capital may vary from industry to industry and from business to business. Fair comparisons can only be made between businesses if they operate in the same industry and have the same characteristics. For example, comparing the rate of return of a shoe manufacturer with that of a bank may not be appropriate.

Question 2.

Leonard & Co manufactures glassware in Hereford. It employs 45 staff and has a reputation for high-quality wine glasses, vases and crystalware. The company has won awards for innovation in recent years but is facing pressure from overseas competitors.

Simpsons plc is a sheet glass retailer. It operates from a huge site in Bradford and mainly serves traders such as builders and glaziers. In the last year it has taken over a local rival and the integration of the two businesses raised costs for the year.

Argo Ltd makes a range of glass products such as glass tables, show cases and cabinets. It employs seven staff and operates from an industrial unit in Sunderland. The company was bought from the previous owner by the present manager two years ago. Some financial information for the three companies is shown in Table 3.

Table 3: Financial information for Leonard & Co, Simpsons plc and Argo Ltd

	Leonard & Co	Simpsons plc	Argo Ltd (£)
Capital invested	2,340,000	7,800,000	1,400,000
Net profit	245,000	466,000	156,000

(a) Explain what is meant by return on capital.
(b) Calculate the return on capital for the three businesses in the case.
(c) Comment on and compare the returns calculated in (b).
(d) How useful are the comparisons made in (c)?

Methods of improving profitability

All businesses will want to improve their performance. An improved performance is likely to benefit all stakeholders. The returns on capital can be increased by making more profit with the same level of investment. This might be achieved by growth funded externally. This means the business increases sales using fresh capital.

Increasing profit margins will also improve performance. If profit margins can be raised, the business will make more profit at the existing level of sales. The profit margins can be improved in two ways.

Raising prices If a business raises its price it will get more revenue for every unit sold. If costs remain the same then profitability should improve. However, raising price might have an impact on the level of sales. Generally, when price is raised demand will fall. However, if demand is not too responsive to changes in price, the increase in price will generate more revenue even though fewer units are sold. Raising price is always risky because it is never certain how competitors will react.

Lowering costs A business can also raise profit margins by lowering its costs. It can do this by buying cheaper resources or using the existing resources more effectively.

- Using existing resources more efficiently. It might be possible to buy raw materials and components from new suppliers that offer better prices. It may also be possible to find new providers of essential services such as telecommunications, electricity, insurance and IT support. For example, there has been increased competition recently in the supply of gas, electricity and telecommunications. Another option might be to find ways of using cheaper labour. For example, some businesses have moved overseas to take advantage of cheap labour in places like China and eastern Europe. However, these measures may have drawbacks. When taking on new suppliers the possibility that they are cheaper because they are not as good should be considered. The quality of raw materials might be inferior, they may be unreliable and supply might not be guaranteed. For example, a number of new, and cheaper, broadband providers have not been able to guarantee supply. Moving abroad to take advantage of cheap labour may be disruptive. It may also damage the image of the company if it lays off large numbers of staff in the UK. Consequently, when looking to acquire cheaper resources, a business must be cautious and understand the pitfalls.
- Buying cheaper resources. Making better use of current resources will improve efficiency and lower costs. A business might do this by introducing new working practices or training staff. This would help to raise labour productivity. It could upgrade its machinery by acquiring newer, more efficient models. This would raise capital productivity. A business might be able to reduce waste by recycling materials, for example. Some of these measures

might also have drawbacks. For example, the workers might resist new working practices and new technology often has teething problems. This could disrupt the business.

The difference between cash and profit

It is important for businesses to recognise the difference between cash and profit. At the end of a trading year it is unlikely that the value of profit will be the same as the cash balance. Differences between cash and profit can arise for a number of reasons.

- During the trading year a business might sell £200,000 worth of goods with total costs of £160,000. Its profit would be £40,000. However, if some goods had been sold on credit, payment by certain customers may not yet have been received. If £12,000 was still owing, the amount of cash the business had would be £28,000 (£40,000-£12,000). Thus, profit is greater than cash.
- A business may receive cash at the beginning of the trading year from sales made in the previous year. This would increase the cash balance, but would not affect profit. In addition, the business may buy resources from suppliers and not pay for them until the next trading year. As a result its trading costs will not be the same as cash paid out.
- Sometimes the owners might introduce more cash into the business. This will increase the cash balance, but will have no effect on the profit made. This is because the introduction of capital is not treated as business revenue in the profit and loss account. The effect will be the same if a business borrows money from a bank.
- Purchases of fixed assets will reduce cash balances, but will have no effect on the profit a company makes. This is because the purchase of assets is not treated as a business cost in the profit and loss account.
- Sales of fixed assets will increase cash balances but will have no effect on profit unless a profit or loss is made on disposal of the asset. This is because the cash from the sale of a fixed asset is not included in business turnover.
- The amount of cash at the end of the year will be different from profit because at the beginning of the year the cash balance is unlikely to be zero. If, at the beginning of the year, the cash balance for a business is £23,000, then the amount of cash a business has at the end of the year will exceed profit by £23,000.

It is possible for a business to trade for many years without making a profit. For example, Oxford Biomedica, a biopharmaceuticals company, began trading in 1995 and has never made a profit. The company survives because it has been able to generate cash. Extra cash has been introduced by shareholders on several occasions (a total of £117 million over the life of the company). In 2006 the company lost £17.62 million. However, the company had £33 million in liquid assets – including about £8 million in cash.

On the other hand it is possible for a profitable business to collapse if it runs out of cash. This is likely to happen if a business has to meet some substantial unexpected expenditure or if a bad debt occurs.

KEYTERMS

Gross profit – total sales revenue or turnover minus cost of sales, the direct costs of production.
Gross profit margin or mark-up – gross profit expressed as a percentage of turnover.
Net profit – total sales revenue or turnover minus cost of sales and overheads.
Net profit margin – net profit expressed as a percentage of turnover.
Profit margins – profit expressed as a percentage of turnover.
Return on capital – the amount of profit expressed as a percentage of the capital invested in a business.

KNOWLEDGE

1. How reliable is the size of profit as a performance indicator?
2. Explain the difference between net profit and gross profit.
3. What does an increase in the net profit margin tell a business?
4. Why would an investor expect a greater return on capital when investing in a business compared with depositing money in a bank?
5. What might be a negative impact of raising price to improve the net profit margin?
6. State two ways in which a business can lower costs.
7. State two reasons why profit and cash may not be the same in a business.

Case Study: *Compton Foods*

Compton Foods is a food-processing company. It buys fresh fruit and vegetables from farmers and produces a wide range of packaged products, including mangetout, beans, baby carrots, mushrooms and bean sprouts. It adds value to some products by slicing and dicing fruit and vegetables before packing. It also produces variety packs where several vegetables or mixed vegetables are combined in the same pack. All of Compton Foods' products are sold to supermarkets in the south of England.

The processing plant is located in Reading. Around 50 people are employed in the plant, most of whom are unskilled. In 2006, the company's shareholders provided an injection of fresh capital. £300,000 was raised to pay for a computerised packing machine and the introduction of new shift patterns. Unfortunately, this resulted in seven staff being laid off, affecting the relationship between the owners and the workers. The workers benefited financially from the new shift patterns, but they resented their colleagues being laid off. This was the first time in the history of the company that staff had been made redundant. A worker representative said 'Working here will never be the same. There used to be an atmosphere of a family company, but that's all changed now. The company is dominated by the accountants.'

Table 4: Financial information for Compton Foods

	2004	2005	2006	2007 (£)
Turnover	2,440,000	2,820,000	3,190,000	3,210,000
Net profit	235,000	242,000	246,000	331,000
Capital invested	1,500,000	1,500,000	1,500,000	1,800,000

(a) Calculate the net profit margins for the four years. (8 marks)
(b) Using this case an example, explain why the size of profit might be misleading when measuring the performance of a business. (6 marks)
(c) How might you account for the changes in the net profit margin between 2006 and 2007? (8 marks)
(d) At the end of the trading year in 2007, Compton Foods had

£378,000 in the bank. Explain the difference between cash and profit for the year. (8 marks)
(e) Calculate the returns on capital between 2006 and 2007. (8 marks)
(f) Do you think the measures taken to improve the performance of the company were worthwhile? (12 marks)

Organisational structures

Each business has its own ORGANISATIONAL STRUCTURE or BUSINESS STRUCTURE. The structure is the way in which positions within the business are arranged. It is often know as the **internal structure** or FORMAL ORGANISATION of the business.

The organisational structure of the business defines:
- the workforce roles of employees and their job titles;
- the route through which decisions are made;
- who is responsible and who is accountable to whom, and for what activities;
- the relationship between positions in a business;
- how employees communicate with each other and how information is passed on.

Different businesses tend to have different objectives, relationships and ways in which decisions are made. So they may have different structures. But there may also be some similarities. For example, small businesses are likely to have simple structures. Larger businesses are often divided into departments with managers.

Structure is important to all businesses. It helps them to divide work and co-ordinate activities to achieve objectives. But it may be more important for larger businesses. For example, a two person plumbing business is likely to have fewer problems deciding 'who does what' than a business operating in many countries.

One method of organising a business is where managers put people together to work effectively based on their skills and abilities. The structure is 'built up' or it 'develops' as a result of the employees of the business. In contrast a structure could be created first, with all appropriate workforce roles outlined, and then people employed to fill them. It has been suggested that the entrepreneur Richard Branson worked out a complete organisation structure for his Virgin Atlantic airline before setting up the company and then recruited the 102 people needed to fill all the positions.

Workforce roles

The positions in an organisation will have particular workloads and jobs allocated to them.

Directors Directors are appointed to run the business in the interest of its owners. In smaller businesses, owners may also be directors. But in larger businesses owned by shareholders, for example, they may be different. Directors are in overall charge of activities in an organisation. They meet, as the **Board of Directors**, to make major decisions that will affect the owners. Some directors, known as executive directors, will be involved in the running of a business. Non-executive directors may play little part in its running. The **managing director** (MD) will have overall responsibility for the organisation and have AUTHORITY over specific directors, such as the **finance** or **marketing director**.

Managers Managers are responsible for controlling or organising within the business. They often make day-to-day decisions about the running of the business. The sales manager, for example, would have responsibility for sales in the business and be responsible to the marketing director. Businesses often have **departmental** managers, such as the marketing, human

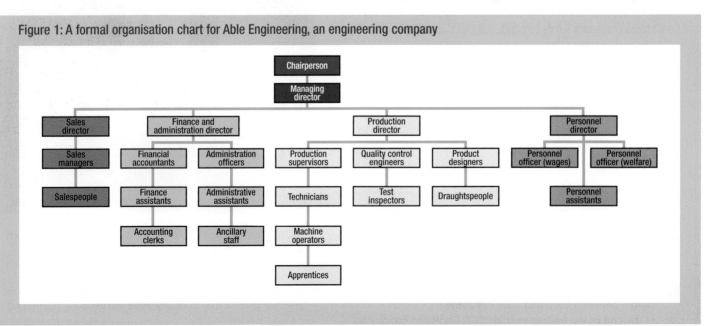

Figure 1: A formal organisation chart for Able Engineering, an engineering company

resources, finance and production manager. There may also be **regional** managers, organising the business in areas of a country or **branch** managers, organising particular branches or stores.

Team leaders Team leaders are members of a team whose role is to resolve issues between team members and co-ordinate team efforts so that the team works effectively. A team leader may be part of a permanent cell production team or a team set up for a particular job, such as investigating staff morale. A team leader may also take responsibility for representing the views of a team to the next higher reporting level, for example to report the findings of a market research team.

Supervisors Supervisors monitor and regulate the work in their assigned or delegated area, for example stock supervisor or payroll supervisor. Supervisors may be given some of the roles of managers, but at a lower level. Their roles in this case may be to hire, discipline, promote, punish or reward.

Professionals These are positions for staff with high levels of qualifications and experience. The job roles are likely to involve a degree of decision making and responsibility for ensuring that task are carried out effectively to a high standard. Examples might include doctors, architects, stockbrokers, product designers, chefs and accountants.

Operatives These are positions for skilled workers who are involved in the production process or service provision. They carry out the instructions of managers or supervisors. In their own area of activity they may have to ensure targets are met and tasks are carried out effectively. Examples of operatives in business might include staff in:

- production, for example assembling a car or manufacturing furniture;
- warehousing, for example checking invoices against goods and ensuring effective deliveries;
- IT, for example giving technical support for machinery.

General staff There is a variety of positions in business which are carried out by staff with non-specific skills. They follow instructions given by superiors to carry out particular tasks and are an essential part of the production process or service provision. Examples might include checkout staff and shelf stackers in supermarkets, cleaners and receptionists in offices. They might also include general jobs on a farm or building site, such as cleaning out.

Although there may be similar generic job roles, there will be differences between organisations in the precise nature of these roles, relationships between various job roles, how they are managed and how decisions are made.

Organisation charts

Businesses often produce ORGANISATION CHARTS. These

Figure 2: Different chains of command and spans of control

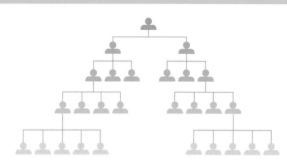

(a) A long chain of command and a narrow span of control. A production department may look like this. One manager is helped by a few assistant managers, each responsible for supervisors. These supervisors are responsible for skilled workers, who are in charge of a group of semi-skilled workers. Close supervision is needed to make sure quality is maintained. This is sometimes referred to as a tall organisational structure.

(b) A short chain of command and a wide span of control. A higher or further education department may look like this, with a 'head' of department, a few senior staff and many lecturing staff. Staff will want a degree of independence. This is sometimes referred to as a flat organisational structure.

illustrate the structure of the business and the workforce roles of people employed with the business. Figure 1 shows a 'traditional' type of chart. It is a chart for an engineering firm, Able Engineering. It illustrates the formal relationship between different workforce roles and people in the business. Why do businesses draw such charts?

- To spot communication flow problems. An organisation chart indicates how employees are linked to other employees in the business. If information is not received, the business can find where the communication breakdown has occurred by tracing the communication chain along the chart.
- Organisation charts help individuals see their position in a business. This can help them appreciate the responsibilities that have been delegated to them, who has authority over them and who they are accountable to.
- Organisation charts allow firms to pinpoint areas where specialists are needed. For example, in Figure 1 Able Engineering recognises it needs designers and draughtspeople as part of the production 'team'.
- Organisation charts show how different sections of the firm relate to each other. For example, the chart for Able

Engineering shows the relationship between salespeople and technicians. They are both at the same level in the hierarchy, but work in different departments and are responsible to different managers.

Simply producing an organisation chart is of limited use to a business. The business will only achieve its objectives if it understands the relationships between employees and other parts of the business.

Key elements of organisational structures

Chain of command The HIERARCHY in a business is the levels of management in a business, from the lowest to the highest rank. It shows the CHAIN OF COMMAND within the organisation - the way authority is organised. Orders pass down the levels and information passes up. Businesses must also consider the number of links or levels in the chain of command. R. Townsend, in his book *Up the Organisation*, estimated that each extra level of management in the hierarchy reduced the effectiveness of communication by about 25 per cent. No rules are laid down on the most effective number of links in the chain. However, businesses generally try to keep chains as short as possible.

Span of control The SPAN OF CONTROL refers to the number of subordinates working under a superior or manager. In other words, if one production manager has ten subordinates his span of control is ten. Henri Fayol argued that the span of control should be between three and six because:
- there should be tight managerial control from the top of the business;
- there are physical and mental limitations to any single manager's ability to control people and activities.

A narrow span of control has the advantage for a firm of tight control and close supervision. It also allows better co-ordination of subordinates' activities. In addition, it gives managers time to think and plan without having to be burdened with too many day-to-day problems. A narrow span also ensures better communication with subordinates, who are sufficiently small in number to allow this to occur.

A wide span of control, however, offers greater decision-making authority for subordinates and may improve job satisfaction In addition, there are likely to be lower costs involved in supervision. Figure 2 shows two organisation charts. In the first (a), there is a long chain of command, but a narrow span of control. The second (b) shows a wide span, but a short chain.

Authority and responsibility Employees in the hierarchy will have RESPONSIBILITY and authority. However, these terms do not mean the same thing. Responsibility involves being accountable or being required to justify an action. So, for example, managers who are responsible for a department may be asked to justify poor performance to the board of directors. The personnel department may be responsible for employing workers. If a new worker was unable to do a particular job, they would be asked to explain why.

Authority, on the other hand, is the ability to carry out the task. For example, it would make no sense asking an office worker to pay company debts if she did not have the authority to sign cheques. Employees at lower levels of the hierarchy have less responsibility and authority than those further up. However, it may be possible for a superior to delegate (pass down) authority to a subordinate, eg a manager to an office worker, but retain responsibility. Increasingly, businesses are realising the benefits of delegating both authority and responsibility.

Line, staff and functional authority Line, staff and functional authority are terms used to describe the type of relationship that managers may have with others in the hierarchy.

Question 1.

Figure 3 shows part of an organisation chart for a UK engineering company.

Figure 3: Part of an organisation chart of a UK engineering company

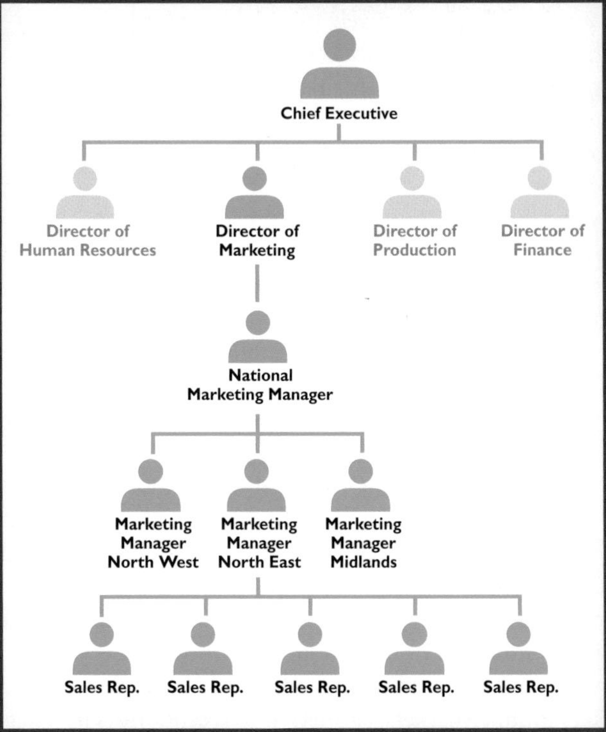

(a) The company sells into regional markets. How can this be seen from the chart?

(b) Describe the chain of command from Chief Executive to UK sales representative.

(c) How large is the span of control of the Marketing Manager?

(d) Who is immediately subordinate to the Director of Marketing?

(e) The Chief Executive is considering reducing the number of sales reps from five to three. How might this affect the Marketing Managers?

Question 2.

During 2007 BP aimed to cut overheads and re-energise the oil and gas company. Tony Hayward, the chief executive, insisted the overall strategy was not about 'cost reduction and cull', but about a radical change in culture. There were no specific numbers for how many staff would be cut, but Mr Hayward said it 'could be thousands over several years'.

The BP boss sent a message to his 100,000 staff outlining other plans to streamline the business into two basic units. This would be exploration and production on one side and refining and marketing on the other, similar to the type of structure at Exxon. The third segment, gas, power and renewables, is to be incorporated mainly into the other two.

A city analysts said, 'I think it is really good. This is copying the Exxon model of keeping things simple and ensuring unit managers are given responsibility but held accountable too.'

Mr Hayward promised that in future, corporate infrastructure would be 'rigorously' reviewed and up to four layers of management would be shed. 'Managers will be listening more acutely, particularly to frontline staff. We will make sure individuals are fully accountable for things they control,' he said.

Source: adapted from www.guardian.co.uk, 12.10.2007.

(a) Explain how the changes might affect:
(i) employees at the businesses; (ii) management at the businesses; (iii) clients of the business.
(b) Discuss to what extent BP might experience resistance from managers and employees.

- **Line authority** is usual in a hierarchy. It shows the authority that a manager has over a subordinate. In Figure 1, the production director would have line authority over the designers. Communication will flow down from the superior to the subordinate in the chain of command. The advantage of this is that a manager can allocate work and control subordinates, who have a clear understanding of who is giving them instructions. The manager can also delegate authority to others if they feel this will make decision making more effective. In large organisations, the chain of command can be very long. This means that instructions given by those at the top of the chain of command may take time before they are carried out at a lower level.
- **Staff authority** might be when a manager or department in a business has a function within another department, for example, giving specialist advice. A marketing manager may give advice to the production department based on market research into a new product. Personnel managers have responsibilities for personnel matters in all departments. Although the specialist can give advice, they have no authority to make decisions in the other department.
- **Functional authority** is when a specialist has the authority to make a line manager accept his or her advice. It is different from staff authority, where the specialist can only advise. For example, the finance manager may have overall authority over the budget holder in the marketing department.

Problems may occur in a business if people do not understand where authority and responsibility rest. This means that managers must know whether their authority is line, staff or functional. Unfortunately, this can lead to friction. Line managers are sometimes thought of as 'first class citizens' and staff managers are thought of as costly 'overheads' who are not contributing anything of worth to the organisation. Also, the authority of functional managers is not accepted by line managers at times.

Delegation Managers are increasingly being asked to carry out strategic activities that affect the whole business. This has resulted in the need to DELEGATE activities for certain tasks to employees further down the hierarchy. Delegation can provide benefits to a business, as explained in the next section. When is delegation likely to be effective?

- Researchers such as Spetzer (1992) have suggested that employees need to be empowered in order to make effective decisions. They need to be given self-confidence and control of what they do.
- If managers only delegate when they are overloaded, subordinates may be resentful.
- Delegation requires planning. Managers must be clear about what needs to be done. Instead of freeing time, poor delegation may take up managers' time as they try to correct problems.
- Managers must take time to explain delegated tasks clearly. Employees may waste time or make mistakes because of lack of information. Telling subordinates why the work is important helps to create shared values.
- Allow participation. It is useful to discuss the task with those to whom it has been delegated. Subordinates will then know from the start what the task will include. It also helps managers to decide if delegation is appropriate. A person may feel they do not have the skills to carry out the task.
- The employee given a delegated task should also be given the authority and responsibility to carry it out. Managers must tell others in the business that the delegated person is acting on his or her behalf. This will avoid difficulties, such as the questioning of authority.
- Managers must avoid interfering with delegated tasks.
- Delegated tasks should be given to suitable employees. It would be inappropriate to delegate a marketing task to an employee in personnel. Employees must also have the training to carry out the task.
- Provide support and resources. If an employee is delegated a task without suitable support and resources this could lead to anxiety, frustration and the task being badly done.

Research has shown that when factors like these are taken into account, delegation was four times as likely to be successful.

Different forms of business structure

Despite the variety of formal business organisation that exists, there are four main types of structure most often found.

The entrepreneurial structure In this type of business structure, all decisions are made centrally. There are few collective decisions and a great reliance on 'key' workers. It is often found in businesses where decisions have to be made quickly, such as newspaper editing. Most small businesses also have this type of structure, as illustrated in Figure 4(a). These businesses rely on the expertise of one or two people to make decisions. Decision making is efficient up to a point because:

- decisions can be made quickly;
- subordinates understand to whom they are accountable;
- little consultation is required.

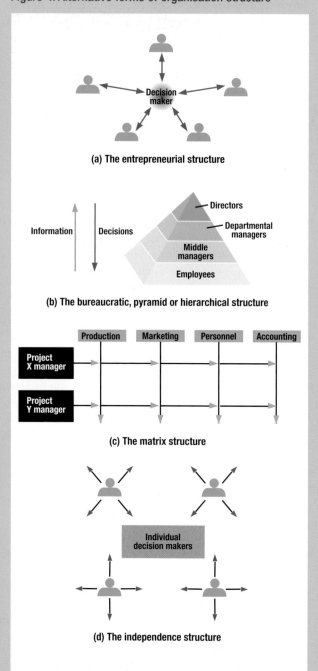

Figure 4: Alternative forms of organisation structure

(a) The entrepreneurial structure

(b) The bureaucratic, pyramid or hierarchical structure

(c) The matrix structure

(d) The independence structure

However, as the business grows, this structure can cause inefficiency as too much of a load is placed on those making decisions.

The bureaucratic, pyramid or hierachical structure This is the traditional hierachical structure for most medium-sized and large businesses and perhaps the most well known. It is illustrated in Figure 4(b). Decision making is shared throughout the business. Employees are each given a role and procedures are laid down which determine their behaviour at work. Specialisation of tasks is possible. This means that a departmental structure, with finance, personnel, production and marketing employees, can be set up. Specialisation may allow the business to enjoy economies of scale. Recently, this type of structure has been criticised for its inability to change and meet new demands.

The matrix structure This emphasises getting people with particular specialist skills together into project teams, as illustrated in Figure 4(c). Individuals within the team have their own responsibility. The matrix structure was developed to overcome some of the problems with the entrepreneurial and bureaucratic structures. Matrix management involves the co-ordinating and support of specialist teams within a matrix structure.

Managers often argue that this is the best way of organising people, because it is based on the expertise and skills of employees and gives scope for people lower down the organisation to use their talents effectively. For example, a project manager looking into the possibility of developing a new product may draw on the expertise of employees with skills in design, research and development, marketing, costing etc. A college running a course for unemployed people may draw on the skills of a number of lecturers in different departments. In this way, a matrix structure can also operate within a business that has a bureaucratic structure. The matrix model fits in with managers who have a Theory Y view of employees It is suggested that this structure improves flexibility and motivation of employees. It has recently lost favour because it often needs expensive support systems, such as extra secretarial and office staff. There may also be problems with co-ordinating a team drawn from different departments and the speed of decision making.

The independence structure This emphasises the individual and is almost a 'non-organisation'. The other three methods put together the contributions of a number of people so that the sum of their efforts is greater than the parts. All efforts are co-ordinated so that the business benefits. The independence structure is a method of providing a support system. Barristers' chambers and doctors' clinics have worked in this way. It is attractive to independent people who are confident of their ability to be successful. This form of organisation tends to be unsuitable for most types of business because of the lack of control and co-ordination.

Question 3.

The Manchester Film Association is an SME in the centre of the city's 'cultural quarter'. Its main activities are video, film and multimedia production. It employs nine full-time staff. Mike joined the company six months ago. He recently graduated, but has little work experience. However, he has proven so far in the work that he has done for clients to be innovative. He often has ideas that no-one else has considered. Shoaib has worked for the business for 15 years. He has built up considerable production and post-production skills. Lisa had previously set up her own website design and consultancy operation. She has experience in managing projects, working to deadlines and taking responsibility for clients' requests. The managing director of the business, Paula, has been approached by a fast growing leisure company to produce an innovative multimedia training programme on CD Rom for newly recruited employees. The company wants the programme to be interactive, but it must be ready within two months. Paula decided to ask Mike to look after the project.

Source: adapted from company information.

(a) Explain what type of organisational structure do you think might best reflect the business needs of Manchester Film Association.

Informal business structure

Organisation charts show the formal organisation of a business. However many relationships between employees in business are informal. The INFORMAL BUSINESS STRUCTURE is the network of relationships that develops between members on the basis of their common interests and friendships. These relationships can affect the way a business operates. A study of informal networks in the banking industry, for example, found three types of relationship.

- Advice networks – who depends on who to solve problems and provide information.
- Trust networks – which employees share potential information and back each other up in times of crisis.
- Communication networks – which employees regularly talk to each other on work related matters.

They recommended that businesses use informal structures to solve problems. For example, a study showed that a bank's task force group was unable to find ways of improving the bank's performance. The leader of the task force held a central position in the 'advice network'. Employees relied on her for technical advice. However, she only had one 'trust link' with a colleague. Management did not want to label the group as a failure or embarrass a valued employee by dismissing her as team leader. Instead, it redesigned the task force in line with the informal organisation of the business by adding a person in the trust network to share responsibility for group leadership.

KEYTERMS

Authority – the right to command a situation, a task or an activity.
Chain of command – the way authority and power are passed down in a business.
Delegation – authority (and sometimes responsibility) to pass down from superior to subordinate.
Formal organisation – the relationships between employees and the organisational structure determined by the business, as shown in an organisation chart.
Hierarchy – the order or levels of management of a business, from the lowest to the highest.
Informal business structure – the relationships between employees that are based on the common interests of employees.
Organisation chart – a diagram which illustrates the structure of an organisation.
Organisational or business structure – the way in which a business is organised.
Span of control – the number of subordinates working under a superior.

KNOWLEDGE

1. What are the features of the internal structure of a business?
2. How might an organisation chart be used in a firm's induction programme?
3. Draw a simple organisation chart showing:
   (a) a partnership with two partners and six employees;
   (b) a large company with a board of directors, six departments, and two more levels in the hierarchy.
4. What is meant by a 'wide span of control'?
5. What problems might a 'wide span of control' have for a business?
6. Explain the difference between line, staff and functional authority.
7. What factors influence effective delegation?
8. Why is empowerment important when tasks are delegated?
9. What problems might a matrix structure cause for a business?
10. What type of business might be organised with:
    (a) an entrepreneurial structure;
    (b) an independence structure?
11. Why is it important for businesses to understand their informal business structures?

Case Study: *Avalanche*

Avalanche control operations at the Lake Louise Ski Area have a history spanning nearly 30 years. Lake Louise is in the Banff National Park in Canada. The area currently receives half a million guests per year for skiing, snowboarding and related activities. Safety is a key aspect and part of that relates to the danger of avalanches of snow burying skiers in their wake. The ski resort covers over 17 square kilometres and there are over 100 places where avalanches can occur. In addition, some skiers deliberately go outside the resort area for the thrill of skiing in uncrowded, uncontrolled areas. But this increases the number of potential avalanche areas.

In the 1980s, there were effectively three separate departments working on the mountain. The main responsibility of the Ski Patrol was pre-hospital care for skiers who had accidents. For the Warden/Ski Patrol Avalanche Crew, it was monitoring and controlling avalanches. For the Trail Crew, it was managing the slopes, including putting up fencing. However, there was overlap between the three departments. Members of the Trail Crew, for example, would organise help if they were first on the scene at an accident.

These three departments were then reorganised into one Snow Safety Department. This was partly prompted by budget costs. The previous three departments had over 40 staff in total. The new single department now consisted of just 25 staff. Efficiency gains were possible because staff were used more intensively. In particular, on the mountain, patrollers were expected to perform any of the functions which before had been the main responsibility of just one of the departments.

Under the new structure, shown in Figure 5, a Snow Safety Manager was put in charge of the whole department, answerable to the Area Manager for the ski resort. Beneath the Snow Safety Manager in the hierarchy are three Snow Safety Supervisors. Two of these are Avalanche Forecasters and one is a Patrol Leader. Working under the the Snow Safety Supervisors are four Senior Avalanche Patrollers. Their main duties are as Team Leaders in snow research and avalanche control. In addition, they have become involved in other facets of the department, such as training and acting as roving 'troubleshooters'. They are not scheduled into the daily routine of run checks and accident coverage or to patrol specific areas. In addition, there are five Senior Patrollers and 13 Patrollers who have as their primary responsibilities pre-hospital care and risk management (in the form of run checks and trail work). These 18 people also act as Avalanche Team Members on a rotating basis wherever needed. Generally, between two and five teams are used daily for research and control, depending on conditions.

Adapted from a paper by Mark Klassen, Skiing Louise Ltd, Alberta, Canada.

(a) Explain what is meant by the terms: (i) 'hierarchy'and (3 marks)
    (ii) 'department' (3 marks).
(b) (i) Explain what is the span of control of the Snow Safety Manager shown in Figure 5. (3 marks). (ii) Explain to whom the Patrol Leader, who is one of the three Snow Safety Supervisors, might delegate a task. (3 marks)
(c) Analyse how the change in structure between the 1980s and the 1990s described in the data has affected job roles, responsibilities and communication. (8 marks)
(d) Discuss the possible costs and benefits of delegating greater authority and responsibility further down the hierarchy. (10 marks)

Figure 5: Organisation chart: Snow Safety Department

1 Area Manager

1 Snow Safety Manager

3 Snow Safety Supervisors

4 Senior Avalanche Patrollers

5 Senior Patrollers

13 Patrollers

27 | Measuring the effectiveness of the workforce

Measuring personnel effectiveness

Advocates of human resource management (HRM) claim that the performance of the workforce is enhanced through adopting appropriate personnel policies. In many other areas of business, such as finance or production, there is a large number of possible measures of performance, from sales revenue to profit after tax to output per day. In personnel, there are fewer key measures. Some of these only point indirectly at key variables. For example, it is not possible to measure directly:

- the motivation of a workforce;
- the ability of a workforce to accept and implement change;
- the teamworking capabilities of workers;
- the commitment of workers to the business;
- the contribution of £1 spent on personnel such as higher pay or spending on training to profit.

However, there are a few measures which can be used, including labour productivity, absenteeism rates, labour turnover, working days lost for health and safety reasons and wastage rates.

Labour productivity

Labour productivity is defined as output per worker. As a formula:

$$\text{Labour productivity} = \frac{\text{Total output (per period of time)}}{\text{Average number of employees (per period of time)}}$$

Labour productivity is an important measure of the efficiency of a workforce. For example, if there are two teams of workers in a factory, each with identical equipment and the same number of workers, then the team with the highest productivity could be identified as the most effective team.

Figures for labour productivity need to be used with caution. For example, differences in labour productivity between factories or plants may be accounted for by differences in equipment used rather than the efficiency of the workforce. A plant with newer equipment is likely to have higher labour productivity than one with old equipment. Equally, productivity differs widely between processes within a business and between businesses in different industries. A highly automated section of a factory is likely to have much higher labour productivity than a labour-intensive packing section in the same factory using little capital equipment. Manufacturing industry may have a higher average labour productivity than service industries simply because more capital is used per employee in manufacturing.

A business wishing to improve the labour productivity of groups of workers can adopt a number of strategies.

- Improving the capital equipment with which they work.
- Changing the way in which workers are employed, for example, moving from an assembly line production system to a cell production system.
- Disappointing labour productivity may be due to a lack of training on the part of workers. Increased training may therefore raise productivity.
- Changing the reward system may increase motivation and commitment and so improve productivity. There are many other ways that motivation may be increased. These include changing the structure of the business and devolving decision making power down the chain of command.

Increasing labour productivity is generally assumed to increase the competitiveness of a business. Higher labour productivity should drive down costs, allowing a business either to lower its prices and so gain higher sales, or to keep its prices the same but increase its profit margins.

However, businesses sometimes find that they become less competitive despite increasing their labour productivity. This may occur for a number of reasons.

- Rival businesses may increase their productivity at an even faster rate.
- New rival businesses may set up which pay considerably lower wages. Many UK manufacturing businesses have become less competitive over the past ten years due to the emergence of competition from low wage, low cost businesses in the Far East and eastern Europe.
- Other factors apart from cost may change adversely for a business. For example, a rival business may bring out a far better new product. However, productive the workforce and however low the cost, customers may prefer to buy the new product rather than a cheaper old product.

Absenteeism

Absenteeism is a problem for all businesses for a number of reasons.

- Staff who are absent often claim to be ill. The business then, in most cases, has to pay sick pay.
- If temporary staff are brought in to cover for absent staff, this leads to increased costs. Equally, costs will increase if permanent staff have to work overtime and are paid at higher rates than their basic rate of pay.
- Output may suffer if workers are expected to cover for sick colleagues or if temporary staff are not as productive as the absent workers.
- Prolonged absences can lead to major disruption if the worker is key to a particular area of work or a new project.
- If production is delayed or there are problems with quality, customers can be lost.

Question 1.

The NHS Executive has introduced the labour productivity index for all NHS trusts in England. The index is a measure of the value of the output per trust employee. It is calculated by multiplying each type of activity, eg inpatients, outpatients, health visitor contacts, by its average cost, adding all these costs together and dividing the total by the number of employees in the trust. The index allows trusts to compare their labour productivity with others. It may also be a useful tool in contract negotiations. Theoretically, a trust with a labour productivity index of 6000 can be interpreted not only as being more productive than a trust with an index of 3000, but of being twice as productive.

This simple interpretation however, is not without difficulties. Major areas of activity, such as research and diagnostic services, are excluded, distorting the index. It is also assumed that those activities included are the same in each trust. This does not take into account variations in the quality or effectiveness of different contacts. Another problem is that the effort (cost, labour, etc) to produce one 'unit' of activity will vary across trusts and will depend on patient characteristics such as age or complexity. Further, only full-time staff are included but many trusts subcontract work.

Source: adapted from *British Medical Journal*, 2006.

(a) How is the productivity of employees in the NHS being measured?
(b) Explain how the measurement of employees' productivity can benefit NHS trusts.
(c) Discuss how useful the labour productivity index will be in measuring NHS employees' productivity.

- Absenteeism can be demotivating to staff left to cope with the problems.
- The higher the rate of absenteeism, the more likely it is that workers will report ill. This is because a culture of absenteeism will develop where it becomes acceptable for workers to take extra days holiday by reporting in sick.

The RATE OF ABSENTEEISM or ABSENTEEISM RATE or ABSENTEE RATE can be calculated by dividing the number of staff absent by the total number of staff employed. The rate is expressed as a percentage. It can be calculated as a daily rate using the formula:

$$\frac{\text{Number of staff absent on a day}}{\text{Total number of staff employed}} \times 100\%$$

For example, if 1,000 staff are employed, and 30 are absent on a particular day, then the rate of absenteeism for that day is 3 per cent (100% x 30 ÷ 1,000). If the rate of absenteeism for a year is calculated, the total number of staff days lost through absenteeism must by divided by the number of staff days that should have been worked over the year. This is calculated using the formula:

$$\frac{\text{Total number of staff absence days over the year}}{\text{Total number of staff days that should have been worked}} \times 100\%$$

For example, assume 6,000 staff days were lost through absence. There were 500 staff, each of whom should have worked 240 days during the year. So the total number of staff days that should have been worked was 120,000 (500 x 240). The rate of absenteeism was therefore 5 per cent (100% x 6,000 ÷ 120,000).

Rates of absenteeism can be calculated for a business as a whole and compared to industry averages or national averages. They can also be compared between one part of a business and another or compared over time. Differences in rates of absenteeism occur for a number of reasons.

- Small businesses tend to have lower rates of absenteeism than larger businesses. Arguably this is because there is much more commitment and feeling of teamwork in a small business than in a large business. Workers in large businesses can feel that no-one will suffer if they take a day off work and so absenteeism is acceptable.
- Health and safety is a factor. Businesses which have good health and safety procedures will tend to suffer less illness-related absenteeism than those with poor procedures. Equally, some jobs are inherently more dangerous to health than others and so absenteeism is more likely.
- The nature of the tasks given to workers is another factor. Tasks which are fragmented and repetitive lead to low job satisfaction and demotivation. This encourages workers to report sick. Workers in jobs which are interesting and rewarding tend to have lower absentee rates.
- The culture of a workplace can cause absenteeism. Where workers are overworked, where there is a climate of

intimidation and bullying by superiors of subordinates, and where the needs of workers are ignored, work-related stress becomes much more common. Workers off through stress are a particular problem because they often take months off work at a time.

- Stress-related illness is also more common where workers are oversupervised and feel that they are not trusted by their superiors to accomplish tasks.
- Workers who feel that they are grossly underpaid are more likely to take time off work. They see it as compensation for the lack of monetary reward they receive. Low pay is also a demotivator and so contributes to absenteeism.

Businesses can adopt a variety of methods to reduce absenteeism. Some assume that absenteeism is mainly caused by inappropriate or a lack of human resource management policies. Problems such as lack of commitment, low motivation, bullying, oversupervision and perceptions of low pay can be tackled through methods such as more teamwork, devolving power down the chain of command, more democratic leadership, better reward systems and policies which make bullying and harassment at work a major disciplinary offence. Health and safety issues can be addressed through the rigourous application of a well thought out health and safety policy. Adoption of lean production techniques are also likely to improve absenteeism rates.

The UK government in the early 2000s stressed the importance of a WORK LIFE BALANCE in dealing with a number of HR issues including absenteeism. Absenteeism can be caused by conflicts between work and family commitments, or work and leisure goals. A parent may phone in sick when in fact he or she is having to stay at home to look after his or her ill eight year old. Or a worker may phone in sick on a Monday morning because he can't face work after a weekend's activities. The solution is for more flexible working patterns. For example, workers may be able to take a few hours off work if they work them at some other time in the week or the month. Or workers may have a number of individual days holiday a year which can be taken without giving notice. Or a worker may have the right permanently to the number of hours worked per week, changing for example from full time to three days a week.

On the other hand, a scientific management approach would tend towards the introduction of systems of rewards and punishments. Cutting down the number of days when staff can claim sick pay is one measure. Another is for superiors to monitor closely staff who are absent. Telephoning them or even visiting them in their homes when they are off sick can be effective in deterring absenteeism. Being prepared to sack staff who abuse the system can also be an important deterrent to the rest of the workforce. Some employers offer bonuses to workers who have not had time off work due to illness. A few even offer all their staff a number of paid days off work each year which can be taken when staff don't feel like going into work or have problems with childcare arrangements.

Another policy which is frequently advocated is 'back to work' interviews. Any member of staff who has been absent has to be interviewed by a superior about why they were absent. This can be seen from a human relations school perspective as supportive of the worker. Their superior cares for them enough to want to know why they were away. Equally it can be judged from a scientific management school perspective. The superior

Question 2.

Royal Mail's cure for Britain's £1.75bn problem of absenteeism is simple - a Ford car and holiday vouchers. Its incentive scheme has improved attendance levels by more than 10 per cent in six months, equivalent to 1,000 extra staff. It is so pleased that it is extending the scheme for 12 months. Under the initial scheme staff who worked for six months without a day off work sick were entered for a prize draw. More than half of the 170,000 employees at Royal Mail and Parcelforce Worldwide qualified. Thirty-seven won a new Ford Focus car, worth £12,000 each and 75 won the £2,000 holiday vouchers. Even the 90,000 who qualified for the draw but missed out got a £150 holiday voucher.

Royal Mail will not say how much the scheme cost, but insists it makes financial and commercial sense. 'The employees like it, as a company we like it – we have 1,000 more people every day than we would otherwise have had if nothing had changed. It benefits the customers too because good attendance goes hand in glove with good quality of service', said a Royal Mail spokesperson. Some have estimated the costs at £1.9m before allowing for any discounts.

The company denies it is putting pressure on genuinely ill workers to turn up for work. Its people and operational development director, said 'We must support and reward postmen and women. They deserve it. They do a demanding job to a high standard, day in and day out, in all weathers.'

The Communication Workers Union had a more old-fashioned explanation for the fall in absenteeism – better pay and conditions. The union's deputy general secretary said: 'Giveaways are not the reason why attendance levels have improved and they are certainly not a substitute for continuing to invest in our members' overall employment package.'

Source: adapted from *The Guardian*, 26.4.2005.

(a) Why is it important for the Royal Mail to measure absenteeism rates?
(b) Examine the advantages and disadvantages of the scheme to reduce absenteeism at Royal Mail for (i) the business and (ii) its employees.
(c) Discuss whether the scheme is likely to be more effective than 'better pay and conditions'.

is checking up on the worker to see whether the absence was genuine.

Labour turnover

Labour or staff turnover is another measure of personnel effectiveness. **Labour turnover** is the proportion of staff leaving a business over a period of time. It is measured by the formula:

$$\text{Labour turnover} = \frac{\text{Number of staff leaving over a period of time}}{\text{Average number of staff in post during the period}} \times 100\%$$

For example, if 20 staff left over a year and there were on average 40 on the staff, then the staff turnover would be 50 per cent (100% x 20 ÷ 40).

As with other measures of personnel performance, labour turnover differs from department to department within a business, from business to business within an industry and from industry to industry within an economy. Relatively high labour turnover is caused by a number of factors.

- Relatively low pay leads to higher labour turnover as workers leave to get better paid jobs.
- Relatively few training and promotion opportunities will encourage workers to leave their current jobs.
- Poor working conditions, low job satisfaction, bullying and harassment in the workplace are other factors.
- Some businesses are relatively poor at selecting and recruiting the right candidates for posts. Where workers are ill suited to their jobs, there is more chance that they will leave relatively quickly.
- In a recession, labour turnover tends to fall as the number of vacancies falls and workers become worried that if they leave their job without having got another one to go to, they will become part of the long-term unemployed. In a boom, when there might be labour shortages, there are far more vacancies and so labour turnover tends to rise.

Relatively high labour turnover is usually seen as a problem for businesses for a number of reasons.

- Recruiting new staff can be costly.
- It takes time for new staff to become familiar with their roles and the way in which the business operates. High labour turnover is likely to reduce the human process advantage of a business.
- Larger companies may put on induction programmes which further adds to costs.
- If the post is filled internally, there may be training needs for the worker who gets the job.

However, some labour turnover is usually beneficial to a business.

- New staff can bring in fresh ideas and experience from their work with other businesses.
- Some workers may be ineffective and need to be encouraged to leave. Getting rid of ineffective staff leads to

labour turnover.

- If a business is shrinking in size, reducing the size of the workforce will lead to higher labour turnover.
- Where a business pays low wages, or where conditions of work are poor, it may be more profitable to have a constant turnover of staff rather than raise wages or improve conditions of work.

Businesses can attempt to reduce their labour turnover if they see it as a problem. Higher pay and better working conditions might be one strategy. Another might be offering better internal promotion prospects to workers. Better selection procedures would be appropriate if the problem is poor recruiting. Effective procedures against bullying and harassment could help too. For senior workers, a business might offer bonuses in the future (often in the form of share option schemes) which can only be claimed if they are still employed by the business at the point in time.

Health and safety

The safety of the working environment can be measured in a number of different ways. For example, health and safety could be measured by the number of working days lost through accidents or injuries per thousand employees over a time period.

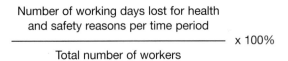

$$\frac{\text{Number of working days lost for health and safety reasons per time period}}{\text{Total number of workers}} \times 100\%$$

For example, if there were 300 days lost through accidents or injury over a year and the workforce were 6,000, then the number of working days lost per thousand employees would be (300 ÷ 6,000) x 1,000, which is 50.

Another measure relates working days lost to the total number of working days that could have been worked over the period, expressed as a percentage.

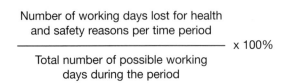

$$\frac{\text{Number of working days lost for health and safety reasons per time period}}{\text{Total number of possible working days during the period}} \times 100\%$$

For example, if 2,000 days are lost due to health and safety reasons over a year, and the number of possible working days for the workforce over the period was 100,000, then the health and safety ratio is 2 per cent (100% x 2,000 ÷ 100,000).

A poor health and safety record may occur for a number of reasons.

- Equipment used may be dangerous. For example, it might be poorly maintained or be too old.
- The working environment itself may be dangerous. For example, unsafe levels of dangerous gases or chemicals may be found in the atmosphere in a factory building.
- There may be a lack of safety equipment. For example, workers should perhaps be wearing safety hats, but these

are not provided by the employer.

- Workers may not receive sufficient health and safety training.
- The business may not enforce its own health and safety procedures. It may turn a 'blind eye' to abuses because otherwise production would be slowed down.
- Work may be contracted out to self-employed workers who prefer to disregard time-consuming health and safety procedures in order to earn more money. In the building industry, the widespread use of subcontractors is sometimes given as a reason for a poor health and safety record.

Improving a poor health and safety record may be achieved by:

- increasing expenditure on buildings and equipment to bring them up to health and safety standards;
- drawing up an appropriate set of health and safety policies and procedures;
- training all staff to ensure that they understand these policies and procedures and can carry them out;
- strictly enforcing health and safety policies, putting safety above profit and output.

Businesses which have poor health and safety records are either poorly organised and managed, or deliberately exploiting the situation to cut their costs. Lower health and safety standards is one way in which some businesses can gain a competitive advantage. One of the criticisms of globalisation is that producers in Third World countries operate under much less stringent health and safety standards than in the UK. Hence, it could be argued that they have an 'unfair' competitive advantage.

A poor health and safety record can be a disadvantage to a business.

- Poor health and safety standards are likely to lead to the demotivation of staff. Their basic needs are being threatened.
- Such businesses are liable to have their operations closed down or be open to prosecution by health and safety inspectors. Equally, they are open to being sued by workers involved in accidents or by customers if products are put at risk. At worst, such a business could be forced to close because of this issue.
- Staff absences due to accidents may have the same costs as absences due to illness, as explained in the last section. Businesses may also be fined or sued as a result of accidents.
- A poor health and safety record could contribute towards

giving a business a poor reputation with customers and so it could affect sales. In the Third World, suppliers to some Western multinationals have to conform to basic standards to win and retain orders. This is because the reputation of the multinationals in their First World markets can be at stake.

KEY TERMS

Rate of absenteeism or absenteeism rate or absentee rate – the number of staff absent as a percentage of the total number of staff employed. It can be calculated for different periods of time, ie daily rates or annual rates.
Work life balance – the relationship between time spent at work and time spent away from work or the time spent at work as a proportion of total time.

KNOWLEDGE

1. How is labour productivity calculated?
2. A component manufacturer makes 10,000 metal washers with ten workers. After employing five extra workers it makes 20,000. Calculate the effect on labour productivity.
3. List four ways in which a business may improve labour productivity.
4. How can a business calculate its rate of absenteeism?
5. List five reasons why rates of absenteeism are different in different industries.
6. State three ways in which a business might reduce rates of absenteeism.
7. What is the relationship between absenteeism and a work life balance?
8. A business finds that its labour turnover falls from 20% to 15%. Should it be concerned?
9. List four factors that might lead to high labour turnover.
10. State five problems of high labour turnover for a business.
11. State two formulae that a business might use to measure its health and safety record.
12. List five factors that may cause a business to have a poor health and safety record.
13. State five possible problems for a business with a poor record of health and safety.

Case Study: *Supermarkets' labour turnover and absenteeism*

First there were duvet days for staff temporarily 'sick' of work - offered by companies trying to reduce absenteeism by gentle persuasion. Then there was time off for everything from a religious festival to a child's first day at school. In 2004 Tesco, opted for the stick approach, cutting sick pay in some of its stores and tested other schemes in an attempt to cut rates of absenteeism. Tesco spokesperson Jonathan Church said that absenteeism '...impacts on our business as well as creating more work for people in the store. These trials are about encouraging people to use planned absence whenever they can. If they need to take little Johnnie to the dentist, then we will bend over backwards to make that possible.'

One scheme, introduced in two stores in the south, meant workers got no pay for the first three days off sick, but after the fourth day would get paid again with compensation for the first three days. That could encourage people to go sick for a whole week. Other options are to offer staff more holiday allowance up front, but reduce it every time they take a day off sick. Tesco said there are fewer absences in stores testing the schemes. 'Our intention is not to penalise people who are genuinely ill. It is to discourage people from taking those odd days.'

Asda offers incentives such as prizes to reward low absenteeism. 'It might be a week's extra holiday or a weekend break or vouchers. It has really helped bring absenteeism down because people think hard about whether they really need to be off.' The company already has 'carers leave' and 'first day/half day' leave for parents taking children to school.

Sick leave costs British companies around £11 billion every year through 166 million lost working days. Stress-related absence is rising, according to the Health and Safety Executive. This has prompted organisations like The Work Foundation for businesses to look more carefully at how they treat staff and the work environment.

In 2003, seasonal workers at Asda at Christmas were entitled to benefits and job security equivalent to those enjoyed by their full-time colleagues, after the supermarket created 10 000 new permanent positions for contract workers. The new 'seasonal squad' would have the same status as permanent staff but with a contract to work an annual, rather than weekly, number of hours. They could work for as little as ten weeks of the year. The contracts would cover Christmas, Easter and the school summer holidays and cover jobs such as greeters, porters, checkout operatives and warehouse workers. 'We recognise that people are looking for flexibility across the working year, not just the working week' said Caroline Massingham, Asda retail people director. 'If you're one of the many people that want to balance long periods of leave with a fulfilling job, the options are limited'. Asda hopes the initiative would encourage more over 50s to join. The supermarket said that since actively recruiting older workers, it has seen absence levels drop, customer service levels rise and labour turnover fall. The flexible working package includes one week's leave for new grandparents, five days leave for IVF treatment and up to two years for a career break. Asda is hoping to make huge savings from the initiative by reducing turnover, as it has spent around £3,500 per person in recruitment costs.

Source: adapted from *The Observer*, 16.5.2004.

(a) (i) Explain why supermarkets may want to reduce rates of absenteeism and labour turnover. (8 marks)

(ii) Examine the factors that might affect rates of absenteeism and labour turnover at supermarkets. (12 marks)

(b) Evaluate the methods used by supermarkets in the article to reduce rates of absenteeism and labour turnover. (20 marks)

Stages of recruitment

Successful businesses are able to develop an effective workforce. The first stage in this process is **recruitment** and **selection**. In a small business, it may seem obvious to the employer what will be required of a new recruit. The employer may put in an advertisement for, say, an 'administrative assistant' and explain at the interview what the job entails. However, where the business is larger, and if there is a personnel department, more formal procedures are likely to be used.

Job description

First, a JOB DESCRIPTION will be drawn up. This gives the title of the job. It is a statement of the tasks to be undertaken and responsibilities of the employee holding that job. The job description may describe the employee's place in the hierarchy of the business. Working conditions may also be specified, such as rates of pay or holiday entitlements. An example of a job description is shown in Figure 1. In many cases, the job description for the new recruit will simply be the job description of the person leaving the job. Large businesses, where many employees do the same job, such as a sales assistant or production line worker, might have a common job description for a particular job.

Job descriptions tell the new employee what is expected of them. It can be used when appraising the performance of a worker. If the worker fails to perform satisfactorily and is threatened with dismissal, it can also be used by the employer as evidence to support the dismissal.

The details about the job included in job description can be found by JOB ANALYSIS. This is a study of what the job entails. It will include the skills needed to do the job, the tasks that are needed to carry out the job, the activities that enable these tasks to be done, the roles and duties of the job holder and the criteria used to measure performance. It is important for a business to gather views of all people associated with the job including the job holders, their superiors and subordinates and other advisors such as work analysts.

Person specification

A job description can be used to draw up a PERSON SPECIFICATION. This is a description (or profile) of the personal qualities that match the requirements of the job specification. The person specification might include the educational and professional qualifications needed for the post. Previous experience required might be outlined. General skills and character traits could also be described.

The person specification can be used to 'screen' applicants. If there are many applicants, selectors will be able to discard those

Figure 1: A job description for a cabin crew assistant with an airline

Job title
Cabin crew member.

Function
Perform ground and air duties that the company may reasonably require. Ground duties apply to any area of work connected to aircraft operational requirements.
Other duties, including boardroom functions and publicity, are voluntary.

Cabin crew must also:
- be familiar and comply with company policy and procedures;
- provide a high standard of cabin service and perform their duties conscientiously at all times;
- not behave in any way that reflects badly upon the company or harms its reputation.

Pay and expenses
Salary will be £13,000 per annum.
Payment will be one month in arrears, paid directly into the employee's bank account.
Expenses will be paid as set out in the current contract.
If flights are cancelled, you will be entitled to a reporting allowance as set out in the current contract.

Work time
You are required to work 20 days in every 28 day roster period.
Days and hours will vary according to the company's requirements.
Details of rest periods and flight time limitations are set out in the staff manual.

Figure 2: Person specification for an administrative assistant in an engineering plant

	Essential/Desirable
Aptitudes/skills/abilities	
Able to take a flexible approach to working conditions and a changing working environment	E
Self-motivated and enthusiastic	E
Ability to work on own initiative	D
Work effectively as part of a team	D
Qualifications/knowledge and experience	
4 GCSE level C or above	E
Computer literate in Word and Excel	E
Good written and verbal communication skills	E
Able to solve problems effectively	E
Planning and organisational skills	D
Experience of working in a manufacturing environment	D

Question 1.

Job Designation: Broadcast Journalist

Grade: Towers Perrin Level 5/7

Ref: 59858

JOB PURPOSE

To initiate and produce, as part of a team, a wide variety of news and current affairs material for Radio and/or Television.

KEY BEHAVIOURS

1. To carry out in-depth research to a broad brief, with minimal supervision across the whole range of Regional Broadcasting news and current affairs output.

2. To write material for programme scripts, bulletins and links, exercising editorial judgment, maintaining professional journalistic standards and adhering to BBC policy and legal and contractual guidelines.

3. To undertake interviewing and reporting duties, under broad direction in both recorded and live situations, in studio or on location, for both Radio and Television.

4. To prepare and present bulletins, including assessing incoming copy, sub-editing news copy and deploying the necessary resources.

(a) Explain what is meant by a 'job description', illustrating your answer with examples from the data.

(b) The job being advertised was for the presenter of the Good Afternoon Show on BBC Radio Leeds. Discuss whether the BBC was likely to recruit internally or externally for the post.

which don't match the person specification. If there are only a few applicants, and none match the specification exactly, the employer may have to compromise and decide which aspects of the person specification are most important. Alternatively, the employer might decide to readvertise the post. An example of a person specification is shown in Figure 2.

Internal recruitment

INTERNAL RECRUITMENT is recruitment from within the business. An employee may be chosen to be offered a post. Or the business may advertise internally, asking employees to apply for the vacancy. The advertisement may be sent round via email or posted on a noticeboard. Larger organisations may have regular newsletters devoted to internal vacancies or notices may be put in the company magazine or on the company website. Internal recruitment has a number of advantages compared to external recruitment.

- It is often cheaper because no adverts have to be placed and paid for at commercial rates.
- Internal recruits might already be familiar with the procedures and working environment of the business. They may, therefore, need less induction training and be more productive in their first year of employment.
- The qualities, abilities and potential of the candidates should be better known to the employer. It is often difficult to foresee exactly how an external recruit will perform in a particular work environment.
- Regular internal recruiting can motivate staff. They might see a career progression with their employer. Even for those who aren't seeking promotion, internal recruitment suggests that the employer is looking after existing staff.

External recruitment

EXTERNAL RECRUITMENT is when someone is appointed from outside the business. External recruitment has two main advantages over internal recruitment.

- The employer may want someone with new and different ideas to those already working in the business. Bringing in experience of working in different organisations can often be helpful in keeping a business competitive.
- External recruitment might attract a larger number of applicants than internal recruitment. The employer then has more choice of whom to appoint.

External recruitment requires the employer to communicate with potential employees. Ideally, every person who is suitable and who might consider the job should apply. That way, the employer will have the maximum number of candidates from which to choose. There is a number of ways in which an employer can do this.

Word of mouth A common method of hearing about a job is through word of mouth. This means a person hearing about a job from someone else, often someone who works in the place of employment. For example, a person might hear about a vacancy for a hospital porter from their next door neighbour who works as a nurse in a local hospital.

Direct application Many jobseekers send their details to employers for whom they would like to work on the off-chance that they would have a vacancy. An employer might then use these to recruit if a vacancy arises.

Advertising The employer may place advertisements in local or national newspapers and specialist magazines and journals. The Internet is another medium for job advertisements. Advertisements may appear on a company website. The largest sector covered by Internet advertising is jobs in IT. Advertisements on a board or window on the employer's premises can also be successful. Advertisements are sometimes costly. But they can reach a wide number of potential applicants. People wanting to change their job are likely to seek out advertisements.

Private employment agencies The business may employ a private employment agency to find candidates. Private employment agencies are probably best known for finding temporary workers (temps). However, many also specialise in finding permanent staff. At the top end of the range, private employment agencies tend to call themselves executive agencies. They specialise in recruiting company executives and finding jobs for executives seeking a change or who have been made redundant. Using an employment agency should take much of the work out of the recruitment process for the employer. But it can be costly because the employment agency charges a fee. Private employment agencies sometimes have a website where specialist workers can look for jobs or advertise their services.

Headhunting For some posts, such as chief executive of a company, it may be possible to headhunt a candidate. This is where the agency draws up a list of people they think would be suitable for a job. Having cleared the list with the organisation making the appointment, the agency will approach those on the list and discuss the possibility of them taking the job. Some will say no. Others will indicate that, if the terms were right, they might take the job. A final selection is then made and one person is offered the job. Nobody has formally applied or been interviewed. Headhunting works best where there is only a limited number of people who potentially could take on the post and where the agency knows about most of those people.

Jobcentres Businesses can advertise vacancies through Jobcentres run by the government. Jobcentres are often used by the unemployed and vacancies tend to pay less than the average wage. So a cleaner's post is more likely to be advertised in a Jobcentre than a chief executive's post. For a business, this is a relatively cheap way of advertising, but it is not suitable for many vacancies.

Government funded training schemes Some businesses take on trainees from government funded training schemes. The current main scheme is called the New Deal. The schemes are designed to give the unemployed a chance to work for six or 12 months with some element of training. Businesses may choose then to offer these workers a permanent job if there is a vacancy and they have proved satisfactory.

Selection

Having advertised the post or gone through an employment agency, a business needs to select the right candidate. Those expressing an interest may be sent details about the post and how to apply or the details may be included on an advertisement. A number of stages will the take place.

Application forms, letters of application or curriculum vitae Sometimes, a business has an application form that it wants to be filled in giving details of the applicant. Or a business may ask candidates to send in a CURRICULUM VITAE (CV), possibly with a letter explaining why they want the post. A CV is a short document which gives the main details about a candidate. Like an application form, it should show information such as their name, address, age, gender, qualifications and job experience.

Long and short lists If a business receives many applications, it is likely to shortlist or longlist candidates. This involves selecting a small or large number of candidates who appear most suitable from their applications.

Interviews Some or all of these candidates might then be asked to an INTERVIEW. Short- and long-listings might reduce the cost of selection for a business as it would be time consuming and costly to interview, say, 200 applicants. At an interview, applicants will be asked questions about themselves and about issues related to the job. Applicants may have the chance to ask their own questions about the job. Almost every selection process involves some sort of interview. Applicants may even be

Question 2.

Pete Roghey owns and runs a small building company with 20 employees. Turnover of staff is relatively high. Skilled workers are constantly in demand and he can find that they have been poached by another company, often on short-term contracts, to work at higher rates of pay.

This week, Pete needs to hire three workers. There is a part time office cleaner's job, working in the evening from 5-7, five nights a week. He is looking for a skilled full time bricklayer. Then there is a general labourer's job, which could suit a young person just starting.

There never seems to be a right way to get hold of new staff. Sometimes, Pete advertises in the local newspaper and gets no replies. Other times, he can be spoilt for choice. More often than not, he gets approached by someone who has heard about the job vacancy from one of his workers. But there is never any guarantee that anyone will turn up this way.

(a) Discuss the advantages and disadvantages for Pete Roghey of using word of mouth to fill job vacancies compared to placing adverts in local newspapers.

(b) What might be the advantages of placing an advert in a local newsagent for the cleaner's job?

put through several interviews with different interviewers or panels of selectors. Interviews may be conducted by the personnel department or by department heads.

Some research has shown that interviews are poor at selecting the best candidate for the job. Some candidates are very good at interviews, but poor at their job. Others are bad at interviews, but are excellent employees. Interviewers tend to look for someone with qualities similar to their own rather than qualities required by the job and person specification. Judgments are often formed within the first few minutes of most interviews.

Because interviews are so unreliable, some businesses choose to use additional selection techniques.

- Candidates may be asked to role play or take part in a simulation relating to the job. This involves interviewees acting out a situation. It gives assessors a better insight into how a candidate might perform in a post.
- Tests may also be used. These could be simple numerical or literacy tests to see whether candidates can perform calculations and write effectively. There could be complicated tests, such as IQ tests. PSYCHOMETRIC TESTS aim to uncover the personality of the candidates. This helps selectors gain insights, for example, into whether a candidate would be good with customers, a useful part of a team, or could cope with stress.
- A number of large organisations today use assessment centres for some of their appointments. These are specialist organisations that deal only with making appointments. They use a variety of selection techniques to gain as wide a picture of candidates as possible. Even so, they can recommend unsuitable appointments, showing that selection procedures are not 100 per cent accurate.

Appointment

The successful candidate for a job will be appointed by the business. Candidates might be offered a job conditionally. For example, if, after the interview, they fail medical tests or police checks the offer of the job may be withdrawn. Employers also usually take up references from previous employers. A current or previous employer may give unflattering references because they don't want to lose the employee or simply out of spite. This is one reason why most employers don't ask for references before the interviews. However, a reference may turn up something like a police conviction which would again mean the offer of the job being withdrawn.

Legal constraints

Businesses recruiting and selecting new staff are bound by various employment laws.

- The Sex Discrimination Act 1975 and the Race Relations Act 1976 state that there must be no discrimination against applicants, whether male or female, or whatever ethnic origin. Discrimination can occur at any stage of the recruitment process. For example, an advertisement saying 'Males only need apply' might be a case of discrimination.

Cases are also brought against employers through employment tribunals (courts which deal with employment law) mainly by women or those from ethnic minorities arguing that jobs were given not to the best applicant, but on gender or race grounds.

- The Disability Discrimination Act 1995 states that it is unlawful for businesses to discriminate against an applicant with a disability, unless there is justification. Justification might be shown if the employer had to take unreasonable measures to allow the person with the disability to work successfully. For example, an employer might not be able to reject a candidate in a wheelchair if there were a few steps at the entrance to the place of work because a ramp could easily and cheaply be installed. However, it might be unreasonable to expect an employer to move premises just to employ the disabled worker.
- The Age Discrimination Act 2006 gives protection against age discrimination, unless it can be justified, for example if there are saftey issues. The laws protect employees of any age against age discrnimation over recruitment, terms and conditions, promotions, transfers, dismissals and training.
- After appointment, employees must be given a contract of employment detailing their duties and their rate of pay, for example.

How recruitment and selection can improve the workforce

Good recruitment and selection procedures can help to improve the workforce of a business and ensure it works effectively. They will identify the type of person required for the a job. This means that a suitable person can be appointed. They will have the skills to do the job and labour productivity may be high. They are likely to make fewer mistakes, which can be costly and time consuming.

Effective procedures may also be able to identify ways in which employees can improve. For example, if training needs are highlighted at an early stage then employees' skills may improve as they are employed for a period and receive training.

If the wrong person is recruited, this can cause problems for a business. The person appointed may find the job boring or too difficult, which could lead to a lack of motivation and poor productivity. If the person leaves, there will be administration costs for the human resource department. The business will face the extra costs of advertising and interviewing. There will also be a settling in period until the new employee has learned the job. Good recruitment and selection procedures can prevent this.

Identifying the most suitable employees may give a business a competitive edge over rivals. Productive and motivated employees will help a business to operate effectively. Business may also develop a good reputation, which can help attract customers. For example, a restaurant that has attentive staff and chefs that cook to a high standard may encourage customers to return.

KEYTERMS

Curriculum vitae – a brief description of an individual's personal details, experience and qualifications.

External recruitment – when an employee looks for applicants for a job from outside the organisation.

Internal recruitment – when an employee seeks to find applicants for a job from inside the organisation.

Interview – a meeting where an applicant answers questions from and asks questions of selectors for a job.

Job analysis – a study of what the job entails, such as skills, tasks and performance expected.

Job description – a statement of the tasks to be undertaken and responsibilities of the employee holding the job.

Person specification – a description (or profile) of the personal qualities that match the requirements of the job specification.

Psychometric tests – tests which aim to uncover the personality of individuals.

KNOWLEDGE

1. What is the difference between a job description and a person specification?
2. Compare the advantages of recruiting internally with recruiting externally.
3. Briefly explain the different ways in which a business might recruit externally.
4. Explain the difference between a short-list and a long-list.
5. What techniques may a business use to select candidates for a post?
6. Briefly explain the legal constraints on employment.

Case Study: *Using online information in recruitment and selection*

The recruitment activities of a business has shortlisted a number of candidates for the job. There appears to be the perfect person for the job at an interview with a perfect CV. An hour before the interview you look on Facebook and find a photo of the candidate looking drunk. What do you do?

CVs, interviews, references and psychometric testing used to be the main tools for selecting candidates. But more and more employers are using web browsers to check out potential staff. According to one recruitment consultancy survey, one in five employers are using information from network sites such as Facebook and MySpace as an aid to recruitment and selection. Employees used to be able to predict how prospective employers would research them, but social networking sites have changed this. Candidates may not realise the effect their websites are having on their job prospects and may not have full control over the details being posted. Employer surveys indicate the key recruitment 'turn-offs' are:

- disparaging a previous employer or disclosing confidential work information;
- disparity between the website and the CV/application form, for example, qualifications;
- intolerance of others that could cause disruption in the workplace;
- criminal activity.

It can be to employers' advantage to use online information. But there are employment law risks. For example, employers could be guilty of not processing personal data fairly under the Data Protection Act 1998 Or they might breach guidelines in the Information Commissioner's Employment Practices Code (DPA Code). Employers also face potential discrimination claims. For example, employers could may discrminate against people using Facebook on the grounds of age, since most users are aged between 18 and 24. Checking existing employees without good reason could breach the implied contract term of trust and confidence.

How can employers reduce the risk? The DPA Code recommends candidates are told that web-checking may be part of the selection process. Employers could also nominate someone removed from the decision making to research and document information. This reduces the scope for unlawful bias. Employers could also give applicants a chance to explain discrepancies in qualifications, for example. Employers could limit checking in this way to those they intend to offer a job to rather than shortlist candidates. And they should consider carefully the information they find. They may be put off by images of drunkenness, but having too many drinks at the weekend does not necessarily mean that a person can not do their job, nor are they an alcoholic.

Employers need to weigh up what message 'web-vetting' sends out about the business. Some will see it as intrusive. Others as a legitimate way of getting a feel for how a person behaves when not in a formal interview.

Source: adapted from *People Management*, 18.10. 2007.

A footwear retailer with a number of branches in the South West is opening three new shops.

(a) **Explain the meaning of the terms:**
    (i) **'shortlist'; (3 marks) (ii) 'recruitment'. (3 marks)**
(b) **Describe two different methods of selecting candidates that the business can use. (6 marks)**
(c) **Explain why the business may want to use network sites such as Facebook and MySpace in the recruitment and selection process. (8 marks)**
(d) **Evaluate the extent to which using such networks might help the business recruit and select effectively. (10 marks)**

Why business train their workforce

TRAINING is the process of increasing the knowledge and skills of workers so that they are better able to perform their jobs. The objectives of training differ from business to business but they include:

- making workers more productive by teaching them more effective ways of working;
- familiarising workers with new equipment or technology being introduced;
- educating workers in new methods of working, such as shifting from production line methods to cell methods;
- making workers more flexible so that they are able to do more than one job;
- preparing workers to move into a different job within the business, which could be a new job at a similar level or a promotion;
- improving standards of work in order to improve quality;
- implementing health and safety at work policies;
- increasing job satisfaction and motivation, because training should help workers feel more confident in what they are doing and they should gain self-esteem;
- assisting in recruiting and retaining high quality staff, attracted by the quality of training offered.

Sometimes, individual employees request training or undertake training without the financial or time support of their employers. For example, a manager may take an MBA university course in her own time. More frequently, training is provided by the employer. The need for training is sometimes identified in the appraisal process.

Induction training

Many businesses put on training for people starting a job. This is known as INDUCTION TRAINING. It is designed to help new employees settle quickly into the business and their jobs. Exactly what is offered differs from business to business and job to job. For example, a small business might simply allocate another worker to look after the new employee for a day to 'show them the ropes'. A young person just out of university might have a year long induction programme to a large company. They might spend time in a number of departments, as well as being given more general training about the business. But most induction training attempts to introduce workers to the nature of the business and work practices, including health and safety issues.

On-the-job training

ON-THE-JOB TRAINING is training given in the workplace by the employer. There are many ways in which this could happen.

Learning from other workers An employee might simply work next to another worker, watch that worker do a task and with their help repeat it.

Mentoring This is where a more experienced employee is asked to provide advice and help to a less experienced worker. The less experienced worker can turn for help and advice to another more experienced worker at any time.

Job rotation This is where a worker spends a period of time doing one job, then another period of time doing another job and so on. Eventually they have received the broad experience needed to do a more specialist job.

Question 1.

Michelle Hallett went from sales assistant to store manager with the help of two training courses available through Modern Apprenticeships. A basic retail training programme led to a National Vocational Qualification level 2 achievement followed by a management course tied to level 3 saw her climb the ladder with Chockers, a small Essex-based shoe retailer. Michelle, said: 'I feel I've benefited in a number of ways. I'm more confident with customers and am better at handling staff. It's all been worthwhile.' Chockers, an eight-store chain with a flagship shop in The Strand in London, is a classic example of a business faced with a training problem in a sector with a high staff turnover.

Rosanne Lewis, area manager co-ordinator, said: 'We couldn't afford to operate a training scheme of our own but now we're able to put more of our sales staff through the apprenticeship programmes.' John Gill, the founder, trained the hard way, on a market stall, before launching the business, but is now committed to using the framework to provide a comprehensive training to add some extra staff polish and performance.

There was some apprehension among young sales assistants at the start.

'Some felt it would be like going back to school but I quickly reassured them on that score. We have a staff of 50 and I want all of them to take up the training programme,' says Ms Lewis.

Michelle did on-the-job training with a supervisor monitoring progress and discussing the finer points of customer relations at the end of a day's work. Her deputy, Hayley Clarke, has followed a similar programme. She said: 'I found it a bit hard at first to fit into the routine but the others in the shop have been really helpful. Being assistant manager now means I have more responsibility.'

Source: adapted from *The Telegraph*, 18.3.2004.

(a) Using examples from the article explain what is meant by on-the-job training?
(b) Explain why there might be potential problems with training staff at Chockers.
(c) Discuss whether Chockers might offer its own training scheme in future.

Traditional apprenticeships In the past, workers in traditional skilled trades, such as carpentry or engineering, would undertake training over, say, three-five years in an apprenticeship. This would involve a mix of training methods. When the business decided they had 'qualified' they would be employed as a full-time worker. Many of these schemes died out due to the cost for the business, the decline in traditional trades, mechanisation and the need for more flexible work practices.

Graduate training Medium- to large-sized businesses may offer graduate training programmes. They are typically designed to offer those with university degrees either professional training, such as in accountancy or the law, or managerial training.

Off-the-job training

OFF-THE-JOB TRAINING is training which takes place outside the business by an external training provider like a local college or university. For example, 16-25 year olds might go to college one day a week to do a catering course or an engineering course. A trainee accountant might have an intensive course at an accountancy college or attend night classes before taking professional exams. A graduate manager might do an MBA (Masters in Business Administration) course at a Business School in the evening and at weekends.

Off-the-job training can provide courses which a business internally would be unable to provide. But it can be expensive, particularly if the business is paying not just for the course but also a salary for the time the employee is attending the course.

Training initiatives

The government promotes training through a variety of initiatives and schemes.

Learning and Skills Councils These are bodies which have been set up by government to cover the whole of the UK. Each area of the UK has its own regional Learning and Skills Council. They are responsible for promoting training and manage funding for a wide range of schemes such as modern apprenticeships (see below). They are funded by the government from taxes. But businesses taking part in training may also be required to contribute towards the cost of training which directly benefits them.

Modern Apprenticeships In the past, apprenticeships were the most common way for a school leaver to become a skilled manual worker with a qualification. In the 1970s, with a sharp decline in employment in manufacturing industry, most businesses scrapped their apprenticeship schemes. Today, the government sponsors Modern Apprenticeships. This scheme aims to give young people an apprenticeship training which will equip them for a specific job in an industry. Businesses run Modern Apprenticeships and then receive a subsidy from the government for each apprentice on the scheme. Typically the Modern Apprenticeship training runs for three years.

Question 2.

Asda operates one of the most rigorous retail training programmes in the UK. New employees spend the equivalent of 25 weeks, mainly in-house, learning how to do their job. In 2004 Asda linked its own programme with National Vocational Qualifications in retailing and Modern Apprenticeships. It hoped this would will help increase productivity, encourage a higher level of internal promotion and reduce a staff turnover rate currently running at 26 per cent. The Learning and Skills Council provided more than £500,000 to the project. Asda, rather than a training provider, would control the money which will be used to cover the cost of outside assessors ensuring that its training is in line with the NVQ programme.

Mrs Sam Smith, people development manager, said: 'We're not doing this for profit but to raise the standard of our training and provide the staff with extra qualifications which will benefit them and the company.' There was extensive discussions between the company, the Learning and Skills Council and City & Guilds to validate the Asda in-house training set-up as a retail NVQ.

Source: adapted from *The Telegraph*, 18.3.2004.

(a) What is meant by (i) a Modern Apprenticeship and (ii) in-house training?
(b) Why is training likely to be so important for a business like Asda?
(c) Discuss whether Asda rather than a training provider should provide training.

The New Deal Since the late 1970s, governments have run a variety of schemes aimed at getting unemployed workers, particularly young workers, into a job. The New Deal, for example, promises to give any young unemployed person under the age of 25 either full-time training or work experience. The New Deal also offers older long-term unemployed workers a similar package.

Investors in People (IiP) IiP is a national standard developed by industry bodies such as the CBI and TUC with the support of the Employment Department, which businesses have to meet if they wish to gain IiP accreditation. To get accreditation, they have to show that the need for training is considered at every level and in every major decision made by the business. Businesses which go through the process of gaining IiP accreditation typically find that there are inefficiencies in the way the business operates because staff have not been trained properly. These training needs then have to be addressed. Gaining IiP is a useful marketing tool for a business. This is because customers perceive that, by gaining IiP accreditation, the business is a modern, forward-thinking business where staff are properly trained to deal with their work.

Labour market failure

It can be argued that, if left to free market forces, too little training would take place. This is an example of MARKET FAILURE. In the labour market, it occurs for two reasons.

- Businesses spend too little money on training because it is often cheaper for them to recruit new workers who have already been trained by another business or on a government training scheme.
- Individual workers don't spend enough on training themselves because they don't want to get into short-term debt. They also fail to realise how much more they could earn if they had better training.

In the past, traditional apprentices might have signed an agreement to stay with their employer a number of years after they became qualified. This meant they could not be 'poached' by a rival business. Today, linking training with staying on in the business is rare. There is nothing to stop a newly trained worker from leaving one business to take up a post at a higher salary elsewhere.

Generally, when there is market failure, it is argued that the government should step in to correct that market failure. Governments have two broad ways of doing this.

- They can provide training themselves and pay for it from tax revenues. Currently, the UK government provides training for the unemployed through its New Deal programme for example. Training is also provided through free college or further education courses.
- The government can pay grants to industry bodies or individual businesses to undertake training. This can be funded from general taxation or by a levy on all businesses in the industry. For example, in the UK construction industry, businesses have to pay a levy (effectively a tax) to pay for the work of the Construction Industry Training Board. This provides training for construction workers.

KEY TERMS

Induction training – training which occurs when a worker starts a job with a business.
Market failure – when the operation of free market forces fails to provide an optimal level of output.
Off-the-job training – training which takes place outside the business through an external training provider like a local college or university.
On-the-job training – training given in the workplace by the employer.
Training – the process of increasing the knowledge and skills of workers so that they are better able to perform their jobs.

KNOWLEDGE

1 List the reasons why a business might train its employees.
2 Why might a business offer induction training?
3 Explain the difference between mentoring and job rotation.
4 What is graduate training?
5 Who benefits from training through the New Deal programme?
6 What is Investors in People?
7 What is the role of Learning and Skills Councils in training?
8 Explain why businesses might spend less on training than is desirable.

Case Study: *Training in social housing*

Kiran Singh argues that his job as a housing officer for a housing association is more than just sorting out anti-social tenants and chasing rent. When he says he works in social housing, his friends think he works with awkward tenants and council homes – a stereotypical view. However there are now many more jobs out in housing than there were 20 years ago, particularly in regeneration. Kiran is responsible for 300 homes managed by the social landlord, East Midlands Housing. Earning £20,000 a year just months after graduating with a housing degree. He hopes to carve himself a successful career in the sector. It is now common for experienced housing managers to earn a minimum £40,000, and it is not unusual for top chief executives or directors to command salaries of up to £100,000.

Unlike other public services, such as the NHS, there are few graduate training programmes in this area, although they are starting to appear in some of the larger organisations. It is not essential to have a housing degree to work in housing. But it does attract graduates from different disciplines such as social sciences, human geography, economics and politics. A Modern Apprenticeship offers another route into the sector. Apprentices are given on-the-job training, but also learn about the historical context of social housing, its management and Housing law. Roger Keller, head of education at the Chartered Institute of Housing, the professional organisation for housing, says: 'An apprenticeship offers a proper understanding of why social housing is important in a country which doesn't have enough housing and how people can get access to housing when prices are rising.' Keller says that the uptake of Modern Apprenticeships in housing is low. 'They aren't widely taken up and you could argue that the sector ought to be recommending more young people take them on.' Once in the sector, it is possible to study for a range of professional qualifications offered by the Institute. Keller estimates that around 90 per cent of people studying for a professional qualification are sponsored by their employer.

The job opportunities within social housing sector have increased over the last 30 years as it has made a greater contribution it makes to public services. In the 1980s social housing was limited, geared towards rent collection and bad neighbours and there was little money available for development. Training may have simply meant learning from a colleague. New job titles today include regeneration officers, tenant participation officers, urban designers, antisocial behaviour managers and financial inclusion officers. These jobs require people to work with agencies like health, education, the police force and the army. There is a need for appropriate people skills and an understanding of different professional perspectives, requiring training and development of staff. With 50,000 people working in social housing sector due to retire by 2014, it may be just the right time to consider a career move into the sector.

Source: adapted from *The Guardian*, 8.11.2007.

(a) What us meant by (i) Apprentices (3 marks) and
    (ii) a graduate training programme? (3 marks)

(b) Outline one of example of 'on-the-job training' and one example of 'off-the-job training' mentioned in the article. (6 marks)

(c) Examine the advantages to an 18 year old of accepting a Modern Apprenticeship in housing rather than doing a university degree. (8 marks)

(d) Evaluate the type of training that might be needed in the future for individuals working in housing. (10 marks)

The satisfaction of needs

If asked, most people who work would probably say they do so to earn money to buy goods and services. However, this is not the only need that is satisfied by working. A list of people's needs that may be satisfied from work might be very long indeed. It could include, for example, the need for variety in the workplace, which may be satisfied by an interesting job. Employees may also need to feel appreciated for the work they do, which could be reflected in the prestige attached to their job.

Individuals are not the same. Therefore, it is likely that lists made by any two people of their needs and how they can be satisfied will be very different. There are some reasons for working that could apply to everyone, such as the need to earn money. However, some reasons have more importance for particular individuals than others. One employee may need to work with friendly colleagues, whereas another might be happy working on his own.

The importance of motivation

Why is it important for a business to find out what satisfies the needs of its employees? It is argued that if an individual's needs are not satisfied, then that worker will not be MOTIVATED to work. Businesses have found that even if employees are satisfied with pay and conditions at work, they also complain that their employer does not do a good job in motivating them. This applies to all levels, from the shop floor to the boardroom. It appears in many companies that employers are not getting the full potential from their employees because they are not satisfying all of their employees' needs. Figure 1 shows one example of how a business might make decisions, having first identified an employee's needs.

It is important for a business to motivate its employees. In the short run a lack of motivation may lead to reduced effort and lack of commitment. If employees are watched closely, fear of wage cuts or redundancy may force them to maintain their effort even though they are not motivated. This is negative motivation. In the long term, a lack of motivation may result in high levels of absenteeism, industrial disputes and falling productivity and profit for a business. So it is argued that well motivated employees will be productive which should lead to greater efficiency and profits for a business.

Maslow's hierarchy of needs

The first comprehensive attempt to classify needs was by Abraham Maslow in 1954. Maslow's theory consisted of two parts. The first concerned classification of needs. The second concerned how these classes are related to each other. Maslow suggested that 'classes' of needs could be placed into a hierarchy. The hierarchy is normally presented as a 'pyramid', with each level consisting of a certain class of needs. This is shown in Figure 2. The classes of needs were:

- physiological needs, e.g. wages high enough to meet weekly bills, good working conditions;
- safety needs, e.g. job security, safe working conditions;
- love and belonging, eg working with colleagues that support you at work, teamwork, communicating;
- esteem needs, e.g. being given recognition for doing a job well;
- self-actualisation, e.g. being promoted and given more responsibility, scope to develop and introduce new ideas and take on challenging new job assignments.

Figure 2 can also be used to show the relationship between the different classes. Maslow argued that needs at the bottom of the pyramid are basic needs. They are concerned with survival. These needs must be satisfied before a person can move to the next level. For example, people are likely to be more concerned with basic needs, such as food, than anything else. At work an

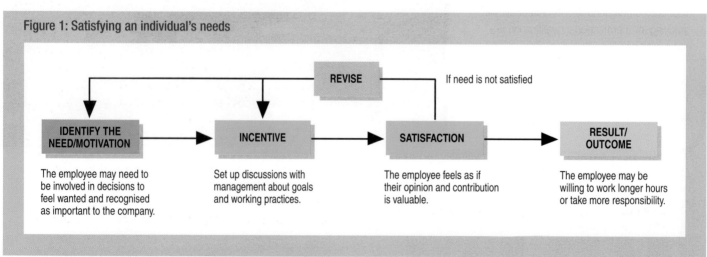

Figure 1: Satisfying an individual's needs

REVISE — If need is not satisfied

IDENTIFY THE NEED/MOTIVATION → INCENTIVE → SATISFACTION → RESULT/OUTCOME

The employee may need to be involved in decisions to feel wanted and recognised as important to the company.

Set up discussions with management about goals and working practices.

The employee feels as if their opinion and contribution is valuable.

The employee may be willing to work longer hours or take more responsibility.

Motivation theories

Unit 30

employee is unlikely to be concerned about acceptance from colleagues if he has not eaten for six hours. Once each level is satisfied, the needs at this level become less important. The exception is the top level of SELF-ACTUALISATION. This is the need to fulfil your potential. Maslow argued that although everyone is capable of this, in practice very few reach this level.

Each level of needs is dependent on the levels below. Say an employee has been motivated at work by the opportunity to take responsibility, but finds he may lose his job. The whole system collapses, as the need to feed and provide for himself and his dependants again becomes the most important need.

Maslow's ideas have great appeal for business. The message is clear – find out which level each individual is at and decide on suitable rewards. Unfortunately the theory has problems when used in practice. Some levels do not appear to exist for certain individuals, while some rewards appear to fit into more than one class. Money, for example, needs to be used to purchase 'essentials' such as food, but it can also be seen as a status symbol or an indicator of personal worth. There is also a problem in deciding when a level has actually been 'satisfied'. There will always be exceptions to the rules Maslow outlined. A well motivated designer may spend many hours on a creative design despite lack of sleep or food.

Taylor's Scientific Management

Research into the factors that motivate individuals had been carried out long before Maslow's 'hierarchy' of needs. Frederick W. Taylor set out a theory of SCIENTIFIC MANAGEMENT in his book *The Principles of Scientific Management* in 1911. Many of the ideas of today's 'scientific management school' come from the work of Taylor.

The turn of the 20th century in the USA was a time of rapid expansion. Compared to today, the organisation of work on the

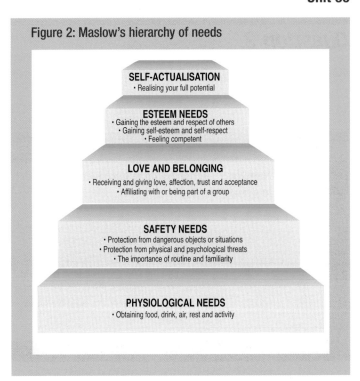

Figure 2: Maslow's hierarchy of needs

shop floor was left much more in the hands of workers and foremen. Workers often brought their own tools and decisions about the speed of machines were left to operators. There were few training programmes to teach workers their jobs and skills were gained simply by watching more experienced colleagues. Decisions about selection, rest periods and layoffs were frequently made by foremen.

Taylor suggested that such arrangements were haphazard and inefficient. Management did not understand the shop floor and allowed wasteful work practices to continue. Workers, on the other hand, left to their own devices, would do as little as possible. 'Soldiering' would also take place (working more slowly together so that management did not realise workers' potential) and workers would carry out tasks in ways they were used to rather than the most efficient way.

Taylor's scientific principles were designed to reduce inefficiency of workers and managers. This was to be achieved by 'objective laws' that management and workers could agree on, reducing conflict between them. Neither party could argue against a system of work that was based on 'science'. Taylor believed his principles would create a partnership between manager and worker, based on an understanding of how jobs should be done and how workers are motivated.

Taylor's approach How did Taylor discover what the 'best way' was of carrying out a task? Table 1 shows an illustration of Taylor's method. Taylor had a very simple view of what motivated people at work – money. He felt that workers should receive a 'fair day's pay for a fair day's work', and pay should be linked to output through piece rates. A worker who did not produce a 'fair day's work' would face a loss of earnings; exceeding the target would lead to a bonus. In 1899 Taylor's

Question 1.

Anmac Ltd is a small expanding high-tech company. It employs approximately 25 workers in two factories, one at Chester and one at Stafford. The employers organise work on a fairly informal basis. Workers work at their own pace, which often results in a variable level of output. Recently orders for their advanced micro-electronic circuit boards have increased rapidly. The firm has decided that, to cope with the orders, increased production is needed. Two suggestions have been put forward.

- Encourage the workers to work overtime at the Chester plant.
- Redeploy some of the workers from Chester to Stafford where there is a shortfall of workers.

The workers at the Chester plant are mainly married women in their twenties, many with young, school-aged children and husbands who also work.

(a) Explain how Taylor's scientific management principles might be used to solve the problems faced by Anmac Ltd.
(b) What problems might Anmac Ltd find in using such principles?

Question 2.

Table 2 shows the results of a survey carried out in Bryant and Gillie, a SME that manufactures children's clothing. The company introduced a piece rate system of work - a system where employees are paid according to the number or quantity of items they produce. Five groups were involved in the new system. Different actions were taken to introduce the system to each group. The table shows the effect on labour turnover and output of these actions.

Table 2: The effect of introducing a piece rate system into a clothes manufacturing business

Group	Number in group	Action taken to introduce system	Resignations within 40 days of introduction	Change in output
A	100	Group told the changes will take place next week	17%	-2%
B	150	Management introduces changes with the help of group to suit their needs	0%	+10%
C	200	Group told the changes will take place next week	7%	0%
D	50	Management explains the need for change to group	2%	+2%
E	100	Management explains the need for change and discusses this with the group	0%	+5%

(a) To what extent do the results support the human relations explanation of workers' motivation?

(b) Using the results of the survey in Table 2, advise the management on the likely action needed to motivate workers when changing work practices.

methods were used at the Bethlehem Steel Works in the USA, where they were responsible for raising pig iron production by almost 400 per cent per man per day. Taylor found the 'best way to do each job' and designed incentives to motivate workers.

Taylor's message for business is simple - allow workers to work and managers to manage based on scientific principles of work study. Many firms today still attempt to use Taylor's principles. In the 1990s for example some businesses introduced **Business process reengineering (BPR)**. This is a management approach where organisations look at their business processes from a 'clean slate' perspective and determine how they can best construct these processes to improve how they conduct business. Taylor's approach is similar in that it advocates businesses finding the best way of doing something to add value to the business.

Problems with Taylor's approach There is a number of problems with Taylor's ideas. The notion of a 'quickest and best way' for all workers does not take into account individual differences. There is no guarantee that the 'best way' will suit everyone.

Taylor also viewed people at work more as machines, with financial needs, than as humans in a social setting. There is no doubt that money is an important motivator. Taylor overlooked that people also work for reasons other than money. A survey in America by the Robb and Myatt in 2004, for example, found that of the top ten factors motivating workers, the first three categories were a sense of achievement, having that achievement recognised, and positive working relationships. This suggests there may be needs that must be met at work, which Taylor ignored, but were recognised in Maslow's ideas which came later.

Human relations

Taylor's scientific management ideas may have seemed appealing at first glance to business. Some tried to introduce his ideas in the 1920s and 1930s, which led to industrial unrest. Others found that financial incentives did motivate workers, and still do today. However, what was becoming clear was that there were other factors which may affect workers' motivation.

The Hawthorne studies Many of the ideas which are today known as the 'human relations school' grew out of experiments between 1927 and 1932 at the Hawthorne Plant of the Western Electric company in Chicago. Initially these were based on 'scientific management' - the belief that workers' productivity was affected by work conditions, the skills of workers and

Table 1: Taylor's method, designed to find the 'best way' to carry out a task at work

- Pick a dozen skilled workers.
- Observe them at work and note down the elements and sequences adopted in their tasks.
- Time each element with a stop watch.
- Eliminate any factors which appear to add nothing to the completion of the task.
- Choose the quickest method discovered and fit them in their sequence.
- Teach the worker this sequence; do not allow any change from the set procedure.
- Include time for rest and the result will be the 'quickest and best' method for the task. Because it is the best way, all workers selected to perform the task must adopt it and meet the time allowed.
- Supervise workers to ensure that these methods are carried out during the working day.

financial incentives. Over the five year period, changes were made in incentive schemes, rest periods, hours of work, lighting and heating and the effect on workers' productivity was measured. One example was a group of six women assembling telephone relays. It was found that whatever changes were made, including a return to the original conditions, output rose. This came to be known as the HAWTHORNE EFFECT.

The study concluded that changes in conditions and financial rewards had little or no effect on productivity. Increases in output were mainly due to the greater cohesion and communication which workers in groups developed as they interacted and were motivated to work together. Workers were also motivated by the interest shown in their work by the researchers. This result was confirmed by further investigations in the Bank Wiring Observation where 14 men with different tasks were studied.

The work of **Elton Mayo** (and Roethlisberger and Dickson) in the 1930s, who reported on the Hawthorne Studies, has led to what is known today as the human relations school. A business aiming to maximise productivity must make sure that the 'personal satisfactions' of workers are met for workers to be motivated. Management must also work and communicate with informal work groups, making sure that their goals fit in with the goals of the business. One way to do this is to allow such groups to be part of decision making. Workers are likely to be more committed to tasks that they have had some say in.

Question 3.

Larry Page and Sergey Brin graduated from America's Stanford University in computer science in 1995. They found common ground in a unique approach to solving one of computing's biggest challenges – retrieving relevant information from a massive set of data. They spent 18 months perfecting their technology, following a path that would ultimately become Google Inc. At Mountain view, California, where Google is based, there is a beach volleyball court, a dinosaur skeleton and gaudy parasols aplenty. There is an abundance of open space, courtyards, quadrangles and forums. The buildings are uncluttered, mixing functionality and hi-tech feng shui. Staff travel between buildings on electric mini-scooters. Whiteboards are dotted throughout and the famous 'help yourself' juice counters are also in evidence. Lunch is free for employees and there's more choice than one would find in a small town. Open a laptop in Mountain View anywhere and you are invited to join the free Google wi-fi network. Everywhere there are examples of the legendary 20 per cent scheme that Google operates - letting engineers spend a fifth of their time pursuing personal projects. On one plasma screen a spinning globe shows search engine queries to Google made in real time. It was created by one of the engineers in his 20 per cent time. Google also has its on-site gym, on-site dentist and on-site celebrity chef who previously served the Grateful Dead.

Source: adapted from www.matr.net, www.bbc.co.uk.

(a) Outline the various ways that Google uses to motivate its staff.
(b) Using a motivation theory, examine why Google is successful at motivating its employees.

CRITIQUE

Motivation theories may not work in practise for a number of reasons.
Different circumstances If the business is geared towards hierarchy and authority, and work is routine, people may choose to do such work in return for financial rewards, for example to enjoy themselves away from work. At other times, job interest and involvement may outweigh financial rewards. This may be true, for instance, in worker buyouts, when employees are prepared to accept lower financial rewards to maintain job security and have a say in the running of the business.
Different types of operation It is also argued that many motivation theories were developed in earlier times, when work conditions were different. Work methods did not need the advanced levels of technological knowledge and problem-solving skills that they do today. These skills change the relationship between management and the shop floor, for example by empowering workers.
Capitalism Theories of motivation based on the ideas of Marx suggest that getting people motivated will always be a problem under capitalism. This is because, although we depend on each other to produce wealth, private ownership of business allows owners to exploit those employees who must sell their labour in order to live. Though profits are only made through labour, the interests of owners and workers, diverge since labour is a cost to be minimised if profits are to be maximised.

There are examples of these ideas being used in business. The Volvo plant in Uddevalla, opened in 1989, was designed to allow workers to work in teams of eight to ten. Each team built a complete car and made decisions about production. Volvo found that absenteeism rates at Uddevalla averaged 8 per cent, compared to 25 per cent in their Gothenburg plant which used a production line system. Other examples have been:

- Honda's plant in Swindon where 'teamwork' has been emphasised - there were no workers or directors, only 'associates';
- McDonald's picnics, parties and McBingo for their employees where they were made to feel part of the company;
- Mary Kay's seminars in the USA, which were presented like the American Academy awards for company employees.

Problems There is a number of criticisms of the human relations school.

- It assumes workers and management share the same goals. This idea of workplace 'consensus' may not always exist. For example, in the 1980s Rover tried to introduce a programme called 'Working with Pride'. It was an attempt to raise quality by gaining employee commitment. This would be achieved by greater communication with employees. The programme was not accepted throughout the company. As one manager stated: 'We've tried the face-to-face communications approach. It works to a degree, but we are not too good at the supervisory level ... enthusiasm for the Working with Pride programme is proportionate to the level in the hierarchy. For supervisors

Figure 3: Herzberg's two factor theory

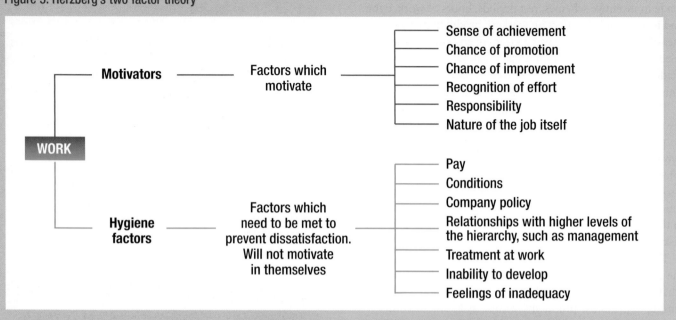

it's often just seen as a gimmick ...'
- It is assumed that communication between workers and management will break down 'barriers'. It could be argued, however, that the knowledge of directors' salaries or redundancies may lead to even more 'barriers' and unrest.
- It is biased towards management. Workers are manipulated into being productive by managers. It may also be seen as a way of reducing trade union power.

Herzberg's two-factor theory

In 1966 Fredrick Herzberg attempted to find out what motivated people at work. He asked a group of professional engineers and accountants to describe incidents in their jobs which gave them strong feelings of satisfaction or dissatisfaction. He then asked them to describe the causes in each case.

Results Herzberg divided the causes into two categories or factors. These are shown in Figure 3.
- **MOTIVATORS.** These are the factors which give workers **job satisfaction**, such as recognition for their effort. Increasing these motivators is needed to give job satisfaction. This, it could be argued, will make workers more productive. A business that rewards its workforce for, say, achieving a target is likely to motivate them to be more productive. However, this is not guaranteed, as other factors can also affect productivity.
- **HYGIENE or MAINTENANCE FACTORS.** These are factors that can lead to workers being **dissatisfied**, such as pay or conditions. Improving hygiene factors should remove dissatisfaction. For example, better canteen facilities may make workers less dissatisfied about their environment. An improvement in hygiene factors alone is not likely to motivate an individual. But if they are not

met, there could be a fall in productivity.

There is some similarity between Herzberg's and Maslow's ideas. They both point to needs that have to be satisfied for the employee to be motivated. Herzberg argues that only the higher levels of Maslow's hierarchy motivate workers.

Herzberg's ideas are often linked with **job enrichment**. This is where workers have their jobs 'expanded', so that they can experience more of the production process. This allows the workers to be more involved and motivated, and have a greater sense of achievement. Herzberg used his ideas in the development of clerical work. He selected a group of workers in a large corporation. Performance and job attitudes were low. Herzberg redesigned these jobs so that they were given more responsibility and recognition.

Problems Herzberg's theory does seem to have some merits. Improving pay or conditions, for example, may remove dissatisfaction at first. Often, however, these things become taken for granted. It is likely that better conditions will be asked for in following years. Evidence of this can be seen in wage claims which aim to be above the rate of inflation in some businesses every year. Job enrichment may also be expensive for many firms. In addition, it is likely that any benefits from job improvements will not be seen for a long time and that businesses will not be able to continue with such a policy in periods of recession.

Surveys that have tried to reproduce Herzberg's results have often failed. This may have been because different groups of workers have been examined and different techniques used. Also, there is a problem in relying too much on what people say they find satisfying or dissatisfying at work as this is subjective. For example, if things go wrong at work individuals have a tendency to blame it on others or factors outside of their control. On the other hand if individuals feel happy and satisfied when they are at work then they tend to see it as their own doing.

Hawthorne effect – the idea that workers are motivated by recognition given to them as a group.
Hygiene or maintenance factors – those things that can lead to workers being dissatisfied.
Motivated – being encouraged to do something.
Motivators – those things that can lead to workers being satisfied.
Self-actualisation – a level on Maslow's hierarchy where an employee realises his or her full potential.
Scientific management – a theory that suggests that there is a 'best' way to perform work tasks.

KNOWLEDGE

1. Why is it important for business to satisfy workers?
2. Name five needs in Maslow's hierarchy that an individual might have at work.
3. What are the aims of Taylor's scientific management theory?
4. According to Taylor, how are people motivated?
5. What is meant by the human relations school of thought?
6. What, according to the human relations school, is the main motivator at work?
7. Explain the difference between Theory X and Theory Y.
8. How is Theory X like Taylor's view of scientific management?
9. According to Herzberg's theory, what factors are likely to:
(a) increase job satisfaction; (b) reduce dissatisfaction at work?
10. What general conclusions can a business draw from the criticisms of motivation theory?

Case Study: *Mendelsons*

Lee Worsnip has worked as an assistant in the financial analysis department of Mendelsons Insurance for two years. He is 24 years of age and joined Mendelsons from college with good exam results. Lee also obtained some extra qualifications by taking night school courses. He started as junior clerk, and quickly moved to a more senior post, which paid a better salary. However, he has been in this post for a while now.

Lee's aim was to use the job as a stepping stone to one of the sales teams. The business was pleased that Lee looked on the job in this way, as it is in favour of encouraging people to get on. However, it is difficult to get onto one of the sales teams, particularly when the company has placed so much emphasis on its graduate recruitment. This may be one of the things that seems to be bothering Lee. Recently the Unit Trust team hired a graduate trainee instead of Lee, although he did accept that the new recruit had an advantage as she was a qualified actuary.

Until a few months ago, Lee had been an above average employee. He was always cheerful, enthusiastic and willing, and picked things up quickly. Lee used to make an excellent contribution to regular weekly meetings. And he was prepared to do one-off projects, always seeming to be able to squeeze in the extra work. He was also quite prepared to work late.

Lately, however, he seems to lack motivation. He has missed some meetings and taken days off. He complained that other members of the meetings had more senior posts and felt they did not listen to his views. He said, 'I shouldn't be treated as a worker who is satisfied just by basic physiological needs.'

The other day, Lee refused to take on a low level task. He suggested that he was fed up doing routine work and not leaving the office every day until 8 o'clock. Lee also argued that he was never allowed to make decisions and his work was always checked, as if he wasn't trusted. In the end some of these tasks had to be given to other members of staff, increasing their workload. Lee's absences have put additional pressure on the team.

Lee has also started being offhand. He was overheard several times being rude to people who asked him for information or help. Last week, at a team meeting about new procedures, Lee suggested that they had been drawn up in secret behind his back.

(a) What is meat by the terms:
(i) lack of motivation (3 marks) and
(ii) physiological needs. (3 marks)
(b) Explain the problems that (i) Lee and (ii) the business might have as a result of a lack of motivation. (10 marks)
(c) Using a motivation theory, examine reasons why Lee may lack motivation. (12 marks)
(d) Suggest ways in which the business might improve Lee's motivation. (12 marks)

Financial and non-financial rewards

A number of theories have tried to explain the factors that motivate people at work. Some of these theories stress that money is the most important factor. The scientific approach, in particular, argues that workers respond to financial rewards. It is argued that such rewards are necessary to motivate a reluctant workforce. Employees see work as a means to an end. As a result they are far more likely to be interested in **financial rewards.** In contrast, the human relations view argues that workers are motivated by a variety of factors. An employee working in a car assembly plant, for example, may be highly motivated by working as part of a team. Poor pay may lead to employees being dissatisfied, which can make other **non-financial rewards** less effective in motivating them. The next two units examine how financial and non-financial rewards can be used.

Salaries and wages

For nearly all workers, the main reason for going to work is to earn money to buy goods and services. Most workers in the UK are either paid a wage or a salary.

Wages WAGES tend to be associated with lower paid workers and BLUE COLLAR WORKERS (i.e. MANUAL WORKERS). Wages are typically expressed as hourly TIME RATES of pay, such as £5.50 an hour or £12.75 an hour. This then forms weekly rates of pay, such as £250 a week, for a fixed number of hours work, such as 38 hours. The 38 hours would then be the basic working week. Time rates are useful when a business wants to employ workers to do specialist or difficult tasks that should not be rushed. Employees can ensure that work is of a high quality without worrying about the time they take.

Waged employees often have the opportunity to work OVERTIME. These are hours worked over and above the basic working week. To motivate workers to accept overtime, employers often pay higher rates of pay. If the basic wage is £10 an hour, overtime might be paid at time and a quarter (£12.50 an hour) or time and a half (£15 an hour). Saturday or Sunday overtime working might be paid at higher rates than weekday overtime, to encourage people to work at weekends.

Salaries SALARIES tend to be associated with better paid workers, particularly WHITE COLLAR WORKERS (i.e. NON-MANUAL WORKERS). Salaried staff are typically paid each month. Some salaried staff might earn overtime because they are only expected to work a fixed number of hours per week. However, most salaried staff are paid to do a particular job. There might be a recommended number of hours work per week, like 38 hours. But they are often expected to work as many hours as it takes to complete the job. A yearly salary is usually higher than that which could be earned by workers if they were in a less senior job and paid a wage.

The main long-term factors which determine the level of wages and salaries are the forces of demand and supply. Businesses have to pay the 'market rate' for the job if they want to retain existing staff and recruit new staff. Paying below the market rate can also demotivate staff. They might feel that they are not valued by their employer. Paying above the market rate can be motivating. Workers might feel that their contribution is being rewarded by higher pay.

Workers are sometimes paid a basic wage or salary and a BONUS at the end of the year or other period if **targets** are reached, or for attendance or punctuality. Sometimes the 'best employee' over a period may be rewarded with a bonus. This is usually a money payment, although Richer sounds, the electronics retailer, has rewarded the retail outlet that performed bets over a period with the use of a classic car such as a Rolls Royce. A problem with regular bonuses is that they are often seen as part of the employee's basic pay. As a result, they may no longer act as a motivator.

Many employers have found that payment based on a fixed working week can be inflexible. For example, half the year employees may be idle after 3 p.m. every day, but are still paid for a 'full day's' work. The other half of the year they may work into the evening and be paid overtime. To cater for fluctuations in demand some employers pay staff on the basis of a certain number of hours to be worked in a year. These are known as ANNUALISED HOURS CONTRACTS. For annualised hours contracts, the number of hours to be worked each year is fixed. However, the daily, weekly or monthly hours are flexible. So employees may have a longer working day at peak times and work less when demand is slack. An employee's pay is calculated on the basis of an average working week, for example 35 hours, which is paid regardless of the actual number of hours the employee works. There are certain advantages of annualised hours. An employee has a guaranteed income each week. Employers often see this as a way of avoiding overtime, reducing costs, increasing flexibility and improving efficiency.

Piece rates, commission and fees

Not all workers are paid wages or salaries. Some are paid piece rates, commission or fees.

Piece rates Piece rates are payments for each unit produced. They are an example of PAYMENT BY RESULTS. For example, a worker might be paid £0.50 per parcel delivered or £1.00 per kilo of strawberries picked. PIECE RATES were recommended by Frederick Taylor, founder of the scientific management school. He thought they were an ideal way to motivate workers. Workers who produced more were more highly paid. However,

Question 1.

(a) Compare the different payment systems shown in the advertisements.

(b) What fringe benefits were being offered?

(c) Discuss what might happen if any of the employers advertising were offering a remuneration package which was below the market rate for the job.

---

piece rates are only suitable for jobs where it is easy to identify the contribution of an individual worker. It would be difficult to devise a piece rate system for, say, secretaries or managers. Piece rates have been criticised on health and safety grounds. They might encourage workers to take dangerous short cuts in a bid to reduce the amount of time taken for each item. Rushing production might also affect the quality of the product.

Commission COMMISSION is a payment system mainly used with white collar workers. Commission, like piece rates, is a payment for achieving a target. For example, car salespeople may get a commission of £100 for each car they sell. Some white collar workers are paid entirely on commission. A salesperson, for example, may be paid entirely on the basis of their sales record. Alternatively, a worker may be paid a basic salary and then receive commission on top. Commission based pay systems are intended to 'incentivise' workers by tying in pay with output.

Fees Fees are payments made to people for 'one-off' tasks. Tasks tend to be geared towards the needs of the client, rather than a standard service or product. The amount paid will depend on a variety of factors. These might include the time taken to finish the task or the difficulty of the task. Often fees are paid to people providing services, such as solicitors, performers etc.

Fringe benefits

FRINGE BENEFITS are benefits received over and above that received from wages or salaries. Fringe benefits are payments 'in kind' rather than in cash. Typical examples of fringe benefits include contributions to pensions, a company car, private health insurance, subsidised meals including luncheon vouchers, and subsidised loans or mortgages.

One reason why fringe benefits are given is because they are a tax-efficient way of rewarding employees. It may cost a business less to give the fringe benefit than the equivalent sum of money needed to buy it by the employee. Some fringe benefits help the running of the business. For example, private health care might reduce the number of days off sick by employees and give the business greater control about when an employee has an operation.

Businesses also give fringe benefits as a way of motivating staff. They can act as a motivator in two ways.

- Many satisfy the basic physiological and safety needs of workers, as outlined by Maslow. They also meet the hygiene factors as outlined in Herzberg's two-factor theory.
- The awarding of fringe benefits can be linked to achievement and promotion. Free private medical health care insurance, for example, is sometimes only available to more senior members of staff within an organisation.

Performance related pay

PERFORMANCE RELATED PAY(PRP) is a pay system designed specifically to motivate staff. Introduced in the 1980s and 1990s, it is now used widely in the UK among white collar workers,

Table 1 Examples of fringe benefits that have been used by businesses

Company	Function	Fringe benefit
Dyson Appliances	Vacuum cleaner manufacturer	Dyson cleaner at reduced rate for new employees
Text 100	PR Agency	2 'Duvet days' (unscheduled holidays) a year
Air Products	Industrial gas supplier	Free exercise classes and subsidised gym and yoga classes, free annual medical checks
Saatchi & Saatchi	Advertising agency	Company pub – 'The Pregnant Man'
Virgin Group	Travel, entertainment, media, retail and financial services	24 hour parties
Body Shop	Cosmetics manufacturer and retailer	£100 a year to 'buy' a training course in new skill of their choice
Tesco	Food retailer	SAYE tax-free share option scheme
Google	Internet search engine provider	Free meals for staff

especially in the financial services industry, such as banking, and in the public sector.

PRP gives workers extra pay for achieving targets. The extra pay may be a lump sum such as £1,000 or it could be a percentage of salary. Some PRP systems make distinctions between levels of achievement. For example, one worker may be rated 'excellent' and receive a 10 per cent bonus, another 'good' and receive a 5 per cent bonus, another 'satisfactory' and receive no bonus.

The targets are likely to be set through a system of APPRAISAL. This is where the performance of individual staff is reviewed against a set of criteria. These criteria could include factors such as arriving for work on time, ability to get on with other workers, improving skills through training or achieving a particular task within the job. Staff are likely to have a performance appraisal interview where someone more senior, such as their line manager, conducts the appraisal.

PRP is widely used because it directly links performance with pay. According to the scientific management school, it should motivate workers to achieve the goals set for them by the organisation.

However, PRP and performance appraisal have been widely criticised for a number of reasons.
- The bonus may be too low to give workers an incentive to achieve their targets.
- Achieving the targets may have far more to do with the smooth running of machinery or technological systems, or how a group of workers perform than the performance of an individual. For example, a worker may set a goal of increasing forms processed by 5 per cent. But the number of forms she receives may depend on how many are processed by other members of her team or whether the printing machines are working smoothly. Where

teamworking is an important management tool, it is likely to be better to give bonuses based on the output of a team rather than an individual.
- Targets may be difficult or even impossible to achieve in the eyes of workers. If this is the case, then they are unlikely to make any effort to achieve them.
- Few staff see appraisal as an independent objective procedure. Staff are quite likely to put their failure to achieve a grade in an appraisal interview down to the unfairness of the interviewer. This is particularly true when there are already problems in the relationship between, say, a worker and his or her boss. Staff who do achieve highly in appraisal interviews may be seen by others as 'favourites' of the interviewer.

Failure to receive a high enough grade in the appraisal process may act as a demotivator of staff. Instead of staff wanting to improve their performance, they may simply give up attempting to change their behaviour and attitudes. Failure to receive a PRP bonus could challenge the physiological needs of staff in Maslow's hierarchy of needs because it deprives them of money. It could also make them feel less 'loved' by the organisation, challenging their need for love and belonging. It will almost certainly knock their self-esteem.

Profit sharing

Some businesses have PROFIT SHARING schemes. In a company, profits would normally be distributed to shareholders. Profit sharing occurs when some of the profits made are distributed to workers as well as shareholders.

Profit sharing can motivate workers to achieve the objectives of the business. Shareholders want higher profits. So too do workers if they are to receive a share of them. Profit sharing therefore unites the goals of both owners and workers for extra money. Profit sharing can also be a way of showing staff that they are appreciated. In Maslow's hierarchy of needs, it may help satisfy the need for love and belonging.

However, most individual workers will have little or no control over how much profit their company makes. If they make extra effort to raise sales or reduce costs, the benefit of that extra effort will be shared between all the other workers. There is no link between individual effort and individual reward in profit sharing. Profit sharing is also unlikely to motivate financially if the amount received is fairly small.

A UK business which uses profit sharing is the John Lewis Partnership, which owns the John Lewis department stores and the supermarket chain Waitrose. The John Lewis Partnership is owned in trust for its workers. So all the profits after tax and retentions are distributed to its workers. The amount given varies according to the salary of the worker. In a good year,

Question 2.

Nick Barnes runs a small printing company in Norwich. It prints cards, leaflets and catalogues for local businesses. It has three design staff and two staff who work as printers. The business pays all its staff the same salary, although at peaks times it might ask employees to work overtime. The business is a limited company and all the shares are owned by Paul and his brother, Wes, who is the company secretary and handles the marketing.

Recently the business has expanded into printing larger posters and designs for exhibitions. Nick has asked Natalie, his longest serving employee, if she will take responsibility for this. He knows that it will be a very profitable venture and wants someone who is experienced and motivated. He is concerned, however, that if he pays her more for the work than other staff they could become demotivated.

Paul has suggested that if this area of the business expands, Natalie could be given a small part-ownership of the business. She would be allowed to buy shares and benefit in future. Nick is still concerned that others in the business may feel that they also deserve shares, as they have all worked for a number of years, although not as long, currently, as Natalie. Nick wonders whether he should involve others in exhibition design and hopes that the revenue gained will generate enough so that he can raise all wages.

(a) Outline ONE advantage and ONE disadvantage of Nick paying his staff overtime.

(b) Explain why a financial rewards system at the business can be a problem.

(c) Discuss whether Nick should use share ownership as a means of financial incentive.

Waitrose workers will receive a profit share handout of more than 20 per cent of their salary. This is a substantial sum. Whether it motivates John Lewis Partnership workers to work harder is debatable.

Share ownership

Some have argued that workers would be motivated by owning a share of their business. They would then have an incentive to work hard because their efforts would contribute to profit. They would benefit from high profits because they would get part of those profits. The value of their shares in the business would also rise if the business were successful.

There are many ways in which employees might acquire shares. One is through **save-as-you-earn schemes**. Here, employees are able to save a regular amount of money from their pay over five years. At the end of five years, they are able to buy shares in the company at the price that they were five years previously. If the share price has gone up over the five years, the saver will make a capital gain.

The granting of **share options** has become a common way of rewarding senior managers and chief executives of large companies. A member of staff is given the option to buy shares in the company at a fixed point in the future, say three years, at a price agreed today. This price may be below, above or at the same level as today's share price. Share options are supposed to be an incentive to senior management to act in a way which will raise the share price significantly. This means that senior management have the same objective as shareholders.

Share options have been controversial. Some chief executives have been able to earn millions of pounds from **exercising** their share options (i.e. buying the shares at the end of the period and then, usually, selling them immediately, make a large capital gain). But when the stock market is rising, the performance of a company can be average and still its share price will rise. So chief executives can earn large amounts even though their company has not done particularly well.

Problems with financial rewards

There is a number of problems that financial incentives schemes have.

Operating problems For financial incentives to work, production needs to have a smooth flow of raw materials, equipment and storage space, and consumer demand must also be fairly stable. These conditions cannot be guaranteed for long. If raw materials did not arrive or ran out, for example, the worker may not achieve a target and receive no bonus for reasons beyond his control. If this happens the employee is unlikely to be motivated by the scheme, and may negotiate for a larger proportion of earnings to be paid as guaranteed 'basic' pay.

Fluctuating earnings A scheme that is linked to output must result in fluctuating earnings. This might be due to changes in demand, the output of the worker or machinery problems. As in the case above, the worker is likely to press for the guaranteed part of pay to be increased, or store output in the 'good times' to prevent problems in the 'bad'. Alternatively, workers may try to 'slow down' productive workers so that benefits are shared out as equally as possible.

Quality The need to increase output to gain rewards can affect quality. There is an incentive for workers to do things as quickly as possible and this can lead to mistakes. Workers filling jars with marmalade may break the jars if they work too quickly. This means the jar is lost and the marmalade as well, for fear of splinters. For some businesses, such as food processing, chemicals or drug production, errors could be disastrous.

Changes in payment Because of the difficulties above, employers constantly modify their incentive schemes. Improved financial reward schemes should stop workers manipulating the system and may give renewed motivation to some workers. However, constant changes mean that employees do not always understand exactly how to gain rewards.

Quality of working life Financial rewards based upon payment by results require a certain type of job design. This often means tight control by management, routine and repetition. The scientific management school argues that production will only be efficient if workers know exactly what to do in any situation and their activities are tightly controlled by management. The result of this is that boredom and staleness may set in and the worker's 'standard of life' at work may be low.

Jealousy Individual workers may be jealous of the rewards earned by their colleagues. This can lead to problems in relationships and a possible lack of motivation. Increasingly, businesses are using group or plant-wide incentives to solve this.

Measuring performance For incentives to work effectively it must be possible to measure performance. For example, a business must be able to measure the number of components made by a worker if she is paid a bonus after 20,000 are made a month.

Team-based rewards Problems may take place if rewards are based on the performance of a team, but some workers are more productive then others in the team.

Given these problems, why are financial incentive schemes still used by many firms? Managers may find a use for a certain scheme. For example, financial rewards may be used to overcome resistance to change. A business introducing new technology, such as computers, may offer an incentive for staff to retrain or spend extra time becoming familiar with the new system. Employees often see benefits in such systems of payment. They may feel that they are gaining some control over their own actions in the workplace, being able to work at their own pace if they so wish. Furthermore, many businesses believe that financial rewards ought to work as it is logical to assume that employees work harder if they are offered more money.

KEYTERMS

Annualised hours contracts – a payment system based on a fixed number of hours to be worked each year, but a flexible number of hours each day, week or month.

Appraisal – where the performance of an individual worker is reviewed against a set of criteria.

Blue collar (or manual) workers – workers who do mainly physical work, like assembly line workers.

Bonus – an extra payment made in recognition of the contribution a worker has made to the company.

Commission – payment made, typically for achieving a target such as a sales target.

Fringe benefits – payment in kind over and above the wage or salary paid, such as a company car or luncheon vouchers.

Overtime – time worked over and above the basic working week.

Payment by results – payment methods that reward workers for the quantity and quality of work they produce.

Performance related pay (PRP) – a payment system, typically where workers are paid a higher amount if they achieve certain targets set for them by their employer.

Piece rates – a payment system where employees are paid an agreed rate for every item produced.

Profit sharing – where workers are given a share of the profits made by the company which employs them.

Salary – pay, usually of non-manual workers, expressed as a yearly figure but paid monthly.

Time rates – rates of pay based on an amount of time, usually per hour.

Wages – payments made to employees for work done, usually given weekly to manual workers.

While collar (or non-manual) workers – workers who do non-physical work like office workers or teachers.

KNOWLEDGE

1. Explain the difference between payment systems frequently found for blue collar workers and white collar workers.
2. Explain the difference between piece rates and commission.
3. Why might fringe benefits motivate workers?
4. Explain the role of targets in performance related pay systems.
5. How might profit sharing schemes motivate workers?
6. Explain the difference between a save-as-you-earn scheme for buying shares and share option schemes.
7. Identify five problems of financial reward schemes.

Case Study: *Incentives for Value Added Resellers*

Value Added Resellers (VARs) are businesses which take a manufacturer's product and add their own value before selling it. For example, a VAR might take an operating system, add its own specialist software for, say, architects, and then sell the bundle to architect businesses. Manufacturers offer VARs a number of incentives to sell their products.

'The best incentive is money in the pocket' said one VAR. Most incentive schemes are based on money and commissions. Other means are used, but do they work? 'Freebies' such as day trips and air miles are commonly on offer. But in the day-to-day slog of running a business, motivation to take advantage of such benefits can be hard to muster. 'We don't really bother with these schemes' said one VAR. 'They create more administration than they're worth. 'Luxury rewards are still available as part of wider packages. For example, the top performing VAR for SolidWorks, was invited to Hawaii.

Opinions on whether rewards for individuals are effective will depend on to whom you speak. There will always be salespeople who thrive on beating the competition and who want to gain recognition for doing so. Peter Dickin, marketing manager at Delcam, feels that a more inclusive approach is required. 'Incentives targeted just at salespeople neglect the contribution of others, which can be demotivating. We tend to favour schemes that foster team building.'

Incentive schemes that reward a group of high-performing VARs have to be carefully structured to create a level playing field to give companies of different sizes and locations a chance. Clearly this is not always being achieved. One disgruntled VAR said 'I have never, ever been incentivised by any scheme I have worked with in the past. Overpaid VAR managers justify their own existence, even so far as coming up with jollies that they had no prior interest in, such as driving racing cars and sailing around the Leeward Isles.'

Schemes based mainly on the volume of sales can have negative implications for all parties. 'The aims of the incentives that we work to are not those that suit our long-term business goals, nor the needs of our customers,' said one VAR. 'They are generally incentives to motivate short-term business.'

The opportunity to gain marketing funds is another regular element of incentive schemes, particularly where a business wants to make inroads into a particular market. IBM, for example, offers a special marketing fund to companies who join its Top Contributor Programme and commit themselves to selling $100,000 of software to the SME (small and medium-sized business) market.

As free trips and luxury gifts are used less, terms such as 'active business management' have crept into the language of incentives. 'We don't incentivise on volume' explains John Mitchell, Manager of Indirect Channels, Europe, PLM Solutions. 'We incentivise VARs to invest in their business and improve the quality of their service to our customers.'

Many VARs are dubious about whether the incentives on offer

actually made them do anything differently. Not offering incentives doesn't go down well either. One VAR said "Our own main vendor doesn't offer any incentive schemes (or even buy drinks at the bar at sales events). So we will have to do our best focusing upon making money for ourselves.'

Source: adapted from retailsystemseller.com.

(a) What is meant by the terms:
   (i) luxury rewards (3 marks);
   (ii) incentivise on volume? (3 marks)
(b) Describe the different financial rewards in the article. (10 marks)
(c) Examine the advantages and disadvantages of each financial reward scheme for VARs. (12 marks)
(d) Assess which financial rewards are likely to be most motivating to VARs selling products such as computers for manufacturers to small businesses. (12 marks)

The need for non-financial rewards

Financial rewards have often been used in the past by firms in an attempt to motivate employees to improve productivity. However, increasingly businesses have realised that:

- the chance to earn more money may not be an effective motivator;
- financial incentive schemes are difficult to operate;
- individual reward schemes may no longer be effective as production has become organised into group tasks;
- other factors may be more important in motivating employees.

If other factors are more important than pay in motivating workers, it is important for firms to identify them. Only then can a business make sure its workforce is motivated. Figure 1 shows some of the factors that employees might consider important in their work environment. Many of these have been identified by the **human relations approach**. A business may consider introducing non-financial incentives to help employees satisfy these needs.

Job design and job redesign

The dissatisfaction with financial incentive schemes reached its peak in the 1960s and 1970s. In response the 'Quality of Working Life Movement' began to develop ideas which were based around the **human relations school**, as first outlined by the Hawthorne studies. It was argued that workers were likely to be motivated by non-monetary factors and that jobs needed to be DESIGNED or REDESIGNED to take these factors into account. Five principles were put forward which any incentive scheme needed to consider.

- The principle of closure. A job must include all tasks necessary to complete a product or process. This should ensure that work is meaningful for employees and that workers feel a sense of achievement.
- Control and monitoring of tasks. Jobs should be designed so that an army of inspectors is not needed. The worker, or the team, should take responsibility for quality.
- Task variety. There should be an increase in the range of tasks that a worker carries out. This should allow job rotation to occur and keep the workers interested in their work.
- Self-regulation. Employees should have control of the speed at which they work and some choice over work methods and sequence.
- Interaction and co-operation. The job structure should allow some social interaction and the chance for an employee to work in a group.

Various methods were devised to try and put these principles into practice. They included job enrichment, job enlargement, job rotation, quality control circles and employee participation in groups. These are examined in this unit.

Poor job design may mean that employees do not achieve their full potential. This means that the firm's output may suffer as a result. For example, an architect who is constantly having her work checked for accuracy is unlikely to be as productive as possible, due to constant interruptions. Also, jobs that do not meet workers' needs are likely to lead to poor motivation,

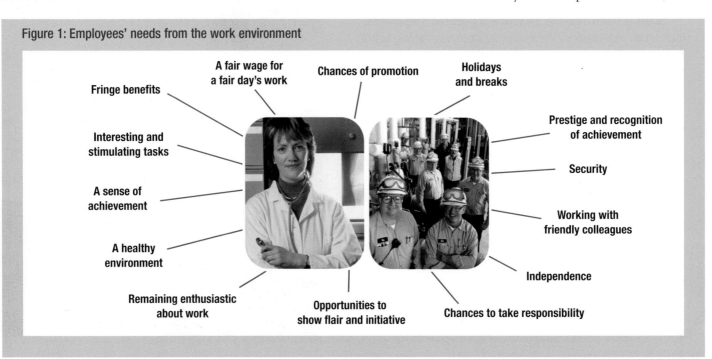

Figure 1: Employees' needs from the work environment

Fringe benefits

A fair wage for a fair day's work

Chances of promotion

Holidays and breaks

Prestige and recognition of achievement

Interesting and stimulating tasks

Security

A sense of achievement

Working with friendly colleagues

A healthy environment

Independence

Remaining enthusiastic about work

Opportunities to show flair and initiative

Chances to take responsibility

Table 1: Problems of job redesign

- Employees may be familiar with the old approach to doing a job and may resent new changes. They might not want the extra duties that result from job redesign.
- Job redesign may be expensive. New methods often require extra training. In addition, redesigned jobs might lead employees to claim extra pay for new responsibilities. There is no guarantee that the redesign of jobs will increase productivity in the long term.
- The introduction of new machinery can make job redesign more difficult. Certain jobs have had to be redesigned almost totally as new technology has changed production processes. In some cases employees have had to learn totally new skills, such as when newspaper page design on computer screens replaced old methods of cutting and pasting type onto pages. At other times skills may be made redundant.
- Effects on output and productivity. Redesigned jobs need to be evaluated to gauge whether they have actually motivated the workforce to increase output.

absenteeism and a lack of quality in work. The process of redesigning existing jobs is often difficult to carry out in practice for a number of reasons, as shown in Table 1.

Job enlargement

JOB ENLARGEMENT involves giving an employee more work to do of a similar nature. For example, instead of an employee putting wheels onto a bicycle he could be allowed to put the entire product together. It is argued that this variety prevents boredom with one repetitive task and encourages employees' satisfaction in their work, as they are completing the entire process. Job enlargement is more efficient if workers are organised in groups. Each worker can be trained to do all jobs in the group and job rotation can take place. Other forms of job enlargement include job rotation and job loading.

Critics of this method argue that it is simply giving a worker 'more of the same'. It is often called the problem of **horizontal loading** - instead of turning five screws the worker turns ten. In many businesses today such tasks are carried out more effectively by machines, where repetitive tasks can be completed quickly and efficiently without strain, boredom or dissatisfaction. It could even be argued that allowing employees to complete the entire process will reduce efficiency. This is because the fall in productivity from carrying out many tasks more than offsets any productivity gains from increased worker satisfaction.

Job rotation

JOB ROTATION involves an employee changing jobs or tasks from time to time. This could mean, for example, a move to a different part of the production line to carry out a different task. Alternatively, an employee may be moved from the personnel to

the marketing department where they have skills which are common to both. From an employee's point of view this should reduce boredom and enable a variety of skills and experience to be gained. An employer might also benefit from a more widely trained workforce.

Although job rotation may motivate a worker, it is possible that any gains in productivity may be offset by a fall in output as workers learn new jobs and take time to 'settle in'. Worker motivation is not guaranteed if the employee is simply switched from one boring job to another. In fact some workers do not like the uncertainty that job changes lead to and may become dissatisfied. Although used by firms such as Volkswagen in the past, where employees carried out a variety of production tasks, job rotation has been less popular in the last decade.

Job enrichment and job loading

The idea of JOB ENRICHMENT came from Herzberg's two factor theory. Whereas job enlargement expands the job 'horizontally', job enrichment attempts to give employees greater responsibility by 'vertically' extending their role in the production process. An employee, for example, may be given responsibility for planning a task, quality control, work supervision, ordering materials and maintenance.

Job enrichment gives employees a 'challenge', which will develop their 'unused' skills and encourage them to be more

Question 1.

Instyle is a fashion design company. It has placed an advertisement on a recruitment website. Part of the advertisement included the following.

Instyle is a modern fashion design company. We want a tailor with at least one year's experience to help with making up our bespoke fashion designs. The main duties will include making up clothing such as suits, shirts, dresses and trousers, including sewing parts together, adding buttons and pressing. You will also work as part of a small team dealing directly with customers. This will involve measuring clients, making a draft of a master pattern and altering patterns to fit customers.

(a) Explain the term 'job design' using an example from the advertisement.
(b) How might the business be making use of job enlargement?
(c) Discuss how the business might make use of job enrichment techniques.

productive. The aim is to make workers feel they have been rewarded for their contribution to the company. Employees will also be provided with varied tasks, which may possibly lead to future promotion. It is not, however, without problems. Workers who feel that they are unable to carry out the 'extra work', or who consider that they are forced into it, may not respond to incentives. In addition, it is unlikely that all workers will react the same to job enrichment. Trade unions sometimes argue that such practices are an attempt to reduce the labour force, and disputes about the payment for extra responsibilities may arise. In practice, job enrichment has been found to be most successful in administrative and technical positions.

Job loading is where workers are given extra tasks when colleagues are off sick or if they have left and not been replaced. It can be particularly important in manufacturing, where absence can disrupt an assembly line for example.

Empowerment

Delegated decision making can be more successful if employees were empowered. EMPOWERMENT of employees involves a number of aspects.

- Recognising that employees are capable of doing more than they have in the past.
- Making employees feel trusted, so that they can carry out their jobs without constant checking.
- Giving employees control of decision making.
- Giving employees self confidence.
- Recognising employees' achievements.
- Developing a work environment where employees are motivated and interested in their work.

Many businesses now recognise the need to empower employees. There is a number of advantages of this for a business and for employees.

- Employees may feel more motivated. They feel trusted and feel that businesses recognise their talents. This should improve productivity and benefit the business in the long term, for example by reducing absenteeism.
- Employees may find less stress in their work as they have greater control over their working lives. This could reduce illness and absenteeism.
- Decisions may be made by those most suited to make them. Also, employees may feel less frustrated that senior staff who are less equipped to make decisions are making them.
- There may be greater employee skills and personal development.
- Businesses may be able to streamline their organisations and delegate decision making.
- Workers may feel less frustrated by more senior staff making decisions which they feel may be incorrect.

However, empowerment is sometimes criticised as simply a means of cutting costs and removing layers from the business. Passing decision making down the hierarchy might allow a company to make managers redundant. Employees are given more work to do, but for the same pay. Some businesses argue that they want to empower workers, but in practice they are unable or

---

Question 2.

St Luke's Communications is a London Advertising Agency owned by its staff. It was formed on St. Luke's day 1995 and has expanded from 35 to 75 staff. It is renowned for its innovative approach to stimulating staff. Teams are a core part of what the advertising agency does. People can sit anywhere and work anytime, but it is their personal responsibility to see that their behaviour doesn't damage the team. In a more traditional structure, empowerment means the handing down of power. If the organisation is owned by everyone, then everyone can 'rise to true freedom from the concepts of authority and power'. Asserting power would seriously damage this concept, so that discipline is through peers, not from above.

Staff are encouraged to contribute to projects other than those to which they have been specifically assigned. Everyone has the right to stumble into meetings. At meetings staff can mention incomplete ideas. It is argued that such thoughts may inspire others. There is also no owned space. Computers are available to all, and if there are not enough to go around, staff may bring in their own. It has been suggested that business has a turnover rate of around 10 per cent, although only around 1 per cent go to competitors. A turnover rate of 25 per cent is typical for advertising agencies.

Source: adapted from www.flexibility.co.uk, harvardbusinessonline, www.fastcompany.com, *The Sunday Times*.

(a) **Using examples from the article, explain how the business motivates employees.**
(b) **Explain how this will benefit (i) employees and (ii) the business.**

---

unwilling to do this. For example, a manager may feel insecure about subordinates making decisions that might affect his position in the business. Feeling that they may 'make the wrong decision' might lead to constant interruptions which are counter-productive. A further problem is the cost involved to the business, such as the cost of training employees or changing the workplace.

Team working

The Swedish car firm Volvo is a well quoted example of a company that has effectively introduced 'teamwork'. In both its plants at Kalmar and Uddevalla, it set up production in teams of eight to ten highly skilled workers. The teams decided between themselves how work was to be distributed and how to solve problems that arise. It is arguable whether these practices led to an increase in productivity, but the company firmly believed that this method of organisation was better than an assembly line system. A similar system has been used at Honda UK. Team working has a number of benefits.

- Productivity may be greater because of pooled talents.
- People can specialise and draw on the skills and knowledge of others in the team.
- Increasingly businesses are finding that the abilities of teams are needed to solve difficult business problems.
- Responsibility is shared. People may be more prepared to take risks.
- Ideas may be created by brainstorming.
- It allows flexible working.

However, in practice team work does not always produce the desired results. Part of the problem may lie in the way teams are organised. Members may fail to work well together for several reasons, from lack of a sense of humour to clashing goals. Studies of teams in the US have shown a number of problems with team work.

- Too much emphasis on harmony. Teams probably work best when there is room for disagreement. Papering over differences sometimes leads to vague or bland recommendations.
- Too much discord. Tension can destroy team effectiveness.
- Poor preparation. It is important that team members prepare for meetings by focusing on the facts. Members should have a detailed knowledge of the issues at hand and all work with the same information.
- Too much emphasis on individualism. For example, teams may fail to deliver results if the emphasis of the company is placed on individualism.
- A feeling of powerlessness. To work well, teams must be able to influence decisions.
- The failure of senior management to work well together. This creates problems because team members may walk into meetings with different priorities.
- Meeting-itis. Teams should not try to do everything together. Too many meetings waste the team's time.
- Seeing teams as the solution for all problems. Some tasks are better accomplished by individuals, rather than groups.

Quality control circles

QUALITY CONTROL CIRCLES or QUALITY CIRCLES are small groups of workers (about 5-20) in the same area of production who meet regularly to study and solve production problems. In addition, such groups are intended to motivate and involve workers on the shopfloor. Unlike job enlargement and job enrichment, they allow the workforce directly to improve the nature of the work they are doing.

Quality control circles started in America, where it was felt workers could be motivated by being involved in decision making. The idea gained in popularity in Japan and was taken up by Western businesses. Examples of their use can be found in Japanese companies setting up plants in the UK in the 1990s. Honda at Swindon has had 52 teams of six people looking at improvements that can be made in areas allocated to the groups, for example, safety.

Quality control circles are only likely to work if they have the support of both management and employees. Businesses have to want worker participation and involvement in decision making, and set up a structure that supports this. Workers and their representatives also need to support the scheme. Employees must feel that their views within the circle are valued and must make a contribution to decisions.

Multiskilling

MULTISKILLING is a term used to describe the process of enhancing the skills of employees. It is argued that giving individuals the skills and responsibilities to deal with a greater variety of issues will allow a business to respond more quickly and effectively to problems. So for example, a receptionist might have been trained to pass on calls to other people in a business. Multiskilling this job could mean that the receptionist now deals with more straightforward enquiries himself. This would result in a quicker response to the customer's enquiry. It would also free up time for other people to work on more demanding activities.

Certain motivation theories suggest that giving individuals more skills and responsibilities can improve their work performance. A criticism of multiskilling is that individuals are only given more skills so that they are expected to work harder without any extra pay. Problems may also result if workers are not trained adequately for their new roles.

Achieving a work-life balance

Recently there has been a stress on the need for employers to deal with the work-life balance of employees. Life is becoming faster and more complex, but without the support of communities or extended families. It is suggested that unless employers are sympathetic and supportive of employees' external needs, there could be an increase in health related absences such as stress. This could affect the operation and efficiency of the business.

Organisational structure, financial and non-financial rewards

There is a link between the motivational techniques used by managers in business and the organisational structure of a business. For example, a business with a traditional and rigid hierarchy will often make use of financial rewards. Each level of the hierarchy will have an associated level of financial reward, which is clear to employees in the organisation. Employees can see this and be motivated into working to achieve promotion or move through the levels of the business.

In a hierarchy non-financial rewards may also be motivating in certain circumstances. As workers achieve a certain living standard with which they are comfortable, they may find that other factors are more motivating, such as the ability to make their own decisions or to have flexibility in their work. These factors can be motivating for higher level posts. Job enrichment and empowerment further down the hierarchy may also be motivating to employees, especially if their jobs are repetitive and boring. However, a manger must take care when empowering workers as not all employees want to or feel able to take extra responsibility.

In other forms of organisational structure non-financial rewards may be particularly motivating. For example, in a matrix structure workers are working in teams. The support of other members of the team or respect from colleagues may be important as a motivation factor. Managers may have to generate a sense of team belonging to motivate staff. In an independent structure the ability to make decisions is likely to be very motivating to employees.

KEYTERMS

Empowerment – to give official authority to employees to make decisions and control their own activities.

Job design – the process of organising the tasks and activities required to perform a job.

Job redesign – changing the tasks and activities of a job, perhaps in an attempt to motivate workers.

Job enlargement – giving an employee more work to do of a similar nature.

Job enrichment – an attempt to give employees greater responsibility and recognition by 'vertically' extending their role in the production process.

Job rotation – the changing of jobs or tasks from time to time.

Multiskilling – the processes of enhancing the skills of employees.

Teamworking – Employees working in small groups with a common aim.

Quality control circles or Quality Circles – small groups of workers in the same area of production which meet regularly to study and solve all types of production problems.

KNOWLEDGE

1. State five possible non-financial rewards that may be an incentive for individuals.
2. What principles would a 'good' job have according to the 'Quality of Working Life Movement'?
3. State four methods of job redesign.
4. 'Job enlargement is simply a method of horizontal loading.' Explain this statement.
5. Under what circumstances might job rotation not lead to an increase in productivity?
6. Suggest four problems of working in teams.
7. Why is job enrichment said to extend an employee's role in the firm vertically?
8. What are the advantages to an employee of quality control circles?
9. State three features of empowerment.
10. What is meant by achieving a work-life balance?

Case Study: *Zinx*

Zinx is an independent boutique hotel and restaurant in the South East of England. It employs 60 staff. It has always had a very traditional organisation with senior managers, departmental managers, supervisors, head waiters, bar staff, cleaners and administrators. It has read the following article about staff in independent hotels and is considering changing its operations to increase staff motivation.

'Empowerment is a frequently used buzzword, not just in the hospitality industry. Empowerment means staff can make decisions. If hotels want to remain successful, they need to be driven by their staff on customer service. Independent hotels have to go "above and beyond" and work harder in a competitive environment. This helps to ensure survival through a high percentage of repeat business, while fostering growth of new clients.

Guests appreciate dealing with people who are empowered. The last thing an arriving guest needs is to be given the runaround, going through "layers" of management to get what they need. Empowerment means, rather than becoming defensive, staff assume accountability mistakes and put them right.

Essential to empowerment is the practice of "trust, but verify". A balance is necessary because empowerment can backfire especially in the wrong application or misguided interpretation. Owners and managers cannot give responsibility to staff without empowering them. But attention should be given to training staff to be ensure empowerment works. Empowerment can work against you if you have a staff member too empowered without direction.

In the hotel industry employees should be seen as part of a team. The terms employee and management create divisions. Such a divide in organisational structure does not foster a sense of teamwork. It's a

"them and me" situation rather than a "we or us". Terms such as staff member illustrate better and reinforce working together. This creates a culture of "leadership teamwork" for the staff working with guests. Having fluid organisational structures reduce levels of management, separating President/CEO/General Manager from guests. The more layers you have, the more distant you remain from the guest and from the pulse of the staff.'

Source: adapted in part from www.hotelinteractive.com.

(a) Explain the meaning of the terms (i) empowerment (3 marks) and (ii) teamwork (3 marks).
(b) Explain TWO ways in which the organisation at Zinx might change to help motivate employees. (6 marks)
(c) Explain how greater empowerment at Zinx can affect (i) employees, (ii) clients and (ii) the business. (8 marks)
(d) Discuss whether Zinx should increase empowerment at the business. (10 marks)

Operational decisions and targets

OPERATIONS MANAGEMENT is the organisation and control of the process by which inputs, such as labour, materials and machinery, are transformed into final products or by which services are provided to customers. Production managers, for example, are responsible for making decisions about:

- what production methods are to be used;
- what levels of input of labour, machinery and materials are needed to produce a given quantity of output;
- how best to utilise the firm's capacity;
- what stock levels are required to support production;
- how to ensure that work is completed on time;
- how best to ensure quality.

Decisions about the entire business that affect production also need to be made. For example:

- What is the optimal size for a business? Should there be five employees, 500 or 500,000?
- Where should production take place? On one or two sites? In the UK or the Far East?

Good operations management can help a business to be more effective. One approach which operations managers are likely to use is to set OPERATIONAL TARGETS. Setting targets can help managers monitor the performance of the production department. A number of key targets might be used, as shown in Figure 1.

Unit costs

Unit cost is the cost of producing a single unit of output. It is the same as average cost. It can be calculated as:

$$\text{Unit cost} = \frac{\text{Total cost}}{\text{Output}}$$

So, for example, if a computer manufacturer produced 12,000 laptop computers in a year at a total cost of £3,480,000, the unit cost would be given by:

$$\text{Unit cost} = \frac{£3,480,000}{12,000} = £290$$

This means that each single laptop computer cost £290 to make.

Production managers may set operational targets for unit costs. These costs can be measured at the end of a production run and compared with the targets. If actual unit costs are higher than the targets, the production manager is likely to search for reasons why so that appropriate action can be taken. Generally, businesses are always looking for ways to *control* or reduce unit costs.

Figure 1: Operational targets

Unit costs · Productivity · Capacity utilisation · Operational targets · Quality · Stock levels

Capacity utilisation

CAPACITY UTILISATION is about the use that a business makes from its resources. If a business is not able to increase output, it is said to be running at full capacity. Its capacity utilisation is 100 per cent. So if a 52 seater coach from London to Edinburgh has 52 passengers, it is operating at full capacity. If it had 32 passengers it would be operating at less than full capacity and so it would have EXCESS, SURPLUS, SPARE or UNUSED CAPACITY.

Businesses do not always operate at full capacity. It may not be possible to keep all resources and machinery fully employed all the time. However, most businesses would wish to be operating at close to full capacity, such as 90 per cent.

In some cases businesses even choose to operate at less than full capacity in order to be flexible. For example, they might want to have capacity to cope with increased orders from regular customers. Without this, a business might let down its customers and risk losing them.

Capacity utilisation can be measured by comparing actual or current output with the potential output at full capacity using the formula:

$$\text{Capacity utilisation} = \frac{\text{Current output}}{\text{Maximum possible output}} \times 100$$

A printing operation might be able to operate for ten hours, six days a week using shifts. If it only had enough work to operate for 48 hours last week, the capacity utilisation would be:

$$\text{Capacity utilisation} = \frac{48}{(10 \times 6)} \times 100 = 80\%$$

Another example might be a printing machine that is capable of printing 10,000 leaflets in a time period but only prints 9,000. It has a capacity utilisation of (9,000 ÷ 10,000) x 100 = 90 per cent. In this case the machine has unused, excess, surplus or spare capacity of 10 per cent.

Costs and capacity utilisation

A business can lower its unit or average costs if it can increase its capacity utilisation. This is because some of its costs are fixed. Higher levels of capacity utilisation and higher levels of output, will make a business more efficient. Table 1 shows capacity utilisation output, variable cost, fixed cost, total cost and average cost (unit cost) for a component manufacturer. When capacity utilisation is raised from 60 per cent to 80 per cent, for example, average cost falls from £2.42 to £2.31. This is because the fixed costs of £50,000 are spread over more units of output. This explains why firms will always be keen to raise capacity utilisation.

Table 1: Capacity utilisation, output, variable cost, fixed cost, total cost, unit cost for a component manufacturer

Actual output (units)	120,000	160,000
Maximum possible output (units)	200,000	200,000
Capacity utilisation	60%	80%
Variable costs (£2 per unit)	£240,000	£320,000
Fixed costs	£50,000	£50,000
Total cost	£290,000	£370,000
Unit cost	£2.42	£2.31

Improving capacity utilisation

A business will make better use of its resources if it increases its capacity utilisation. Its unit costs will be lower and profits will be higher. How can firms increase capacity utilisation?

Reduced capacity A business might decide to cut capacity. It might do this by RATIONALISING, for example. This involves reducing excess capacity by getting rid of resources that the business can do without. There is a number of measures a business might take.
- Reducing staff by making people redundant, employing more part-time and temporary staff and offering early retirement.
- Selling off unused fixed assets such as machinery, vehicles, office space, warehouses and factory space.
- Leasing capacity. Debenhams has leased unused floor space in its stores to other retailers, for example. Parts of a factory could also be leased to another manufacturer. The advantage of this is that the space may be reclaimed if demand picks up again.
- Moving to smaller premises where costs are lower.
- MOTHBALLING some resources. This means that fixed assets, such as machinery, are left unused but are

Question 1.

Oliver Handy make mattresses. It is an established business and operates from a small factory in Swindon. It employs twelve staff and has recently appointed a new production manager. In 2006, the then manager retired after 25 years of service to the company. He was replaced by the current manager. Within two months of the new manager arriving some sweeping changes were made to production methods and working practices. The new manager emphasised the importance of production targets, unit costs, staff rewards and operations management. Table 2 shows some financial information for Oliver Handy.

Table 2: Financial information for Oliver Handy

	2004	2005	2006	2007 (£)
Total output	12,000	13,500	14,000	17,000
Total cost	252,000	297,000	305,200	297,500

(a) What is meant by operations management?
(b) (i) Calculate the unit costs for the four years.
    (ii) What impact has the new production manager had on unit costs?
(c) How can setting operational targets help a business like Oliver Handy?

maintained, so that they can be brought back into use if necessary.

Increased sales If a business sells more of its output, it will have to produce more. Therefore capacity utilisation will rise. A business might need to spend money on promotion to increase sales, for example. If these costs are not covered by the extra revenue generated, raising capacity utilisation in this way may not be viable.

Increased usage A problem that many businesses face is dealing with peak demand. Train operators can find that capacity utilisation is close to 100 per cent during the 'rush hour', but perhaps as low as 10 per cent late at night. Such businesses would like to increase capacity utilisation during 'off-peak' hours. This might explain why discounts are offered for 'off-peak' travel.

Subcontracting Capacity utilisation can vary considerably within a business. Where capital equipment has low utilisation rates, it might be more efficient for the business to SUBCONTRACT or OUTSOURCE the work. This means hiring or contracting another business to do work which was previously done in-house.

For instance, a business might run a small fleet of delivery vans which on average are on the road for four hours per day. It is likely that it would be cheaper for the business to sell the vans and employ a company to make the deliveries. The delivery company would be more efficient because it would be running its vans for much longer during the day. There may also be cost savings in terms of staff. If the business employed full-time drivers for the vans, they would have been under-utilised if they only worked four hours per day.

Subcontracting can also lead to other cost advantages. The delivery business will be a specialist business. It should operate its delivery service more efficiently than a business with a few vans and little knowledge of the industry. If nothing else, it should have greater buying power. It might be able, for instance, to negotiate lower prices for its vans because it is buying more vans. If it is a very small business, its hourly wages may be less than, say, a union-negotiated rate at the larger business.

An alternative outsourcing strategy is to take on outsourcing contracts for other businesses. For example, a major manufacturer of soap could accept contracts from rival soap manufacturers to improve its capacity utilisation. Outsourcing then becomes a strategy for increasing demand for the business.

Redeployment If a business has too many resources in one part, it may be possible to deploy them in another part. For example, a bank may ask some of its employees to work in another branch for a short period.

Advantages and disadvantages of working at full capacity

Advantages Working at full capacity has some benefits.
- Average costs will be minimised because fixed costs will be spread across as many units of output as possible. This will help to raise profits.
- Staff motivation might be good if workers feel secure in their jobs.
- A busy operation can improve the company's image. As a result, customers might be more confident when placing orders.

Problems However, there may be some drawbacks when a firm is unable to increase output any more.
- The pressure of working at full capacity all the time might put a strain on some of the resources. For example, workers might be doing too much overtime, resulting in tiredness and stress. This might cause accidents or absence.

Question 2.

Zaman & Nazran is a business which specialises in the manufacture of diecast zinc and aluminium products. It produces components for a variety of industries. Since being founded in the mid-1990s, it has grown to today's workforce of 14 employees. Sales were up 7 per cent last year and 50 per cent up from five years ago. It is confident that in the next five years, it can increase its sales by another 50 per cent.

Table 3 shows the number of hours that machinery and equipment were used during each week between July and August 2008. Management works on the assumption that 60 hours per week represents full capacity for the business. This reflects the maximum number of hours that the existing labour force would be prepared to work, including overtime.

Currently, equipment in a typical week is used to 75 per cent capacity. Working to 100 per cent capacity in any week, such as in the second week of July 2008, is unusual and difficult to maintain because machines break down or employees are off work sick. In fact, in the second week of July, the business was forced to sub-contract some of the work to rival companies because it couldn't cope with delivery deadlines set by customers. Seasonal factors affect demand. Orders often fall in late July and early August because customers tend to produce less due to their workers taking summer holidays.

Management has considered rationalisation to reduce costs. Equally the business is committed to an investment programme to buy the latest equipment, which will increase productive efficiency and allow for expansion of sales in the future.

(a) Explain what is meant by:
  (i) 'capacity utilisation';
  (ii) 'rationalisation'.
(b) Calculate capacity utilisation for weeks 3–4 in July and weeks 1–4 in August.
(c) Analyse two ways in which the business could increase capacity utilisation.
(d) Discuss whether the business would perform better in the long term if it sold off half its plant and equipment, moved to smaller premises, sacked half the workforce and used subcontractors to complete work which it could not manufacture to meet delivery deadlines from customers.

Table 3

	July				August			
Week	1	2	3	4	1	2	3	4
Hours worked	44	60	47	31	41	45	45	47
Capacity utilisation (%)	73	100	?	?	?	?	?	?

Machines may also be overworked to breaking point.

- The business might lose lucrative orders from new customers.
- There may be insufficient time for staff training and important maintenance work.

Matching production to demand

A production manager has to make sure that production levels tie in with the level of demand. If production levels exceed demand there will be a build up of stocks. This may be expensive because stock holding costs can be very high indeed. Also, if the stocks are not being sold, there will be a drain on resources. However, if production levels are too low, the business may not be able to satisfy demand. This could lead to a loss of trade if customers are kept waiting and decide to buy from a rival. Matching production with demand often means that operational methods should have some flexibility built in. This can be achieved in a number of ways.

Offering overtime Production managers could ask staff to work overtime if orders increase. Overtime is often popular with workers because overtime rates are usually higher than basic wage rates. They may be time and half or double time. However, not all workers will want to work overtime because they have other commitments.

Hiring part-time or temporary staff A business might use temporary or part-time staff to deal with surges in demand. Temporary staff can be 'hired and fired' according to demand levels. They will be employed on very short-term contracts. However, temporary staff will have to be trained and may not be as reliable as permanent staff. Part-time staff are generally more flexible than full-time staff. They can often adapt to changes in the hours they work.

Making flexible use of capital Fluctuations in demand may also mean that capital needs to be flexible. This might be achieved by leasing machinery and equipment in the short-term. For example, vehicles, tools and machinery can be leased to cope with increases in demand.

Using suppliers Businesses will need flexible suppliers. When orders increase a business might need to call on suppliers to make emergency deliveries. Suppliers that cannot offer flexibility and reliability might be avoided.

Adjusting production Production levels can also adjusted to match demand through rationalisation and subcontracting. This is discussed above.

Holding finished stocks A common way of matching production and demand is to hold stocks of finished goods. If

demand increases, orders can be satisfied from stocks. If demand falls, then stocks can be accumulated. However, stock holding costs need to be taken into account when using this approach.

Some businesses have to cope with **seasonal demand**. These could be businesses operating farms, hotels and other leisure activities, for example. They have to organise their operations to deal with 'peak' demand in the high season and very low demand out of season. The methods discussed above are likely to be even more important to such businesses.

Non-standard orders

It is not unusual for businesses to receive **non-standard orders**. These are orders for goods that the business does not normally produce. For example, a publisher may be asked for a particular book to be available in the Welsh language. To meet such an order businesses may need to reset machines, use different labour skills, different raw materials and possibly different tools. In the example above the publisher would need to employ someone to translate the text, typeset the whole book again and organise a small production run. To meet non-standard orders extra costs will be incurred and a business may charge a premium price. Non-standard orders might be irritating but refusing such orders might lead to a loss of custom. However, accepting non-standard orders might gain new long-term customers.

KEYTERMS

Capacity utilisation – the use that a business makes of its resources.

Excess or surplus capacity – when a business has too many resources, such as labour and capital, to produce its desired level of output.

Mothballing – when machines, equipment or building space are left unused but maintained so they could be brought back into use if necessary.

Operations management – the organisation and control of the process by which inputs, such as labour, materials and machinery, are transformed into final products or by which services are provided to customers.

Operational targets – the goals set by a business that must be achieved in the production of a product or provision of a service.

Rationalising – reducing the number of resources, particularly labour and capital, put into the production process, usually undertaken because a business has excess capacity.

Subcontracting or outsourcing – hiring or contracting another business to do work which could be done in-house by a business.

KNOWLEDGE

1. State four decisions a production manager might have to make.
2. State four operational targets that might be set by a business.
3. Explain what is meant by unit cost.
4. Why will unit costs fall if capacity is better utilised?

5. State three ways in which a business might reduce capacity.
6. What is meant by redeployment?
7. What are non-standard orders?
8. State four measures that a business might take to help match production with orders.

Case Study: Gibson's Golf Buggies Ltd

Gibson's has manufactured golf buggies for 27 years. The company employs 48 staff and has a factory in Manchester. Its standard product has the following features.

- Double-seated, four-wheeled electric powered
- Twist grip stepless speed control for smooth operation
- Forward/reverse switch conveniently located
- Safe operator controlled speed governor
- Maximum speed restricted to 8mph in consideration of other golfers
- Hill climbing ability: 1:3 gradient
- Battery charging unit simply plugged into rear of buggy
- Two heavy duty batteries – 12V 75 amp/hour coupled in series.

In 2004, the company started to experience some problems. Intense competition from overseas manufacturers, China in particular, resulted in a decline in sales. The company responded by making cost savings and investing in a new marketing campaign. This appeared to halt the decline in sales and boost profit margins. However, the factory was left with a great deal of unused capacity, particularly in the winter when demand always fell. Table 4 shows some production information for Gibson's Golf Buggies Ltd.

(a) Explain what is meant by 'capacity utilisation'. (3 marks)

(b) (i) Calculate the capacity utilisation for Gibson's over the five year time period. (5 marks)

(ii) Comment on the capacity utilisation of Gibson's over this time period. (5 marks)

(c) Why is the capacity utilisation at Gibson's a problem? (6 marks)

(d) How might Gibson's deal with the problem of seasonal demand in the factory? (10 marks)

(e) Evaluate the measures that might be used by Gibson's Golf Buggies Ltd to improve capacity utilisation. (20 marks)

Table 4: Gibson's Golf Buggies Ltd

	2003	2004	2005	2006	2007
Output	14,000	12,000	11,000	10,500	10,900
Total capacity	18,000	18,000	18,000	18,000	18,000

Operational decisions and stocks

Businesses purchase raw materials, semi-finished goods and components. A washing machine manufacturer, for example, may buy electric motors, circuit boards, rubber drive belts, nuts, bolts, sheet metal and a variety of metal and plastic components. These stocks of materials and components are used to produce products which are then sold to consumers and other businesses. Managing these materials is the responsibility of the production or operations manager. Materials management involves:

- the purchasing of stocks and their delivery;
- the storing and control of stocks;
- the issue and handling of stocks;
- the disposal of surpluses;
- the provision of information about stocks.

The nature of stocks

Businesses prefer to minimise stock holding because it is costly. In practice a variety of stocks are held, for different reasons.

Raw materials and components These are purchased from suppliers before production. They are stored by firms to cope with changes in production levels. Delays in production can be avoided if materials and components can be supplied from stores rather than waiting for a new delivery to arrive. Also, if a company is let down by suppliers it can use stocks to carry on production.

Work-in-progress These are partly finished goods. In a television assembly plant, WORK IN PROGRESS would be televisions on the assembly line, which are only partly built.

Finished goods The main reason for keeping finished goods is to cope with changes in demand and stock. If there is a sudden rise in demand, a firm can meet urgent orders by supplying customers from stock holdings. This avoids the need to step up production rates quickly.

Normally, at least once every year, a business will perform a STOCK TAKE. This involves recording the amount and value of stocks which the firm is holding. A stock take is also required for security reasons – to check that the items actually in stock match the stock records kept by the business. The stock take is also necessary to help determine the value of total purchases during the year for a firm's accounts. A physical stock take can be done manually by identifying every item of stock on the premises. Many firms have details of stock levels recorded on computer.

The cost of holding stocks

In recent years stock management has become more important

Question 1.

(a) Look at the photographs. Explain which of them shows: (i) stocks of raw materials; (ii) work-in-progress; (iii) stocks of finished goods.
(b) Explain why businesses hold stocks of finished goods.

for many firms. Careful control of stock levels can improve business performance. Having too much stock may mean that money is tied up unproductively, but inadequate stock can lead to delays in production and late deliveries. Efficient stock control involves finding the right balance. One of the reasons why control is so important is because the costs of holding stocks can be very high.

- There may be an **opportunity cost** in holding stocks. Capital tied up in stocks earns no rewards. The money used to purchase stocks could have been put to other uses, such as buyingnew machinery. This might have earned the business money.
- Storage can also prove costly. Stocks of raw materials, components and finished goods occupy space in buildings. A firm may also have to pay heating, lighting and labour costs if, for example, a night watchman is employed to safeguard stores when the business is closed. Some products require very special storage conditions. Food items may need expensive refrigerated storage facilities.   A firm may have to insure against fire, theft and other damages.
- Spoilage costs. The quality of some stock, for example perishable goods may deteriorate over time. In addition, if some finished goods are held too long they may become outdated and difficult to sell.
- Administrative and financial costs. These include the cost of placing and processing orders, handling costs and the costs of failing to anticipate price increases.
- Out-of-stock costs. These are the costs of lost revenue, when sales are lost because customers cannot be supplied from stocks. There may also be a loss of goodwill if customers are let down.

Stock levels

One of the most important tasks in stock control is to maintain the right level of stocks. This involves keeping stock levels as low as possible, so that the costs of holding stocks are minimised. At the same time stocks must not be allowed to run out, so that production is halted and customers are let down. A number of factors influence stock levels.

- Demand. Sufficient stocks need to be kept to satisfy normal demand. Firms must also carry enough stock to cover growth in sales and unexpected demand. The term BUFFER STOCK is used to describe stock held for unforeseen rises in demand or breaks in supply.
- Some firms stockpile goods. For example, toy manufacturers build up stocks in the few months leading up to December ready for the Christmas period. Electricity generating stations build up stocks of coal in the summer. During the summer, demand for electricity is low so less coal is needed. At the same time, prices of coal during the summer months are lower, so savings can be made.
- The costs of stock holding. The costs of holding stock were described earlier. If stock is expensive to hold then only a

small quantity will be held. Furniture retailers may keep low stock levels because the cost of stock is high and sales levels are uncertain.

- The amount of working capital available. A business that is short of working capital will not be able to purchase more stock, even if it is needed.
- The type of stock. Businesses can only hold small stocks of perishable products. The stock levels of cakes or bread will be very small. Almost the entire stock of finished goods will be sold in one day. The 'life' of stock, however, does not solely depend on its 'perishability'. Stocks can become out of date when they are replaced by new models, for example.
- LEAD TIME. This is the amount of time it takes for a stock purchase to be placed, received, inspected and made ready for use. The longer the lead time, the higher the minimum level of stock needed.
- External factors. Fear of future shortages may prompt firms to hold higher levels of raw materials in stock as a precaution.

Stock control

It is necessary to control the flow of stocks in the business. This ensures that firms hold the right amount. Several methods of stock control exist. They focus on the RE-ORDER QUANTITY (how much stock is ordered when a new order is placed) and the RE-ORDER LEVEL (the level of stock when an order is placed).

- **Economic order quantity (EOQ)**. It is possible to calculate the level of stocks which minimises costs. This is called the economic order quantity. It takes into account the costs of holding stock, which rise with the amount of stock held, and the average costs of ordering stock, which fall as the size of the order is increased. A business must calculate the EOQ to balance these costs.
- **Fixed re-order interval**. Orders of various sizes are placed at fixed time intervals. This method ignores the economic

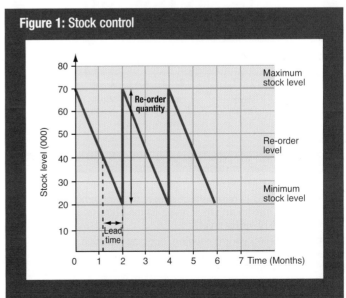

Figure 1: Stock control

order quantity, but ensures that stocks are 'topped up' on a regular basis. This method may result in fluctuating stock levels.

- **Fixed re-order level.** This method involves setting a fixed order level, perhaps using the EOQ. The order is then repeated at varying time intervals.
- **Two bin system.** This simple method involves dividing stock into two bins. When one bin is empty a new order is placed. When the order arrives it is placed into the first bin and stocks are used from the second bin. When the second bin is empty stocks are re-ordered again.

A stock control system is shown in Figure 1. It is assumed that:

- 50,000 units are used every two months (25,000 each month);
- the **maximum stock level**, above which stocks never rise, is 70,000 units;

- the **minimum stock level**, below which stocks should never fall, is 20,000 units, so there is a buffer against delays in delivery;
- stock is re-ordered when it reaches a level of 40,000 units (the **re-order level**);
- the **re-order quantity** is 50,000 units - the same quantity is used up every two months;
- the **lead time** is just under one month. This is the time between the order being placed and the date it arrives in stock.

This is a hypothetical model which would be the ideal for a business. In practice deliveries are sometimes late, so there is a delay in stocks arriving. Firms may also need to use their buffer stocks in this case. It is likely that re-order quantities will need to be reviewed from time to time. Suppliers might offer discounts for ordering larger quantities. The quantities of stocks used in each time period are unlikely to be constant. This might be because production levels fluctuate according to demand.

Too much or too little stock

Why might having too much or too little stock be bad business practice?

Too much stock
- Storage, insurance, lighting and handling costs will all be high if too much stock is held.
- Large stock levels will occupy space in the premises. There may be more productive ways of using this space, such as improving the layout of the factory.
- The opportunity cost will be high. Money tied up in stocks could be used to buy fixed assets, for example.
- Large stock levels might result in unsold stock. If there is an unexpected change in demand, the firm may be left with stocks that it cannot sell.
- Very large stocks might result in an increase in theft by employees. They may feel the business would not miss a small amount of stock relative to the total stock.

Too little stock
- The business may not be able to cope with unexpected increases in demand if its stocks are too low. This might result in lost customers if they are let down too often.
- If deliveries are delayed the firm may run out of stock and have to halt production. This might lead to idle labour and machinery while the firm waits for delivery.
- The firm is less able to cope with unexpected shortages of materials. Again, this could result in lost production.
- A firm which holds very low stocks may have to place more orders. This will raise total ordering costs. Also, it may be unable to take advantage of discounts for bulk buying.

Question 2.

Hahmid & Odusanya is a machine fabrications specialist. It makes large parts for machine tools and special parts machines such as those be found on production lines. It holds stocks of steel. The pattern of its stockholding is shown in Figure 2.

Figure 2:

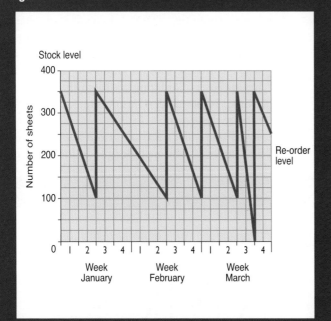

(a) Measured in numbers of sheets of steel, what is
   (i) the maximum stock level; (ii) the buffer stock level;
   (iii) the re-order level?
(b) Explaining your reasoning, suggest in which weeks there was (i) an unexpected large rush order; (ii) very disappointing sales.
(c) Explain what might happen to maximum stock levels if the business began to experience cash flow problems.

Computerised stock control

Stock control has been improved by the use of computers. Many businesses hold details of their entire stock on computer databases. All additions to and issues from stocks are recorded and up to date stock levels can be found instantly. Actual levels of stock should be the same as shown on the computer printout. A prudent firm will carry out regular stock checks to identify differences.

Some systems are programmed to automatically order stock when the re-order level is reached. In some supermarkets, computerised checkout systems record every item of stock purchased by customers and automatically subtract items from total stock levels. The packaging on each item contains a bar code. When this is passed over a laser at the checkout, the sale is recorded by the system. This allows a store manager to check stock levels, total stock values and the store's takings at any time of the day. Again, the system can indicate when the re-order level is reached for any particular item of stock.

Access to stock levels is useful when manufacturers are dealing with large orders. The firm might need to find out whether there are enough materials in stock to complete the order. If this information is available, then the firm can give a more accurate delivery date.

JIT and stock rotation

In recent years many businesses have changed their approach to stock management. To reduce costs, firms have held low levels of stocks. In some cases holdings of both finished goods and raw materials have been reduced to zero. This approach to stock control is the key feature of just-in-time manufacturing (JIT). It is explained fully in the unit on lean production.

Businesses often use systems to control the flow of stocks in and out of their store areas. This flow of stock is sometimes called STOCK ROTATION. One system used to rotate stock is called First In First Out (FIFO). This means that those stocks which are delivered first are the first ones to be issued. This method is useful if stocks are perishable or if they are likely to become obsolete in the near future. A second method of stock rotation is called Last-In-First-Out (LIFO). This system involves issuing stock from the latest rather than the earliest deliveries. This method might be used if the stocks are difficult to handle and it is physically easier to issue the more recent deliveries. However, when using this method it is important that stocks are not perishable. 'Old' stock could remain in store for long periods before it is finally used.

KEYTERMS

Buffer stocks – stocks held as a precaution to cope with unforeseen demand.
Lead time – the time between the placing of the order and the delivery of goods.
Re-order level – the level of stock when new orders are placed.
Re-order quantity – the amount of stock ordered when an order is placed.
Stock rotation – the flow of stock into and out of stores.
Stock take – the process of counting the amount of stock held at a point in time in order to calculate the total stock level held.
Work-in-progress – partly finished goods.

KNOWLEDGE

1. What are the activities involved in materials management?
2. Why do businesses prefer to minimise stock holdings?
3. What is meant by: (a) components; (b) finished goods?
4. What are the costs of holding stocks?
5. Why are buffer stocks held by firms?
6. Why do some firms stockpile?
7. What is meant by LIFO and FIFO?

Case Study: *Regal Jewels*

Regal Jewels is a small chain of jewellers. It has nine outlets in the south east. Each shop has a manager and employs one or two other full-time staff with some part-time staff who help out at busy times, such as Christmas. The shops stock a wide range of rings, earrings, bracelets, necklaces, gemstones and watches. They also produce specialist, tailor made pieces for wealthy customers. The business has flourished by focusing on the old fashioned virtues of personal service and value for money. All managers are members of the HRD Institute of Gemology, Antwerp (Europe's diamond capital). This is a highly regarded professional qualification and gives the business a great deal of credibility. The shop operates at the top end of the market and most of their pieces sell for over £100 – with many pieces going for £1,000s.

Stock is the most valuable asset for the business. After the last stock take, the total value of stocks held by Regal Jewels was £3,560,000. The stock is purchased centrally by the owner of the business. Regal Jewels uses a number of different suppliers, some of them from overseas. However, there have been one or two problems relating to stock management at the business.

One problem is maintaining the supply the supplier of customised carrier backs. All customers leave the shops with their purchases packaged in a specially designed Regal Jewels bag, adorned with gold ribbon and the business logo. Regular purchases of these carrier bags are made every month. The diagram in Figure 2 shows stocks of the carrier bags for a nine month period.

Another problem faced by the business owner is keeping right up to date with the stocks held in each shop. At the moment a manual, paper-based stock system is used. This is proving to be increasingly cumbersome and inefficient as the business grows. She is thinking of setting up an online stock control system. A new online system has been developed which allows small businesses, such as Regal Jewels, to login and manage their stock levels. It is perfect for a business with more than one location. It is possible to monitor stock movements and react to information delivered to a computer from anywhere in the world. The system has a number of benefits.

- Cost effective (no software to purchase/upgrade).
- No new hardware needed.
- Available from multiple locations.
- Easy to use system/set-up system.
- Free support available (unlike all other systems).
- Time saving (no need to produce your own reports or fill in endless paperwork).
- Up/downsizeable for when your business grows or shrinks.

- Easy to train other members of staff.
- 30 day free trials available.

(a) Regal Jewels have monthly stock takes.
(i) What is meant by a stock take? (3 marks)
(ii) Why do you think a stock take is so important for Regal Jewels? (6 marks)

(b) Discuss two stock holding costs that Regal Jewels will incur. (6 marks)

(c) Look at Figure 3. Identify the (i) lead time; (ii) the re-order quantity; (iii) re-order level; (iv) minimum stock level for the carrier bags. (8 marks)

(d) In September 2007, Regal Jewels found a new supplier of carrier bags. Why do you think it took this action? (6 marks)

(e) Do you think Regal Jewels should introduce the online stock system? (10 marks)

Figure 3: Stocks of Regal Jewels carrier bags

Deciding how to produce

A business must decide on the most suitable method to manufacture its goods or to provide services. It is likely that products which are different will be produced differently. For example, a plastic drinks bottle may be produced using automated machinery, but a wrist watch may be assembled by hand. Products that are similar can also be produced in different ways. The Ford Motor Company and Morgan Cars both produce cars, but different processes are used. Ford builds cars using a production line and semi-skilled labour, but Morgan cars are hand built by skilled workers. There are three important decisions that businesses must make when choosing how to produce. These are shown in Figure 1, along with the factors which influence these decisions. In the diagram it is assumed that the firm has already decided 'what' to produce. When deciding how to produce, the objective of the firm will be to minimise the cost per unit of output, i.e. PRODUCTIVE EFFICIENCY.

What production method will be used? Production is sometimes divided into one of three methods. JOB PRODUCTION is where one job is completed at a time before moving on to another. An example might be a costume made for a television play set in the nineteenth century. BATCH PRODUCTION involves dividing the work into a number of different operations. An example would be bread production, where each batch goes through several different baking stages before it is completed. FLOW PRODUCTION involves work being completed continuously without stopping. The production of cars on a production line might be one example.

Some industries may combine different methods of production. For example, a large brewery may produce 'batches' of beer, but then send them to a bottling line for packaging, where flow production is used. Such combinations are particularly common in the food industry.

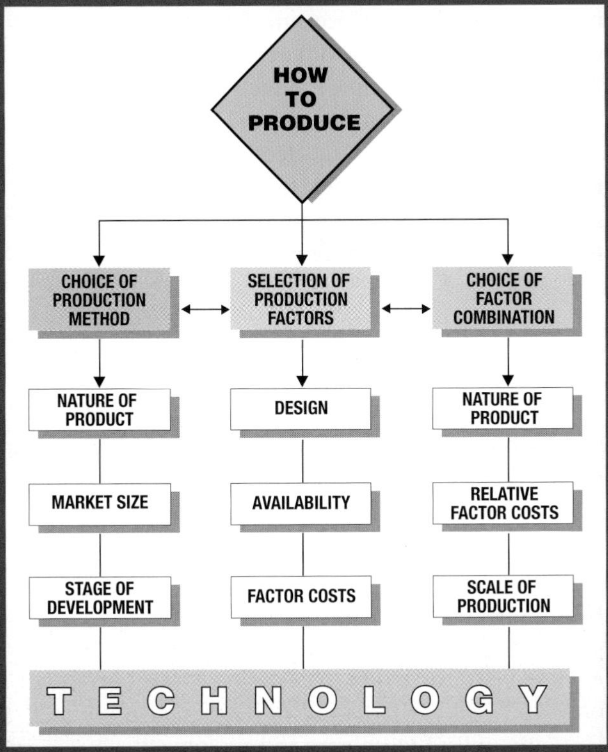

What factors of production will be used? Businesses are often faced with a wide choice between alternative production factors. For example, a builder planning to construct a new house must decide what building materials to buy, which tools to use, which sub-contractors to employ and whether to hire any extra labour. The builder will be faced with a choice in all of these cases. If he decides to hire a labourer, there may be hundreds or even thousands of people to choose from in the area.

How will the factors of production be combined? A third production decision concerns the way in which the available production factors should be combined. For example, should an assembly plant invest in a highly automated assembly operation, or employ a large semi-skilled labour force to undertake the work?

This unit focuses on the types of production a business might choose from.

Job production

Job production involves the production of a single product at a time. It is used when orders for products are small, such as 'one-offs'. Production is organised so that one 'job' is completed at a time. There is a wide variety of goods and services which are produced or provided using this method of production. Small-scale examples include the baking of a child's birthday cake, a dentist's treatment session or the construction of an extension to a house. On a large scale, examples could include the building of a ship, the construction of the Channel Tunnel or the manufacture of specialised machinery. Job production is found in both manufacturing and the service industries. Because the numbers of units produced is small, the production process tends to be labour intensive. The workforce is usually made up of skilled craftsmen or specialists and the possibility of using labour-saving machinery is limited. Many businesses adopt this method of production when they are 'starting up'. The advantages and disadvantages of job production are shown in Table 1.

Figure 1: Factors which affect the decision about how to produce

Table 1: Advantages and disadvantages of job production

Advantages

- Firms can produce unique or 'one-off' orders according to customer needs. For example, a wedding dress may be designed and produced for the individual taste of a client. It is also possible to change the specifications of a job at the last minute, even if the work has actually begun.
- Workers are more likely to be motivated. The tasks employees carry out often require a variety of skills, knowledge and expertise. Their work will be more demanding and interesting. They will also see the end result of their efforts and be able to take pride in their work. Jobs may be carried out by a team of workers aiming to achieve the same objectives. This should help raise the level of job satisfaction.
- The organisation of job production is fairly simple. Because only one job is done at a time, co-ordination, communication, supervision and inspection can take place regularly. Also, it is easier to identify and deal with problems, such as a defective damp proof course in a house or a poorly cooked meal in a restaurant.

Disadvantages

- Labour costs will be high because production tends to be labour intensive. The workforce is likely to be skilled and more versatile. Such employees will be more expensive. The amount of time each employee spends on a particular job will also be long.
- Because there is a variety of work, subject to many specifications, the business would need a wide range of tools, machines and equipment. This can prove expensive. Also, it may not be possible to achieve economies of scale because only one 'job' is produced at a time.
- Lead times can be lengthy. When building a house, the business has to incur costs which cannot be recovered until the house is sold. Sometimes the sale of a house can take a long time.
- Selling costs may also be high. This is likely if the product is highly complex and technical. The sales team will need to be well qualified, able to cope with questions and deal with problems concerning sales and installation. Some firms employ agencies to help reduce their selling costs.
- Once the demand for a firm's product rises, job production may become costly. Firms may prefer to use a method more suited to producing larger quantities. This is not always the case. Even if demand is high, each customer may require a unique order. In addition, many firms believe that the 'personal touch' they can offer in job production is important. As a result, they may choose not to change to other production methods. Other production methods require some degree of product standardisation. This may result in more efficient production, but a loss of 'individuality'.

Table 2: Operations involved in the production of a batch of bread

1. Blend ingredients in a mixing container until a dough is formed.
2. Knead the dough for a period of time.
3. Leave the dough to rise for a period of time.
4. Divide the dough into suitable units (loaves) for baking.
5. Bake the loaves.
6. Allow loaves to cool.

Batch production

Batch production may be used when demand for a firm's product or service is regular rather than a 'one off'. An example might be a furniture factory, where a batch of armchairs is made to a particular design. Production is divided into a number of operations. A particular operation is carried out on all products in a batch. The batch then moves to the next operation. A baker uses batch production when baking bread. The operations in the baking process are broken down in Table 2.

These operations would be performed on every batch of bread. There is some standardisation because each loaf in the batch will be the same. However, it may be possible to vary each batch. The ingredients could be changed to produce brown bread or the style of baking tin could be changed for different shaped loaves.

A great number of products are produced using this method, particularly in manufacturing, such as the production of components and food processing. For example, in a canning plant, a firm may can several different batches of soup, each batch being a different recipe. Products can be produced in very large or very small batches, depending on the level of demand. Larger production runs tend to lower the **unit** or **average cost** of production. New technology is increasingly being introduced to make batch production more efficient. The advantages and disadvantages of batch production are shown in Table 3.

Flow production

Most people will have some idea of flow production from pictures of motor car factories. Production is organised so that different operations can be carried out, one after the other, in a continuous sequence. Vehicles move from one operation to the next, often on a conveyer belt. The main features of flow production are:

- the production of large quantities;
- a simplified or standardised product;
- a semi-skilled workforce, specialising in one operation only;
- large amounts of machinery and equipment;
- large stocks of raw materials and components.

Table 3: Advantages and disadvantges of batch production

Advantages

- Even though larger quantities are produced than in job production, there is still flexibility. Each batch can be changed to meet customers' wishes. It is particularly suitable for a wide range of similar products. The settings on machines can be changed according to specifications, such as different clothes sizes.
- Employees can concentrate on one operation rather than on the whole task. This reduces the need for costly, skilled employees.
- Less variety of machinery would be needed than in job production because the products are standardised. Also, it is possible to use more standardised machinery.
- It often results in stocks of partly finished goods which have to be stored. This means firms can respond more quickly to an urgent order by processing a batch quickly through the final stages of production.

Disadvantages

- Careful planning and co-ordination are needed, or machines and workers may be idle, waiting for a whole batch to finish its previous operation. There is often a need to clean and adjust machinery before the next batch can be produced. This can mean delays. In brewing, one day of the week is used to clean equipment before the next batch begins.
- Some machinery may have to be more complex to compensate for the lower skill levels required from the labour force. This may lead to higher costs.
- The workforce may be less motivated, since they have to repeat operations on every single unit in the batch. In addition, they are unlikely to be involved with production from start to finish.
- If batches are small then unit costs will remain relatively high.
- Money will be tied up in work-in-progress, since an order cannot be dispatched until the whole batch has been finished.

Question 1.

Samiksha Mirza is a chartered accountant. She runs a small business from an office in Kidderminster producing final accounts for sole traders, partnerships and small private limited companies. She has a client base of around 110 businesses and employs a secretary and a young trainee accountant. In addition to preparing accounts she offers other services such as:

- completing tax returns;
- taxation planning;
- advice on the financial management of businesses;
- advice on investment;
- auditing.

(a) Use this case as an example to explain what is meant by job production.

(b) Explain why job production might help to motivate Samiksha and her trainee.

Flow production is used in the manufacture of products as varied as newspapers, food and cement. It is sometimes called **mass production**, as it tends to be used for the production of large numbers of standard products, such as cars or breakfast cereals. Certain types of flow production are known as **continual flow production**, because products such as clothing material pass continually through a series of processes. **Repetitive flow production** is the manufacture of large numbers of the same product, such as plastic toy parts or metal cans.

The advantages and disadvantages of flow production are shown in Table 4. In the 1990s flow production processes were changed in an attempt to solve some of the problems. Japanese manufacturers setting up businesses in the UK introduced methods to improve efficiency. Just-in-time manufacturing, for example, helped to reduce the cost of holding stocks. Some vehicle manufacturers attempted to introduce an element of job production into flow processes by **customising** products for clients. For example, a range of different cars was produced on the same production line. Cars in the same model range differed in colour, engine size, trim and interior design.

Process production

PROCESS PRODUCTION is a form of flow production which is used in the oil or chemical industry. Materials pass through a plant where a series of processes are carried out in order to change the product. An example might be the refining of crude oil into petrol.

Flow production relies on the use of computers. Computers send instructions to machines, control production speeds and conditions, and monitor quality. They allow large numbers of products to be produced continuously to exact standards or control continuous production, which requires many processes.

Choice of production method

Table 4: Advantages and disadvantages of flow production

Advantages
- Unit costs are reduced as firms gain from economies of scale.
- In many industries the process is highly automated. Production is controlled by computers. Many of the operations are performed by robots and other types of machinery. Once the production line is set up and running, products can flow off the end non stop for lengthy periods of time. This can reduce the need for labour, as only machine supervisors are needed.
- The need to stockpile finished goods is reduced. The production line can respond to short-term changes in demand. For example, if demand falls the line can be shut down for a period of time. If it rises then the line can be opened.

Disadvantages
- The set--up costs are very high. An enormous investment in plant and equipment is needed. Firms must therefore be confident that demand for the product is sufficient over a period of time to make the investment pay.
- The product will be standardised. It is not possible to offer a wide product range and meet different customers' needs. However, modern machinery is becoming more flexible and is beginning to overcome this problem.
- For a number of reasons, worker motivation can be a serious problem. Most of the manual operations required on the production line will be repetitive and boring. Factories with production lines tend to be very noisy. Each worker will only be involved in a very small part of the job cycle. As a result of these problems worker morale may be low and labour turnover and absenteeism high.
- Breakdowns can prove costly. The whole production system is interdependent. If one part of the supply or production line fails the whole system may break down.

The method of production chosen might depend on a number of factors.

The nature of the product Many products require a specific method of production. For example, in the construction industry, projects such as bridges, roads, office blocks and sewers must be produced using job production. Cereal farming involves batch production. A plot of land undergoes several processes before it 'produces' a crop.

The size of the market Fast-moving consumer goods like soap, confectionery and canned drinks are normally produced using flow production because the market is so big. When the market is small, flow production techniques are not cost effective.

The stage of development a business has reached When firms are first set up, they often produce small levels of output and employ job or batch production methods. As they grow and enjoy higher sales levels, they may switch to flow production.

Technology The current state of technology will affect all decisions concerning how to produce. As technology advances, new materials and machinery become available. Changes in technology often result in firms adopting new methods of production. For example, the development of computers and robotic welders has radically changed the way in which cars are manufactured. Also, car manufacturers are now able to produce different models on the same production line at the same time.

Question 2.

Uniform+ was established in 1997 and has become a leading supplier of workwear, leisurewear and promotional clothing to businesses and organisations across the UK. In 2006, the company moved to a purpose-built freehold head office and factory in Cannock. Uniform+ supplies over 12,000 garments a week to more than 5,500 customers. The company has an excellent reputation in the industry because of their:

- commitment to offering a wide choice of quality clothing at unbeatable prices;
- dedication to providing excellent customer service and value for money;
- fast turnaround and flexibilty to meet customers' needs;
- unique free logo and delivery service.

Like most companies in the clothes industry, Uniform+ uses batch production. The company can meet a wide range of different orders due the flexibility of its machinery and its multi-skilled workforce.

(a) Use the clothes industry as an example to explain what is meant by batch production.
(b) Why is batch production common in the clothes industry?
(c) How do you think Uniform+ has overcome some of the typical problems associated with batch production?

KEYTERMS

Batch production – a method which involves completing one operation at a time on all units before performing the next.

Flow production – very large scale production of a standardised product, where each operation on a unit is performed continuously, one after the other, usually on a production line.

Job production – a method of production which involves employing all factors to complete one unit of output at a time.

Process production – a form of flow production where materials pass through a plant where a series of processes are carried out in order to change the product.

Productive efficiency – production methods which minimise unit costs.

KNOWLEDGE

1. What are the three main decisions which have to be made regarding the method of production?
2. Under what circumstances might a business become more capital intensive?
3. State three types of products which may be manufactured using job production.
4. Describe the advantages and disadvantages of job production.
5. State three products that are generally manufactured using batch production.
6. Describe the advantages and disadvantages of batch production.
7. Describe four features of flow production.

Case Study: *Nacional*

Nacional is a major breakfast cereal manufacturer in Portugal and forms part of the grain milling Amorim-Lage Group. The popularity of breakfast cereals has grown in Portugal in recent years and one of Nacional's main production facilities was in need of a major update and expansion using new technology and new ideas. Early in 2004, Nacional carried out a major refit and expansion plan that was completed by mid-September. The investment in the new facility was estimated at 11.2 million euros.

Nacional's main product was cornflakes but since the expansion the facility has been able to manufacture a variety of extruded breakfast cereal products for marketing under its own brand names and also for supermarket own-brand labels. The adoption of extrusion techniques (drawing a dough mixture through a shape to produce a continuous strand with an identical cross section which can be cut into shapes such as stars or squares for example) in processing breakfast cereal at the Nacional plant has widened the production possibilities because a variety of grains can now be used. This has allowed the blending of different grains into unique cereal pieces. Extrusion has also made production more efficient by combining several processing steps into a single, continuous flow.

PV Baker has supplied and installed a complete processing plant for Nacional. It incorporates the entire production process, from compounding and mixing the recipe 'dough' through extrusion and cooking to drying and coating the final extruded product shapes. The new facility can make a variety of different products, including corn-balls, coco-balls, choco curls, golden squares, stars and rings, as well as co-extruded filled pillow shapes. All of these extruded shapes, except the pillows, will be coated with a honey, sugar or glucose based glaze.

Most of the products are cut into individual pieces by a die as they leave the extruder. A key design feature of the facility is the ability to change over rapidly between products in response to market demand, including those products involving different raw materials and syrup. For example, to create filled pillow products, which cannot be cut at the die, a mobile crimping unit is wheeled in and out of the line.

Source: adapted from www.foodprocessing-technology.com

(a) State four processes used in the production of breakfast cereals at Nacional. (4 marks)
(b) Explain how Nacional is using both batch production and flow production methods in its factory. (10 marks)
(c) When upgrading its production facilities, what role did technology play at Nacional? (6 marks)
(d) To what extent do you think the 11.2 million euro investment will benefit Nacional? (20 marks)

36 | Quality

What is quality?

Consumers, faced with many goods or services at similar prices, are likely to consider QUALITY when making choices. Quality could be described as those features of a product or service that allow it to satisfy customers' wants. Take an example of a family buying a television. They may consider some of the following features:

- physical appearance – they may want a certain style;
- reliability and durability - will it last for 10 years?
- special features – does it have stereo sound?
- suitability – they may want a portable television;
- parts – are spare parts available?
- repairs – does the shop carry out maintenance?
- after sales service – how prompt is delivery?

They may also consider features which they perceive as important, such as:

- image – is the manufacturer's name widely recognised?
- reputation – what do other consumers think of the business or product?

The importance of quality has grown in recent years. Consumers are more aware. They get information through magazines such as *Which?* that contain reports on the quality of certain products. They also have more disposable income and higher expectations than ever before. Legislation and competition have also forced firms to improve the quality of their products.

Businesses, faced with competition, are also concerned about the quality of their:

- design – the ideas and plans for the product or service;
- production processes – the methods used to manufacture the goods or provide the services.

Poor designs may lead to problems with the materials and the functions of the finished good or service. It costs time and money to redesign poor products. Clients are unlikely to use businesses with poor designs again. Problems also occur with poor quality production processes. Faulty products are costly for a business. Machinery that breaks down or constantly needs to be repaired will also be expensive. Late delivery and ineffective productivity that results in poor quality can harm a business's reputation.

Traditional quality control

Traditionally, in manufacturing, production departments have been responsible for ensuring quality. Their objectives might have been to make sure that products:

- satisfied consumers' needs;
- worked under conditions they were likely to face;
- operated in the way they should;
- could be produced cost effectively;

- could be repaired easily;
- conformed to safety standards set down by legislation and independent bodies.

At Kellogg's, the cereal manufacturer, for example, samples of breakfast cereal have, in the past, been taken from the

Question 1.

Airbus S.A.S. is the aircraft manufacturing subsidiary of EADS N.V., a pan-European aerospace business. Based at Toulouse, France with significant operations in other European states, Airbus produces around half of the world's jet airliners. Airbus employs around 57,000 people at sixteen sites in four European countries. Airbus' customers expect quality in the aircraft they buy. Safety, reliability, comfort and maintenance costs are key areas where quality is crucial in an airline's judgment of an aircraft. To achieve the very highest standards in these and other aspects of an aircraft's performance the question of quality is addressed by Airbus at every stage, from design to final assembly and beyond. Repeated checks are made. Tests are applied. Airbus ensures every supplier of parts meets the strictest standards on quality. Defective work, parts and materials are rejected.

Delivering aircraft on time, on cost and on quality – getting it right first time – is the goal Airbus continually strives for. Airbus has a network of key employees who identify problems at various stages of design, production and assembly and recommend action to eradicate them, pre-empting possible costly delays at a later point. These employees also ensure continuous improvement in standards and efficiency by pinpointing ways in which people could work better or tools and materials could be improved. As it raises production to meet demand, Airbus knows setting even higher standards in quality is critical to maintaining its success.

Source: adapted from www.airbus.com.

(a) (i) What features do customers of Airbus consider important when buying aircraft?
(ii) Which of the features in (i) do you think is the most important?

(b) What measures does Airbus take to meet the high quality aspirations of customers?

production line every half hour and tested. The testing took place in a food review room twice a day and was undertaken by a small group of staff. Each sample, about 50 in total, was compared with a 'perfect' Kellogg's sample and given a grade between 1 and 10. 10 was perfect but between 9.8 and 7, although noticeable to the trained eye, was acceptable to the customer. Below 7 the consumer would notice the reduction in quality. The cereals were tested for appearance, texture, colour, taste etc. More sophisticated tests were carried out in a laboratory where the nutritional value of a sample, for example, was measured.

QUALITY CONTROL in UK organisations, in the past, often meant **quality controllers** or **quality inspectors** checking other people's work and the product itself after production had taken place. By today's standards this is not quality control, but a method of finding a poor quality product (or a problem) before it is sold to the consumer.

Quality assurance

Today businesses are less concerned about 'Has the job been done properly?' than 'Are we able to do the job properly?' In other words inspection is carried out during the production process. This means that problems and poor quality products can be prevented before final production.

Such a preventative approach has been used by Japanese businesses and is known as TOTAL QUALITY MANAGEMENT (TQM). It is now being adopted by many companies in the UK. It involves all employees in a business contributing to and being responsible for ensuring quality at all stages in the production process. QUALITY ASSURANCE is a commitment by a business to maintain quality throughout the organisation. The aim is to stop problems before they occur rather than finding them after they occur.

Quality assurance also takes into account customers' views when planning the production process. For example, customers may be consulted about their views through market research before a product is manufactured or a service provided. They may also be part of a consultation group involved at the design and manufacturing stage.

Total quality management

Errors are costly for business. It is estimated that about one-third of all the effort of British businesses is wasted in correcting errors. There are benefits if something is done right the first time. Total quality management (TQM) is a method designed to prevent errors, such as the creation of poor quality products, from happening. The business is organised so that the manufacturing process is investigated at every stage. It is argued that the success of Japanese companies is based on their superior organisation. Every department, activity and individual is organised to take into account quality at all times. What are the features of TQM?

Quality chains Great stress is placed on the operation of

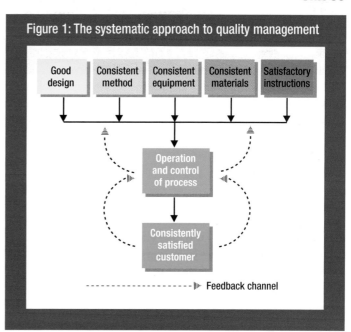

Figure 1: The systematic approach to quality management

QUALITY CHAINS. In any business a series of suppliers and customers exists. For example, a secretary is a supplier to a manager, who is the customer. The secretarial duties must be carried out to the satisfaction of the manager. The chain also includes customers and suppliers outside the business. The chain remains intact if the supplier satisfies the customer. It is broken if a person or item of equipment does not satisfy the needs of the customer. Failure to meet the requirements in any part of the quality chain creates problems, such as delays in the next stage of production.

Company policy, accountability and empowerment There will only be improvements in quality if there is a company-wide quality policy. TQM must start from the top with the most senior executive and spread throughout the business to every employee. People must be totally committed and take a 'pride in the job'. This might be considered as an example of job enrichment. Lack of commitment, particularly at the top, causes problems. For example, if the managing director lacks commitment, employees lower down are unlikely to commit themselves. TQM stresses the role of the individual and aims to make everyone accountable for their own performance. For example, a machine operator may be accountable to a workshop supervisor for his work. They may also be empowered to make decisions.

Control Consumers' needs will only be satisfied if the business has control of the factors that affect a product's quality. These may be human, administrative or technical factors, shown in Figure 1. The process is only under control if materials, equipment and tasks are used in the same way every time. Take an example of a firm making biscuits. Only by cooking in the same way can the quality be consistent every time.

These methods can be documented and used to assess operations. Regular audits must be carried out by the firm to check quality. Information is then fed back from the customer to the 'operator' or producer, and from the operator to the supplier of inputs, such as raw materials. For example, a retailer may return a batch of vehicles to the manufacturer because the gears were faulty. The manufacturer might then identify the person responsible for fitting the gears. An investigation might reveal that the faulty gears were the responsibility of a component supplier. The supplier can then be contacted and the problem resolved. Quality audits and reviews may lead to suggestions for improvements - a different material, perhaps, or a new piece of equipment.

Monitoring the process TQM relies on monitoring the business process to find possible improvements. Methods have been developed to help achieve this. STATISTICAL PROCESS CONTROL (SPC) involves collecting data relating to the performance of a process. Data is presented in diagrams, charts and graphs. The information is then passed to all those concerned.

SPC can be used to reduce variability, which is the cause of most quality problems. Variations in products, delivery times, methods, materials, people's attitudes and staff performance often occur. For example, statistical data may show that worker attitudes may have led to variations in output late on Friday afternoon. Discussion might result in a change in the 'clocking on' and 'clocking off' times to solve the problem.

Teamwork TQM stresses that teamwork is the most effective way of solving problems. The main advantages are:
- a greater range of skills, knowledge and experience can be used to solve the problem;
- employee morale is often improved;
- problems across departments are better dealt with;
- a greater variety of problems can be tackled;
- team 'ideas' are more likely to be used than individual ones.

TQM strongly favours teamwork throughout the business. It builds trust and morale, improves communications and cooperation and develops interdependence. Many UK firms in the past have suffered due to lack of sharing of information and ideas. Such approaches have often led to division between sections of the workforce.

Consumer views Firms using TQM must be committed to their customers. They must be responsive to changes in people's needs and expectations. To do this, information must be gathered on a regular basis and there must be clear communication channels for customers to express their views. Consumers are often influential in setting quality standards. For example, holiday companies issue questionnaires to their customers on the way back from a package holiday. The information can be used to identify the strengths and weaknesses of their operations. Such information can be used to monitor and upgrade quality standards.

Zero defects Many business quality systems have a zero defect policy. This aims to ensure that every product that is manufactured is free from defects. A business that is able to guarantee zero defects in customers' orders is likely to gain a good reputation. This could lead to new clients and improved sales.

Quality circles TQM stresses the importance of teamwork in a business. Many businesses have introduced quality circles into their operations. Quality circles are small groups of staff, usually from the same work area, who meet on a regular and voluntary basis. They meet in the employer's time and attempt to solve problems and make suggestions about how to improve various aspects of the business. Issues such as pay and conditions are normally excluded. After discussions, the team will present its ideas and solutions to management. Teams are also involved in implementing and monitoring the effectiveness of solutions. In order for quality circles to be successful certain conditions must exist.
- A steering committee should be set up to oversee the whole quality circle programme.
- A senior manager should ideally chair the committee. Managers must show commitment to the principle of

Question 2.

Compsoft is a UK-based company which produces tailor-made data management software for high-growth businesses. One of Compsoft's first products was Delta, a market-leading DOS-based database which is still used by many organisations today. Compsoft also developed Equinox, a rapid application development tool and database environment. Equinox is used by SMEs, blue-chip companies and governmental bodies.

Compsoft is committed to quality assurance and has been awarded ISO 9001, the internationally recognised standard for the quality management of businesses. As a result Compsoft has adopted the BSI framework to monitor its business processes to ensure the quality of service provided to its customers. Some of the basic requirements of certification include:
- adapting a set of procedures that cover all key processes in the business;
- monitoring development processes to ensure they are producing quality products;
- keeping records;
- checking outgoing applications for defects, with appropriate corrective action where necessary;
- regularly reviewing individual processes and the quality system itself for effectiveness;
- facilitating continual improvement.

Regular monitoring ensures that these standards are upheld and that Compsoft remains worthy of its title as an accredited ISO 9001 provider.

Source: adapted from www.compsoft.co.uk.

(a) (i) What is quality assurance?
    (ii) How does Compsoft ensure quality in its business?
(b) What role does the BSI play in Compsoft's quality assurance?
(c) What benefits might Compsoft enjoy as a result of ISO 9001 certification?

quality circles.
- At least one person on the committee should be accountable for the programme.
- Team leaders should be properly trained.

Using TQM TQM helps companies to:
- focus clearly on the needs of customers and relationships between suppliers and customers;
- achieve quality in all aspects of business, not just product or service quality;
- critically analyse all processes to remove waste and inefficiencies;
- find improvements and develop measures of performance;
- develop a team approach to problem solving;
- develop effective procedures for communication and acknowledgement of work;
- continually review the processes to develop a strategy of constant improvement.

There are, however, some problems.
- There will be training and development costs of the new system.
- TQM will only work if there is commitment from the entire business.
- There will be a great deal of bureaucracy and documents and regular audits will be needed. This may be a problem for small firms.
- Stress is placed on the process and not the product.

ISO standards

Businesses can work to quality assurance **codes of practice**. These show that a production process has been carried out to a certain standard and to the required specification. Once a business has been assessed and has achieved a certain standard, it is regularly checked by the awarding organisation to make sure standards are maintained. ISO 9000 is an international standard which businesses seek to achieve.

The **British Standards Institution** (BSI) is an independent organisation that attempts to set quality standards in industry. The BSI and other independent bodies, such as Lloyds, offer BS EN ISO 9000 registration. The title reflects the European (EN) and international (ISO) recognition for this series. BS EN ISO 9001 gives quality assurance in design, development, production, installation and servicing and is suitable for businesses which have a large element of design in their operations. BS EN ISO 9002 gives quality assurance in production, installation and servicing, for businesses which produce fairly standard products with little or no design. BS EN ISO 9003 gives quality assurance in final inspection and testing. This standard is suitable for small firms or where customers can check quality themselves through inspection.

Firms seeking certification have to show that their methods and procedures meet the recognised standards and comply with requirements. They are inspected on a regular basis to make sure that standards are being maintained. BS EN ISO 9000

certification can help a business to:
- examine and improve systems, methods and procedures to lower costs;
- motivate staff and encourage them to get things right first time;
- define key roles, responsibilities and authorities;
- ensure that orders are consistently delivered on time;
- highlight product or design problems and develop improvements;
- record and investigate all quality failure and customer complaints and make sure that they do not reoccur;
- give a clear signal to customers that it is taking measures to improve quality;
- produce a documented system for recording and satisfying the training needs of new and existing staff regarding quality.

Product standards

Businesses may include signs and symbols on their products which tell a customer about the product's standards. Certain bodies have also been set up to ensure the quality of goods and services.

British Standards Institution Any business can apply to the BSI for an inspection of its product. Those that achieve and maintain a standard can carry the BSI Kitemark. The Kitemark tells the customer that the product has been tested to destruction, to ensure that it meets with certain safety standards. Products that carry a Kitemark include some cricket helmets, kitchen units, child car safety seats, door locks, curtains, and sofa and duvet covers.

The BSI also issues a number of other product standards. These include ensuring:
- products conform to yachting standards;
- the tensile strength of yarns;
- performance levels for the amount of UV light through sunglasses;
- grades of carpet pile, according to quality and durability.

The British Electrotechnical Approvals Board (BEAB) Now part of Intertek, a global leader in testing, inspection and certification, this is a body which inspects domestic electrical equipment. Manufacturers of domestic electrical appliances will be keen for the BEAB to approve their products. Approval can serve as a recognition of quality that customers will recognise.

The Association of British Travel Agents (ABTA) The Association of British Travel Agents is a trade association which has drawn up a code of practice for its members. The code aims to improve the trading standards of activities related to the sale of holidays. Travel agents are allowed to register with ABTA if they agree to follow its code of practice.

The Wool Marketing Board This allows manufacturers to carry labels such as the Wool Mark if their garments are made entirely of pure new wool. Obtaining a trademark is a way for a firm to give quality assurance to customers. If customers know that the quality of a product is guaranteed, they are more likely to buy the product. Also, there is less need to inspect the product, and returns and re-ordering are reduced.

The British Toy and Hobby Association (BTHA) developed the Lion Mark as a symbol of toy safety to be displayed on toy packaging. Toy manufacturers that want to include the Lion Mark must take out a licence with the BTHA. The manufacturer must sign a strict code of practice which sets standards relating to toy safety and advertising, as well as counterfeiting and markings on toy guns. The Lion Mark was adapted by the BTHA and the British Association of Toy Retailers (BATR) for shops. If the symbol is displayed in a shop it indicates that the retailer has agreed to a strict code of practice. They agree only to offer safe toys for sale and to ensure staff are briefed on toy safety matters such as age warnings.

The Consumers Association This is a body which follows up complaints by people about faulty products or services. It also makes recommendations about products and services to customers. These take into account such things as quality, reliability and value for money. Often survey results appear in its *Which?* magazine.

The Institute of Quality Assurance (IQA) The Institute of Quality Assurance is a professional body in the UK whose purpose is the promotion and advancement of quality practices. The IQA has three main objectives.
- To seek the advancement of quality management and practices and help the exchange of related information and ideas.
- To promote the education, training, qualification and development of people involved in quality assurance and the management of quality.
- To provide a range of services to members and, where appropriate, to the community at large.

Some businesses support their products with WARRANTIES. If goods are warranted, it means that the manufacturer will undertake any necessary work arising from a defect in the product 'free of charge'. Warranties are popular with products such as cars and a wide range of electrical appliances.

A number of laws exist which protect consumers from poor trading practices. They have tended to focus on safety aspects and consumer exploitation. However, increasingly UK laws and EU regulations are taking into account product quality. Existing laws are enforced by local inspectors, called **Trading Standards Officers**.

Costs and benefits of ensuring quality

Firms will want to monitor the costs of quality control carefully. All businesses are likely to face costs when trying to maintain or improve the quality of their products and services.
- The cost of designing and setting up a quality control system. This might include the time used to 'think through' a system and to train staff to use it.
- There might be a cost in terms of lost production. When a business introduces a major new system there may be some serious disruption while the new system is 'bedded-in'. This could lead to a loss of output and damage to customer relations if orders are not met.
- The cost of monitoring the system. This could be the salary of a supervisor or the cost of an electronic sensor.
- There will be costs if products do not come up to standard. Faulty goods may have to be scrapped or reworked. Product failures might also result in claims against a company, bad publicity and a possible loss of goodwill.
- The cost of improving the actual quality. This may be the cost of new machinery or of training staff in new working practices.
- If the whole quality system fails, there may be costs in setting it up again. Time may be needed to 'rethink' or adjust the system. Retraining might also be necessary.
- Quality initiatives will only be successful if the people involved in their implementation are properly trained. This can prove very costly. For example, if TQM is introduced the entire workforce will have to be trained. This may involve sending all staff on specialist training courses or outsourcing training to an expert in TQM.

It has been suggested that between 10-20 per cent of the revenue of a business is accounted for by quality related costs. This means that UK businesses could save billions of pounds by cutting such costs. The vast majority of these costs is spent on appraisal and failure, which add very little to the quality of the product. Eliminating failure will also help to reduce appraisal and failure costs.

Although quality control systems are costly, it is argued that their benefits outweigh the costs. The actual quality of the product should be improved, so customers are more likely to purchase the product. Business costs may be cut if faults in products are identified before the product reaches the market. The costs of failure once the product has reached the market are likely to be much higher than those incurred during manufacture.

Quality, USP and pricing flexibility

Some businesses use quality as a means of developing a unique selling point (USP). If a business can differentiate its product on grounds of quality and persuade the customer that its product is superior to its rivals, it may enjoy some benefits. One of the main benefits is the ability to charge a higher price. If consumers are convinced that a product is superior in quality to those of its rivals, they are often prepared to pay higher prices. This gives a business more flexibility in pricing. For example, Porsche, the performance car manufacturer, has a global reputation for high quality. Consequently it is able to charge premium prices for their range of sports cars.

Case Study: GNY Building Materials

GNY Building Materials is a multi-location ready mix concrete, sand and gravel supplier. It employs over 350 staff and is currently faced with the twin problems of escalating costs and ailing customer service. After an important board meeting it was decided to create a new business culture, a culture which valued quality, customer service and continuous improvement. A business consultant was commissioned to perform a TQM readiness assessment, organise a Quality Steering Committee, train the management and hourly employees in TQM and support the work of the departmentally based Quality Teams and the cross functional Corrective Action Teams.

When the consultant began work it was apparent that the company did not have a history of participative management and reacted slowly to opportunities. Initial interviews confirmed that management was viewed sceptically. Poor internal communication led to employees feeling fear and resentment. Also, the business faced increasingly aggressive competition. A major objective for implementing TQM was to eliminate the waste in delivery and improve the reliability of delivery. The chairman made it plain that the savings from improvements would fund the culture he needed to foster in order to implement TQM.

Implementing TQM

There was a number of steps involved in implementing TQM at the business.

STEP 1 Perform a TQM readiness assessment. Over a five day period all of the senior management team and several hourly employees were interviewed. This highlighted several areas for targeted customer service improvement and cost reduction. TQM training was developed and initial Corrective Action Teams (CATs) were formed.

STEP 2 Communicate the vision to every single employee in the company. The chairman told each employee his vision for the business.

STEP 3 Organise the steering committee and train the management

team. Training was further developed in the six TQM training sessions.

By incorporating their culture, credibility was improved. In addition, training improved the application of TQM ideas and broke down barriers to change. Four groups of twenty employees were then trained. The consultant trained in-house trainers to continue the training of employees. A second, but equally important, task continued parallel to the training. The Corrective Action Team (CAT) used the TQM process to improve the customer service levels and eliminate waste in trucking. It used each of the five critical areas in TQM to generate the needed changes in their trucking operations. These were considered to be the following.

- Customer Focus
- Teamwork
- Problem Solving
- Waste Elimination
- Continuous Improvement

Over three months the business generated cost reduction initiatives worth £600,000 and implemented over £300,000 of cost savings. This major victory by hourly and first line management demonstrated the effectiveness of TQM. GNY Building Materials realised a 25:1 payback on its investment in Total Quality Management. Their premier service reputation was restored and it became the preferred supplier to many contractors. According to the chairman, the company has become much more flexible and responsive. Improvements to the bottom line confirm this.

(a) What is a TQM readiness assessment? (4 marks)
(b) Why did GNY Building Materials introduce TQM? (6 marks)
(c) How important was training in the implementation of TQM at GNY Building Materials? (8 marks)
(d) Examine the likely costs incurred by GNY Building Materials when implementing TQM. (10 marks)
(e) Evaluate the benefits to GNY Building Materials of introducing TQM. (16 marks)

What is customer service?

CUSTOMER SERVICE is about meeting the needs of customers. Customer service can be defined as 'a series of activities designed to enhance the level of customer satisfaction – the feeling that a product or service has met the customer's expectations'. Customer service has become increasingly important in recent years due to market orientation and the belief held by businesses about the importance of customers. If businesses offer good customer service, they are more likely to see customers return. Customers may also recommend products to their friends and relatives if they have enjoyed good customer service. Some businesses aim to exceed customer expectations. This approach should go a long way to satisfying customers.

The nature of customer service can vary quite significantly depending on the type of business providing it. Some examples are given below.

- Being courteous, friendly and helpful to customers.
- Dealing with complaints and problems in a sensitive and practical manner.
- Providing an Internet tracking service so that customers can see how their orders are progressing.
- Providing information, and advice about products.
- Providing assistance such as helping a non-English speaker complete an application form for a sports club.
- Offering extra services, such as a hotel providing free champagne, chocolates, flowers and a bowl of fresh fruit to honeymooners.

Customer service and communication

Call centres Customer service can be provided over the telephone. Many financial institutions such as banks and insurance companies, travel companies and the providers of utilities, use CALL CENTRES to provide customer service. Call centres have large numbers of staff or **call centre agents** who deal with telephone calls from customers. Someone working at a call centre for a bank may deal with a query on a customer's bank statement, for example. People working at call centres generally sit in front of a computer and respond to customers' telephone calls all day. All the information they need to provide customer service, including customers' account details, can usually be accessed from the computer.

However, some customers do not like call centres and their criticisms generally follow a number of common themes, for example:

- operators working from a script – too impersonal;
- non-expert operators;
- incompetent or untrained operators incapable of processing customers' requests effectively;
- overseas locations, with language and accent problems;

Question 1.

Asda, the supermarket chain, provides a variety of customer services.

Instore Greeters Greeters are customer care specialists who are trained to help customers with all their enquiries. ASDA are proud of their warm and friendly Greeters who always give customers a genuine welcome as they walk into the store. They provide a range of help, from selecting the right shopping trolley to suit customers' shopping needs, helping wheelchair users and directing customers to the right aisle.

Trolley range Asda offers customers a wide range of trolleys ranging from smaller smart shoppers to larger 175 litre trolleys with child seats. Its fleet of trolleys also accommodates the elderly and disabled. It has low and high trolleys which attach to wheelchairs along with Senior Citizen trolleys to help less able customers to get around the store.

Electric Karts To help less able shoppers navigate stores Asda introduced Electric Mart Karts to all food stores. ASDA was the first major retailer to introduce them. The Mart Karts are easy to use and all customers are given a demonstration when joining the Asda 'Scooter Club'.

Refund policy If customers are not happy with any purchase of branded items they simply return the product and Asda will offer a full refund or a replacement product. A receipt is preferred but not essential.

Exchange policy When customers purchase an electrical item they can ask for their receipt to be placed into a free Guarantee Wallet. This means that their purchase is guaranteed for a full year. However, customers will need to keep their own receipt to cover the warranty.

Source: adapted from www.asda-corporate.com.

(a) Using examples from the case, explain what is meant by customer service.
(b) How might Asda benefit by training staff in customer service?

- automated queuing systems. This sometimes results in excessively long hold times;
- a lack of communication between different business departments

Online A growing number of businesses have their own websites and provide customer service online. For example, people can get information about products and services. They can also buy products online. One common customer service is to provide answers to a list of FAQ (frequently asked questions). Also, if a person wants further information from a business they can ask questions using email. Email is increasingly used as a means of responding to customers by businesses. In some cases this has replaced the work of call centres. Many businesses prefer to provide customer service in this way because it is cheaper than answering customers' telephone calls.

Methods of meeting customer expectations

Since the provision of customer service has become increasingly important, businesses have developed different ways of identifying customer expectations and meeting them.

Market research In order to meet customer expectations it is necessary to identify them. One obvious way is to carry out market research to find out exactly what customers expect. A wide range of market research techniques could be used. These include exit surveys, telephone surveys, customer satisfaction questionnaires, focus groups, in-depth interviews and online surveys. Online surveys have become very popular with businesses. They can be used to find out what customers thought about the quality of customer service when buying online or how useful customers found the website, for example.

Customer satisfaction surveys are widely used in leisure and tourism. For example, hotels often leave short questionnaires in their rooms for guests to complete before they leave. Tour operators often ask holidaymakers to complete customer satisfaction surveys on the plane during the journey home. Some businesses employ market research agencies to carry out in-depth customer satisfaction surveys. However, these can be very expensive.

Once information from market research has been gathered and analysed, it can be used to design customer service provision. Some businesses will aim to provide customer service which they hope will exceed customer expectations.

Training Businesses are more likely to meet customer needs if staff are trained to deliver good customer service. Staff who come into direct contact with customers might be trained in a variety of skills to help provide better customer service. Some examples are shown in Figure 1.

A business may use off-the-job or on-the-job training methods when improving staff skills in customer service. Large companies are likely to have their own training facilities and courses, some of which are likely to target customer services.

Figure 1: Training to provide effective customer service

Smaller businesses might rely more on experienced staff to teach new recruits 'good practice' while on the job. There is a number of businesses that provide training courses which focus on customer services. An example is shown in Figure 2. This gives details of an introductory course in customer training provided by Activia.

Training in customer service will help staff to do their job more effectively. Without proper training the quality of customer service is likely to be poorer. Training will also motivate staff. Without training they may become frustrated because they cannot do their jobs properly. Training is also likely to make staff more flexible. For example, staff from one

Figure 2: Introductory training course on customer services provided by Activia

This intensive one day training course teaches delegates the basics of customer service. They will learn how to develop and maintain a positive attitude, show extra attentiveness to customers, use customer-friendly language, and deal effectively with customer complaints and problems. Finally, delegates learn how to build rapport with customers, interpret non-verbal communication skills, provide quality customer service over the telephone and communicate effectively through email.

Source: www.activia.co.uk.

department might cover for an absent colleague in another if they have been widely trained. Training is often necessary to bring staff up to date with new technology or new legislation in customer services. For example, staff in a travel agency might be trained in a new computer-based booking system for clients.

Quality assurance, quality control and quality standards

Another way of meeting customer expectations is to adopt recognised quality standards in customer service. A business might also guarantee quality by taking into account customer needs and ensuring that quality is built into processes and systems used when providing customer service. This is called quality assurance. Some approaches to quality assurance and quality standards are outlined below.

Total quality management One of the main approaches to quality assurance used by businesses today is total quality management (TQM). This involves every single person in a business taking responsibility for quality, including those involved in customer service. TQM makes the customer the centre of attention. One of the advantages of using TQM is that the approach involves collecting data for monitoring purposes. Customer service data can be used to help maintain quality standards and also to improve them in the future. This is explained in the next section.

BS 8477:2007 The British Standard Institution (BSI), a body responsible for setting quality standards in industry, has recently published the first British Standard for customer service. It is the BS 8477:2007 Code of practice for customer service. It sets out essential, basic principles for establishing and maintaining effective customer service and provides recommendations for applying these principles. If businesses are granted certification in this standard, it will help to guarantee standards of customer service.

The Institute for Customer Service This organisation is the professional body for customer service. Their aim is to help members raise their customer service standards and individuals achieve professional recognition. In particular it:

*   provides advice and guidance on world-class customer service issues;
*   defines professional customer service standards;
*   promotes a wide understanding of the nature of competent customer service and how individuals can acquire it;
*   spreads authoritative customer service knowledge through breakthrough research papers;
*   offers a range of quality products and services to help organisations and individuals improve customer service.

Businesses that become members of this organisation can use its services to help them maintain quality standards in customer service.

Charter mark Charter Mark is the government's national

standard for customer service excellence. Charter Mark is a powerful, easy to use tool to help everyone in an organisation focus on and improve customer service. Achievement of the standard is recognised by awarding the right to display the prestigious Charter Mark logo. The Charter Mark is awarded for excellence in the provision of customer services by public sector or a voluntary organisation such as a hospital, a police force, a local authority, a prison, a primary school, a Jobcentre or a museum. To qualify for the Charter Mark organisations have to satisfy six criteria.

Monitoring and improving customer service

Many businesses monitor the quality of their customer service. They may do this by gathering data. The data can be analysed and the results used to make recommendations on how to improve the quality of customer service in the future. Businesses can use a number of methods to gather data.

Questionnaires Many businesses gather data using questionnaires. Customers might be asked to complete questionnaires in a follow-up procedure after a sale has been made. Corkills, the Volkswagen car dealer and service centre in Southport, uses a telephone questionnaire to gather information about customer service after customers have had their cars serviced. Questionnaires can be tailored to the needs of different businesses. Figure 3 shows a questionnaire used by Fred. Olsen Travel to gather information about the quality of its customer service.

Figure 3: Customer service survey used by Fred. Olsen Travel

Source: www.fredolsen.co.uk/travel/travelshops/question.htm

Question 2.

TSO (the stationery office) delivers managed print and publishing services to a variety of private and public sector clients. The company is committed to high quality customer service. It sets targets for performance which are outlined below.

- Answer 80% of our telephone calls in 10 seconds, 90% in 20 seconds and 95% in 30 seconds.
- Achieve an abandon call rate of no more than 2% of call volumes answered.
- Average time to answer a call of 6 seconds.
- Process standard written order requests sent by post within an average of 2 working days of receipt.
- Deliver a service that achieves a benchmarked satisfaction score of 83.1%.

- Achieve a fair outcome for customers when things go wrong and receive less than 1.4% of complaints received against overall despatches.

TSO also gathers data to monitor its performance. An extract from its results is shown in Table 1.

Source: adapted from www.tso.co.uk.

(a) How does TSO monitor performance in customer service?

(b) Comment briefly on TSO's performance in customer service provision in 2006.

(c) What are the main advantages of using quantitative data when monitoring customer performance?

Table 1: Performance standards for TSO customer service – an extract from 2006

												2006	
	Target	Jan	Feb	Mar	Apr	May	Jun	Jul	Aug	Sep	Oct	Nov	Dec
% of calls answered in 10 seconds	> 80.0	91.9	93.6	92.9	93	90.9	92.5	92.9	91.5	90.0	93.0	92.9	94.2
% of calls abandoned	< 2.0	0.7	0.6	0.6	0.7	1.1	0.7	0.6	1.0	1.1	1.0	1.29	2.2
Average time to answer (seconds)	6 max	6	6	6	6	7	7	6	8	10	7	7	7
Complaints - % of orders dispatched	< 1.25	1.2	1.3	1	1.3	0.79	1.08	1.18	1.28	1.12	1.4	1.14	1

Gathering performance data Businesses will especially benefit if they can produce quantitative data when monitoring customer service performance. Quantitative data is much easier and quicker to analyse than other types of data. For example, it is easier to make quick comparisons between different years using numeric performance indicators. Businesses that use quantitative data are likely to set performance targets. At the end of the year actual performance can be compared with the targets. Striving for targets will help to improve performance. An example of quantitative customer service performance data is shown in Table 1 in Question 2.

Recording telephone conversations One common way of monitoring the quality of customer service is to record telephone conversations between customers and staff providing customer service over the telephone. By analysing these recordings a business can identify areas for improvement. For example, a recording of a telephone conversation might reveal that a particular member of staff does not know enough about the products the employer is selling.

Complaints A common way of monitoring the quality of customer service is to keep an up to date record of all complaints from customers relating to customer service. By analysing the nature of complaints a business can take measures to improve the quality of its customer service in the future. Businesses generally take complaints quite seriously. If they fail to respond positively to customer complaints they are likely to lose customers in the future. 'Complaints can be used as business feedback to help drive decision making and customers should be able to complain through a variety of channels', says RightNow Technologies, a customer relations management software producer.

Monitoring and improving the quality of customer services are clearly important issues. Businesses can monitor the quality of customer service by gathering information using the methods described above. They must then take measures to improve the quality of customer service by acting on the results shown by an analysis of that data. This might involve retraining staff, modifying systems or introducing new ways of providing effective customer service.

The benefits of high levels of customer service

It has been argued that customer service is generally the critical factor in determining whether a customer buys and is retained. Consequently, the benefits of providing good quality customer service are huge. Some of the benefits of providing high levels of customer service are outlined below.

- Retaining customers through effective customer service enables easier growth. For example, healthier sales volumes and margins can be sustained and a business can expand as a result of word-of-mouth referrals.
- High levels of customer retention through effective customer service also improves staff morale and motivation. No-one enjoys working for a business where customers are not valued and customer service systems are either ineffective or non-existent. When customers are happy, staff are likely to be happier too. As a result they will be more productive.
- Improved staff morale and motivation resulting from reducing customer dissatisfaction also benefits staff retention and turnover, recruitment quality and costs, stress, grievance, discipline and counselling pressures.
- In some industries, where the product is fairly homogenous, the provision of customer service is one of the few ways in which the product can be differentiated. Consequently, providing good customer service is crucial.
- Reduced customer dissatisfaction will obviously reduce legal action from customers and claims that a business is breaking fair trading laws.
- Retaining customers also enables the business to focus more on proactive opportunities such as growth, innovation and development, rather than reactive tasks such as fire-fighting, crisis management and failure analysis.
- Having a culture of delighting and retaining customers improves the image of a business. A company's reputation in the media, and increasingly on the web in blogs and

KEY TERMS

Call centre – an office where large numbers of staff provide customer service over the telephone.
Customer service – a series of activities designed to enhance the level of customer satisfaction.

KNOWLEDGE

1. Give two examples of customer service a bank might provide.
2. How do call centres provide customer service?
3. State two criticisms of using call centres to provide customer service.
4. State two ways in which a business can meet customer expectations in relation to customer service.
5. What is the Charter Mark?
6. State four advantages of using the BS 8477: 2007.
7. State three ways in which a business might monitor the quality of customer service.
8. How can customer service be used to differentiate a product?

forums, for example, can be improved. The converse also applies. For example, one disgruntled customer and a reasonable network of web friends may cause a significant public relations headache.

So providing high levels of customer service will increase sales, assist growth, retain customers, improve staff motivation, reduce costs and improve the image of a business.

Case Study: ScottishPower

ScottishPower uses an intelligent web-based self-service system to enable faster, more accurate answers to customer queries. The system, from Transversal, the UK's leading provider of multi-channel eService solutions for customer-facing websites and contact centres, ensures customers receive rapid responses to their online account queries. 'We are committed to making it easy for our customers to benefit from the flexibility and cost savings of managing their accounts online,' said Nicola Morrison, online manager at ScottishPower. 'As part of our overall aim to be the industry's number one for customer service we needed to ensure that they had fast, accurate answers to their queries. Working with Transversal has not only helped underpin our online growth, but has given us an unparalleled insight into our customers' requirements through the ability to analyse the questions they are asking,' she said. By investigating the type and number of questions asked on its site, ScottishPower has been able to ensure that the right information is immediately available to its customers - without needing to invest in costly market research. For example, after seeing a growing number of queries on energy efficiency, this information was made more visible on the new site.

Increasing the number of its 5.2 million UK customers who manage their gas and electricity accounts online is part of ScottishPower's business strategy to become the UK's best integrated power provider. Some 95 per cent of customer questions are now answered automatically, improving customer service and encouraging consumers to adopt more online services such as meter reading and billing. ScottishPower introduced a new website in February 2007. Customers can enter meter readings online, view and pay bills, change services, update personal details and notify the company when changing address.

Source: adapted from www.e-consultancy.com.

(a) Describe some examples of customer service provided by ScottishPower. (6 marks)
(b) How has the provision of customer service probably changed for ScottishPower in recent years? (6 marks)
(c) How has Transversal helped to improve the quality of customer service at ScottishPower? (10 marks)
(d) How important do you think customer service is to ScottishPower? (10 marks)
(e) Evaluate the benefits to ScottishPower of providing high levels of customer service. (18 marks)

38 Working with suppliers

The role of suppliers in operations

Suppliers are important business stakeholders and will benefit from the success of a business. However, they can also contribute to that success. Operations managers need to find effective suppliers that provide good quality materials and services at competitive prices. Suppliers also need to be thoroughly reliable and offer some flexibility in their services. Having good suppliers, and maintaining effective relations with them, will help to improve the operational performance of a business

Controlling costs Businesses that use just-in-time (JIT) manufacturing techniques depend very heavily on their suppliers. JIT manufacturers need supplies delivered at regular intervals and at specific times. JIT manufacturers do not hold stocks of materials and components, so a break in supply leaves them vulnerable. If a supplier fails to deliver, or delivers the wrong order, the manufacturer may have to close down production for a time. This could be very expensive. Having good suppliers therefore reduces the costs of holding stock. It can also prevent costly delays.

Reliability and customer satisfaction For JIT manufacturers suppliers need to be 100 per cent reliable. Their role is critical. Many suppliers feeding JIT manufacturers have located their own operations very close to their customers. This helps to reduce the chances of a break in supply and fosters good relations. Even businesses that do not operate JIT will need reliable suppliers. For example, most large supermarkets receive daily deliveries of fresh fish. If these supplies did not arrive on time supermarkets might not be able to offer their customers the range of fish they have come to expect. This could result in lost sales and disgruntled customers.

The need for flexibility In some industries businesses need highly flexible suppliers. One reason for this is because some businesses are subject to sharply fluctuating demand. In the events and hospitality industry it is often very difficult to estimate demand. For example, a catering company providing meals at a cricket match might require additional supplies of food if the attendance was unusually high due to very good weather.

Purchasing

In many businesses it is the purchasing department that has responsibility for working with suppliers. Purchasing involves the buying of materials, components, fuel, tools, machinery, equipment, stationery and services by the business. It also includes adopting any method that allows the firm to obtain the

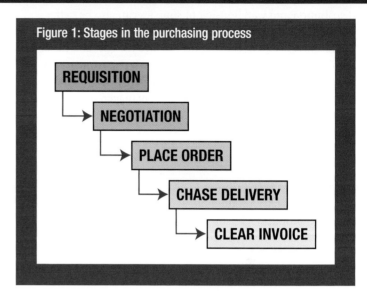

Figure 1: Stages in the purchasing process

REQUISITION → NEGOTIATION → PLACE ORDER → CHASE DELIVERY → CLEAR INVOICE

goods and services it needs, such as hiring.

The various stages in the purchasing process are shown in Figure 1. Purchasing usually begins when the purchasing department is notified of a particular need. For example, a firm's stores or a particular department may send a **requisition form** asking for more stationery. The purchasing department will then act on this. Most purchases are repeat purchases from regular suppliers. Orders are placed with the supplier at previously agreed prices and delivery is accepted under previously arranged terms. New products may need different materials and new suppliers. This will involve a period of search and negotiation, as the buyer tries to find the best deal. If there is a delay in delivery, it is the purchasing department's responsibility to find out why and speed up delivery. Once the goods have arrived the invoice is checked and then payment can be made.

In manufacturing the purchasing department works closely with the production and finance departments. Most purchasing is carried out on behalf of the production department. The finance department needs information about purchases to make payments and record the transactions.

The importance of purchasing is likely to vary according to the nature and size of the business. In many service industries purchasing is not very important. This is because materials are only a small fraction of the total cost of the final product. For example, hairdressing involves very little purchasing, as production involves a skill and uses few materials. However, a large manufacturer requires a large amount of materials, components etc. and so the firm will employ a purchasing department made up of specialists.

Centralised and decentralised purchasing

In some businesses, **centralised purchasing** is used. This is where the purchasing for the whole business is carried out by one department. The advantage of this method is that **economies of scale** can be gained as large-scale buyers enjoy lower rates and market power. Also, the same quality and standard of materials can be set throughout the business. The distribution and warehousing of supplies can also be better planned.

Decentralised purchasing may reduce the cost and burden of administration. Purchasing officers in each department may be more in touch with the needs of that department. In retailing, if purchasing is undertaken by each store manager, the needs of each store can be better catered for. The added responsibility might also motivate store managers.

Choosing effective suppliers

It is important for a business to evaluate suppliers. A poor supplier may delay production, which can be costly. When choosing suppliers a business is likely to use a number of **criteria** to evaluate their reliability.

Price For many businesses the price charged by suppliers will be the most important criterion when choosing a supplier. If businesses can lower the costs of raw materials, components and other services they will make more profit. Price will be particularly important if there is little difference in the quality of the material being purchased. For example, when finding an electricity supplier, only the price is likely to be considered.

Payment terms Payment terms can vary enormously. Payment terms usually refer to the length of the credit period and the method by which payment must be made. Businesses will tend to prefer long credit periods – 90 days or more perhaps. The method of payment is not likely to be a big issue today, although not many businesses will want to pay in cash unless there are significant discounts.

Quality Businesses will need good quality materials and services. They cannot produce good quality products themselves if they use poor quality materials. For example, a business that fits high quality kitchens cannot use poor quality tiles and kitchen units.

Capacity If a business is going to buy very large quantities from a supplier, it will want reassurance that the supplier has the capacity to meet demand. If there is a danger that the supplier may run out of capacity, supplies may be threatened which could disrupt production. A business may also consider the capacity of a supplier if it is likely that the business would be expanding in the near future.

Reliability Businesses want suppliers that deliver goods when they say they will. They also want the correct order first time. Suppliers that are late and prone to making mistakes in orders will be avoided.

Flexibility Many businesses prefer suppliers that can offer a flexible service. For example, can they change orders at the last

Question 1.

McPhersons Ltd is a chain of twenty butchers operating in Scotland and the North of England. Its head office is attached to the shop located in Leeds. All the purchasing is currently undertaken at head office and the meat is delivered in bulk to a warehouse in Leeds. The firm employs a driver to distribute orders to the varios shops twice a week. The board of directors is considering the decentralisation of the purchasing function, since the discounts from bulk buying are not particulary significant. If decentralisation takes place each shop manager will receive a £2,000 p.a. salary increase. The discounts lost from bulk buying are expected to total £20,000 p.a. Cold storage, handling and disitribution costs are expected to fall by £50,000 in total and administration costs will be £5,000 lower in total. It is expected that the quality of the meat will improve when purchasing is the responsibility of the shop managers.

(a) Advise the company whether or not decentralisation is a worthwhile change in operational policy, in purely financial terms.

(b) Explain the non-financial advantages and disadvantages to McPhersons of decentralising purchasing.

minute or can they deliver a day early? Flexible suppliers make operations management easier when planning production.

Vendor rating

The measurement of suppliers' performance is called VENDOR RATING. A business must choose criteria which could be used to measure the performance of a supplier.

A simple vendor rating system is shown in Table 1. The supplier is awarded a mark for performance based on five criteria. For example, the supplier has a good price record, scoring 18 out of a possible 20. Adding the scores gives a total vendor rating of 71/100. When deciding which supplier to choose, a firm is likely to pick the one with the highest rating. If a business feels that some criteria are more important than others, it may give them more value using a weighting system. One problem with this system is how to judge a supplier's performance against given criteria. It may be possible to use records. But sometimes evaluation may simply be based on the subjective opinion of a manager.

Table 1: A simple vendor rating system

Criteria	Maximum Score	Actual Score
Quality	20	17
Price	20	18
Delivery	20	10
Communication	20	12
Flexibility	20	14
Total	**100**	**71**

eSourcing

ESOURCING is the use of Internet technologies and electronic communications in the whole purchasing process. It is a systematic approach that can handle all stages in the purchasing process including identifying appropriate suppliers, tendering, negotiation and award and contract management. The various eSource tools available enable buyers and suppliers to connect and agree a contract quickly and efficiently in order to improve the company's competitiveness. eSourcing significantly reduces the length of time spent on the whole purchasing process. It also reduces the need for paper-based systems and labour-intensive processes. In general, eSourcing helps to improve operational efficiency and can benefit both buyers and suppliers. Buyers benefit from eSourcing for following reasons.

- Faster sourcing process and faster results – time reductions of up to 70%.
- Elimination of face-to-face meetings, travel time, and geographical barriers.
- More transparent, uniform and predictable pricing.
- Improved enforcement of corporate purchasing policies.
- Increased process transparency.
- Better supplier measurement.

Suppliers can also benefit from eSourcing for certain reasons.

- More efficient and objective sourcing process and more level playing field.
- Easier to respond – negotiations and travel are eliminated.
- Lower selling costs.
- Improved convenience for buyers, leading to more transactions.

KEYTERMS

eSourcing – using the Internet in the purchasing process.
Vendor rating – a method of measuring and evaluating the performance of suppliers.

Question 2.

Vi-Spring manufactures high quality beds. A feature of its large range is the ability to offer customers a wide variety of personalised options. It markets its well-known products around the world through a number of large and small retailers. Founded over 100 years ago, the company now employs 180 people and is located in Plymouth, Devon.

The company has recently adopted a just-in-time (JIT) approach to production. Vi-Spring now holds a very low stock of raw materials. Stocks required for production come in on a JIT basis from around two hundred suppliers, of which thirty are key sources. The majority - mainly those providing cotton ticking, padding and webbing - are in the North of England. Delivery of an order is on a next-day basis; other materials are on a longer lead time.

The company prefers to build close and reliable relationships with its suppliers, regarding them as key business partners. If a problem develops, rather than dropping a supplier Vi-Spring will work with it to overcome the issue concerned.

Source: adapted from http://datadialogs.com.

(a) Why is the reliability of suppliers so critical for Vi-Spring?
(b) Do you think Vi-Spring has good relations with its suppliers? Explain your answer.

KNOWLEDGE

1. Why is it important to develop effective relations with suppliers?
2. How important is the role played by suppliers for JIT manufacturers?
3. What are the different stages in the purchasing process?
4. What is the difference between centralised and decentralised purchasing?
5. State two benefits of centralised purchasing.
6. State four benefits of eSourcing to buyers.
7. State three benefits of eSourcing to suppliers.

Case Study: IXO Instruments Ltd

Based in Southampton, IXO Instruments Ltd is a privately owned company. It operates in the market for high-value, handheld test instruments. Its products are sold through a network of national catalogue houses, regional stocking distributors and international master distributors. The company has become one of the largest manufacturers and suppliers of test equipment. It has built an enviable reputation for providing innovative products offering unique and patented designs with features, functions and reliability at an affordable price. IXO is ISO 9001:2000 certified. Its products include portable meters for the measurement and testing of light, sound, temperature, humidity, airflow and water quality.

IXO has a supplier base of 120 but is always looking for new suppliers to keep costs down. The family who own the company set demanding financial targets, which often means that managers continually have to cut costs. At the moment a vendor rating system is used to find new suppliers. Recently a new supplier was found for a component in a new printer. The component is a circuit board and is called FFD 339. Table 2 shows some of the information that was used to find the new supplier.

Unfortunately, last year, the operations manager had to take early retirement due to ill health. A new manager was appointed and it was apparent that she wanted to make a number of operational changes. She was particularly concerned about the treatment of suppliers. She felt that IXO could not develop effective relations with suppliers if they continually looked for cheaper ones. To improve operational performance with regard to suppliers, she was extremely keen to make use of eSourcing in the organisation.

Table 2: Supplier information for FFD 339

Supplier name	Price	Quality	Reliability	Flexibility	Payment terms	Total
Reynolds Ltd	18	8	7	8	6	
AGT	12	8	9	9	5	
Adco	14	6	7	5	8	
Veelle	8	9	9	9	9	
Williams & Co	20	8	6	4	5	

NB All criteria are marked out of 10 except for price which is given more weight and marked out of 20.

(a) (i) How does IXO Instruments Ltd choose effective suppliers? (4 marks)

(ii) Which is the most important criterion for IXO when choosing suppliers? Explain your answer. (6 marks)

(b) Which of the suppliers shown in Table 2 would have been selected by IXO Instruments Ltd? Explain your answer. (8 marks)

(c) Analyse IXO's current relationship with suppliers. (8 marks)

(d) Evaluate the possible benefits to IXO Instruments Ltd if they adopt eSourcing. (14 marks)

The nature and impact of technology

One of the most significant factors affecting how businesses have operated in the twentieth century has been the impact of new TECHNOLOGY. It is easy to see its impact when we consider some of the changes that have taken place in business.

- New products, such as camcorders, compact discs, laptop computers and services such as direct purchasing from television.
- New production processes, such as robotic welding, and computer controlled cutting machines.
- New materials such as silicon chips for computer circuit boards and polystyrene for packaging.
- Changes in business operations and new skills. For example, as a result of automatic cash tills in banking, many staff have been retrained to sell financial services.

There are many ways in which technology can be defined. One approach is to say that it is 'a creative process which uses human, scientific and material resources to solve problems and generate better efficiency'. Some examples make this clear. A business that uses video conferencing to communicate with branches spread all over the country is using technology. So is a plant which uses lasers to detect faults in products as they move along the production line.

How does technological progress take place? It is usually by means of **invention** and **innovation**. Invention is the discovery of something new. Some examples include the laser beam developed in 1960 by Dr. Charles Townes and the micro-processor developed in 1971 by Marcian Hoff in the USA. Inventions are then developed into products. The laser beam has been used for cutting in industry, micro-surgery in hospitals and spectacular lighting shows in displays.

Inventions are sometimes made by creative people 'outside' business. For example, the ball point pen was invented by a sculptor, and the pneumatic tyre by a veterinary surgeon. Today, research is carried out by teams of people working for a business, university or the government. The rewards to inventors can be very high, if their inventions can be used commercially and patented.

In business, innovation is the commercial exploitation of an invention. An invention is not usually in a form that consumers will buy. The product must be developed to meet consumers' needs, so that it can be sold profitably by business. UK firms have, perhaps, been reluctant to do this in the past. For example, the first working computers were developed in the 1930s. Since then Japan and America have led the world in hardware production and computer research. Enormous investment is often required to innovate once a technical breakthrough has been achieved.

Type of technology in primary industry

Primary industry has been affected by the introduction of new technology in a number of ways. In agriculture the use of tractors, combine harvesters, lifting equipment, grain drying machines and automatic milking and feeding apparatus have helped to increase output, reduce time and waste, and improve conditions. Agrochemicals and pesticides have raised crop yields. Biological research has helped to develop plants and crops which are more resistant to disease and more attractive to consumers. Genetically modified foods are argued to have better resistance to disease. In extractive industries, such as mining, cutting, lifting and tunnelling machines have all led to increased output.

Question 1.

Barclays, Britain's third biggest bank, is planning to cut 1,100 jobs in its processing centre in Poole, Dorset, over the next three years. The redundancies are the result of automation in more of its systems. For instance, cheques which were previously processed by hand will now be handled by computers. The cutbacks will leave just 850 employees remaining. The bank will also shut its Barclays House operation in Poole and seek out smaller premises in the town or nearby Bournemouth.

Unite, the newly formed union which incorporates finance branch Amicus, expressed concerned about the 'large reduction of jobs in Poole'. Union official Steve Pantak said: 'Unite does, however, have robust agreements in place and the bank's plans are spread over the next three years, so we will be working with the bank to ensure the maximum number of redeployments and voluntary redundancies.

The new premises will be 100,000 sq ft compared with the 300,000 sq ft currently provided by Barclays House. The bank has had operations in Poole since 1976. The job reductions will affect a number of areas, including cheque processing as well as IT support and some human resources functions.

Source: adapted from *The Guardian*, 10.5.2007.

(a) Using this case as an example, explain what is meant by automation.
(b) What problem does this case highlight when introducing new technology?

There have also been improvements in safety equipment and mining conditions for workers. The extraction of oil now takes place on large oil rigs with computer controlled drilling equipment. This improves the speed and accuracy of production. In fishing, the introduction of refrigerated boats has helped to improve productivity. Forestry has benefited from cutting, lifting and haulage equipment.

One problem with the use of more efficient technology is that resources are used up more quickly. It may be possible to control this in the case of **renewable resources**, such as timber, by replanting and managed forestry. However, unless new forms of power can be developed, there are likely to be problems in future with extracting large amounts of the world's finite resources such as coal and oil. There have also been criticisms of genetically modified food and its possible effects on humans.

Type of technology in secondary industry

New technology has led to major changes in manufacturing. Many factories and production lines employ complex mechanical, electrical and electronic systems. Even smaller manufacturing businesses have benefited from the introduction of new equipment and processes. Examples of new technology can be found in a number of areas.

Robots Robots are increasingly used on assembly and production lines. They have some form of arm, which moves to instructions given by a computer. Repetitive tasks, such as installing components, can be carried out many times with great accuracy. Such tasks may lead to boredom, lack of motivation, tiredness and human error if undertaken by employees. Robots may also increase the flexibility of a business. For example, in 1998 small robots, each with its own set of paint cans, were installed in the paint shop of the Volkswagen-Audi car plant in Germany. The robot could be activated at a few minutes' notice when a customer wants a colour which is not included in the current program. Using the robot means that customer demand for less popular colours can be satisfied without having to clean out the pipes of the main painting apparatus, which would be costly.

Computer aided design COMPUTER AIDED DESIGN (CAD) is now used by businesses in the design process, before a product is manufactured. Examples of products designed using CAD include vehicle bodies, plastic containers to hold milk and oil, furniture and clothing. Designing on computer allows a business to produce accurate drawings, which can be viewed in 3D and altered cheaply and quickly for a client. Designs can be accurately measured and tested on computer for faults, such as unsuitable components or dimensions, which might have caused problems during manufacture.

Computer numerically controlled machines Products can be manufactured using COMPUTER NUMERICALLY CONTROLLED (CNC) machines. Instructions are given to the CNC machine by the operator. The machine then carries out its instructions, controlled by a computer. An example might be a CNC milling machine which is used to cut out a mould of a mouse in plastic. The computer controls the cutting to produce the shape of a mould. In the textile industry computer controlled sewing, cutting and printing machines are used. Some CNC machines make use of probes and **coordinate measuring machines** (CMMs). These are designed to make simple or complex measurements, check batches or components one at a time and inspect geometric or irregular shapes. CMMs are accurate to within a few microns. CNC machines can produce shapes and cut quickly and accurately. They can also carry out repetitive tasks without human error. The instructions can be changed easily to carry out different tasks. For example, JCB uses CNC machines to cut a wide range of patterns from metal plates for its mechanical diggers.

Computer aided manufacture In many factories computers are used to design products and the information is then fed into CNC machines. This automated operation is known as COMPUTER AIDED MANUFACTURE (CAM). For example, a manufacturer of telephones may design a new shape using a CAD software program on computer. The instructions may be taken from the CAD program and inputted into CNC machines. These machines will reproduce the shapes, guided by the information contained in the computer. Other examples of CAM include computer controlled manufacture of plastic bricks at Lego, computer controlled assembly lines at Sony and computer controlled temperatures, flow rates and ingredients for pizza production at McCain Foods. The computer controlled weaving system produced by Bonas stores designs on computer in one part of a factory and sends production information to looms in other parts of the factory. These then weave the designed fabric.

Computer integrated manufacture Some businesses have integrated the entire design and production process. Computers are used to guide and control the production of a good. Employees supervise the manufacturing part of the operation, checking that it is working effectively and repairing faults. This system is known as COMPUTER INTEGRATED MANUFACTURE (CIM). There is a number of stages in the operation. They are shown in Figure 1.

- Orders are received via email, fax or letter and inputted into the system. Costings are carried out on computer using spreadsheet programs. Customers are stored on databases. Accounts are kept on computer and regularly updated. Orders which are received are processed and invoiced at a later date.
- The design department uses CAD packages to design the product for a client, making changes on computer. The instructions to manufacture the design are produced and fed through to the production part of the system.
- Production is planned and scheduled. Parts and materials are ordered as required by the computer, which monitors

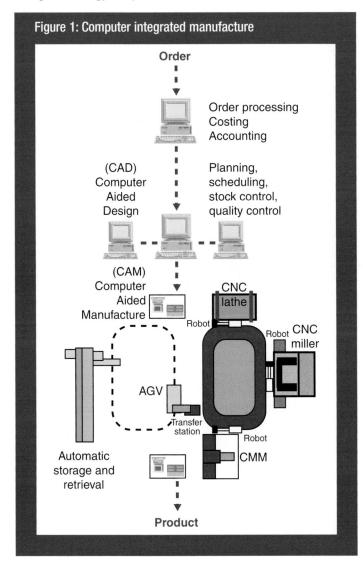

Figure 1: Computer integrated manufacture

Order

Order processing
Costing
Accounting

(CAD)
Computer
Aided
Design

Planning,
scheduling,
stock control,
quality control

(CAM)
Computer
Aided
Manufacture

CNC
lathe

Robot

Robot CNC
miller

AGV

Transfer
station

Robot

Automatic
storage and
retrieval

CMM

Product

stock and automatically reorders where necessary.
- The instructions for production are passed to CNC machines which manufacture the product. CMM machines monitor the quality of the work.
- Robots are used to transfer products from one CNC machine to another.
- Automatically guided vehicles (AGVs) take components to the machines.
- Finished products are taken to the stores or sent for dispatch.

Type of technology in tertiary industry

The supply of services has in the past been relatively more labour intensive than in the primary and secondary sectors. This is because supplying services often requires direct and personal contact with customers. However, today the use of technology in the tertiary industry is becoming more widespread in a number of areas.

Government and private services There is a range of services provided by government or private alternatives. New technology

used in health care and dental care has improved services considerably. Developments in new vaccines and drugs have reduced suffering and cured diseases that not long ago may have led to deaths. Surgeons can carry out exact operations using lasers, viewing them on television screens with the use of fibre optics. Replacement teeth can be produced for patients which exactly fit jaw shapes from materials which will last for years. Government information can now be found easily on the Internet.

Financial services Businesses selling financial services match customers with appropriate financial products. For example, client information can be fed into a computer to identify the most suitable insurance policy or savings plan. The sale of financial products such as ISAs, pensions and insurance policies is increasingly carried out on the Internet. Some banks offer online banking services. Many financial organisations now have cash dispensers outside their premises. These can be used by customers who want to take out cash with a minimum of fuss or out of normal working hours. Some banks have cash dispensers inside, and customers can enter the bank in non-business hours using 'swipe cards' to open doors. This gives extra security to customers using the facilities.

Distribution The introduction of containers has made the handling of freight quick and easy. They can be hauled onto trailers and locked in position. This prevents movement during transport and possible damage and theft. At port or rail terminals, containers can be loaded safely and quickly onto trains or ships using cranes. Refrigerated containers allow perishable goods to be transported long distances without deteriorating.

Personal services Dating agencies use computers to match couples using personal information held on databases about clients' characteristics and preferences. Agencies also make use of video technology to record messages from clients. Online dating agencies allow people to register on the Internet.

Post and communication Technology has helped to improve the speed and efficiency of postal and packaging delivery. Many businesses have franking machines that weigh and record the required postage. Bar codes allow a free postal or business service to be provided by firms. A customer can return a leaflet or envelope without charge to a business. Machines at the post office will read the bar code and bill the business providing the service. Post offices make use of video and television to advertise their services.

Most business now make extensive use of email to communicate. Emails can also have attachments. These can be documents that have been scanned or saved as jpeg files. This means that the post does not have to be used, preventing delays in communication.

Hotels, restaurants and transport In the travel industry technology allows customers to travel without a ticket. They can book a flight over the telephone or the Internet using a credit card. The same card is then used to pick up a boarding pass from an airport machine or a check-in counter. Travellers to Australia can obtain an 'electronic visa'. Entry can be organised by giving passport details to a travel agent. These details are sent electronically to the appropriate port of entry. Booking for hotels or theatre tickets can also be made by credit card. Meals at restaurants can be paid for by a 'swipe or switch' card. The transaction is recorded by a machine and the money is automatically transferred from the current account of the customer.

Advertising In advertising, television makes increasing use of advances in filming technology and special effects to make adverts more sophisticated and entertaining. There is also a growing selection of advertising media. For example, advertisers have used electronic messaging on the 'touchlines' of sporting events and in city centres on the sides of buildings. The Internet provides worldwide advertising, but only to Internet users.

Retailing Retailing has benefited in many ways from new technology.

- The packaging of goods has changed greatly in recent years. New materials such as polystyrene and strong plastic wrap have improved the way in which goods are packaged. The materials have been lighter and stronger, have provided better protection, and have been easier to handle. Many firms have redesigned the packaging of goods to increase sales. In some cases new technology has helped. For example, Lucozade and other soft drinks have been packaged in flexible bags instead of cans and bottles.
- There has been a growth in home shopping. Computers and televisions have been linked together to enable shoppers to browse at home and then place orders by telephone or through a link. The Internet is a growing means of direct selling to customers at home.
- Payment has been made easier. Bar codes and hand-held recorders allow customers to register the prices of goods as they shop. This saves time and queues at the checkout. Goods can be paid for by credit or 'swipe cards', increasing security as the customer does not have to carry cash.
- Some supermarkets have unstaffed checkouts where customers can scan their own shopping and choose from a variety of payment methods.

Information and communication technology

INFORMATION AND COMMUNICATION TECHNOLOGY (ICT) is the recording and use of information by electronic means. Some of the uses of **information technology** (IT) have already been explained in the previous sections. However, there are some common uses of ICT which may apply to businesses operating in primary, secondary or tertiary industries.

Administration Many routine tasks can be carried out quickly

Question 2.

Coilcolor is one of the largest independent paint coating lines in the UK, specialising in organic coating of steel and aluminium coils. It offers a wide range of protective finishes and colours to suit its customer's requirements. The company has the ability to produce both extremely low and high volume quantities, a wide choice of colours and short lead times. Among their prestigious clients are B&Q, Ikea and Jaguar.

The original stock control and sales processing system was implemented in 1992. Since then Coilcolor's business model has undergone substantial changes. The original system, with its ageing technology base, no longer serviced the demands of this highly competitive industry. Consequently the company had to invest in an upgrade. A company called Computerisation developed two highly sophisticated, bespoke systems for Coilcolor – a Sales Order Processing System and a Stock Control System. The new systems efficiently manage Coilcolor's complex product portfolio. This consists of many product variables including stock code, material, colour etc.

The new systems were created to work alongside Sage MMS, a computerised accounts system. This has reduced administration time and costs by avoiding the need for multiple data entry. Coilcolor has achieved a sustainable competitive advantage through its quick turnaround times within the intensive manufacturing process. Improved administration has enhanced that advantage which was made possible by the implementation of Computerisation's systems. From a customer service aspect its new systems provide the company with the ability to monitor stock efficiently, satisfying customer demand with low minimum order quantities.

Source: adapted from www.computerisation.co.uk.

(a) Explain how Coilcolor makes use of computers in its operations.
(b) What benefits has Coilcolor enjoyed as a result of using computers?

---

by computer. These may include customer invoicing or billing. Standard letters or memos may be produced which can be easily changed if necessary. Large amounts of information about customers may be stored on databases.

Personnel Personnel files are now easily kept on databases. They can be regularly updated. Spreadsheets also allow calculations of salaries and deductions.

R&D Computer aided design can be used to research new materials or new product ideas. For example, tests may be carried out on the endurance of materials using a CAD simulation. Recording, monitoring, regulating, forecasting and analysing data are all tasks that can be carried out more easily.

Finance Many firms record all financial transactions on spreadsheets. Some allow instant production of financial information such as profit and loss accounts or income statements, cash flow forecasts, budgets and financial ratios. It is also possible to make checks on outstanding payments that are due from customers so that credit control will be effective.

Communications Developments in information and communications technology mean that information can be collected, stored and sent electronically in a fraction of a second. This saves money and makes sure information is passed correctly. Mobile telephones, faxes and email mean that people can work from a variety of locations. Information can be sent over great distances and at any time. The Internet provides wide ranging communication opportunities, including promotion, online buying and emailing.

Production information Information may be stored about the terms of suppliers. Production costs may be calculated on spreadsheets. The ordering of stocks or components may be carried out by computer. Purchasing may be undertaken using eSourcing, where the whole purchasing process is handled by online purchasing systems.

Stock control Technology is increasingly used to control stock. For example, retailers such as supermarket chains have a very sophisticated stock control system called EPOS (electronic point of sale). The system holds a record of every single stock item in the store. When a customer passes through the checkout every item purchased is subtracted automatically from the stock list. At any time a manager can enter the system to see how much of an item is left in stock. The system may even reorder stock automatically. Businesses may also have systems to reorder stocks online from suppliers, perhaps using intranets or extranets.

Information and sales Many businesses now have their own website on the Internet, providing company information. Some are using sites to provide information or to sell products to customers. A readers' survey by Marketing Technique about use of the Internet by businesses found 75 per cent of respondents worked for companies with their own site. Two-thirds of respondents used the Internet to monitor competitors' activities.

Benefits of new technology

There is a number of benefits to business of using new technology.

Reducing costs One of the main benefits of new technology to businesses is lower costs. If a task or activity is automated, people are replaced by machines which can operate more cheaply. For example, the cost to banks of dispensing cash has fallen considerably since ATMs were introduced.

Improving quality The quality of products is often improved when new technologies are introduced. This is because machines are usually more precise and consistent than humans. For example, robotic welders in car factories can maintain a consistent and high quality weld indefinitely once they have been programmed. This will help to improve the quality of the car.

Increased productivity More can be produced with less and, as a result, businesses may gain higher profits. In addition, fewer of the environment's resources may be used up.

Reducing waste Introducing new technology often results in time being saved and fewer materials being used. For example, technology has created printing machines which waste less paper when printing books or magazines. The ways in which resources are used have attracted a great deal of attention in recent years. As the world's population continues to grow it will be necessary to improve resource use even further.

Improving the working environment Statistics on accidents at work show that the working environment is safer as a result of new technology. Mining and manufacturing in particular have benefited. Modern equipment has made work easier and more tolerable. For example, fork lift trucks mean workers no longer need to load goods by hand. These improvements also help to remove workers' dissatisfaction.

Benefits to society Many new products have come onto the market in recent years. Personal stereo systems, video recorders, satellite and digital television, high performance cars and microwave ovens are some examples. New products mean wider consumer choice and possibly higher living standards. Other developments have helped to make our lives easier, such as ATMs, online shopping and mobile telephones.

Improvements in communications Faster means of transport (such as the jet aircraft), answerphones, email, computer network links and fax machines are all examples of inventions which have helped to improve the speed of communications.

Higher incomes If firms enjoy greater profits they can afford to pay higher dividends to shareholders and higher wages to employees. Also, if efficiency is improved then products may be sold at lower prices. As the country's income increases the government collects more tax revenue. This could be used to improve the quality of public services or alternatively to reduce the overall level of taxation or government borrowing.

Problems with new technology

The introduction of new technology can also cause problems for both business and society.

Cost Development, installation and maintenance can often prove costly. Also, businesses may have to lay off and retrain staff, leading to redundancy payments and retraining costs. If firms borrow to meet these costs, they will have to pay interest. Reorganisation may also be needed. Production may be changed from batch to flow production, job descriptions may be changed and in some cases a larger or smaller plant may be needed.

Labour relations In the past, trade unions have resisted the introduction of some new technology because of the threat to their members' jobs. The growth of union and business partnerships after the year 2000 may have made the introduction of new technology easier.

Job skills New technology creates jobs which require new, technical skills, but replace manual jobs. These new jobs cannot be done by the existing workforce unless it can be retrained. Often, this is not possible.

Breakdowns Automated production lines are interdependent. If one part of the line breaks down the whole process may stop. There may also be teething problems. Breakdowns often occur when technology is first installed. For example, it is argued that the Stock Exchange Automatic Quotation (SEAQ) share dealing system was partially to blame for the 1987 Stock Exchange crash. The system automatically triggered selling instructions, causing big falls in some share prices.

Motivation Some staff may dislike working only with machines. This may affect their motivation.

Management The management of technological change is considered very difficult. One reason is due to the rapid pace of the change. When new technology becomes available business managers have to decide whether or not to purchase it, or wait for the next important breakthrough. Deciding when to invest in new technology is very difficult. The management of the human resources leading up to the change, and during the change, requires great skill. People are often unhappy about change in their lives.

Unemployment and employment Much new technology is labour saving. Tasks once carried out by people will be done by machines. As a result people may become unemployed. For example, in automated production lines tasks such as assembly and quality checks are done by robots and CMMs. One or two employees may act as supervisors. On the other hand technology has to be designed, manufactured, installed, programmed, operated, serviced and replaced, which may create new jobs.

IT problems Computer software can become infected by viruses. A computer virus is a programme written to deliberately damage or destroy software and files. Such viruses are very damaging. It is possible for businesses to use software to check the existence of viruses. They can then be blocked from entering the computer system if included on emails, for example. If a virus has entered the system, it can be removed. Computer software has other problems which can affect a business. They may have to constantly buy the latest software to be compatible with clients or suppliers who use more modern versions. Modern machines may not run older software. New software may not be able to convert older programs.

Leisure time People have gained more leisure time as a result of new technology. They need to learn how to use this extra time in

KEYTERMS

Computer aided design – the use of computers when designing products.
Computer aided manufacture – the use of computers in the manufacture of products.
Computer numerically controlled machines – machines which have their operations controlled by a computer program.
Computer integrated manufacture – the use of computers to control the entire production process.
Information and communication technology – the recording and use of information by electronic means.
Technology – a creative process which uses human, scientific and material resources to solve problems and improve efficiency.

KNOWLEDGE

1. What is meant by technology?
2. What is the difference between invention and innovation?
3. State four areas of a business that might benefit from new technology.
4. How has new technology been used in marketing?
5. How might a business exporting products abroad make use of new technology?
6. How has information technology been incorporated in production?
7. How has business security used information technology?
8. Why was the Data Protection Act introduced?
9. In what ways has new technology benefited (a) business owners; (b) management?
10. Briefly explain problems that (a) workers and (b) management may face with the introduction of new technology.
11. How might business exploit the Internet?

a constructive way. Businesses are taking advantage of this. For example, it is argued that there is enough demand in the UK for many more golf courses.

An ageing population Medicine has benefited greatly from new technology. One effect of this is that the population of many countries is now 'ageing'. As a result the pressure has increased on those in work to support the aged. Demands on public funds will also increase and the government will have to find money for facilities which are needed for the elderly.

Data protection The rapid development in the use of IT has led to legislation about the collection, storage, processing and distribution of data. The **Data Protection Act, 1998** lays down a number of conditions with which users must comply. For example, personal data should be obtained and processed fairly and lawfully and can only be held for specified and lawful purposes. There is also some legislation regarding the use of the Internet. EU legislation prevents the downloading of copyright music and allows businesses to block downloading. For example. EU legislation in 2003 made it illegal to send junk email, known as spam, by businesses to individuals.

Case Study: *Minco Manufacturing*

Minco Manufacturing is an American company. It produces over 250,000 fuser rollers a month for more than 400 models of copiers, printers and facsimile machines at its state-of-the-art production plant in Colorado. Its products include sleeved, silicone and hard coated upper fuser rollers, and silicone coated lower pressure rollers.

As a result of adopting 16 new Stäubli robots in its production cells the company has improved product quality and reduced costs. The robots are used for a variety of tasks such as operating lathes. Robots keep labour costs down, allowing Minco to compete internationally. 'By using robots and reducing labour costs, we can compete with companies that make parts in China, for example.' said Brian Duff, manufacturing engineer. 'We are able to keep the work in the United States and still be competitive with the cheaper labour rates in Asian countries.'

'Once the robots have been programmed they just run. … That frees up the operator to do inspections and move parts in and out of the cell, instead of having all these people loading lathes for 10 to 12 hours a shift,' Duff said. Stäubli robots are known for high-speed performance, and this speed also generated savings. Before the robots were installed, this process required an additional finish turning lathe. We had an operator manually feeding two lathes to work the ends and then feeding a third lathe to do the finish turn work. The finish turning machine was actually capable of twice the production that was possible by hand,' Duff explained. 'With three robotic cells currently running, we've saved three lathes that we can transfer into making another cell.'

They've also saved about 50 per cent more floor space. 'It allows us to design extremely compact work cells,' Duff said.

The quantity of fuser rollers produced and the level of quality needed, demanded repeatability as well as speed. 'Repeatability is key to the robot's performance in this application because of how we are locating the part into the draw tube. If we didn't place the part against the stop very accurately then we would have too much fluctuation and we could not control the quality of the roller,' Duff said. 'We need to meet a length accuracy of less than .005 of an inch, but we're not seeing even that much variation. We're seeing .002 or less.'

After the initial 16 robots are installed, Minco's plan is to integrate robots into other processes that could benefit from automation. Then the company will start replacing their older robots. 'We've talked to Stäubli about adding robots to load the initial paint station. It is very labour-intensive, because every roller we make gets painted. Rollers weigh up to eight pounds so it is exhausting work. We get a lot of operator fatigue and production begins to drop,' he said.

Minco Manufacturing is also considering installing robots to unload rollers off a conveyor after the coating has cured. 'This is very labour intensive, but also has to be done very carefully. At this stage the rollers cannot get nicked or scratched,' Duff said. Robots are also ideally suited for Minco's packaging process.

Source: adapted from www.roboticsonline.com.

(a) Explain how robots are used in operations. (6 marks)
(b) Explain why the introduction of robots is an example of automation. (6 marks)
(c) How will workers benefit from the introduction of more robots? (6 marks)
(d) Discuss the benefits enjoyed by Minco Manufacturing as a result of employing more robots. (10 marks)
(e) Discuss the problems Minco Manufacturing could encounter when making more use of robots. (12 marks)

What is marketing?

A **market** is any set of arrangements that allows buyers and sellers to exchange goods and services. It can be anything from a street market in a small town to a large market involving internationally traded goods. But what is meant by the term MARKETING?

Marketing is not just about selling products to customers. Before selling products, many businesses carry out a range of activities to find out consumer preferences, including market research and testing of products on consumers. Similarly, marketing and advertising are not the same. Advertising is just one of a number of promotion methods used by businesses. Other methods involve giving 'free' gifts and running competitions.

A widely accepted definition of marketing, from the Institute of Marketing, is that 'Marketing is the management process involved in identifying, anticipating and satisfying consumer requirements profitably.' Some others are shown in Table 1.

Table 1: Marketing definitions

Marketing is about supplying the right products, to the right customers, at the right price, in the right place, at the right time.
Anon

'The basic function of marketing is to attract and retain customers at a profit.'
P. Drucker, The Practice of Management (1993)

'Marketing is the process of planning and executing the conception, pricing, promotion and distribution of ideas, goods and services to create exchange and satisfy individual and organisational objectives.'
American Marketing Association (1985)

The purpose of 'Marketing is to establish, maintain and enhance long term customer relationships at a profit, so that the objectives of the parties involved are met. This is done by mutual exchange and fulfilment of promises.'
C. Gronroos, 'Marketing redefined', Management Decision, 1990.

Marketing effectively

Effective marketing will have certain features
- **A process.** It does not have a start and an end, but is ongoing all the time. Businesses must be prepared to respond to changes that take place. This is shown in Figure 1. For example, a business marketing office furniture would be unwise not to take into account consumers'

reactions. If the business sold modern designs, but sales were poor, it might consider designs for offices that had a traditional look.
- **A business philosophy.** It is not just a series of activities, such as advertising or selling. It is more a 'way of thinking' about how to satisfy consumers' needs. A business selling good quality products, cheaply, may be unsuccessful in its marketing if it has dirty, badly organised or poorly lit facilities. Retailers such as Ikea and Asda have large 'superstores' with restaurants and play areas for children. They could be said to cater for all their consumers' shopping needs.
- **Building relationships with customers.** Profitable businesses are often built upon good customer relations. This might involve dealing with customer complaints in a considered manner. Customers, as a result, are likely to develop a favourable view of the business and buy its products over a long period of time. RELATIONSHIP MARKETING is now used by some businesses, such as Tesco. This is an approach to marketing which stresses the importance of developing relationships with customers which last longer than the short-term.

The purposes of marketing

There is a number of reasons why businesses carry out marketing.

To satisfy consumers A product has a far greater chance of being a success if it satisfies consumers' needs. Businesses which make satisfying their customers a main concern are more likely to be effective at marketing. Marketing should affect all aspects of a business. A production department, for example, would not continue making a product that did not satisfy the needs of the

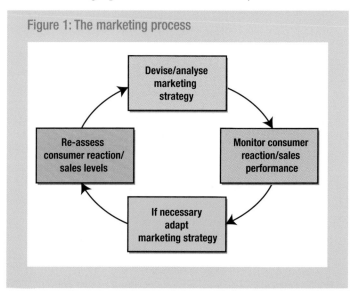

Figure 1: The marketing process

Devise/analyse marketing strategy → Monitor consumer reaction/sales performance → If necessary adapt marketing strategy → Re-assess consumer reaction/sales levels →

consumers at whom it was aimed.

To identifying consumer requirements Marketing should find out what consumer needs and requirements are and make sure that products meet them. Market research is often used by businesses for this purpose. Managers, however, also place stress on having a 'feel' for the market.

To anticipate consumer requirements Businesses have to understand what customers want in advance. In some cases this is easy. For example, supermarkets and butchers stock up with turkeys before Christmas. In other cases it is more difficult. What colours of clothes will be fashionable this year? A chain of stores with the wrong colours might find it difficult to sell its stock. Tastes and fashions in today's markets are changing faster than ever before. Marketing must anticipate and respond to these changes. Toy manufacturers, for example, try to be aware of the next 'craze'. In addition, rapid technological change has taken place in recent years and continues to do so. Firms constantly invent, design and launch new and advanced products onto the market. One example is the electronics industry which has introduced DVD players, digital camcorders, MP3 players and high definition televisions to the market in recent years.

To compete effectively The number of products competing for the consumer's attention is constantly increasing. Businesses today are finding it easier to change their products and enter new markets. Also, there has been increased competition from foreign products in UK markets. This means that businesses have to work even harder to be competitive. Effective marketing should help a business to achieve this.

To make a profit Most businesses today regard making a profit as their main aim. Businesses must make a profit in the long run to survive. Those that do not will cease to operate. Marketing that satisfies consumers' needs profitably is therefore essential. Even when profit is not the main objective, marketing has a vital role to play. Charities, such as Oxfam, and many public sector organisations such as colleges and hospitals, adapt and change the marketing of their services to satisfy their consumers' needs.

Consumer and business to business marketing

CONSUMER MARKETING is where a business is marketing to consumers. There are numerous examples of consumer marketing, including the marketing of the vast majority of products sold in retail outlets such as supermarkets, department stores and high street clothing stores.

BUSINESS TO BUSINESS MARKETING is where one business is engaged in marketing its products to another business. Examples of business to business marketing might include:
* an office furniture manufacturer marketing to business users;
* a car manufacturers providing company cars to a business;
* a local newspaper offering advertising space to local

businesses;
* a software supplier providing software geared up to the needs of businesses.

Product and market orientation

Some businesses are said to be relatively product orientated or market orientated.

Product orientation Many businesses in the past, and some today, could be described as PRODUCT ORIENTATED. This means that the business focuses on the production process and the product itself. It puts most of its efforts into developing and making products which it believes consumers want and which will sell well.

In the past, businesses producing radios and televisions could be said to have been relatively product orientated. It was their novelty and the technical 'wonder' of the product that sold them. There were few companies to compete against each other, and there was a growing domestic market. There were also few overseas competitors. The product sold itself.

Some industries today are still said to be product orientated. The machine-tool industry, which produces machines used in the production of other goods, has to produce a final product which exactly matches a technical specification. However, because of increased competition, such firms are being forced to take consumers' needs into account. The technical specification to which a machine-tool business produces might be influenced by what customers want, for example.

Question 1.

Levens Farm is a fruit farm in Sussex. It allows customers to 'pick your own fruit'. But increasingly it is selling to retailers, encouraged by the news that Britain is fast becoming a nation of berry lovers.

Sales of British strawberries, blackberries and raspberries broke records in 2007 and many suppliers were struggling to keep up with demand. The soft fruits, which are credited with staving off cancer, saw sales of £204 million in the UK. 'It's because people are becoming more aware of the health benefits of eating fresh fruit, especially berries,' said Laurence Olins, the chairman of British Summer Fruits (BSF), which represents nearly all of Britain's soft fruit growers.

Strawberry sales accounted for £165 million, a 5 per cent sales increase from the previous year. In comparison, sales of blackberries shot up by 31 per cent to £4 million while raspberry sales were up 26 per cent to £35 million. Such is the demand that none of Britain's home-grown fruit is exported. And in July and August, when demand was at its highest, berries had to be imported from Europe.

Source: adapted in part from *The Independent*,18.12.2006.

(a) Explain why Levens Farm is selling to (i) consumer markets and (ii) business to business markets.
(b) Explain how the information in the article might help Levens Farm to: (i) identify customer requirements, (ii) anticipate customer requirements; (ii) make a profit.

Product orientated businesses thus place their emphasis on developing a technically sound product, producing that product and then selling it. Contact with the consumer comes largely at this final stage. There will always be a place for product orientation. A great deal of pure research, for example, with no regard to consumers' needs, still takes place in industry, as it does in the development of pharmaceuticals.

Market orientation A business that is MARKET ORIENTATED business is one which continually identifies, reviews and analyses consumers' needs. It is led by the market. A market orientated business is much more likely to be engaged in effective marketing if it is market orientated. Henry Ford was one of the first industrialists to adopt a market orientated approach. When the Ford motor company produced the Model T, it did not just design a car, produce it as cheaply as possible, and then try to sell it to the public. Instead, in advance of production, Ford identified the price at which he believed he could sell large numbers of Model Ts. His starting point was the market and the Model T became one of the first 'mass-market' products. This illustrates the market orientated approach – consumers are central to a firm's decision making. Sony is one of many modern businesses that has taken a market orientated approach. The Sony Bravia High Definition television is an example of a product being developed in response to the wishes of consumers.

A more market orientated business may have several advantages over one which is more product orientated.

- It can respond more quickly to changes in the market because of its use of market information.
- It will be in a stronger position to meet the challenge of new competition entering the market.
- It will be more able to anticipate market changes.
- It will be more confident that the launch of a new product will be a success.

What effect will taking a market orientated approach have on a business? It must:

- consult the consumer continuously (market research);
- design the product according to the wishes of the consumer;
- produce the product in the quantities that consumers want to buy;
- distribute the product according to the buying habits and delivery requirements of the consumer;
- set the price of the product at a level that the consumer is prepared to pay.

The business must produce the right product at the right price and in the right place, and it must let the consumer know that it is available. This is known as the **marketing mix**.

The adoption of a market orientated approach will not always guarantee success. Many well-researched products have been failures. Coloroll was a business which started in the wallpaper market and expanded into home textiles and soft furnishings. Its attempt to enter the DIY burglar alarm market, however, was a failure. The company's reputation and design skills had little value in that section of the DIY market compared with other companies, whose reputations were based on home security or electronics. Whether a business places a greater emphasis on the product or on the market will depend on a number of factors.

The nature of the product Where a firm operates in an industry at the edge of new innovation, such as bio-technology, pharmaceuticals or electronics, it must innovate to survive. Although a firm may try to anticipate consumer demand, research is often 'pure' research, i.e. the researcher does not have a specific end product in mind.

Policy decisions A business will have certain objectives. Where these are set in terms of technical quality or safety, the emphasis is likely to be on production. Where objectives are in terms of market share or turnover, the emphasis is likely to be on marketing.

The views of those in control An accountant or a managing director may place emphasis on factors such as cash flow and profit forecasts, a production engineer may give technical quality control and research a high priority and a marketing person may be particularly concerned with market research and consumer relations.

Question 2.

Beverly Morgan started her home-based business, Kitz 4-U Inc. in Hamilton, Ontario, by selling first aid kits to fundraising organisations. She has also developed three other affordable 'Everything You Need In A Pinch' kits - the Bowling Kit, the Golf Kit, and the Travel Kit. The kits are also unique gifts and promotional items. Companies buy the kits to give away as a 'Thank You' to clients or as appreciation gifts to staff.

The challenges Beverly faced starting Kitz 4-U Inc. were those that every new business faces, including product development and defining the market. To produce the kits, she had to find the answers to questions such as, 'What will I put in each kit? What will the packaging look like? Where will I purchase the products I need? Who will do the graphic design? Who will make the packaging?'

To determine which products her potential customers would like to see in the kits, she carried out several market surveys, which she describes as 'very time consuming, but very important.' Once the product list was set, she had to find suppliers, which also took some searching. 'Some wouldn't sell to me, while others took a chance.'

Beverly prepared and rejected several designs before deciding on the final product. The graphic design for the packaging took the longest. Beverly almost went to print before she found the information she needed on packaging laws, which would have been an expensive lesson. Just in time, she discovered that everything was incorrect and the entire design had to be redone.

Source: adapted from http://sbinfocanada.about.com.

(a) Explain why Kitz 4-U Inc is likely to be selling to a niche market.
(b) Examine two problems that the business may have faced operating as a niche market.
(c) Discuss whether the business might grow to become a mass marketing organisation in future.

Figure 2: Product vs market orientation

More product orientated | More market orientated

Examples
Coal mining business
Wheat farmer
Water supply business

Examples
Clothing retailer
Soap powder manufacturer
Supermarket chain

The nature and size of the market If production costs are very high, then a company is likely to be market orientated. Only by being so can a company ensure it meets consumers' needs and avoid unsold goods and possible losses.

The degree of competition A company faced with a lack of competition may devote resources to research with little concern about a loss of market share. Businesses in competitive markets are likely to spend more on marketing for fear of losing their share of the market.

The distinction between product and market orientation could better seen as a spectrum, as in Figure 2. Most business are somewhere along the spectrum. For example, supermarkets may be more market orientated and a copper mining company more product orientated.

Asset-based or asset-led marketing

Both market and product orientated approaches have their limitations. Many businesses have failed because they have offered a high quality product, but have not met the needs of their customers. Perhaps the product was too expensive or the business failed to persuade enough retailers to stock it. Equally, market orientated businesses might fail because they put great effort into certain aspects of marketing, but fail to get the right product to the customer.

Another approach is ASSET-LED or ASSET-BASED MARKETING. A business which is asset-led is responsive to the needs of the market. But equally it takes into account its own strengths and weaknesses when producing a good or providing a service. Its strengths, for example, might include its product, production techniques, goodwill and branding, experience and knowledge.

A tobacco company, for example, might come up with the idea of offering life insurance to smokers. It could offer lower premiums (prices) to its customers than other insurance companies which group smokers and non-smokers together. It also might have a large customer database of users who could be contacted to advertise the insurance. However, selling insurance is a very different business from manufacturing and selling cigarettes. There are likely to be few **synergies**, or links, between the different businesses. The tobacco company has great expertise in the production of cigarettes, but little in selling insurance. Simply because market research shows there is a potentially profitable business opportunity does not mean

to say that a business should take it up.

Mass and niche marketing

In order to undertake effective marketing a business needs to consider whom it will be aiming its products at. One way of thinking about this is in terms of niche and mass marketing.

Mass marketing MASS MARKETING occurs when a business offers almost the same products to all consumers and promotes them in almost the same way. Examples of products that are generally mass marketed include Coca-Cola and Microsoft computer software. Mass marketing has a number of features and benefits. Products are usually sold to large number of consumers. They may also be marketed in many different countries, a process known as **global marketing**. This means that a business can manufacture large quantities and the average costs can be reduced as the business gains **economies of scale**. High sales and lower average costs can lead to high profits.

However, there can be problems. It is often expensive to set up production facilities to provide mass marketed products. Such products also face competition in parts of the market from producers who might be more effective in targeting market segments. So mass marketing does not necessarily guarantee profitable products.

Niche marketing NICHE MARKETING involves a business aiming or **targeting** a product at a particular, often small, segment of a market. It is the opposite of mass marketing, which

CRITIQUE

Supporters or marketing argue that it benefits both businesses and their consumers. Businesses that market effectively make profits. Customers who buy the products of these businesses have their requirements met. But some argue that businesses don't seek to meet consumer requirements as their first objective. Instead, they are more interested in profits. They point to the way that some businesses are alleged to 'harm' their customers. Examples might be businesses that make profits by selling foods that may possibly contribute to a poor diet or to obesity.

Critics of marketing would also question the extent to which businesses respond to consumer needs as opposed to creating them. Many would argue that businesses actively work to create the need to consume more, rather than just responding to what consumers want and need. They suggest that consumer needs in general would be better met if businesses encouraged them to spend less rather than more. So while marketing may make sense for individual businesses and their relationships with individual consumers, it does not necessarily work at a wider level. One consequence of this so-called pressure on consumers is that individuals spend beyond their means. This has led to many people taking on more debt than they can manage. Another consequence is more rapid use of the world's resources and the creation of higher levels of environmental damage.

Question 3.

Mark Boyd works as an electrical engineer and plays guitar in groups at weekends. His ambition has been to build and sell his own guitars. After years of testing he has designed a new style of pick-up for a guitar which will reduce noise. Together with his friend Tony, who currently makes hand made acoustic guitars, he wants to build hand made electric guitars which incorporate these new pick-ups. They have some interesting ideas for modern designs, but the guitars will be very labour intensive to build.

After researching the market, Mark and Tony produced the perceptual map shown in Figure 3. They have included mass manufactured guitars with traditional designs by Fender, modern designs such as Parker, and hand made designs by TCM Guitars.

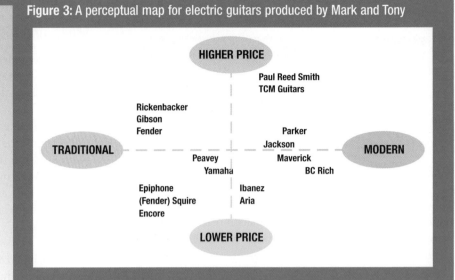

Figure 3: A perceptual map for electric guitars produced by Mark and Tony

(a) How might Mark and Tony have collected the information to produce the perceptual map of electric guitars?
(b) Explain how the information in the perceptual map might help Mark and Tony when they are making marketing decisions about their new products.

involves products being aimed at whole markets rather than at particular parts of them. Why do firms attempt niche marketing?

- Small firms are often able to sell to niche markets which have been either overlooked or ignored by other firms. In this way, they are able to avoid competition in the short run at least.
- By targeting specific market segments, firms can focus on the needs of consumers in these segments. This can allow them to gain an advantage over firms targeting a wider market.

There is, however, a number of problems with niche marketing.

- Firms which manage successfully to exploit a niche market often attract competition. Niche markets, by their very nature, are small and are often unable to sustain two or more competing firms. Large businesses joining the market may benefit from economies of scale which small firms are unable to achieve.
- Many small firms involved in niche marketing have just one product aimed at one small market. This does not allow a business to spread its risks in the way that a business producing many goods might be able to.
- Because niche markets contain small numbers of consumers, they tend to be faced by bigger and more frequent swings in consumer spending than larger markets. This may mean a rapid decline in sales following an equally rapid growth in sales.

Perceptual maps

The positioning of a brand is influenced by customer perceptions rather than by those of businesses. For example, a business may feel its brand is a high quality, up-market product. But if

customers see it as low quality and down-market, it is their views that will influence sales.

So, if a business wants to find out where its brand is positioned in the market, it might carry out market research. This will help it to understand how customers see the brand in relation to others in the market.

A business may also wish to launch a new brand. Having decided the target market, market research might show what characteristics the brand must have to succeed in that market. It could reveal the price that customers are prepared to pay. It could also suggest what sort of promotional support will be needed. For example, will a national television advertising campaign be used? Will promotion to retailers be a better strategy?

The results of market research can be displayed on PERCEPTUAL MAPS (sometimes also called MARKET MAPS or POSITIONING MAPS). Typically, the maps are drawn in two

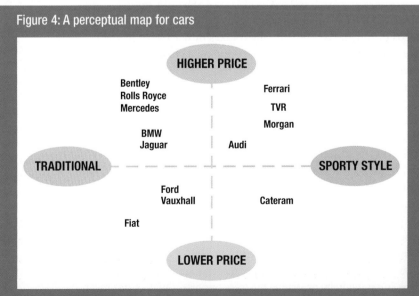

Figure 4: A perceptual map for cars

dimensions, as in Figure 4. This allows two of the attributes of the brand to be shown visually. More maps need to be drawn if more than two attributes are shown.

Figure 4 shows a perceptual map for cars. Two characteristics are displayed - the price of a new car and its 'sportiness'. So Bentley cars might be highly priced, but considered traditional. Morgans might be less costly, but considered more sporty. Cateram produces cheaper sporty 'kit cars' which must be self-assembled.

Drawing maps can help a business make marketing decisions about new or existing brands. Market mapping reveals the extent to which brands are similar to or different from those of rivals. A business can then choose to emphasise those similarities or differences through promotion. Or it can change the characteristics if current sales are poor. It could, for example, change its price or its method of promotion. Perhaps the brand itself needs redesigning. Changing the characteristics will help **reposition** the brand in the market.

KEYTERMS

Asset-led or asset-based marketing – where a business combines its knowledge of the market with an understanding of its strengths and weaknesses to decide what products to bring to market.
Business to business marketing – where a business markets its products to other businesses.
Consumer marketing – where a business is marketing to consumers.
Marketing – the management process involved in identifying, anticipating and satisfying consumer requirements profitably.
Market orientation – an approach to business which places the requirements of consumers at the centre of the decision making process.
Mass marketing – the marketing of a product to all possible consumers in the same way.
Niche marketing – the marketing of products to a particular, small segment of the market.
Perceptual maps, positioning maps or market maps – typically a two dimensional diagram which shows two of the attributes or characteristics of a brand and those of rival brands in the market.
Product orientation – an approach to business which places the main focus of attention upon the production process and the product itself.
Relationship marketing – an approach to marketing which seeks to strengthen a business's relationships with its customers.

KNOWLEDGE

1. What is meant by the term marketing?
2. What are the features of effective marketing?
3. Distinguish between marketing and advertising.
4. Why is marketing described as a process?
5. Why might product orientation still be important today?
6. What are the main advantages of a market orientated approach?
7. Why might a market orientated approach still be unsuccessful?
8. What is the difference between mass and niche marketing?

Case Study:
House on the Hill Software

House on the Hill Software is a highly successful software business based in Marple near Manchester. The company was established by Iain and Trudy Broadhead in 1993 with the aim of helping businesses to manage their help desks through the use of specialised cost effective computer software. In the fast changing world of IT they provide customers with regular updates, which can be collected from the House on the Hill website and make every effort to adapt and amend their software in response to customer enhancement requests.

In the 14 years the business has been in existence House on the Hill Software has developed a large, diverse customer base spanning over 40 countries. Iain Broadhead explained the reasons for the success of the business as follows: 'Initially our software was developed based upon our own experience of working in the IT business, with sometimes only a partial understanding of the needs of our different customers groups. Gradually, however, we have come to understand what our customers want from our products. Accordingly we've been very careful to respond to these wishes. I think this has been central to our success. We've also never stood still and we are always looking for new ways of developing our products and meeting the evolving needs of our customers'.

One of the biggest selling items produced by House-on-the-Hill is a piece of software called SupportDesk. The driving force behind the continuing development of SupportDesk has been customer feedback based upon longstanding relationships with customers who appreciate the prompt and friendly support offered by the company.

The businesses House on the Hill supply products to are wide and varied and include manufacturing businesses, further education colleges, providers of adventure skills programmes and medical research institutes. House on the Hill maintains regular and close contact with its customers and has become aware of a number of key features it is looking for in SupportDesk. These include functionality (doing what it says it can do), value for money, allowing help desks to become more efficient, enabling help desks to provide quicker responses and being at the forefront of technology.

The business has discovered that one of the main ways in which it gains new business is through word of mouth recommendations from existing customers. 'Our customers are important to us and we pride ourselves on the individual care and attention that we provide. We have long-standing relationships with our customers' said Trudy Broadhead.

Source: www.houseonthehill.com and networkcomputing.co.uk.

(a) Identify whether House on the Hill is engaged in business to business or consumer marketing. Explain your answer. (3 marks)
(b) (i) Explain whether House on the Hill is selling to a niche or mass market. (3 marks) (ii) Explain TWO benefits of this approach to the business. (6 marks)
(c) Examine the factors that may have affected the change in approach to marketing at the business. (8 marks)
(d) Discuss whether the approach to marketing at House on the Hill is effective. (10 marks)

The markting mix

In order to market its products effectively a business must consider its MARKETING MIX. The marketing mix refers to those elements of a firm's marketing strategy which are designed to meet the needs of its customers. There are four parts to the marketing mix - product, price, promotion and place. These are often known as the four 'Ps', as illustrated in Figure 1. To meet consumers' needs and to create an effective marketing mix, businesses must produce the right product, at the right price, make it available at the right place, and let consumers know about it through promotion.

Product Businesses must make sure that their products are meeting the needs of their customers. This means paying close attention to a number of features of the product.

- How consumers will use the product. A furniture manufacturer, for example, would market different products for home use than it would for office use. Products created for the office would need to be sturdy, functional, able to withstand regular use and be long lasting. Products created for the home would need to stress features such as the quality of the fabric, the design and the level of comfort.
- The appearance of the product. This is likely to involve a consideration of such things as colour. Food manufacturers, for example, go to great lengths to ensure that their products have an appealing colour. In some cases this means adding artificial colourings to alter the appearance. There are many other factors to be taken into account during the product's design. These include shape, taste and size. Deodorant manufacturers and toilet cleaning fluid producers among others might also consider aroma.
- Financial factors. There is little point in a firm producing a product which meets the needs of consumers if it cannot be produced at the right cost. All things being equal, a good produced at high cost is likely to be sold for a high price. Unless consumers are convinced that a product is value for money, they are unlikely to purchase it. They might take into consideration factors such as the quality of the product or after-sales service.
- The product's life cycle. After a period of time the sales of all products rise and then later start to fall. A business must decide whether to allow the product to decline and cease its production or to try to revive it in some way.
- A product's UNIQUE SELLING POINT or PROPOSITION. This is the aspect or feature of the product that may differentiate it from its rivals. It may help a business to gain a competitive advantage over competitors.
- Market position. This is the view that consumers have of a product compared to that of its competitors. For example, a product might be seen as 'up-market' or alternatively 'low cost' by buyers.

Price The pricing policy that a business chooses is often a reflection of the market at which it is aiming. Prices will not always be set at the level which will maximise sales or short-run profits. For example, a business may charge a high price because it is aiming to sell to consumers who regard the product as exclusive rather than because production costs are high. However, factors such as production costs can also influence pricing.

Promotion There is a number of promotional methods a business can use including above the line promotions, such as TV advertising, and below the line promotions such as personal selling. A business will choose a promotion method it feels is likely to be most effective in the market in which it operates. For example, methods such as '10 per cent off your next purchase' are used with 'fast-moving consumer goods', such as canned food and packets of biscuits. National television advertising will only be used for products with a high sales turnover and a wide appeal.

Place This refers to the means by which the product will be distributed to the consumer. The product must get to the right place, at the right time. This means making decisions about the way in which the product will be physically distributed, i.e. by air, sea, rail or road. It also means taking into account how the product is sold. This may be by direct mail from the manufacturer or through retail outlets such as supermarkets.

When considering the marketing mix of services, the 4Ps are sometimes argued to be 7Ps. The importance of the following is also stressed.

- The people involved in providing the service.

Figure 1: Elements of the marketing mix

MARKETING MIX

PRODUCT	PRICE	PLACE	PROMOTION
Appearance Function Cost	Cost based Competitor based Consumer based	Retailers Wholesalers Distribution	Advertising Sales promotion Personal selling

- The process, i.e. the mechanisms, activities and procedures involved in delivering the services, such as delivery time of a meal.
- Physical evidence, such as the appearance of the environment in which the service is provided.

Choice of marketing mix

Each business must decide upon its own marketing mix. It is important that the right balance between price, product, promotion and place is achieved if this is to be as effective as possible. It could be argued that as businesses become more market orientated all elements are important. However, at times businesses may stress one or more elements of the mix. What is important for a business is that its marketing mix is integrated. This means that the different parts of the marketing mix must fit together well .

Take, for example, a business launching a new range of hand-made, luxury organic cheeses priced at over 50 per cent higher than rival cheeses, promoted in specialist food magazines, packaged by hand in high quality materials and with a taste, texture and smell positively commented upon by food experts. It would not make sense to distribute such cheeses through discount supermarkets, such as Aldi and Netto, or through discount cheese stalls at local street markets. Such a strategy would suggest a marked lack of integration between the product, price and promotion on the one hand and place on the other. Instead, if it is to be effective, each element of the marketing mix should support the other. In the example above it may mean distributing the cheeses through high quality specialist cheese shops and delicatessens. The marketing mix a business chooses will depend upon certain factors.

Finance available Some new products are launched onto the market with the backing of large businesses and with huge financial back-up. There is a huge range of choice as to the components of the marketing mix to be used to support these products. Other businesses with more restricted finances have far fewer options available to them.

Technological developments Technological developments have enabled businesses to adapt and develop their marketing mixes in ways that wouldn't previously have been possible. For example, the use of the Internet and mobile phone texts are relatively recent additions to the promotional techniques available to businesses. Information technology developments have allowed businesses to develop much more sophisticated pricing strategies, with prices rising and falling according to demand. This has been a particular feature of airline and rail travel businesses. In addition, the Internet has revolutionised the place many products are sold. Many consumer goods are now more likely to be purchased on the Internet than they are in shops.

The findings from market research As well as informing

Question 1.

Biome Lifestyle is an online shopping site (www.biomelifestyle.com) that offers eco-friendly and ethically-sourced products for the home. The emphasis of the business is upon products that are carefully chosen for how they look and for being made from recycled, sustainable, organic or fairly-traded materials. The business has grown rapidly since its launch in December 2005, but its founder Alexandra Bramham says it has not been easy. She spent the year before the official launch developing the idea and then had to wait for the public to cotton on. 'When we first started I was a bit naïve and thought people would flock to it. I quickly found that you have to develop ways of reaching the public,' she says.

One of those ways is a recently launched wedding list service for the eco-conscious couple. Another is online advertising. Although there are frustrations, Bramham insists she is enjoying trying to get the business off the ground. For the moment, she is keeping control of costs by outsourcing elements such as design and web development, but she has big plans. 'I want to be a one-stop shop for ethical products,' she says. The business' products are not always at low prices and include handmade recycled teddy bears for £32. There are also Eco Shopper Bags for £6 and recycled wrapping paper at £1.50 per sheet.

Source: adapted from the *Independent*, 5.7.2007 and www.biomelifestyle.com.

(a) Identify elements of the marketing mix from the article.
(b) Explain how these elements might help Biome Lifestyle to gain a competitive advantage over its rivals.

consumers about the nature of a product itself, market research can also help a business to decide on the make up of its marketing mix. Indeed, it is likely that an effective marketing mix will have been informed by market research. For example, market research may allow a business to find out about how consumers will respond to different prices and where a product should be made available.

The type of product it is selling For example, a business marketing highly technical products is likely to emphasise its products' qualities rather than giving a free good as a promotion. However, a business marketing a product very similar to that of its competitors may wish to emphasise a lower price or use some method of promotion.

The market it is selling to Businesses selling consumer goods aimed at the mass market are likely to emphasise the promotional and pricing aspects of their marketing mix. Firms selling machinery or industrial goods are likely to stress the product itself.

The degree of competition A business operating in a competitive market, with many close rivals, is likely to stress the importance of price in its marketing mix. In less competitive markets price might not be seen as being so important.

Question 2.

In 2003 Jenny Bodey set up the smallest of small businesses in a single shop. It was a wedding shop in Bootle, Liverpool, called The Bridal Lounge. By Christmas 2003 and January 2004 she had experienced record days of sales. Perhaps this was due to her choice of business. The profit margins on products in this market are very high. Dresses that are bought for £119 can be sold for £449 and still remain competitive. In the first year sales were predicted to be £56,000 but turned out to be nearer £80,000. She could now easily look at opening a second shop within a couple of years, although she needed to be careful because the area where her current shop is sited had very low overheads.

Jenny also has some advice for others looking to start up. She says budding entrepreneurs should not be too keen to offer discounts and promotions. 'I was giving people £100 of accessories with certain deals, but I've halved that. People don't expect a deal to be so generous. She also says 'I did quite a lot of advertising from regional based wedding magazines to wedding brochures and the local press. If I had a stall at a wedding fair I would take an advert in the brochure as everyone who visited my stall would take the brochure away with them.'

Source: adapted from *en*, February, 2004.

(a) Suggest reasons why the marketing mix of this business has been successful.

The marketing mix of competitors Businesses cannot afford to ignore the mix chosen by competitors. For example, confectionery manufacturers lay particular emphasis upon the availability of their products in a wide range of retail outlets. These include petrol stations, newsagents, off-licences and DIY stores. The emphasis here is on place. Any business wishing to compete in this market would, therefore, be unable to overlook the importance of place in its marketing mix.

The position of a business within an industry Businesses that are leaders within their industries tend to have a greater degree of freedom over the particular marketing mix which they choose. Such businesses include Nike and Coca-Cola. Other businesses are in less strong positions, but may operate in industries with strong market leaders. Where this occurs the relatively weaker businesses often choose to 'mimic' the marketing mix of the dominant business.

The marketing mix and small businesses

For many small businesses, particularly sole proprietors, sophisticated marketing strategies are beyond their means. As indicated above, financial factors restrict their choices in terms of creating an effective marketing mix. They often have so much work keeping their businesses ticking over on a day-to-day basis, they do not get the chance to think strategically about their marketing.

Nevertheless, it is vital that even small businesses consider all aspects of their marketing mix. For example, a cake maker employing two staff would still need to think carefully about:

- the type of cakes, the **product**, that consumers would buy in the local area and how these migth be different from those of competitors;
- a **price** that would encourage local business to buy from a local business rather than a national distributor, but still allow the business to make a profit
- the type of **promotion** that would be most effective. Certain elements of the marketing mix may be more important for small business owners. For example, a survey by Barclays Bank found that 60 per cent of small businesses depend upon word of mouth to promote themselves;
- how to distribute to local shops and restaurants (**place**), for example, directly.

KEYTERMS

Marketing mix – the elements of a business's marketing that are designed to meet the needs of its customers. The four elements are often called the 4 'Ps' – price, product, promotion and place.

Unique selling point or proposition – the aspect or feature of the product that differentiates it from its rivals.

KNOWLEDGE

1. Identify the four main elements of an effective marketing mix.
2. What is a unique selling point?
3. What features of a business's product are important in the marketing mix?
4. Explain the difference between price and place in the marketing mix.
5. State five factors that influence a business's choice of marketing mix.
6. 'The size of a business is likely to affect its marketing mix.' Explain this statement.

Case Study: *A woman's own story*

W*oman's Own* has relaunched at the age of 75. The average age of its readers is 48. It is one of dozens of women's weeklies fighting for the over-35s in the UK national market. How has it survived? Forty seven per cent of the total magazine market in the UK is taken up with women's weeklies. They entertain readers with friendliness and real-life dramas. *Woman's Own* is a major brand, but not one that, up to now, has captured the 'excitement pushing-up circulation figures' elsewhere. All that, according to the title's publishers, IPC Connect, is about to change. The magazine, which was launched in 1932 with a cover showing three wraps of wool, relaunched in April, 2007 with a £2 million marketing budget that was to include TV and billboard advertising.

The new *Woman's Own* is the result of eight months of research into the sort of woman who buys the title and what she wants out of it. Its editor, Karen Livermore, and her team found a 'gap' between how the readers, typically women aged 35-plus, saw themselves (confident, outgoing, loves to gossip and shop) and how they saw other *Woman's Own* readers (settled, middle aged, mumsy, loves cooking and is a loyal friend and neighbour). This is the attitude gap Ms Livermore intends to tackle. But she has a battle on her hands, as these old-fashioned perceptions of the title are almost certainly shared by the wider marketplace. In fact, though more restrained than many rivals, *Woman's Own* has not been 'mumsy' and 'middle aged' for years. If it had, sales would have dropped even further than they have. Circulation has fallen in the past 10 years, from 808,311 in 1996 to 356,811 in December 2006. Despite this, it is still the 21st biggest-selling magazine on the UK news-stand.

In the late Eighties, two German companies, Bauer and Gruner and Jahr, launched their own titles into the UK market. *Best* and *Bella*, brought shorter, snappier stories and a new, 'value-for-money' feel. In 1990 Bauer launched *Take a Break*, and suddenly 'real-life stories were the undisputed currency of women's weeklies. *Woman's Own* responded by relaunching with its own strong true-life stories. Further competition came with the launch in 2002 of Emap's *Closer*, with its celebrity gossip and paparazzi pictures. When *Grazia* came along a few years later, calling itself a 'weekly glossy', yet another genre was born. For traditional titles to survive, reinvention has been the name of the game for the past 20 years. So what is so different about the relaunched *Woman's Own*?

'*Woman's Own* had lost connections with its readers. Their median age is 48 and that hasn't changed — what has changed is that women in their 40s are very different now. Yes, lots of our readers are housewives and they have homes to run, but they don't want to be reminded of it. Weekly readers can be an unforgiving lot. They are no one's fools — they are savvy and clued up. They're sick of tired old magazine speak — if they're on a diet, they don't want to be told to get off the bus one stop early for the exercise. Our challenge has been to launch the magazine as if it's launching for the first time in 2007. 'We have completely pulled it apart. We'd develop a section, try it out at two or three customer focus groups and then use the information to

redesign it and test a different version the following night,' says Ms Livermore.

Last week's issue definitely looked different, with bolder colours and cleaner, fresher lines. The cover is a glamorous shot of Sharon Osbourne. The content is not so different, but somehow the tone of the magazine is livelier, brighter and cheekier. The cover price has risen from 78p to 85p, the paper stock has been upgraded and there is a new, seven page section of news, views and celebrity gossip. Where magazines used to compete for reader loyalty, these days research shows that women are buying across the market, picking up several titles each week, a practice termed 'repertoire buying' by the marketing teams.

So is there room for the all-new *Woman's Own* in today's crowded market? The biggest hurdle is not so much producing a great magazine. It's getting across to the reader that *Woman's Own* is no longer about knitting a nice sweater and finding a good recipe for dinner.

Source: adapted from the *Independent* 22.4.2007.

(a) What is meant by the term marketing mix? (3 marks)
(b) How would you describe *Woman's Own's* unique selling point? (4 marks)
(c) Identify elements of *Woman's Own's* marketing mix using examples from the article. (6 marks)
(d) Using evidence from the article, explain the factors that may have influenced *Woman's Own's* marketing mix. (10 marks)
(e) Discuss whether IPC connect should place so much emphasis in its marketing mix upon the nature of *Woman's Own* as a product. (10 marks)

The product life cycle

Product is one part of the marketing mix. For marketing to be effective a business must be aware of its PRODUCT LIFE CYCLE. The product life cycle shows the different stages that a product passes through over time and the sales that can be expected at each stage. By considering product life cycles businesses can plan for the future. Most products pass through six stages – development, introduction, growth, maturity, saturation and decline. These are illustrated in Figure 1.

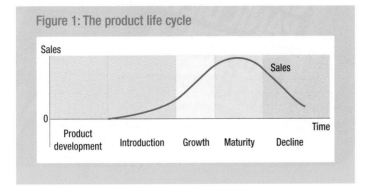

Figure 1: The product life cycle

Development During the development stage the product is being **researched** and **designed**. Suitable ideas must be investigated, developed and tested. If an idea is considered worth pursuing then a prototype or model of the product might be produced. A decision will then be made about whether or not to launch the product. A large number of new products never progress beyond this stage and will **fail**. This is because businesses are often reluctant to take risks associated with new products. During the development stage it is likely that the business will spend to develop the product and **costs** will be high. As there will be no sales at this stage, the business will initially be spending but receiving no revenue

Introduction At the start of this stage the product will be **launched**. As the product is new to the market. sales initially are often slow. Costs are incurred when the product is launched. It may be necessary to build a new production line or plant, and the firm will have to meet promotion and distribution costs. A business is also likely to spend on **promotion** to make consumers aware of the new product. Therefore, it is likely that the product will still not be profitable. **Prices** may be set high to cover promotion costs. But they may also be set low in order to break into the market. Few outlets may stock products at this stage. The length of this stage will vary according to the product. With brand new technical products, e.g. computers, the introduction stage can be quite long. It takes time for consumers to become confident that such products 'work'. At first the price of such products may be quite high. On the other hand, a

product can be an instant hit resulting in very rapid sales growth. Fashion products and some **fast moving consumer goods** may enjoy this type of start to their life.

Growth Once the product is established and consumers are aware of it, sales begin to grow rapidly, new customers buy the product and there are repeat purchases. Costs may fall as production increases. The product then becomes **profitable**. If it is a new product and there is a rapid growth in sales, **competitors** may launch their own versions. This can lead to a slowdown of the rise in sales. Businesses may need to consider their **prices and promotion**. For example, a high price charged initially may need to be lowered, or promotion may need to increase to encourage brand loyalty.

Maturity and saturation At some stage the growth in sales will level off. The product has become established with a stable market share at this point. Sales will have peaked and competitors will have entered the market to take advantage of profits. As more firms enter the market, it will become saturated. Some businesses will be forced out of the market, as there are too many firms competing for consumers. During the maturity and saturation stages of the product life cycle many businesses use extension strategies to extend the life of their products. These are discussed below.

Decline For the majority of products, sales will eventually decline. This is usually due to changing consumer tastes, new technology or the introduction of new products. The product will lose its appeal to customers. At some stage it will be withdrawn or sold to another business. It may still be possible to make a profit if a high price can be charged and little is spent on promotion or other costs.

Different product life cycles

Many products have a limited life span. Their product life cycles will look similar to that shown in Figure 1. For some products there is a very short period between introduction and decline. They are sometimes called **fads**. The slope of the product life cycle in the introduction and growth period will be very steep and the decline very sharp. Examples of such products include Micropets in 2003, Heelies in 2006 and Pokemon cards in 2005. Once consumers lose interest in a product and sales fall, a business may withdraw it from the market. It may be replaced with another new product. Sometimes poor selling products are withdrawn in case they damage the image of the company. However, businesses must take care not to withdraw a product too early. Over time, certain products have become popular again. For example, skateboards, which were popular in the 1980s regained popularity in the mid-1990s and the early 2000s.

Question 1.

Figure 2

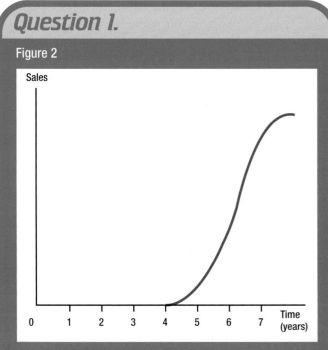

Figure 3

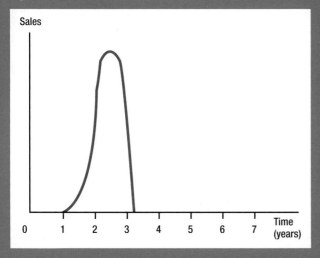

(a) Examine Figures 2 and 3. For each of these, name a product which you think might have a similar product life cycle.

(b) Why do some products have a very long life cycle (greater than 50 years)?

(c) Sketch the current product life cycle of three of the following products:
   (i) A compact disc or downloadable song by a leading performance artist/group (you will need to specify the name of the song and the performance artist);
   (ii) Walkers cheese and onion crisps;
   (iii) Coca-Cola;
   (iv) Hovis bread;
   (v) Rice Krispie bars;
   (vi) Golden Compass DVD;
   (vii) the Facebook website;
   (viii) a football strip of a Premier League team (you will need to specify the team).

Some businesses still enjoy profits from products which were launched many years ago. The Oxo cube was launched in 1910, Kellogg's Cornflakes were launched in 1906 and Theakston's Old Peculier, a strong ale, was launched in the eighteenth century. These products still sell well today in a form fairly similar to their original.

Because of the high cost of investment, car producers often set product life cycles of ten years for their models. For many products, life cycles are getting shorter, especially in areas like electronics. In the computer industry, some models and software have become obsolete within a very short period as new versions appear which are more technically advanced. For example, in 1995 Microsoft launched its operating software Windows 95. It was later replaced by Windows 98, Windows 2000 and Windows XP.

Extension strategies

It is clear from the product life cycle that the sales of products decline, although at different rates. Firms can attempt to extend the life of a product by using EXTENSION STRATEGIES. They may decide to use one or more of the following techniques.

- Finding new markets for existing products. Over the last 20 years there has been a boom in the sales of sports clothing. This has been largely due to the use of sports clothing as fashion wear.
- Developing a wider product range. Lucozade was originally sold as a product to those recovering from an illness. By extending the product range to include a 'Sports' version, a huge increase in sales has been achieved. Lego constantly develops new versions of a product that started out as a plastic set of building blocks.
- Gearing the product towards specific target markets. Mobile phone companies have packages geared to the needs of teenagers. Banks have accounts for young people.
- Changing the appearance, format or packaging. Coca-Cola is available in individual cans, in glass or plastic bottles, or in multipacks. Chocolate bars such as Toblerone are sold in standard sizes, in large bars or in mini sizes.
- Encouraging people to use the product more frequently. Manufacturers of what were previously known as 'breakfast cereals' have used promotional campaigns to encourage the use of their products at different times throughout the day.
- Changing the ingredients or components. Many microwaveable food products are available as 'weight watchers' or 'low fat' meals, as well as more traditional meals. Many cars are equipped with CD or MP3 players and air conditioning as standard.
- Updating designs. Car manufacturers regularly update models. Makers of computer gaming systems bring out new versions after a period of time.

The effect that an extension strategy can have on the product life cycle is shown in Figure 4. As the market becomes saturated and sales begin to fall, the decline in sales is delayed by the use of

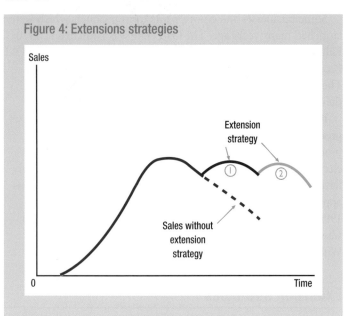

Figure 4: Extensions strategies

an extension strategy. It would be sensible for a business to try to extend the life of a mature product before sales start to decline. Firms that can predict falling sales from market forecasts may attempt to use extension strategies before the decline takes place, i.e. in the maturity stage.

The product life cycle and capacity

Capacity utilisation is the extent to which a business uses the capacity that it has to produce a particular product. It is the relationship between what a business actually produces and what it is capable of producing. A business working at full capacity that is unable to produce any more of a product will be at maximum capacity utilisation. A business that can still produce more with its existing technology and machinery is likely to be working at less than full capacity.

The product life cycle is linked to capacity utilisation.

- At launch, sales of a product are likely to be limited. So a business will have spare capacity.
- When a product is at its growth stage a business will often be expanding its production and using up spare capacity to meet the rising demand for the product.
- When a product is in its maturity stage a business may be operating at full capacity. If sales continue to grow it must decide whether to invest to expand capacity.
- In the decline stage the capacity that a business has to produce a product will often be underutilised. This is because sales and therefore production may be cut back.

So during the development, growth and growth phases a business will have to make decisions over its capacity.

Creating new capacity A business may decide to build new capacity to deal with sales of a new product. New capacity could be created as sales grow. This would delay outflows of cash until they were needed. There would be less risk that the new capacity would be greater than sales. But, if sales were higher than

expected, the business might find it difficult to invest quickly enough to prevent shortages. Alternatively, new capacity could be created before sales take place. But this carries the risk that the investment would be wasted if sales did not grow in line with expectations. The cash to pay for the investment would flow out of the business earlier. Average costs would be higher too, because the cost of creating and running spare capacity at launch would have to be paid for. However, it would easier to deal with unexpectedly high sales than if investment took place when sales actually happened.

Utilising existing capacity There is less risk if a business uses existing capacity. If a business is operating at less than full capacity, it could use the spare capacity to launch a new product. This would help reduce cash outflow associated with new products. Or a business may be working at full capacity, but have products which are at the end of their life cycle. These could be taken out of production and replaced by the new lines.

A problem with this approach is that the average costs of

Question 2.

Rachel's is a manufacturer of organic dairy products. The business is very much a farm based enterprise. In 1952, Brynllys, a farm in Wales, began the process which made it into the first organic farm in the UK. Initially, its dairy production was confined to selling organic milk. But in 1982 it branched out into making and selling cream and butter, initially sold locally. 1984 saw the first commercial production of yoghurt. By 1987, Marigold, a leading London health food supplier, was an enthusiastic buyer and, in 1989, Rachel's yoghurts were on sale in Harrods.

In 1990, the owners of the business, the husband-and-wife team of Gareth and Rachel Rowlands, decided to expand. They borrowed the money, using their farm as collateral, to build a state-of-the-art dairy. It was capable of processing not just the 330,000 litres of organic milk a year from their farm, but 3 million litres – the entire organic output of Wales. Their decision to take this risk was helped by their first large contract to supply a supermarket chain, Sainsbury.

In 1999, they sold the business to Horizon Organic, the biggest wholly organic dairy supplier in the US. Horizon has introduced three new yoghurt flavours: low fat vanilla, whole-milk with maple syrup and Greek-style with honey. This month sees the debut of Rachel's organic fat-free yoghurt and a Welsh butter with bilingual packaging. However, Horizon promised not to alter Rachel's yoghurts in content or concept.

Source: adapted from *The Financial Times*, 24.11.2001.

(a) Discuss whether the introduction of (i) organic yoghurt in 1984 and (ii) organic fat-free yoghurt in 2001 were examples of a new product being brought to the market or an extension strategy for an existing product.

(b) Discuss the cash flow requirements of Rachel's yoghurts during and after the decision in 1990 to build a new state-of-the-art dairy.

production, excluding the cost of any investment, may be higher than if new capacity had been built. For example, it may cost 60p to produce an item on old machinery but only 40p if the latest equipment is used. The decision about whether to buy new equipment will depend upon the relationship between the cost of the new equipment and the saving on running costs. If a business only saves £10,000 a year on running costs by buying £100,000 of new equipment, then it probably won't buy. If it saves £90,000 on running costs for an investment of £100,000, it will probably purchase the new equipment.

As explained above, average costs of production may be higher at launch and during the growth phase if existing capacity to cope with high levels of sales is set aside for use at launch. But again, if sales exceed expectations, the business is more likely to cope if there is spare capacity.

The product life cycle and cash flow

Figure 5 shows the cash flow of a business over a product life cycle.

- Before product launch a business will spend to develop the product and yet no money is coming into the business from sales. So cash flow is likely to be negative.
- At launch, at point A, a product begins to sell. Cash flowing out of a business is still likely to be greater than cash flowing in, so cash flow will be negative. Sales have yet to take off and a business might be spending on promoting the product.
- In the growth period, eventually revenue from the product will be greater than spending (point B) and so cash flow becomes positive. This is because sales will be increasing and average costs may be falling as output increases.
- In the maturity stage cash flow will be at its highest. The product will be earning its greatest revenue.
- In the decline stage, sales will fall and so cash flow will decline.

Uses and problems of the product life cycle

Why might a business be interested in analysing the product life cycle of its existing products or anticipating the life cycle of new products?

- It will illustrate the broad trends in revenue that a product might earn for the business.
- It will identify points at which businesses may need to consider launching new products, as older ones are in decline.
- It will identify points at which extension strategies may need to be introduced.
- It may help a business to identify when and where spending is required, e.g. on research and development at the start, or on marketing at the introduction and when extension strategies are required.
- It may help to identify points at which a business should no longer sell a product.
- It will help a business to manage its product portfolio – its mix of products. This is discussed in the next section.
- It will give an indication of the profitability of a product at

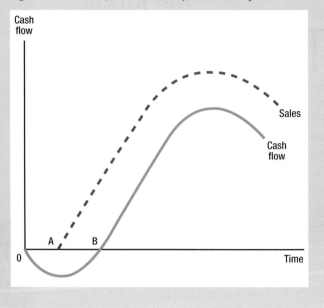

Figure 5: Cash flow, sales and the product life cycle

each stage in its cycle.
- It will allow a business to plan different styles of marketing that a product might need over its life cycle.

There may be problems, however, when using this model. It can be used to show changes over the life of a product. But it may not be effective in **predicting** the future sales of a product and how sales will change in future. In practice, every product is likely to have a slightly different product life cycle. Furthermore, it is important that the model does not **determine** decisions. For example, a product that is in the decline stage does not automatically have to be withdrawn. Sales may be falling due to a lack of promotion or poor distribution. The decline in sales may be more to do with management decisions than where the product is in its life cycle.

KEYTERMS

Extension strategies – methods used to extend the life of a product.
Product life cycle – shows the different stages in the life of a product and the sales that can be expected at each stage.

KNOWLEDGE

1. Briefly describe the various stages in the product life cycle.
2. Why might a product have a 'steep' life cycle?
3. Name three uses of the product life cycle.
4. How can a firm extend the life of its products?
5. State three ways in which the product life cycle is linked to capacity utilisation.
6. Name three links between the product life cycle and cash flow.

Case Study: *The KitKat*

The KitKat was launched as Rowntree's Chocolate Crisp in 1935 and renamed KitKat in 1937. The following year it was the company's most popular product. It first became a national favourite in the war years of the 1940s, when the government endorsed it as a healthy, cheap food. Ever since it has been the most popular chocolate bar in the UK. It was one of the main reasons behind the takeover of Rowntree by Nestlé in 1989. It maintained its supremacy even when faced with competition from Nestlé's own Smarties and Black Magic. According to the KitKat website, 47 bars are eaten every second in the UK and a year's production would stretch around the London Underground more than 350 times.

However, in 2003 sales fell by 5 per cent from nearly £123 million in 2002 to £116 million by the end of 2003. 'Saying the business is in crisis is extreme', argued a consumer brands analyst at the time, 'but maintaining its position in the UK confectionery market is going to be a challenge. It's a cut-throat market.' There was concern that saturation point had been reached.

Nestlé fought back by introducing a number of variants to the KitKat market as from 2004. These included an orange and mint flavour, a lemon and yoghurt flavour and a Halloween variant, Blood Orange. In addition, in 2005 a caramac KitKat was launched and the KitKat Dark has now established itself as a permanent addition to the KitKat range. Both the two and four finger versions of the KitKat have remained popular and they have been joined by the KitKat Chunky as mainstays of the KitKat product range.

There are many different variants upon the KitKat theme in those countries where the product remains popular. In Malaysia there is a hot weather version that is less likely to melt in the heat and in Japan a range of flavours, including green tea, passion fruit and lemon cheesecake, have been introduced. Japanese school children regard the KitKat as a lucky charm for exams and tests and take them into school on test days.

In England, health scares regarding childhood obesity have led to a school ban on vending machines selling crisps, chocolate and fizzy drinks as part of what has been termed the 'great KitKat clampdown'. These and other health moves have seen food manufacturers such as Nestle criticized for encouraging youngsters to eat what are seen as unhealthy foods. Health campaigners have also singled out the KitKat

chunky for particular criticism.

Source: adapted from *The Guardian* 10.9.2007, *The Independent*, 15.2.2004; www.nestle.co.uk and www.news.bbc.co.uk

(a) Using information from the article, draw and label the product life cycle for KitKat. (3 marks)
(b) Identify significant periods in the product life cycle of KitKat using examples from the article. (6 marks)
(c) Using information from the article, explain the product extension strategies used by Nestle in relation to the KitKat. (8 marks)
(d) Discuss how changes made in the future might affect the product life cycle of KitKat. (8 marks)

The nature of products

A PRODUCT is anything that can be exchanged and is able to satisfy customers' needs. It might be a tangible physical GOOD, such as a car or a packet of peas. Or it might be an intangible, non-physical SERVICE, such as a foreign holiday, a medical examination or defence.

A distinction can be made between PRODUCER (or INDUSTRIAL) PRODUCTS and CONSUMER PRODUCTS. Producer products are used to make other goods and services or in the operation of A business. For example, a coffee machine and a building are two producer products used by Starbucks to make a cup of coffee served to consumers. Producer products are sold by one business to another through business to business marketing. The cup of coffee is a consumer product because it is bought by individuals or households for personal use. A car bought from a dealer by an individual would be a consumer product bought in a consumer market. In contrast, a car bought by a business for use as a company car would be a producer product.

Consumers buy products because of the benefits given by these attributes. TANGIBLE BENEFITS are benefits which can be measured. For example, the benefit of a train journey might be that it gets you from London to Glasgow in four hours. The benefit of a washing machine might be that it will wash for five years without breaking down. INTANGIBLE BENEFITS are benefits which, though present, cannot be measured. Some products are bought because of the image they convey. For example, wearing a t-shirt in the colours of a national football team might have been considered fashionable during the World Cup of 2006. Other intangible benefits might be pleasure or peace of mind. Cadbury's advertisements stress the pleasure gained from eating a Cadbury's Flake. Insurance to cover funeral expenses is often sold to give peace of mind to the person who is going to die.

What are the characteristics of a 'good' product?
- It should be functional and fulfil the needs of customers. For example, food should taste good. A train service should be fast, frequent and reliable. A television set should give good quality pictures. A lawn mower should cut grass well.
- It should be aesthetically pleasing. Good design is not just about working properly. It is also about how a product looks to the customer. In some industries, such as clothing, cars and kitchen equipment, aesthetics and design have a great effect on how consumers spend their money.
- It should be affordable. Many people would like to take a journey into space, but at present it is too expensive for all but a few. On the other hand, a furniture company like Ikea has become extremely successful because it sells goods which are affordable to most. So the product should be capable of being produced within the purchasing budgets of the target market.
- The product must conform to legal requirements. Toys, for example, should not contain lead paint. Food sold to people should be fit to eat.
- Ideally, products should be environmentally and socially friendly. Increasingly, products are being bought by consumers on the strength of their 'ethical' credentials. For example, people want paper made from recycled paper. They might also refuse to buy trainers made in factories with poor working conditions in low income countries.

Unique selling points of products

Successful products will have a **unique selling point** or **unique selling proposition** (USP). This is a characteristic of a product that makes it different from other products. The USP is often promoted by businesses to customers as being the 'best'. For example, cars may be advertised as being the safest, giving the smoothest ride or having the most space. Identifying and promoting the USP of a product can have a number of benefits.
- For consumers, it helps them to differentiate one product from others, which can make choices easier.
- For businesses, it helps differentiate its products from others. It will aim to show consumers that it is offering something that other products are not. This can increase sales and help to build up BRAND LOYALTY.

The product portfolio

Product life cycle analysis, outlined in the previous unit, shows businesses that sales of products eventually decline. A well organised business with one or more products will attempt to phase out old products and introduce new ones. This is known as managing the PRODUCT PORTFOLIO or PRODUCT MIX. The product portfolio will be made up of PRODUCT LINES. A product line is a group of products which are similar. For example, televisions are a product line including flat screen, HD widescreen and portable televisions. With a constant launch of new products, a business can make sure a 'vacuum' is not created as products reach the end of their life.

Figure 1 shows how a business can manage its product portfolio. Say that a business over a particular time period aims to launch three products. By organising their launch at regular intervals, there is never a gap in the market. As one product is declining, another is growing and further launches are planned. At point (i), as sales of product X are growing, product Y has just been launched. This means that at point (ii), when sales of product X have started to decline, sales of product Y are growing and product Z has just been launched.

This simple example shows a 'snapshot' of three products only. In practice, a business may have many products. It would hope that existing products remain in 'maturity' for a long period. The profit from these mature products would be used to 'subsidise' the launch of new products. New products would be costly at first, and would make no profit for the business.

Examples of businesses that have successfully managed their product portfolios are sweet manufacturers. Companies such as Nestlé produce a wide range of products, including KitKat, Milky Bar and Yorkie, and constantly look to launch new products.

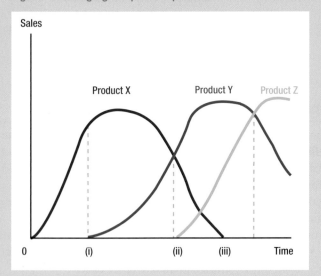

Figure 1: Managing the product portfolio

Sales

Product X   Product Y   Product Z

0   (i)   (ii)   (iii)   Time

Product portfolio analysis and the Boston Matrix

One problem for firms when planning their product portfolios is that it is very difficult in practice to tell what stage of the life cycle a product is at. Also, there is no standard lifetime for products. For example, young people's fashion clothing has life cycles which can be predicted with some certainty. Other poducts are less reliable. Who, for example, could have predicted the lengthy life cycles of products such as Heinz baked beans and the VW Beetle, or the short life cycle of products such as the Sinclair C5 – a sort of 'mini-car' introduced in the 1980s?

A useful technique for allowing firms to analyse their product portfolios is the Product Portfolio Matrix developed by the Boston Consulting Group. It is sometimes called the BOSTON MATRIX. This is shown in Figure 2. Products are categorized according to two criteria.

- **Market growth.** How fast is the market for the product growing? The market may be declining or it may be expanding. Sales of a product in a fast expanding market have a better chance of growing than a product in a stagnant or declining market.
- **Relative market share.** How strong is the product within its market? Is it a market leader that other products follow? Is it a product that is twelfth in terms of sales? To measure this the market share of a product is compared with the strongest rival product. For example, if Product X had a market share of 10 per cent and the market leader had 40

per cent then the relative market share of Product X is 0.25 (10 per cent ÷ 40 per cent). If Product Y is a market leader with 50 per cent market share and the next most important product had a market share of 25 per cent, the relative market share of product Y is 2.0 (50 per cent ÷ 25 per cent).

Using these criteria the products of a business can be placed into one of four categories on the Boston Matrix.

Stars A star is a product with a high market growth and a relatively high market share. Stars are valuable to businesses. The product will be in a strong position in its market as it has a high market share and the business can take advantage of a fast growing market. A star is already likely to be **profitable** as it has a relatively high market share. But a business will need to **invest** in the product to cope with a growing market and growing sales. This could mean investing in new production facilities or promotion to fend off competition. **Cash flow** may be nearly zero. This is because although profits will be high, bringing money in, spending will also be high, leading to outflows.

Cash cows A cash cow is a product with a relatively high market share. It is therefore well positioned in the market and likely to be **profitable**. But the market it is in will have weak growth. So there will be little chance of increasing sales and profits in future. There will be little need for **investment**. With slow growth in sales there should be little need for new premises for example. Cash cows have strong positive **cash flow**. Money coming into the business from profits will not be taken out via investment.

Problem children Problem children, also know as question marks or wildcats, are products with a relatively low market share in a fast growing market. This can be a problem for a business because it is unclear what should be done with these products. If a product is performing weakly it is unlikely to be **profitable**. But as it is in a fast growing market, there is potential to turn it into a star. **Cash flow** is likely to be zero or negative. Weak relative market share means that it will not be profitable. But **investment** will be needed to cope with expanding sales in a fast growing market.

Dogs These are products with a relatively low market share in a market with low growth. Dogs have poor prospects for future sales and **profits**. They may generate some **cash flow** because they will need little **investment** but may earn some profit. But if they make little or no profit, cash flow may be zero or even negative.

Businesses can make use of the Boston Matrix to manage their product portfolios.

Balancing product lines Businesses must ensure that their product portfolios do not contain too many items within each category. Naturally, they do not want lots of 'Dogs', but they should also avoid having too many 'Stars' and 'Problem children'. Products on the top of the Boston Matrix are in the early stages of the product life cycle and are in growing markets. But the cost of developing and promoting them will not yet have been recovered. This will drain resources. Balancing these with 'Cash cows' will mean that the revenue from the 'Cash cows' can be used to support products in a growing market. The development cost of 'Cash cows' is likely to have already been recovered and promotional costs should be low relative to sales. This does not mean though that a business would want lots of 'Cash cows' and few 'Problem children' and 'Stars'. This is because many of the 'Stars' and perhaps some 'Problem children' might become the 'Cash cows' of the future.

Taking appropriate decisions Products in different categories in the Matrix may require different approaches.
- Stars have great future potential. They are future cash cows. A business will need to **build** the brand of these products so that sales increase and competition is fought off successfully.
- Cash cows might be **milked** for cash, which can then be

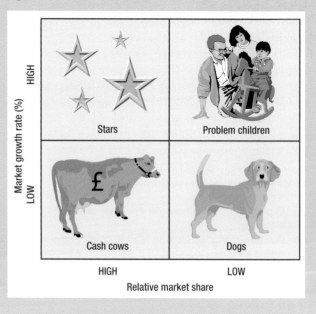

Figure 2: The Boston Matrix

Market growth rate (%) — HIGH / LOW
Stars
Problem children
Cash cows
Dogs
Relative market share — HIGH / LOW

used to develop other products. Or the business may decide to spend just enough on promotion and development to maintain sales and market share, known as **holding**.
- For problem children a business has choices. It can **build** the brand, hoping to turn it into a star, **harvest** the product by raising price and cutting promotion so that profits are increased, or **divest** itself of the product, withdrawing it or selling it because it is not making a profit.
- Dogs may be divested if they are not making a profit or in some cases harvested.

New product development

Planning the product portfolio requires the continual development and launch of new products. New products are needed to replace products coming to the end of their life cycles and to keep up with changes in the market. This is called **new product development**.

In some business sectors the need to plan ahead is very important. In the chemical industry, development work is done on products which might not reach the market for over ten years. In the motor industry many cars take over five years to develop. New products normally pass through five stages when they are being developed.

Generating ideas The first stage is when firms generate ideas. Ideas for new products come from a variety of sources.
- Identifying gaps in the market, perhaps through market research. An example of this has been the development of vegetarian microwave dishes by food producers. An important issue here for businesses is in identifying the unique selling point of a product.
- Scientific research. Pharmaceuticals businesses devote huge

Question 2.

The origins of the iPhone can be found in Steve Job's (the Apple Chief Executive) instruction to Apple engineers in 2003 to investigate touch screens. He believed that mobile phones were going to become important devices for portable information access and was determined to create a device that integrated a mobile phone, Internet access and an iPod. When it was launched in the UK in November, 2007 it was widely regarded as being far superior to anything else on the market with its multitouch technology and wide range of uses. Apple anticipate selling 10 million iPhones worldwide by 2008.

Source: adapted from adapted from *The Guardian*, 5.11.2007, www.wikipedia.org and www.apple.co.uk

(a) Explain TWO influences on the development of the iPhone.
(b) Discuss, using the Boston Matrix. whether the Iphone would be categorised as (i) a star or (ii) a problem child in future.

amounts to research and development expenditure. As a result they have developed products to tackle a range of ailments from heart disease through to cancer.
● Generating creative ideas through open discussions. Products such as the jet engine have come about as a result of this.
● Analysing other products. When developing new products many businesses will analyse products manufactured by competitors. They aim to include, adapt or improve upon the best features of these products in their own designs. Some businesses adapt their own successful products to make new products.

Analysis The second stage is the analysis of those ideas generated in the first stage. There are a number of questions a firm might ask. Most importantly, it must find out if the product is marketable – if enough consumers wish to buy it to allow the firm to make a profit. Businesses must also decide if the product fits in with the company's objectives, if it is legal and if the technology is available to produce it.

Development The third stage is the actual development of the product. This may involve technical development in the laboratory or the production of a prototype. Such work will be carried out by the research and development department. An important part of this process is the actual design of the product. Some preliminary testing may be carried out to find out whether or not the product actually meets consumers' needs.

Test marketing TEST MARKETING occurs when a new product is tested on a small, representative section of the total market. The test market area should share characteristics which are similar to those found in the market as a whole. The benefit of test marketing is the high degree of reliability of results

gained. It is carried out because of the high cost and risk of launching a product in a large, usually national, market. Test marketing can itself be costly, but not as expensive as a national launch which fails. One problem is that it allows competitors to see the new product and gives them the chance to take counter-action before a national launch.

Commercialisation and launch The final stage is the launch and commercialisation. Here any problems found during test marketing must be solved. The firm will then decide on the 'marketing package' it will use to give the product launch the greatest chance of success.

At each of the five stages, many ideas are rejected. This means that very few ideas generated in the first stage will actually end up as a product launched onto the market. In Figure 3, an example is shown where 40 ideas were put forward for a new product. In this company the majority of ideas do not get beyond the first stage. The pass rate at this stage is only 1 in 5, with 4 out of 5 ideas being rejected. After that, the number of ideas which survive from one stage to the next increases as the pass rate falls from 1 in 5 ideas to 1 in 2. At the end of the process, only 1 out of a total of 40 ideas has survived to be launched onto the market.

Influences on new product development

There is a wide range of influences on businesses developing new goods and services. These influences may encourage a business to go ahead with a new product or, alternatively, restrict the development of one or more new products.

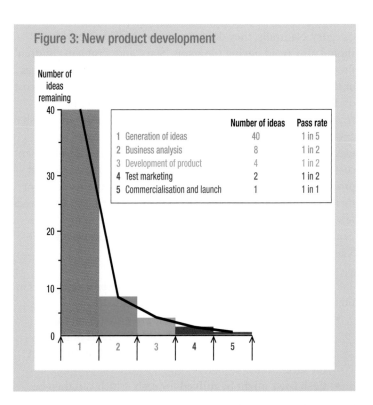

Figure 3: New product development

	Number of ideas	Pass rate
1 Generation of ideas	40	1 in 5
2 Business analysis	8	1 in 2
3 Development of product	4	1 in 2
4 Test marketing	2	1 in 2
5 Commercialisation and launch	1	1 in 1

Availability of finance and resources In highly competitive markets businesses find that their profit margins are squeezed. This means that financial and human resources are often not available to develop new products. An example of this is in the market for budget fashion clothing. Businesses in this market tend to copy products developed for designer labels. Other businesses may find that they have a number of mature products generating a healthy stream of income. Such businesses may invest this income in new product development, hoping to create the 'cash cows' of the future.

Technology The development of technology can affect the type of product or service provided. One hundred years ago computers did not exist. Today they are sold in a variety of ways to different businesses. Internet cafes and laptop computers are now standard products for a range of consumers. There are now many opportunities for new goods and services, such as the online retailing of music that are linked to these new technologies. Just ten years ago such opportunities for new products like these did not exist.

Cost Even when businesses have resources, the cost of developing new products may be prohibitive. The development of products in the electronics market can cost millions of pounds. As technological boundaries have been pushed forward, the cost of even modest new product development has risen sharply. Also, in many markets products have increasingly shorter life spans. This means that less time is available to recover development costs. Conversely, in those markets, such as the market for computer games consoles where technological developments are moving at a fast pace, there can be enormous rewards for successful new products. This creates a clear incentive for new products even when the costs are high.

Competitors' actions The behaviour of a business' competitors can strongly influence new product development. In some cases an innovatory competitor can act as a spur to other businesses in the same sector in their efforts to create new products. Some would argue, for example, that the new products produced by the Apple Corporation, such as the iPhone and iPod, have caused competitors to raise their game. Other businesses respond to innovatory competitors by copying, as far as possible within copyright and patent laws, their competitors' products.

Market constraints There is little point in a business developing a new product unless consumers are prepared to purchase it at a price which can cover development and production costs. Many so-called 'tremendous ideas' for new products have been abandoned. This is because firms believe they cannot find a profitable market for the product. In addition, consumers can be resistant to change. This is often because of the time and effort consumers need to spend in getting to know how new products 'work'. There is also evidence that consumers are resistant to new products which represent a radical departure from existing products. New versions of existing products are sometimes more popular with consumers than totally new ideas for this reason.

Entrepreneurial skills of managers and owners Some businesses are more likely to engage in new product development because of the skills and attitudes of their managers and owners. More entrepreneurial managers and owners of businesses are likely be more inclined to take risks rather than continue doing what they know best. Steve Job, for example, Chief Executive of the Apple Corporation, has been widely credited as being the driving force behind the revolutionary new products produced by Apple, including the iPod, iMac and iPhone.

Legal constraints Firms cannot develop whatever new products they wish. Legislation must be taken into account. For example, a pharmaceutical company wishing to develop a new product must be sure that it adheres to health legislation.

KNOWLEDGE

1. What is a product?
2. What is the difference between a consumer and a producer product?
3. Explain how a business can prevent a 'vacuum' in its product portfolio.
4. What is meant by a product line?
5. What is meant by the Boston Matrix?
6. How can the Boston Matrix help a business to manage its product portfolio?
7. What is meant by new product development?
8. State two ways in which a business can generate new product ideas.
9. State six factors that can influence the development of new products.

KEYTERMS

Brand loyalty – the extent to which customers of a brand repeat purchases of that brand rather than others.

Boston Matrix – a 2 x 2 matrix model which analyses a product portfolio according to the growth rate of the market and the relative market share of products within the market.

Consumer products – goods or services sold to individuals to households for personal consumption.

Goods – physical products.

Intangible benefits (of a product) – benefits that cannot be measured.

Producer or industrial products – goods or services that are sold by one business to other businesses.

Product line – a group of products which are very similar.

Product portfolio (product mix) – the particular portfolio of products which a firm is marketing.

Product – anything that can be exchanged and is able to satisfy customers' needs.

Services – non-physical products.

Tangible benefits (of a product) – benefits that can be measured.

Test marketing – testing out a product on a small section of a market prior to its full launch.

CRITIQUE

Critics of the Boston Matrix argue that the Matrix can cause businesses to focus too much upon pursuing increases in market share as opposed to, for example, attempting to consolidate market share or improve other aspects of the performance of a product. It is also suggested that the model fails to take account of the way in which products within a business can support one another. For example a business might sell a dog, but this might affect sales of other products it supports which could be stars or cash cows. Cash flow and profit can also be different for individual products. A dog may have strong cash flow and be profitable despite falling sales. A star might have negative cash flow if there is fierce competition.

Case Study: *Stubble trouble*

The Fusion Power Stealth is a razor with five pivoting blades and one at the back, a lubrication strip, a rubber guard to stretch the skin, a battery to make it vibrate and a microchip to control the level of vibration. It will also tell you when the battery's flat. It has a striking black and orange box to house the rubberised handle. Sports stars sell it to you, including David Beckham and Roger Federer. And it has a killer name.

It is, claims Gillette, the closest shave a man can get. They did, of course, say that about the last thing they came up with before Fusion Power Stealth - the one just called Fusion Power. Before that, it was just primitive old Fusion. And they said the same for the Mach3 Power, which came after Mach3 Turbo, which followed Mach3, and overtook Sensor Excel, Sensor, Atra Plus and TracII Plus. The latter appeared in 1971 and seems positively primeval; it was smooth, it was safe, it meant you didn't leave the sink covered in blood and your face speckled with tissue paper. Nothing could better it, for a while at least.

The Fusion Power Stealth, which began appearing at chemists and supermarkets in September 2007, will probably only be 'the best' shaving system for a couple of years. After that, Gillette have other plans, which they are not keen to divulge as 'other people may be reading your story,' says Kevin Powell, Gillette's laboratory director, by which he means Wilkinson Sword. Gillette has 74 per cent of the total razor market in the UK, followed by Wilkinson Sword.

The razors aren't just thrown together by a marketing department in an attempt to sell us something we didn't know we needed. They are the result of years of called cutting-edge science and the endeavours of biologists, dermatologists, physicists, polymer scientists, biometricists and neurologists. There is a team concerned solely with how to make a razor vibrate just the right amount, and other people employed to optimise handle grip in a slippery bathroom environment. Only when these people have done their work (Fusion Power Stealth has taken four years to appear from the initial prototype), do the people who design the packaging and advertising slogans go to work.

Before the concept of the Fusion system went to Gillette's global HQ in Boston, it was tested on about 9,000 men throughout the world. When Fusion was tested against its predecessor Mach3, 30 per cent of men in the trials said they preferred their existing system. But the majority preferred it in 69 respects, including 'giving the closest shave without irritation'; 'blades shaving as close on the first stroke as the last'; 'the colour of the razor'; 'the texture of the handle'; and 'ease of rinsing'.

Source: adapted from *The Guardian*, 23.11.2007.

(a) Explain the unique selling points of the Fusion Power Stealth. (3 marks)

(b) Using information from the article, explain TWO influences on the development of the Fusion Power Stealth. (6 marks)

(c) Examine, using the Boston Matrix, the position in the market of the Fusion Power Stealth a couple of years after its launch and the decision about the product that Gillette may face. (8 marks)

(d) Discuss whether Gillette should have launched the Fusion Power Stealth when it had 74 per cent of the total razor market in the UK. (10 marks)

44 | Promotion

What is promotion?

PROMOTION is the attempt to draw attention to a product or business in order to gain new customers or to retain existing ones. There are many different forms of promotion. One way of distinguishing between these different forms is in terms of whether or not a business is promoting its products via independent media such as newspapers and TV. ABOVE-THE-LINE promotion is through independent media, such as television or newspapers. These allow a business to reach a wide audience easily. Most advertising is carried out 'above the line'. Some advertising, however, is carried out by methods over which a firm has direct control, such as direct mailing and branding. Such methods are known as BELOW-THE-LINE promotions.

The objectives of promotion

A business must be clear about exactly what it is trying to achieve through its promotion. The main aim of any promotion is to obtain and retain customers. However, there is a number of other objectives, some or all of which any successful campaign must fulfil.

- To make consumers aware or increase awareness of a product.
- To reach a target audience which might be geographically dispersed.
- To remind consumers about the product. This can encourage existing consumers to repurchase the product and may attract new consumers.
- To show a product is better than that of a competitor. This may encourage consumers to switch purchases from another product.
- To develop or improve the image of a business rather than a product. Much corporate advertising is carried out with this in mind, and is dealt with later in this unit.
- To reassure consumers after the product has been purchased. This builds up confidence in the product and may encourage more to be bought at a later date.
- To support an existing product. Such promotions may be used to remind consumers that a reliable and well thought of product is still available.

Businesses sometimes consider their promotion using **models**.

- AIDA is a method used to consider advertising. It suggests that effective advertising will raise Awareness (A) and encourage Interest (I), Desire (D) and Action (A), so that consumers buy the products.
- The DAGMAR (Defining Advertising Goals for Measured Advertising Results) model is also used to measure the effect of advertising. A business can measure how far the

group that is targeted has progressed along the scale:

Unawareness...Awareness...Comprehension...
Conviction...Action

- A similar model by Lavidge and Steiner suggests six stages – awareness, knowledge, liking, preference, conviction and purchase.

Above-the-line promotion

Above-the-line promotion is ADVERTISING. Advertising is often placed into different categories.

- INFORMATIVE ADVERTISING is designed to increase consumer awareness of a product. Examples include the classified advertisements in local newspapers, new share offers, grants available to small firms and entries in the *Yellow Pages*. New products may be launched with informative advertising campaigns to make consumers aware of their presence. It is argued that this type of advertising helps consumers to make a rational choice as to what to buy.
- PERSUASIVE ADVERTISING tries to convince consumers to purchase a product, often by stressing that it is more desirable than others. It is argued that this type of advertising distorts consumer buying, pushing them to buy products which they would otherwise not have bought. In reality, a great deal of advertising is persuasive to some extent.
- REASSURING ADVERTISING is aimed at existing customers. It tries to persuade them that their purchase was correct and that they should continue to buy the product. Banks and building societies often use this method to assure customers that their investments are safe.

There is a wide range of ADVERTISING MEDIA that firms can choose from in order to make consumers aware of their products including:

- commercial television, whether terrestrial such as ITV1 or Channel 4, or satellite such as BSkyB;
- commercial radio, which in the UK is local radio;
- national newspapers, such as *The Sun* or *The Times*;
- regional newspapers, such as the *London Evening Standard* or the *Birmingham Evening Post*;
- magazines, such as *Cosmopolitan* or *Loaded*;
- trade newspapers and journals, such as *The Grocer* or *Accountancy Age* which are read by workers or businesses in a particular industry, trade or profession;
- directories, including the telephone directories *Yellow Pages* and *Thomson Directory*;
- posters and transport, such as billboards by the side of the road or advertisements on the side of buses;
- the Internet.

The medium that is chosen will depend on a variety of factors including:

- **Cost** – most businesses could not afford television adverts, for example. Cost also has to be measured against effectiveness – how much extra new business will be generated by each £1 of advertising expenditure?
- **Media reach** – what media will best get to the audience the advertiser wishes to reach?
- **Delivery of the chosen message** – what media would best persuade consumers to change their brand of washing powder, for example, or give customers a telephone number to call if their washing machine broke down?
- **The marketing mix** – an advertising campaign may be part of a wider campaign using other elements of the marketing mix, such as below-the-line promotion or pricing. These other elements may help determine which media to use for advertising.
- **The law** – there are legal restrictions on the use of different media for advertising certain products, such as cigarettes.

Promotion below the line

Promotion below the line is any promotion that is not advertising. Above-the-line advertising in newspapers means that the promotion is seen by most of the readers, even though some will not be interested. With below-the-line promotions, firms aim their message at consumers who are either known to them or who have been chosen in advance, and who are interested. For example, businesses promoting through exhibitions, such as the Boat Show, can be certain that the majority of those attending will be interested in the products on show.

There may be problems that result from below-the-line promotions. As with advertising, they are expensive and their outcome can be difficult to predict. Also, they are often 'one-off' events, which have an impact for a limited period. Further, some types of promotion, such as direct mail and direct selling, are disliked by consumers.

Public relations PUBLIC RELATIONS is a attempt by a business to communicate with groups that form its 'public'. Such groups may include the government, shareholders, employees and customers. The aim is to increase sales by improving the image of the business and its products. This can be done directly by the business itself through a public relations activity or a television programme or a newspaper could be used. Because of the importance of maintaining good relations with the media, a business may appoint a **publicity manager**. As well as promoting favourable press stories, publicity managers must respond to criticisms and try to ensure that there are no unfavourable press notices.

Consumers appear to attach great importance to messages conveyed through public relations. For example, a new restaurant may promote a positive image of itself through promotional materials. Such communications may be taken 'with a pinch of salt' by consumers. However, a good write-up in

Question 1.

Anna Lever runs a shop which sells imported comics and graphic novels from the USA and Europe. She stocks well known comics by Marvel and DC, such as X-Men and Batman, and also a small line of European comics. Anna also sells comics by independent publishers in the UK. The market for comic sales in the UK tends to be a niche market, selling to specialist collectors, teenagers, students and children, and older people who Anna argues 'want to recapture their youth, by reading the stories they read when they were children and teenagers.'

There is a small number of chains selling comics in the UK, such as Forbidden Planet, but many other independent shops. The nearest competitor for Anna's shop is over 50 miles away. Anna often tries local mailing in the area. General mailing to all people tends to be a waste of time, so she must carefully target her audience. She also keeps clients regularly updated via emails. Most regular customers are happy to receive information about the latest issues although some newer customers have objected to this 'spam'.

Every month Anna makes the trip to the nearest city and puts up a stall in the comic mart on Sundays. She tends to see the same faces there all the time, and can build up contacts. There may also be people coming to 'have a look' on their day off and some have become regular clients. She has also occasionally taken a stand at the large fair held at the NEC in Birmingham a few times a year. She finds the trip is tiring, takes a lot of time out of her week and does not always pay for itself.

Source: adapted from company information.

(a) Why might it be important for Anna's business to use a trade fair as part of its promotional mix?

(b) Assess whether a trade fair might be more successful than direct mail advertising in promoting and selling comics.

a newspaper or restaurant guide is likely to be taken much more seriously by consumers. Businesses use a variety of methods to attract publicity.

- **Press conferences.** These might involve inviting journalists to a company presentation, where they are given information. The business may take the opportunity to launch a new or updated product. Sometimes, businesses provide free products for conference members to try out. Conferences may also be used for presentations to trade customers.
- **Press releases.** These are written accounts of events or activities which may be considered newsworthy. For example, new multi-million pound contracts gained by firms such as British Aerospace are announced on TV news bulletins. Such news stories usually originate from press releases issued by businesses.
- **Donations.** These can range from a small contribution to a college mini bus appeal to a large donation to Comic Relief's 'Red Nose Day' or the 'Children in Need' appeal . While some make payments anonymously, others take advantage of the opportunity for a good public relations event. The approach of a business to such an event is likely to be determined by its particular ethical stance.
- **Sponsorship.** This is popular in the sporting world. Examples have included the links between Coca-Cola and the Olympic Games, McDonald's and the World Cup, and Nike and Tiger Woods. Other types of sponsorship take place in the arts world with ballet, opera and theatre being sponsored by businesses.
- **Company visits.** Jaguar Cars and Warburtons Bakeries have allowed members of the public to visit their manufacturing and research plants as part of their public relations activities.

Branding A BRAND is a name, term, sign, symbol, design or any other feature that allows consumers to identify the goods and services of a business and to differentiate them from those of competitors. Some examples are shown in Table 1. A brand can be one product, a family or range of products or the actual business itself. So, for example, a Nestlé KitKat is an individual product produced by Nestlé. KitKat Chunky and KitKat Kubes are also part of the KitKat family. Nestlé is the name of the company which produces KitKats, other confectionery products,

---

Table 1: Examples of brands

- The use of the 'Mc' name by McDonald's in its products.
- The Nike 'swoosh' logo.
- The Apple on Apple computer and other products.
- The use of the colour orange in promotions by the Orange communications company or B&Q.
- The slogan 'Vorsprung Durch Technik' used for Audi cars.
- The 'tune' which accompanies references to the Intel Pentium Processor fitted into computers.

---

such as Milky Bar and Smarties, and foods such as breakfast cereals.

Brand names are the parts of the brand that can be spoken, such as the name of the product, ie Heinz Baked Beans or a Bratz doll. A **brand mark** is the design or symbol used in the brand, such as the apple used on Apple Macintosh computers. It is possible to protect the use of trademark by copyright. A company might use its **trade name** as a brand, such as Virgin, Disney or Starbucks. In some cases the company name might be as well known as its products or even more well known such as Sony or Ford.

There is a number of reasons why businesses use branding.

- **To create brand loyalty.** Consumers often have a high degree of **brand loyalty** to popular, well-established, brands. In many markets it can be difficult for firms to compete unless they have a strong brand identity.
- **To differentiate the product.** Especially in markets where products are fairly similar, it is important for a firm that its own products can be clearly distinguished from others. A clear brand identity can help to achieve this.
- **To gain flexibility when making pricing decisions.** The greater the loyalty of consumers to a particular brand, the more room for manoeuvre a firm will have in its pricing decisions. A survey by Business Marketing Services found that consumers were reluctant to switch from well-known brands in the hotel, car hire, computer and transatlantic flights markets. For example, in the car hire market pricing discounts of over 20 per cent were required to persuade consumers to switch from Hertz or Avis to one of the lesser known companies.
- **To help recognition.** A product with a strong brand identity is likely to be instantly recognised by most consumers. This may mean consumers trust the product and are therefore more willing to buy it. Some brand names are used to describe whole classes of products, such as Sellotape and Hoover. PESTER POWER can be important. Children often put pressure on parents to buy particular brands.
- **To develop a brand image.** It is argued that customers respond to brand images with which they identify. Some consumers respond to brands that allow them to pursue multiple goals. Volvo, for example, stresses that its cars not only protect but allow the user to escape to remote places. Consumers also react to brands that offer 'extreme consumption experiences' such as Häagen-Dazs ice cream or Starbucks coffee.

A brand must be **positioned** in the right place in the market for it to be successful. A business, for example, might sell a 'high quality' brand. It is more likely to be successful if the target market is people with high incomes looking for a superior product than those looking for a bargain. The marketing mix of the business is important to positioning the brand. So, for example, high quality jewellery is likely to be a product manufactured from high quality materials and design, sold for a premium price, promoted in a way that reflects the status of the product, sold in places that reflect the

Question 2.

How many copies of the *Sunday Times* can a delivery boy or girl carry? The answer is five. The reason for this is the polybags that now accompany newspapers. For newspapers delivering news is not enough. Added value is required in the form of supplements, additional sections and gifts. During 2006 the *Daily Mail* added 37,000 new customers. This was largely ascribed to a drive to increase homesales deliveries but was also linked to the free gift of two major DVDs per month. In the same year the *Sun* experienced a 0.6 per cent rise in readers partly linked, it is thought, to a 20p price cut in the South of England. The *Daily Mirror*, by contrast, suffered a 4.7 per cent drop in readers over the same period despite its free collection of 13 classic Ladybird books. The *Daily Star Sunday* leaped by 12 per cent as it music CD series continued, while the *People* plummeted by 12 per cent despite offering free cross channel ferry tickets.

Source: adapted from *The Independent*, 12.11.2007.

(a)   Identify the diferent promotional methods described in the article.

(b)   Explain whether the methods are above-the-line or below-the-line methdos of promotion.

(c)   Discuss whether a local newspaper should use this type of promotional method.

product's features, such as high quality jewellery stores.

Large retail chains may offer OWN BRANDS for sale. These are products that are manufactured by suppliers but sold under the name of the retailer. They are an attempt by the retailer to use the brand name of the company to sell products. They are often lower in price than BRAND LEADERS, although the retailer will try to match the quality of the leading brand. Retailers may gain from this as:

- it helps them to be competitive against other retailers;
- own brands can have higher profit margins than leading brands.

Merchandising MERCHANDISING is an attempt to influence consumers at the POINT OF SALE. The point of sale is anywhere that a consumer buys a product. It may be, for example, a supermarket, a department store, a bank or a petrol station. Consumers are intended to buy based on 'what they see' rather than from a sales assistant. The aim of merchandising is to encourage sales of a product and therefore to speed up the rate at which stocks are turned over. There is a number of different features of merchandising.

- **Display material.** A good display should attract attention, enhance certain aspects of a product and encourage the 'right frame of mind' to make a purchase. Department stores lay great stress on window displays. Banks make sure that the services which they offer, such as insurance and loan facilities, are well displayed in their branches.
- **The layout of products at the point of sale.** Many retail outlets, such as supermarkets, design the layout of their stores very carefully. Their aim is to encourage consumers to follow particular routes around a store. Retail outlets often place popular items at the back or sides of a store. Consumers, on their way to these, are encouraged to walk past other items which they might buy. Another tactic is to

---

Table 2: Sales promotions

- **Coupons and loyalty cards** involve either providing money off or refunds on specific purchases or allowing savings to be made over time for being a loyal customer. The Nectar card which includes Sainsbury's and PC World is now used by hundreds of retailers in this way.
- **Competitions.** Prizes are sometimes offered for competitions. To enter, consumers must first buy the product. Tabloid newspapers often use this type of promotion. They try to attract customers through large cash prizes in their 'bingo' competitions.
- **Product endorsements** are widely used by a range of manufacturers, where well-known personalities are paid to use products. For example, sports products companies will sign up teams and successful sports personalities to promote their products. The competition between sports companies has often been reflected by the teams they supply – Real Madrid has worn Adidas while Manchester United and Barcelona have worn Nike.
- **Product placing** involves a firm paying for product brands to be placed on the sets of films and TV programmes. Car manufacturers are often eager to see their vehicles driven by Hollywood stars in popular movies.
- **Free offers.** A free 'gift' may be given with the product. An example of might be music magazines, which regularly offer readers free CDs of featured artists.
- **Special credit terms** have been increasingly used by firms. They include offers such as interest free credit and 'buy now pay later' schemes.

place related products next to each other, so consumers buy both.

- **Stocks.** A firm must make sure that stock levels are maintained and shelves are quickly restocked. Shelf space is usually allocated according to the amount of a product which a business expects to sell. For example, a supermarket will give more space to products on special offer.
- **Appropriate lighting and the creation of desirable 'smells'.** Generally lighting is kept soft where browsing is encouraged and bright where there is a need to suggest cleanliness as, for example, at a cosmetics counter. Smells are used to encourage the right atmosphere. Bread smells are often wafted into supermarkets and food retailers.

Sales promotions SALES PROMOTIONS are the incentives offered to consumers to encourage them to buy goods and services. They are used to give a short-term 'boost' to the sales of a product. This is different to building up brand recognition and loyalty, which may be a longer-term aim. There is a variety of sales promotions that a business can use, as shown in Table 2. Why have these methods become popular?

- Sales promotions can be used as a method to break into a new market or introduce a new product into an existing market. They can also be used as a means of extending the product life cycle of an existing product.
- They encourage consumers to sample a good or service which they might not have bought otherwise. Once the initial good has been purchased it is likely that further goods will be bought. Many magazines offer free gifts ranging from CD ROMS to make-up in their first issues hoping that their consumers will continue to buy.
- Customers feel 'rewarded' for their custom. They may, as a result, develop a loyalty to a particular product or business.
- Customers identify products or businesses with things that they like or are attracted to. A customer is therefore more likely to purchase a product.
- Sales promotions provide businesses with feedback on the impact of their marketing expenditure, for example, through the number of coupons returned or the amount spent on loyalty cards.

Sales promotions are not without problems. The free flight offer of Hoover in 1992 is one example. It offered two free flights to the US with the purchase of products worth over £200. The company misjudged the number of people taking advantage of the offer. This meant extreme pressure on the company to produce the goods consumers were demanding. Also many consumers did not receive the holidays on dates or at times they wished. By 1993 there were so many complaints that Maytag, Hoover's US parent company, had to intervene to make sure flights or compensation were provided. It was estimated that the cost of dealing with these problems was £21.1 million.

Direct selling Direct selling or personal selling occurs when a company's sales team promotes a product through personal contact. This can be done over the telephone, by setting up

Question 3.

A firm from Walsall in the West Midlands has won an order to provide electrical wiring for the world-beating Subaru rally cars raced by drivers such as Richard Burns. Teepee Electrical Systems said that the wiring had been subjected to extensive testing to ensure it met the standards of reliability and performance needed for rally cars. Teepee Electrical Systems sells electrical wiring to other businesses. It is involved with a range of industries, from railway rolling stock, to conveyor belt systems at airports and even the submarine controls in a James Bond film. Kevin Jones, managing director of the company, put the success of the company down to the skills its workers bring to the business. 'A wiring loom is a wiring loom, but our people add engineering skills from widely diverse fields.'

Source: www.teepee-electrical.co.uk and www.expressandstar.com.

(a) In what ways might branding benefit Teepee Electrical Systems.
(b) Suggest why Teepee might find it difficult to establish a strong brand in this market.

meetings, in retail outlets, or by 'knocking on doors'. In general, the more highly priced, technically complex or individual the product, the greater the need for personal selling. Most firms supplying industrial markets rely upon personal selling in the form of sales representatives. The main reason for using personal selling rather than other methods is that individuals can be given personal attention. Most forms of promotion tend to deliver a 'standard message' to a 'typical' consumer. With personal selling the individual consumer's needs can be dealt with and the product shaped to meet these needs. There are other reasons for using direct or personal selling.

- Creating awareness of and interest in a product.
- Explaining the functions and technical aspects of a product.

- Obtaining orders and, in some cases, making deliveries.
- Encouraging product trials and test marketing.
- Providing rapid and detailed feedback from the consumer to the producer via the sales representative.

A disadvantage with personal selling is that it can be expensive. The cost of maintaining a team of sales representatives can be very high. Another problem is the dislike of 'callers' by consumers. There are also legal and ethical issues about the way products are sold that need to be considered.

Direct mailing Direct mailing involves sending information about a product or product range through the post. The consumer can usually buy the product by placing an order by post or telephone. Although sometimes unpopular with the public, direct mail is a fast growing area of promotion. It has proved very effective for firms trying to reach a target audience. Some companies use direct e-mailing, where consumers or businesses receive product information through their email inbox. Systems, however, exist for unwanted emails to be blocked as this method of selling has proved unpopular for some people. Direct mail is one means of **direct marketing**, which is often seen as part of a firm's distribution network.

Packaging A product's packaging is important in its overall marketing. This is because consumers often link the quality and design of a product's packaging with the quality of the product itself. Unsuitable packaging may affect sales. What factors should firms consider when deciding upon how to package their product?

- **Weight and shape.** These can affect the cost of distributing a product. For example, bulky packaging may mean high distribution costs.
- **Protection.** Products must not be damaged in transit or in storage. They must also be protected against light, dust and heat.
- **Convenience.** The packaging must be easy to handle by the consumer and distributors.
- **Design.** The design of the packaging should be eye-catching and help the consumer to distinguish it from others. It should also fit in with the overall marketing of the product and project the brand image. Colour is likely to be important here.
- **Information.** It is likely that the package will contain information required by the consumer. For technical products, the packaging will need to include information about how the product should be used. For food products, there are legal requirements about the information that must be on the package, such as details of the ingredients contained.
- **Environmental factors.** Manufacturers are facing increasing pressure to cut down on the amount and type of packaging placed around products. Consumers and pressure groups stress the wastefulness of this and its impact upon the environment. The response of some manufacturers to this pressure has been to use recyclable materials.

Exhibitions and trade fairs Exhibitions and trade fairs are used by firms to promote their products. They are visited by both industrial and ordinary consumers. Examples of better known fairs and exhibitions include the Motor Show, the Boat Show, the Ideal Homes Exhibition and BETT (the British educational technology exhibition). Why do businesses find them useful?

- They give the chance to show how a product actually works. This is important in the case of bulky or complex technical products. Business to business marketing, including the promoting of industrial and agricultural machinery is often done through trade fairs.
- Consumer reaction to a product can be tested before it is released onto the market.
- Some trade fairs and exhibitions are held overseas. They can form a part of a firm's international marketing strategy.
- A fair or exhibition may attract press coverage. New products may be launched to take advantage of this. The Motor Show is widely used for this purpose.
- They allow customers to discuss a product with members of the management team. It is not unusual for the managing directors of a business to attend a trade fair. For industrial consumers, in particular, this can be a valuable point of contact.
- Technical and sales staff are available to answer questions and discuss the product.

The promotional mix

Businesses usually use a range of different types of the promotional methods described above at any one time. This range is the PROMOTIONAL MIX employed by the business. For example, a business launching a new product might advertise it on television, but also send press releases to newspapers and magazines that it thinks might cover the story. There is a number of influences on the promotional mix that a business decides to employ.

The type of product Some products are better suited to some promotional methods than others. For example, trade fairs and exhibitions are strongly suited to business to business marketing and, in particular, for the promoting of business specific products such as machinery, equipment and software. On the other hand fast moving consumer goods are often better suited to different forms of advertising so that their qualities can be communicated to a wide audience.

The type of market This includes it size, geography, socio-economic characteristics and whether it is a consumer or business to business market. For example, a small business such as a small decorating business might rely upon an occasional advertisement in a local newspaper or a listing in the *Yellow Pages*. This is partly because such a business restricts its operations to a small locality and so promotional methods designed to reach a regional or national market would not be appropriate.

Cost Many small businesses find that they are restricted by considerations of cost when deciding upon use of promotional methods. Many forms of advertising, such as in national newspapers or on television or radio may not be affordable to such businesses. This means that their choice of promotional method will be strictly limited by considerations of cost.

The promotional mix of competitors If competitors are spending a great deal on advertising, for example, a competitor may feel the need to match this. Many small businesses restrict their promotions to word of mouth and personal selling, but the use of other methods by a competitor may cause a business to reconsider this strategy.

The stage of a product in its life cycle The promotional needs of a product at its launch may be very different from those used in its decline stage. Many business, both small and large, make use of public relations when first launching a product on to the market.

Legal and social constraints There is a variety of legislation that affects promotion, particularly advertising, which may influence the choice of media by a business.

- There are laws which affect the nature of advertisements. For example, the **Trade Descriptions Act 1968** states that products must correspond to claims made for them on advertisements.
- The **Advertising Standards Authority (ASA)** is the main independent body in the UK which regulates and controls advertising. It ensures that business correspond with the **British Code of Advertising, Sales promotion and Direct Marketing**, the CAP code. If the ASA finds that an advertisement breaches the code it will ask the business to withdraw the advertisement, to which they usually comply. Although it has no legal powers to force the business to withdraw the advertisement it can put pressure on it by publishing its findings or ask the media to refuse the carry the advertisement. It can also refer the advertisement to the Office of Fair Trading.
- Certain **pressure groups** seek to influence advertising. FOREST, for example, campaigns for the right of people to

smoke. ASH, on the other hand, seeks to make public the health risks of smoking.
- People may resent certain types of promotion. Email campaigns are often resented by people with computers.

KEYTERMS

Above-the-line promotion – promotion in the form of advertising.

Advertising – a form of communication between a business and its customers where the business uses visual, oral or pictorial images in the media to encourage the purchase of products.

Advertising media – the various means by which advertisements can be communicated to the public.

Informative advertising – advertising which primarily seeks to provide consumers with information about a product.

Below-the-line promotion – promotion that is not media advertising.

Brand – a name, term, sign, symbol, design or any other feature that allows consumers to identify the goods and services and differentiate them from those of competitors.

Brand leader – a brand with the high sales or sometimes the brand with the highest sales in the market.

Merchandising – a promotion specifically at the point of sale of a product.

Persuasive advertising – advertising which seeks to influence and persuade consumers to buy a product.

Own brand – a product sold under the brand name of a retailer but manufactured by a supplier of the retailer.

Pester power – the ability of children to persuade parents to buy products.

Promotion – an attempt to retain and obtain customers by drawing attention to a firm or its products.

Promotional mix – the mixture of promotional techniques used by a business to promote its products.

Point of sale – any point where a consumer buys a product.

Public relations – an organisation's attempts to communicate with interested parties.

Reassuring advertising – a method used to assure consumers about their purchases and encourage them to make repeat purchases.

Sales promotions – methods of promoting a product in the short term to give a boost to sales.

KNOWLEDGE

1. What is above the line promotion?
2. What choices of advertising media do firms have?
3 What is below the line promotion?
4. What is direct mailing?
5. Why do businesses promote their products at trade fairs and exhibitions?
6. Identify four different types of sales promotions.

7. Identify five features that a brand might have.
8. Where is merchandising likely to take place?
9. Which aspects of their merchandising should businesses pay attention to?
10. What is the main advantage of personal selling?
11. What is public relations?
12. Identify five factors that might influence the promotional mix.

CRITIQUE

Critics of marketing question the extent to which businesses respond to consumer needs as opposed to creating them. Promotion is a major part of this. Many would argue that promotions actively seek to create the need to consume more, rather than just responding to what consumers want and need. They suggest that consumer needs in general would be better met if businesses encouraged them to spend less rather than more. So whilst promoting their products strongly may make sense for individual businesses and their relationships with individual consumers it does not necessarily work at a wider level. One consequence of this so-called pressure on consumers is individuals spending beyond their means. This has led to many people taking on more debt than they can manage. Another consequence is more rapid use of the world's resources and the creation of higher levels of environmental damage.

Case Study: *Advertising*

Retailers signalled a big push for Christmas sales in 2007 with the launch of TV advertising campaigns. Leading the way was Marks & Spencer, which signed up A-list movie star Antonio Banderas to front adverts that recreate memorable moments from classic Hollywood films. But competing for screen space will be retailers who traditionally do not use TV advertising such as John Lewis and Next. Many retail chiefs have forecast trade is going to be tough this Christmas and they are pouring cash into advertising to persuade shoppers to part with their cash. Last year's M&S Christmas campaign had a James Bond theme and starred Dame Shirley Bassey. Banderas – who starred in the Mask of Zorro – will appear with M&S's usual roster of models: Twiggy, Erin O'Connor, Laura Bailey, Lizzie Jagger and Noemie Lenoir. M&S's advertising, masterminded by marketing director Steve Sharp, has been credited with helping to rebuild the reputation of the retailer.

Next week also sees the launch of a John Lewis advertising campaign. It is spending more than £6 million to promote the 27-strong chain of department stores - three times last' year's advertising spend - and will be using TV adverts for only the second time in its history. The move is the brainchild of the company's new marketing director, Gill Barr, who joined the company in January and was made a member of the board in June. The television advertisement, which is set to 'Morning Serenade', the theme from Prokofiev's ballet Romeo and Juliet, is deliberately understated to contrast with other retailers' celebrity focused Christmas ads. It shows a diverse group of people carefully arranging John Lewis products in such a way that the combined shadow casts the outline of the person for whom the gifts are intended. The image will also be used for billboards and press and in cinema and online advertising. The spend – up from £1.75 million last year – signifies a departure for the department store chain which has traditionally invested little on advertising, believing the brand has grown essentially through word of mouth and that it was not necessary to 'boast about it'.

Ms Barr, a former business development director at Woolworths, said that when she joined the company there wasn't a tradition of advertising, but there was 'an ambition to be more articulate about the brand and to talk to customers more'. She added: 'This campaign is directional for the John Lewis brand. "The creative execution is stylish, intriguing and intelligent. The media plan is more comprehensive than ever before, reinforcing the core idea with three different shadows in press and outdoor. The TV advertisement will also run in cinemas.'

Next recently unveiled its first national television advertising campaign for more than a decade. It is pouring £20 million into advertising this year – double last year's marketing budget. Chief executive Simon Wolfson said recently that he was 'acutely aware that the full effect of recent interest rates has not yet filtered through to our customers' and despite the advertising push forecasts a dip in sales of up to 3.5 per cent, compared to last year, over the current six months. She added that the ad intended to use the extent of the company's range, which includes 350,000 products, to inspire customers with their Christmas shopping. The television ad, which will run from next Tuesday, differs widely from the glitzy ads of Marks & Spencer, which star Shirley Bassey, Twiggy and Myleene Klass, and Next, which launched its first major television ad campaign in September. Next is spending £18 million more than usual on advertising this year, including £2 million more on its Christmas window displays.

Source: adapted from *The Guardian*, 3.11.2007 and the *Independent*, 2.11.2007.

(a) Identify the different promotional methods used in the case study. (6 marks)
(b) Explain, using examples, how the methods of promotion might be made:
(i) persuasive; (ii) informative; (iii) reassuring;
for customers of the businesses. (6 marks)
(c) Examine the factors which might affect the choice of promotional method for each business. (10 marks)
(d) In the light of the information in the article, evaluate the potential promotional methods available to a small independent fashion clothing business. (12 marks)

Influences on pricing

The pricing strategies used by a business may be influenced by a number of factors.

Objectives The pricing strategy chosen by a business is likely to reflect the extent to which it wants to maximise profits or sales. A business seeking to maximise short-term profits may use more aggressive and perhaps risky pricing strategies.

The marketing mix The price chosen by a business must complement the marketing mix. This means that the price must fit in with the nature of the product itself and the way in which it is being promoted and distributed to consumers. For example, a low quality product being sold in retail outlets at the bottom end of the market is likely to be sold at a fairly low price.

Costs A business which cannot generate enough revenue over time to cover its costs will not survive. In the long run, a business must charge a price which earns enough revenue to cover its total cost of production at any level of output. This means that businesses must take account of all of their costs when setting price. In the short run a business may not expect to cover the fixed costs of its factory or machinery. Providing its price is high enough to generate revenue that covers its variable costs, the firm will stay in business. Revenue below this will cause the business to cease production. As a result businesses may have greater flexibility in the short term when making pricing decisions.

Competition Competition can affect pricing decisions For a market trader, the price of her goods is largely determined by prices on nearby stalls selling similar goods. Such a trader will have little room for manoeuvre compared to a business which faces less competition. A monopolist that dominates the market may be able to charge higher prices.

Demand The higher the price set the lower the quantity sold. The effect that a higher prices has on sales is dealt with in the unit titled 'Elasticity of demand'.

Consumer perceptions Businesses must pay attention to what consumers think a product is worth. A product priced above what consumers consider its value to be may generate low sales because of doubts about its value for money. A product priced too low may also generate low sales. This is because consumers often suspect that such products have something wrong with them or that they are of inferior quality. In some cases businesses actually encourage consumers to think of their products as expensive to encourage high income earners to buy them.

Market segment Businesses that produce a range of products are likely to have some aimed at particular market segments. This is true, for example, of all major car manufacturers. They are, therefore, likely to charge different prices for each segment. However, the price which they charge to one segment of the market will affect the prices charged to other segments. A product competing in the top end of the market will need to have a different price from one aimed at the middle or bottom end of the market.

Laws and regulations The price of a number of products is affected by government. Taxes can raise the price above the level that might have been set by manufacturers. Products affected greatly by taxation include cigarettes, alcoholic drinks and petrol. There is also a number of products which are offered to consumers below the price that producers would normally charge. Such products are subsidised by the government. Maximum prices can also be set. For example, the price of products such as water and gas in the UK are determined by regulatory bodies.

Question 1.

The price of each product in a market will be influenced by a variety of factors. For some products, the ability of a business to set its price is limited. For others, there will be more scope for a business to set the price it wants to charge.

(a) What factors may have influenced the prices of the products in the photographs?

213

Question 2.

A range of prices being offered by various retailers for a Fuji S9600 FinePix Digital Camera is shown in Table 1.

Table 1: Prices of Fuji S9600 FinePix Digital Camera in December 2007

Cameras2u.com	£205.20
Amazon.co.uk	£206.00
Littlewoods Direct	£339.00
Argos	£249.99
Jessops.com	£279.99
Computerwebstore.com	£234.37

(a) Describe the pricing tactic that might be being used by Argos.
(b) Compare the pricing strategies of Cameras2u.com with Jessops.com.

Pricing strategies

A strategy is a set of plans designed to meet objectives. PRICING STRATEGY is part of the marketing strategy of the business. Other strategies such as product and distribution strategy also make up a marketing strategy. Marketing strategy is then part of the corporate strategy of the business. Other strategies include production and financial strategy.

Pricing strategy is therefore a set of plans about pricing which help a business to achieve its marketing and corporate objectives. For example, a corporate objective might be to double in size over the next five years. A marketing objective to achieve this might be to take the products of the business 'up-market'. The pricing strategy developed from this could be to increase the average price of the products made by the business.

- Some pricing strategies can be used for: **new products**, such as market skimming or penetration pricing.
- Some strategies are more suitable for **existing products**, such as price.

Price skimming or creaming

If a business realises that its product has a **unique selling point** it may be in a position to charge a high price for a limited time in order to take advantage of the newness of the product. This is known a PRICE or MARKET SKIMMING or CREAMING skimming. New generation mobile phones with fast Internet connections, email facilities and music facilities are priced much higher than 'traditional' phones as mobile phone companies skim this new market. The aim is to gain as much profit as possible for a new product while it remains unique in the market. It usually means selling a product to the most profitable segment of the market before it is sold to a wider market at a lower price.

There are two reasons why businesses adopt skimming. They may try to maximise revenue before competitors come into the market with a similar product. Often new techniques or designs mean that entirely new products, or new versions of a product can be offered. Examples include new fashions in clothes, new children's toys and new inventions. When first launched, a basic digital watch could cost as much as £50 or £60. Now they often sell for as little as a few pounds. Price skimming can also be used to generate revenue in a short period of time so that further investment in the product can be made. Companies in the electronics and pharmaceutical industries often use skimming for this reason.

Penetration pricing

A business may set its price deliberately low in order to gain a footing in the market. This could also be used when a business is launching an existing product into a new market, for example. This is known as PENETRATION PRICING. It involves pricing a product at a low level so that retailers and consumers are encouraged to purchase the product in large quantities.

There are two main reasons why businesses use penetration pricing.
- Consumers are encouraged to develop the habit of buying the product, so that when prices eventually begin to rise they will continue to purchase it.
- Retailers and wholesalers are likely to purchase large quantities of the product. This should mean that they will not buy from other suppliers until they have sold most of their stock. Businesses can thus gain a significant slice of the market.

Penetration pricing, because of its high cost, is often used by large businesses operating in mass markets, such as those selling biscuits, sweets, washing powder and canned drinks. It is also a policy used by new businesses or established businesses in other areas to break into a new market. It is not a policy that is suitable for products with short life cycles. There is usually not enough time to recover the cost of lost revenue from the initially low price.

Price leaders

In some markets, often controlled by a small number of large companies, or just one large business there is an accepted PRICE LEADER or PRICE MAKER. They will decide first to increase or lower prices, knowing that other companies will soon follow. It occurs when one dominant business establishes a position of price leadership within a market. Other firms will follow suit when the price leader changes its prices. This type of policy can be seen when a petrol company changes the price of a gallon of petrol or when banks and building societies change interest rates.

Price takers

In very competitive markets a business might decide to follow closely another firm's price increases or reductions. The business is a PRICE TAKER or PRICE FOLLOWER. This is an example of COMPETITION-BASED PRICING or GOING RATE PRICING, where a business takes into account competitor's prices. The retail market for 'white goods' such as fridges and freezers is an example. It also occurs in markets where businesses are reluctant to set off a price war by lowering their prices and are concerned about a fall off in revenue if prices are raised. Price taking is an example of pricing based upon competition. Where businesses are price takers they may be frustrated by their inability to control prices more closely. A strategy often used in such circumstances is to establish a strong brand identity and to differentiate it from others on the market. An oil company's decision to upgrade all of its service stations is an example of an attempt to achieve this. A strong brand identity and unique product features allow firms much greater scope for choosing their own price levels.

Destroying competition or capturing the market

The aim of **destroyer pricing** is to eliminate opposition. It involves cutting prices, sometimes greatly, for a period of time long enough for your rivals to go out of business. It could be argued that the offering of low price airline tickets by Ryanair and easyJet in the 1990s was designed to drive out competition from the national European airline carriers and force some of them out of business. Some responded by setting up their own low-price carriers and cutting prices. Others, like Sabena and SwissAir, did go out of business.

Price discrimination

Price discrimination occurs when a firm offers the same product at different prices when consumers can be kept separate. An example is BT's policy of charging different prices to business and residential users at different times of the day and the weekend. This allows BT to take into account the differences in cost which exists at peak and off-peak times. So, for example, calls may be charged at a higher rate on Monday to Friday, 8am-6pm, than at weekends.

This price discrimination is **time based**. The price you pay for a phone call is based upon the time of day or the day of the week when you use the service. Other businesses which use this policy are rail companies (cheaper off-peak travel), and holiday firms which charge higher prices for their product during school holidays. Price discrimination can also be **market based**. This involves offering different market segments the same product at different prices. An example of this is students being given discounts on coach and bus travel. Price discrimination is an example of MARKET-ORIENTATED PRICING, where a business takes into account conditions in the market when setting prices.

Customer value pricing

This is pricing according to what the consumer is wiling to pay. It involves charging the price that consumers are prepared to pay. Products which have prestige names attached to them, such

as Rolex, may be able to command a higher price because of the status of these names. Products for one-off events, such as music festivals or sports finals, may be given a high price because they are unique. Businesses sometimes use PRESTIGE or PREMIUM PRICING. This is where a high price is charged for luxury, up-market products to reassure customers about their quality and that they are buying 'the best'.

Cost-based pricing

All businesses are influenced by their costs when determining prices with costs acting as a 'bottom line' when choosing a price. But some use COST-BASED PRICING as their strategy for price setting. Businesses using cost-based pricing are those where the influence of cost is more important than other factors such as market conditions or competitors' pricing. Many small businesses such as the local garage repair business or domestic repair services like electricians and plumbers are likely to take a cost-based approach.

Cost-plus pricing. This involves setting a price by calculating the average cost of producing goods and adding a MARK-UP for profit. If a business produces 10,000 goods costing £50,000, the average cost would be £5.00. A mark-up of 20 per cent would mean goods would cost an extra £1.00 and the price would be £6.00 per product. Retailers often use this method of pricing. Say that a department store buys a colour TV from wholesalers for £200 and its mark-up to allow for a profit is 100 per cent. The retail price to consumers will be £400. The attractiveness of cost-plus pricing is that it is a quick and simple way of setting a selling price. It also ensures that sales revenue will cover total costs and generate profit. A criticism, however, is that a fixed mark-up does not allow a business to take market needs into account when setting prices. In addition, no attempt is made to allocate indirect costs to particular products. This means they do not reflect the resources being allocated by the business to that particular product or product range. Cost-plus pricing is shown in Figure 1.

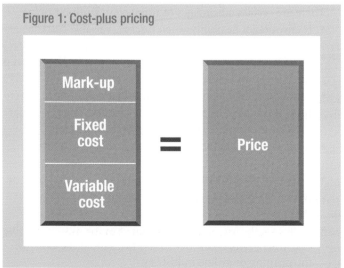

Figure 1: Cost-plus pricing

Mark-up / Fixed cost / Variable cost = Price

Contribution (or marginal) pricing The costs of a business can be divided into two types. **Variable costs** are costs which change as output changes. For example, leather is a variable cost for a shoe manufacturer. The more shoes that are made, the more leather is used. **Fixed costs** are costs which stay the same whatever the level of output. For example, the shoe manufacturer may rent a factory. The rent is a fixed cost because it has to be paid whether a million pairs of shoes are made or zero.

Say that the variable costs for an order of 5,000 pairs of shoes were £40,000. If the order were priced over £40,000, it would cover its variable costs of production and make a **contribution** towards the fixed costs and profit of the business. Contribution is defined as:

$$\text{Contribution} = \text{revenue} - \text{variable costs}$$

So, if the order were priced at £50,000, it would make a £10,000 contribution. If it were priced at £65,000, it would make a £25,000 contribution.

CONTRIBUTION PRICING can be used to decide whether to accept a lower price. This is shown in Figure 2. The usual price of shoes might be £20. If fixed costs were £8 per pair, costs would be £18 (variable costs of £10 + fixed costs of £8). Profit may be £2 per pair. Should the business accept a lower price for an order?

This pricing method would suggest that it could accept any price as long as it was at least £10, the variable cost of production. At a price of £12, for example, each pair makes a loss of £6 (£12 price - £18 costs). But it still makes a contribution of £2 per pair (£12 price - £10 variable cost). If it doesn't take the order, the business will be worse off. There will be no £2 contribution per pair of shoes.

In the long run, businesses have to cover all their costs and make a profit to survive. So the total contribution on sales has to be greater than fixed costs. But in the short run, the contribution method of pricing suggests that businesses might accept orders where the price fails to cover total costs, so long as the contribution is positive.

There are certain advantages of using contribution pricing.

- It encourages flexibility when pricing. Variable costs represent the minimum acceptable price. After that, the business can try to maximise the amount of contribution it can earn from any single sale.
- Products in high demand can be sold at high prices. Where there is intense competition, or the product is not popular with customers, the price can be lower.
- It may lead to one-off orders being accepted at a lower price.
- It may be used to break into new markets. Products can be sold at lower prices to attract initial customers (known as **entry pricing**).
- It may encourage the use of **excess capacity** at times of the year when there is low demand. This is often the case in the printing or airline industries.

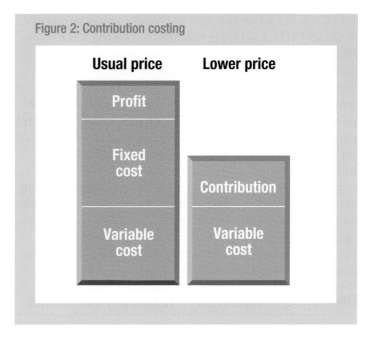

Figure 2: Contribution costing

Usual price	Lower price
Profit	
Fixed cost	
	Contribution
Variable cost	Variable cost

The main disadvantage is that those in charge of sales can focus too much on sales and not on selling at a profit. If all businesses in an industry adopt contribution pricing, this may lead to widespread selling below full cost. Businesses compete with each other for sales and the business with the lowest price can often increase market share. This puts a downward pressure on prices.

Pricing tactics

Once a company has decided upon its overall pricing strategy, it can also use price as a tactical promotional tool. PRICING TACTICS usually involve temporary, changes in prices to attract customers to specific products for a period. These pricing tactics may include the following.

Loss leaders LOSS LEADERS are products priced at very low levels in order to attract customers. The price of a loss leader is set lower than the average total cost of producing the product. The company selling the product makes a 'loss' on each product sold. Businesses use this pricing technique because they expect the losses made on the loss leader to be more than compensated for by extra profits on other products. It is often used by larger supermarkets which sell everyday products such as baked beans, bananas and corn flakes for very low prices. They aim to attract more customers into their stores, drawn in by the low prices. The 'captive' customers will then buy more highly priced and profitable items. Baked beans, bread and whisky have all been used by food and drink retailers as loss leaders in recent years.

Psychological pricing Many businesses seek to take account of the psychological effect of their prices upon consumers. This is known as psychological pricing. A common example is the use of prices just a little lower than a round figure, such as £199.99 rather than £200, or £29.99 rather than £30 for a period of time. Businesses using these slightly lower prices believe that they will influence the consumers' decision as to whether or not to purchase. Such slightly lower prices also suggest that consumers will be looking for value for money. For this reason, the producers of high status products such as prestige cars or designer clothing tend to avoid such prices. Instead, they often choose prices which psychologically match their consumers expectations of higher quality. So, for example, a price of £100 may be charged for a designer shirt rather than £99.99.

Special promotional offers These include offers such as buy one, get one free. Waterstone's, for example, has offered three paperback books for the price of two and Morrisons two pizzas for £5.

Discounts on normal prices In many industries businesses have fixed prices for products. For example sometimes there are manufacturers **recommended prices** or **list prices**. A discount might be offered on this price. This might be for a period of time, such as just before Christmas, for regular customers, such as special offers for loyalty card holders, or for people who buy larger quantities, for example schools getting discounts on supplies of pens, paper and stationery.

Introductory offers This is where the price a customer pays for the first purchase is lower than for subsequent purchases. For example, Broadband has been offered by service providers at £7.50 per month for the first three months and then £15.50 per month after three months.

Sales Sales are typically used to sell stocks of goods which have proved difficult to sell. For example, shops have sales in January for stock which has not sold in the peak selling season of September to Christmas. In some cases, businesses will run a sale on all their stock, whether it has been selling slowly or not. This attracts customers who are seeking a bargain.

KNOWLEDGE

1. State five pricing strategies a business might use.
2. Identify four different pricing tactics that a business might use.
3. What is price skimming?
4. Why might a firm use penetration pricing?
5. What is the difference between cost-plus pricing and contribution pricing?
6. Explain the difference between a price leader and a price taker.
7. What types of business might use pricet skimming as a pricing strategy?
8. Why might a business sell a product as a loss leader?
9. What is meant by psychological pricing?

KEYTERMS

Competition-based pricing – where a business takes into account competitors' pricing when setting its price.

Cost-based pricing – methods of pricing products which are based upon costs.

Contribution pricing - when a business sets its price to cover all of its variable costs, but only a contribution is made to its fixed costs and profit.

Going rate pricing – where price is set equal to the price of similar products in the market.

Loss leaders – products with prices set deliberately below average total cost to attract customers who will then buy other, more profitable, products.

Mark-up – that part of a price which seeks to provide a business with profit as opposed to covering its costs. It is used in cost-plus pricing.

Market-orientated pricing – where a business takes into account conditions in the market when setting prices.

Penetration pricing - when a business sets a low price in an attempt to enter a new market.

Prestige or premium pricing – where high prices are charged to reinforce the quality and luxury image of a product.

Price leader or price maker – a business that sets prices that other businesses follow.

Price or market skimming or creaming – where a product has a unique selling point may have a high price for a limited time in order to take advantage of the newness of the product.

Price taker or price follower – a business that is unable to choose the price it sets and follows the market price.

Pricing strategies – the pricing policies or methods of pricing adopted by businesses.

Pricing tactics – ways of using price as a promotional tool usually over a short period of time.

Tender – a bid to secure a contract for work.

Case Study: *Finding a deal that will float our boat*

With the summer travel season approaching, another ferry service is being introduced across the English Channel, raising the prospect of a price war on the more expensive western routes into France. LD Lines, which will run from Newhaven to Le Havre from May, is offering summer return prices from £142 for a family plus car. This route into Normandy costs less than a third of peak season prices into the Brittany ports further west along the coast.

It might only be a narrow strip of water, but there are huge variations in the cost of taking a car across – with some routes seven times more expensive for a crossing on the same day. Long criticised for their complex charging structures, ferries have become much more like airlines – with websites showing a much more transparent range of port-to-port prices. And after years in the doldrums, ferries have been making a modest revival, boosted by the soaring number of French holiday homes bought by Britons and by a disenchantment with the overcrowding and stress of airports in summer. While ferries might be a more relaxing way to travel, they can also be extremely expensive.

The great divide in this cross-channel market is between the west and the east. On the 'eastern' route, there are the short ferry crossings from Dover and the tunnel crossing at Folkestone into north-eastern France and the Pas de Calais. And on the 'western Channel' routes there are longer crossings to St Malo and Cherbourg.

These are two different holiday markets – one about high-volume, price-sensitive shuttling of passengers; the other a more leisurely, more expensive trip, with restaurants and cinemas.

On the highly competitive Dover route, passenger numbers are rising. Last year, 13.7 million people travelled through the port to Calais, Boulogne and Dunkirk. And the arrival of operators such as Speedferries and Norfolk Line has brought the budget airline pricing model, with one-way crossings for a car plus five passengers from £15.

A car with two adults and two children could travel off peak on the P&O Dover-Calais ferry route for £85 return. And depending on how flexible you could be about crossing times, there are still Eurotunnel summer fares for £98.

But on the western Channel routes it's been a different story, with Brittany Ferries dominating after competitors such as P&O pulled out. And the strategy has been to go upmarket rather than compete with the budget airlines. In terms of prices, the off-peak fare for a return trip from Portsmouth to St Malo, for two adults and two children, can be £300. And for some overnight sailings, accommodation is an additional, compulsory part of the booking. If you were travelling from the west country on the Plymouth to Roscoff route, a summer return could cost £689, if a cabin was included.

Spokesperson Steve Tuckwell says that rather than only focusing on price, passengers are ready to pay a premium for 'floating hotel' services. And although the budget airlines have 'eaten into our business' for short break trips, he says for longer summer holidays people prefer to take their cars on the ferry.

Source: adapted from *The Guardian*, 17.3.2007.

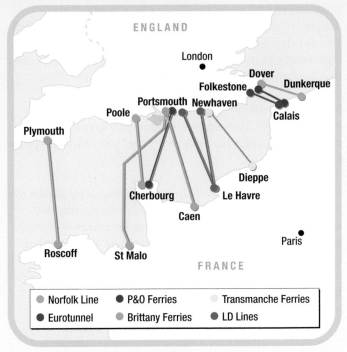

Source adapted from www.drive-alive.co.uk

(a) Using examples from the article, explain what is meant by:
   (i) price discrimination. (3 marks)
   (ii) cost-plus pricing. (3 marks)

(b) Explain the pricing strategy used by Brittany Ferries on its 'western' routes. (6 marks)

(c) Explain, using examples, why prices are higher on the 'western routes' than on the 'eastern' routes across the channel. (8 marks)

(d) Discuss how budget airlines might respond to the strategies used by their ferry competitors. (10 marks)

46 | Elasticity of demand

Demand

DEMAND for a product is the quantity bought over a given time period. For example, demand for cars in the UK in 2006 was 2.4 million vehicles. The quantity bought of a product is affected by a number of factors. These include:

- price – the lower the price, the higher tends to be the quantity demanded; the higher the price, the less tends to be bought;
- the income of customers – for most goods, the higher the income of customers, the more will be bought and vice versa. However, there are some goods, called **inferior goods**, where customers buy less of the good as their incomes rise;
- the price of other goods – for example, if one chocolate bar goes up in price by 10 per cent, demand for other chocolate bars is likely to increase if their price remains constant;
- advertising – successful advertising can increase demand for a product;
- seasonal factors – many goods, from ice creams and beer to toys and foreign holidays are affected by the time of year and the weather. For example, hot summer weather increases demand for ice creams and beer. The run up to Christmas is the peak selling time for toys and clothing.

Price elasticity of demand

Demand theory suggests that quantity demanded varies with price. The higher the price, the lower the quantity demand and vice versa. But it doesn't say by **how much** the quantity demanded will fall or rise if there is a change in price. This varies from product to product. The relationship between the effect of a change in price on quantity demanded is known as PRICE ELASTICITY OF DEMAND.

If there is a **large** percentage change in quantity demanded when price changes by a small percentage, there is said to be ELASTIC DEMAND. The word 'elastic' is used to give an idea that there would be a large response. Think of an elastic band. When you pull it, can you easily double its length? Then it is 'elastic'. But if it is thick, it may be difficult to change its length. It is 'inelastic'. This is also the case with price elasticity. If a large percentage change in price brings about only a **small** percentage change in quantity demanded, there is said to be INELASTIC DEMAND.

Take the example of a Mars Bar made by Mars Corporation. If it puts up the price by 10 per cent, and there is a fall in quantity demanded of 30 per cent, then the demand for Mars Bars is elastic. The percentage change in quantity demanded of Mars Bars is much bigger than the percentage change in price which caused it. But if quantity demanded fell only 5 per cent

when prices went up by 10 per cent, then there would be inelastic demand. The percentage change in quantity demanded is smaller than the percentage change in price.

It is important to realise that price elasticity compares **percentage** changes in quantity and price. Percentages allow the relative changes to be measured and compared.

The formula for price elasticity of demand

The exact value of price elasticity of demand can be calculated by using the formula:

$$\text{Price elasticity of demand} = \frac{\text{\% change in quantity demanded}}{\text{\% change in price}}$$

For example, say that the price of Mars Bars increases by 10 per cent.

- If the quantity demanded falls by 20 per cent as a result of the 10 per cent price rise, then price elasticity of demand is:

$$\frac{-20 \text{ per cent}}{+10 \text{ per cent}} = -2$$

- If the quantity demanded rises by 5 per cent as a result of the 10 per cent price fall, then price elasticity of demand is:

$$\frac{+5 \text{ per cent}}{-10 \text{ per cent}} = -0.5$$

Price elasticity of demand is always negative. This is because a rise (+) in price is always followed by a fall (-) in quantity demanded and vice versa. A plus divided into a minus is a minus. Because it is always minus, the sign is normally left out when talking about price elasticity of demand.

Elastic and inelastic demand

It is possible to give a more precise definition of elastic and inelastic demand using the formula for price elasticity.

Price elastic demand Demand is **price elastic** when it is **greater than 1**. This means that the percentage change in quantity demanded (on the top of the formula) is greater than the percentage change in price (on the bottom of the formula). A 12 per cent rise in quantity demanded resulting from a 10 per cent fall in price would give a price elasticity of +12 per cent ÷ -10 per cent or -1.2. This would be an example of elastic demand.

Price inelastic demand Demand is **price inelastic** when it is **less than 1**. This means that the percentage change in quantity demanded (on the top of the formula) is less than the

Question 1.

A stationery shop selling fibre tipped pens has estimated the following demand schedule for its products.

Table 1: Demand for fibre tipped pens

Price (£)	Quantity demanded
2	800
3	600
4	500
5	400
6	350
7	300
8	260
9	225
10	200

(a) Calculate the change in total revenue for fibre tipped pens of:
   (i) an increase in price from £2 to £3;
   (ii) an increase in price from £7 to £10;
   (iii) a decrease in price from £5 to £3.
(b) Explain why the business might be reluctant to raise prices above £7 per pen.

percentage change in price (on the bottom of the formula). An 8 per cent fall in quantity demanded resulting from a 10 per cent rise in price would give a price elasticity of -8 per cent ÷ +10 per cent or -0.8. This would be an example of inelastic demand.

Estimating price elasticity

There is no easy way to find out the exact price elasticity of demand for a particular product. The business environment is constantly changing. So when the price of a product changes, it is likely that other factors will change too. For example, competing businesses may all change their prices at roughly the same time.

One way of estimating the price elasticity of demand is to assume that all these other factors remain the same. Then a business could consider the impact of its price changes on demand in recent years. If it has changed price four times in four years, it could estimate the impact this has had on quantity demanded each time and calculate a price elasticity figure for each price change. These four figures might be averaged to provide an approximate price elasticity.

Alternatively, a business could use market research. It could ask customers how much they would buy of a product at different prices. Price elasticity of demand for the sample could then be calculated. A problem is that what respondents actually do can be different from what they say they will do in a survey.

A business could consider the behaviour of its customers. For example, the price elasticity of demand for the gas that British

Gas sells to households might be inelastic. A 10 per cent rise in price is likely to have little effect on quantity demanded. This is because households tend not to turn off their central heating when the price of gas rises. Most customers, also, won't switch to another gas company.

In contrast, a small clothing manufacturer might face elastic demand. All its work could come from larger companies that only want limited quantities of dresses or trousers. There are many UK businesses doing this sort of work and others in countries like India or China. So if it quotes a slightly higher price for a contract it is unlikely to get the order. In this industry, businesses find it difficult to raise their prices without losing many customers.

Price elasticity and sales revenue

Price elasticity of demand is important when developing a **pricing strategy**. This is because the price of a product affects **sales revenue**. Sales revenue is the amount a business receives from the sale of its products. It is calculated by multiplying the price of the product by the quantity sold. For example, a business selling 1 million products at £10 each would have sales revenue of £10 million (£1 million x £10).

Sales revenue is affected by the price at which a product is sold and price elasticity of demand. Assume that the product sold at £10 has a price elasticity of 2.

* This means that a 10 per cent increase in price would lead to a fall in quantity demanded (and therefore sales) of 20 per cent. Sales revenue would then fall from £10 million (1 million x £10) to £8.8 million (800 000 x £11).
* If, on the other hand, price was lowered by 10 per cent, quantity demanded (and therefore sales) would rise by 20 per cent. Sales revenue would then rise from £10 million (1 million x £10) to £10.8 million (1.2 million x £9).

This is an example of a more general rule. If demand is price elastic, then putting up price will lead to a fall in sales revenue. The increase in price will be more than offset by a decrease in sales. Conversely, lowering price when demand is price elastic will lead to a rise in sales revenue. The fall in price will be more than offset by an increase in sales.

Equally, the opposite relationship applies if price is inelastic. A rise in price will lead to a rise in sales revenue whilst a fall in price will lead to a fall in sales revenue. For example, if price elasticity of demand is 0.7, then a 10 per cent rise in price leads to a 7 per cent fall in sales. This leads to an approximate 3 per cent rise in sales revenue. This relationship between price elasticity and sales revenue is shown in Table 2.

Changing the price can therefore affect sales revenue. But the

Table 2: Effect on sales revenue of a change in price

	Elastic demand	Inelastic demand
Price increase	Revenue down	Revenue up
Price decrease	Revenue up	Revenue down

exact effect, and whether it leads to an increase or decrease, depends on the price elasticity of demand.

Price elasticity and profit

Price elasticity also has an effect on **profit**. Profit is calculated as sales revenue minus costs. Costs are likely to change with sales. The more that is produced, the higher the costs.

If demand is price inelastic, a rise in price will lead to lower sales but increased sales revenue as explained earlier. But the lower sales will mean lower costs. So profits will increase, not just from higher sales revenue but also from lower costs.

If demand is price elastic, an increase in sales revenue can be achieved by lowering price and raising sales. But higher sales also mean higher costs. In this situation, higher profits will only occur if the increase in sales revenue is greater than the increase in costs.

Factors affecting price elasticity of demand

The value of price elasticity of demand for a product is mainly determined by the ease with which customers can switch to other similar SUBSTITUTE PRODUCTS. A number of factors is likely to determine this.

Time Price elasticity of demand tends to fall the longer the time period. This is mainly because consumers and businesses are more likely to turn to substitutes in the long term. For example, fuel oil is highly price inelastic in the short term. If the price of petrol goes up 20 per cent in a week, the fall in quantity demanded is likely to be only a few per cent. This is because car owners have to use their cars to get to work or to go shopping. But over a ten year period, car owners will tend to buy more fuel-efficient cars. Businesses with boilers using fuel oil may replace these with gas boilers. Homeowners with oil-fired central heating systems might install more insulation in their houses to cut running costs or change to gas boilers. As a result, demand for oil in the long run is likely to be price elastic.

Competition for the same product Some businesses face highly price elastic demand for their products. This is because they are in very competitive markets, where their product is either identical (i.e. are perfect substitutes) or little different from those produced by other businesses. Farmers, for example, when selling wheat or potatoes are in this position. If they push their prices above the market price, they won't be able to sell their crop. Customers will simply buy elsewhere at the lower market price.

Branding Some products are **branded**. The stronger the branding, the less substitutes are acceptable to customers. For example, many buyers of Kellogg's corn flakes do not see own label brands, such as Tesco or Asda cornflakes, as good substitutes for Kelloggs. They will often pay 50 per cent more to buy Kelloggs rather than another brand. Successful branding therefore reduces the price elasticity of demand for the product.

Product types vs the product of an individual business Most

products are made and sold by a number of different businesses. Petrol, for example, is processed and sold by companies such as Shell, Esso and Total. The major supermarkets also sell petrol which they have bought from independent refiners. The demand for petrol is price inelastic in the short term. But the demand for Shell petrol or Esso petrol is price elastic. This is because petrol has no real substitutes in the short term. But Esso petrol is a very good substitute for Shell petrol. In general, a product category like petrol, carpets or haircuts has a much lower price elasticity of demand than products within that category made by individual businesses.

However strong the branding and however little the competition that an individual product faces, it is still likely that a business will sell at a price where demand is price elastic. To understand why, consider a product which has inelastic demand. As explained above, raising the price of the product would increase sales revenue. It would also reduce sales and costs of production would fall. So profits would rise. A profit maximising firm should therefore continue raising price until demand is price elastic.

If demand is price elastic, raising price leads to a fall in sales revenue, but also a fall in costs because less is sold. At the profit maximising point, any further increase in price would see the fall in sales revenue being greater than the fall in costs.

This would suggest that even strongly branded goods, such as Coca-Cola or McDonald's meals, have a price elasticity of demand greater than one at the price at which they are sold. It also suggests that luxury brands, such as Chanel or Gucci, also have elastic demand at their current price.

Problems of measuring price elasticity of demand

There may be problems for small businesses in calculating the price elasticity of demand for their products.

Collecting data A business wanting to know about the price elasticity of its products would need to collect data on demand changes in relation to price for its own products to know the price elasticity of demand for these products. This would mean that they would need to experiment with price changes and to

Question 2.

Kaldor Ltd manufactures reproduction juke boxes which play CDs. Jukeboxes that play old 45 records can cost around £1,000 or a great deal more. Large jukeboxes in pubs can cost thousands of pounds as well. But Kaldor had seen other 'reproduction' jukeboxes that did not cost as much and were far smaller. It decided to manufacture smaller jukeboxes that stand on a table. They sold for £200 and hold three CDs at a time. The jukeboxes have been selling well and so the business raised the price to £240. As a result sales fell from 800 to 600 per month. Kaldor is now questioning the decision to raise the price.

(a) Discuss whether or not the decision to raise the price was a good choice by the business.

monitor consumer reaction. For many small businesses, especially those with a very small number of customers this would be impractical. The dangers of experimenting in this way could lead to a loss of business that would be difficult to recover. Small businesses also often do not have the time or resources to research such matters.

Predicting human behaviour Human behaviour is notoriously difficult to predict and the way that people respond on one day of the week, for example, may be different to how they will respond on others. In addition, consumers do not always act as they say they will. For this reason small businesses attempting to research their price elasticity of demand by observing and talking to their customers may not always find it easy to collect reliable data.

Interpreting data When seeking to research their price elasticity of demand it is not always easy for small business to make sense of the data they collect. Take, for example, a small business selling ice cream from one retail outlet. Were this business to trial a new higher price for its ice creams on one particular day it might find that sales actually rose. They might conclude from this that their ice cream is relatively price inelastic. However, on this same day there could have been because several large coachloads of pensioners swelling the total number of potential consumers and especially high temperatures also inflating demand. In this case it would be difficult for the business to isolate the effect of the price change.

For these reasons many small business estimate their price elasticity of demand rather than calculate it based upon actual research. They will do so based upon their observations of how their customers behave, information from similar businesses and actual sales levels.

KEY TERMS

Demand – the quantity of a product bought over a given time period.
Price elasticity of demand – the responsiveness of quantity demanded to changes in price. It is measured as percentage change in quantity demanded ÷ percentage change in price.
Price elastic demand – when price elasticity is greater than 1, which means that the percentage change in quantity demanded is greater than the percentage change in price which caused it.
Price inelastic demand – when price elasticity is less than 1, which means that the percentage change in quantity demanded is less than the percentage change in price which caused it.
Substitute product – a product which has similar characteristics to another good. For example, gas is a substitute for oil as a fuel in heating systems. Shell petrol is a good substitute for BP Amoco petrol for use as a fuel in cars.

KNOWLEDGE

1. Explain, without using the formula, what is meant by 'price elasticity of demand'.
2. 'The demand for journeys taken on the London Underground is price inelastic.' Explain what this means.
3. (a) What is the formula for price elasticity of demand?
   (b) How does it differ from the formula for income elasticity of demand?
4. How can a business estimate the price elasticity of demand for one of its products?
5. Explain why a rise in price would lead to higher revenues if demand for the product were price inelastic.
6. Explain the link between price elasticity of demand and profit.
7. Explain why strongly branded goods such as Coca-Cola or Chanel perfumes are likely to be price elastic at the price at which they are currently sold.

Case Study: *Taxi pricing*

Bill Finch is a London taxicab driver. Towards the end of 1999, all the talk amongst taxicab drivers was about the new Millennium - whether they were going to drive or be out partying on New Year's Eve. In November 1999, the government, which sets London taxicab fares, announced that London taxis would be able to charge double rate for journeys taken between 8 pm on December 31 and 6 am on January 1st. Those taking journeys long enough to cost more than an ordinary fare of £25 would have to pay a flat rate £25 supplement. This compared to the usual New Year supplement of £3 per journey.

Bill decided he would drive on the Millennium eve, expecting that demand would be highly price inelastic. But he was disappointed with his takings. Many party goers had decided to stay at home because restaurants, pubs and clubs as well as taxis were charging double or more on the night. There was a general feeling amongst the public that they were going to be ripped off if they went out. Where journeys were

necessary, many took a private car and agreed in advance which of the party goers would be the non-drinking driver. Bill Finch found that he carried 30 per cent fewer passengers than he typically did on a normal Saturday night in the winter months. None of his journeys on the Millennium eve exceeded the £25 limit.

(a) Explain what is meant in the passage by 'demand would be highly price inelastic'. (3 marks)
(b) Explain (i) why it was expected that demand for taxi cab rides would rise on Millennium eve; (4 marks)
(ii) how this might have affected the ability of travellers to get a taxi cab ride on that night if fairs had NOT risen from their normal levels. (6 marks)
(c) Using the concepts of price elasticity of demand, revenue and profit, discuss whether Bill made the right decision to drive on Millennium eve. (11 marks)

47 Place

Place and the marketing mix

Place is one of the 4Ps of the marketing mix. It is no less important than the other Ps of product, price and promotion. However good the product, if it isn't available to customers to buy at the right place and at the right time, it won't sell.

The right place Products need to be available to customers in the place where they want to buy. For example, 75 per cent of all groceries in the UK are now bought from large supermarket chains. So if a grocery product is not available in a supermarket, its sales will be severely restricted. Equally, a car manufacturer might insist that parts are delivered to its plant by the component manufacturer. Unless the business agrees to deliver, it won't get the order.

The right time Products need to be available to customers at the time they want to buy. For example, often at Christmas there is a toy which becomes popular. Supplies may run out in shops. The manufacturer of the toy knows that unless it can increase supply to meet demand before 25th December, the sales it could have made will be lost. Equally, if there is a strike at the printers of a daily newspaper and a day's production is lost, those sales will never be recovered. Nobody will want to buy yesterday's newspaper today.

Coca-Cola has become the world's largest soft drinks distributor by making sure that its drinks are available to consumers not just in the right place, but also at a time when consumers want to buy. Coca-Cola vending machines, for example, are part of this strategy.

Distribution channels in consumer markets

The DISTRIBUTION CHANNEL for a product in a **consumer market** is the route it takes from manufacturer to the consumer. Figure 1 shows some common channels of distribution. They can be distinguished by the number and type of intermediary involved. A MARKETING INTERMEDIARY is a business or individual which acts as a link between the producer and customer.

Manufacturers to consumers DIRECT MARKETING involves a business selling its product straight to consumers. A manufacturer might advertise its products directly for sale to the public through advertisements in magazines. It might also operate a mail order catalogue or offer online ordering through a website on the Internet. It might even sell via its own sales representatives. Some manufacturers have factory shops where consumers can buy products. **Services** are also usually distributed straight to the customer, for example solicitors or accountants.

Manufacturers to consumers via retailers A RETAILER is a service business which sells goods to consumers. Retailers are typically called **shops**. But there are many other names for retailers, such as department stores, supermarkets and hypermarkets, superstores and convenience stores. Jewellers, butchers, grocers and hardware stores are also examples of shops.

Retailers provide certain services. First, they BREAK-BULK. They buy large quantities from suppliers and sell in smaller quantities to consumers. For example, a supermarket chain might buy 1 million packets of butter from a food manufacturer, but sell butter to consumers in single packets. Breaking-bulk is a service both to manufacturers and consumers. Most manufacturers don't want to sell in small quantities to consumers. Equally, consumers don't want to buy large quantities from manufacturers.

Figure 1: Examples of channels of distribution

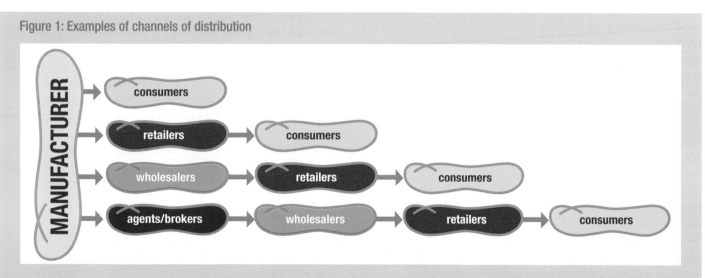

Question 1.

KFM Ltd manufactures interactive whiteboard software. Interactive whiteboards are used in education to support teaching and in business for conferences and presentations. KFM started as a small operation selling direct to customers from an industrial estate in Milton Keynes. It would place adverts in specialist magazines and often tailor products to the specific needs of customers.

Recently the business has expanded and now wants to sell more standardised products in greater quantities. KFM has been approached by a retail chain which wants to stock its product range in stores under the 'business and education' section. The retailer feels that the growing market in interactive whiteboards means that more customers will be looking for this type of software. KFM has also been looking to expand in the USA. It is interested in adapting its products for the US market. However, it is aware that legislation might affect its product specification and also that it lacks knowledge about the US market. It has considered a number of alternatives – using an agent to find a retail chain to stock the products, selling to a warehouse business or licensing the product to a US manufacturer.

(a) Examine the factors that might affect KFM's channel of distribution:
(i) as a small operation; (ii) as it expands in the UK;
(iii) as it expands abroad.
(b) Which channel of distribution would you advise KFM to use? Explain your answer.

Retailers also sell goods in locations which are convenient to consumers. A yoghurt manufacturer may have a plant in Wales, for example. But consumers in London don't want to travel to Wales every time they want to buy a yoghurt.

Retailers also provide other services which add value to the good being sold. These may include home delivery, repair services, extra guarantees and gift wrapping.

Manufacturers selling to customers via retailers is a **one level channel** because there is a single intermediary between manufacturers and consumers.

Manufacturers to consumers via wholesalers and retailers
A WHOLESALER is a business which buys goods from manufacturers and sells them to retailers. Some wholesalers call themselves a **cash-and-carry** because their customers, usually small shops, visit the premises and take away what they have purchased. In most cases, though, wholesalers deliver to retailing customers.

Like retailers, wholesalers provide two main services. They break-bulk and they are located or deliver to a location which is convenient to the retailer. They may also offer services such as trade credit.

The use of wholesalers is an example of a **two level channel** because there are two intermediaries between manufacturers and consumers.

Manufacturer to consumers via agents and/or wholesalers and retailers A manufacturer may use an intermediary called an

AGENT or BROKER. They bring buyers and sellers together. Agents are often used when selling into a foreign country. They often have better knowledge of the laws, needs of consumers and trading conditions in that country.

The choice of distribution channel

Which distribution channel is used depends upon a variety of factors.

Cost The longer the supply chain, the greater may be the cost to the final consumer. This is because each intermediary has its own costs to cover and wants to make a profit. Large supermarket chains often reduce these costs by cutting out the wholesaler and buying directly from the manufacturer.

However, in some cases short supply chains can be more costly than long supply chains. For example, a small upmarket food manufacturer may find that supermarkets will not stock its goods. To survive, it might have to supply directly to the customer, by mail order or the Internet. But the cost of a catalogue, an Internet site and delivery may be far more than the cost of supplying through a retailer. Some businesses employ sales representatives to sell directly. These can also be very costly.

Distribution Manufacturers may find it difficult to reach large numbers of consumers without an intermediary. This might be because the manufacturer lacks resources. It may not be able to afford to run a sales team, for instance. Equally, a manufacturer such as Heinz or Kellogg's may want to sell to every household in the country. The only way it can achieve this might be to use the large network of retailers, including supermarket chains.

Another factor may be knowledge of the market. A UK company that wants to sell a small quantity of goods to Australia may know nothing about this market. By using an agent to sell the goods, it will gain the agent's expertise.

Control Some manufacturers want to control the distribution channels they use carefully. For example, manufacturers of luxury goods or up-market brands, such as Chanel or Levis, don't want their goods being sold in supermarkets. This is because the place of sale can give important messages to consumers about the product. Expensive perfumes or jeans sold in Tesco or Asda detract from the exclusive image of the brand, according to their manufacturers. It is then going to be more difficult to sell these luxury goods at a high price and high profit margin.

Safety may be another issue. Some products require careful installation or maintenance. The manufacturer may find it easier to control safety aspects if it sells directly to the customer.

Legal factors The law may affect how a product is distributed. For example, drugs which need a doctor's prescription can only be sold through licensed chemists.

Distribution channels in business to business markets

The distribution channel for a good in a **business to business market** is the route it takes from the manufacturer to another business. As in consumer markets, there can be none, one or more intermediaries. For example, some businesses sell directly to others using their own 'sales reps'. Small tradespeople and businesses in the building industry, such as plumbers or carpenters, often buy from builders' merchants or building wholesalers. These intermediaries distribute products for the building industry. Agents might also be used by a producer dealing with a manufacturer in a foreign country.

Services are often distributed straight from one business to another, for example cleaning services, or through an agent, such as secretarial help.

The number of intermediaries depends upon a variety of factors, including cost and ease of distribution.

Distribution targets and objectives

A business that wants to be successful is likely to have clear **marketing objectives**. These are the goals that the business wants to achieve through its marketing, such as increasing sales.

When choosing which distribution channels it will use, a business will set DISTRIBUTION TARGETS. These are plans which might include, for example, the quantity to be sold over a future time period and to whom products will be sold. They will take into account marketing objectives. For example, a toy manufacturer that has the objective of increasing sales may set a target of selling 5,000 extra toys a month. It might decide that

Question 2.

Sales of CDs slumped by 8 per cent in the UK in the first half of 2007 but strong growth in legally downloaded music helped offset some of the decline. The collapse in CD and DVD sales on the UK high street has come into focus after music chain Fopp closed its 81 outlets last week. Retailers such as HMV and Virgin have come under intense pressure from low-cost online competitors as well as illegal downloading of music. However, the overall decline in CD sales was not quite as dramatic as the music retailers' woes suggest. The latest data from the BPI, the UK music industry trade body, showed that 60 million albums were sold in the first half of the year, down from 65 million in the same period in 2006. Nearly 97 per cent of those albums were sold as CDs.

Geoff Taylor, the BPI chief executive, said: 'CDs remain very attractive to consumers because of the flexibility and outstanding value for money they offer, and for this reason they represent the overwhelming majority of sales. Consumers vote with their pay packets and 58 million CD album sales in just six months is a very significant number indeed.'

The UK market for CDs is holding up better than other markets such as the US, helped by strong sales of UK artists such as Amy Winehouse and the Kaiser Chiefs. The BPI said that UK music fans buy more CDs per capita than anywhere else in the world, with the UK market accounting for more than 150 million sales for four years running.

The BPI also said the UK was 'ahead of the curve' in terms of legally downloaded music, with digital album sales partially offsetting the decline in physical sales. It said that 2.1 million albums were downloaded in the first half, with more than 100,000 sales a week achieved during June. Digital sales have also breathed life into the flagging singles market, helping to drive a 23 per cent increase in single sales in the first half of the year.

Source: adapted from *The Independent*, 11.7.2007.

(a) Identify the channels of distribution for music referred to in the article.
(b) Analyse the possible responses of a small UK based record shop/CD retailing business to the information in the article.

KEYTERMS

Agent or broker – an intermediary which arranges contracts for the sale of products between a supplier and a customer.

Break-bulk – dividing a larger quantity of goods ordered from a supplier and selling them in smaller quantities to customers. A key function of retailers and wholesalers is to break-bulk.

Direct marketing – selling by manufacturers direct to consumers without passing through retailers or wholesalers.

Distribution channel – the path taken by a product as it goes from manufacturer to the ultimate customer.

Distribution targets – goals set by a business for future sales of goods, for instance, through particular channels of distribution.

Marketing intermediary – a business or individual which acts as a link between the producer and customer.

Retailer – a type of business which buys goods from manufacturers and wholesalers and sells them, typically in smaller quantities and in a place convenient to the buyer, to customers.

Wholesaler – a type of business which buys goods from manufacturers and sells them in smaller quantities to retailers.

the best way to do this is to sell in bulk to wholesalers. Or a new computer magazine may want to target computer users. It may

decide to sell directly over the Internet for a charge, allowing buyers to download and print out the magazine.

KNOWLEDGE

1. Explain why it is important for businesses to have goods available for sale (a) at the right price and (b) at the right time.
2. What is the difference between a zero level channel of distribution and a two level channel of distribution?
3. Explain why a mail order catalogue is an example of direct marketing.
4. What is the difference between a retailer and a wholesaler?

5. What services do retailers provide to consumers?
6. What services do wholesalers provide to retailers?
7. What factors determine which channel of distribution is used by a manufacturer?
8. What channels of distribution might there be in producer markets?
9. Why are distribution targets important for achieving marketing objectives?

Case Study: *Sunny side of the street*

Kamil Soud is the proprietor of Matrix Mobiles a business selling mobile phones through their website cheaphonesonline.co.uk. 'With e-retailing you are always fighting to provide the lowest price, so I thought it might be good to get a shop' explains Soud.

'I could tell from the traffic on my website what type of people bought from us', Soud said and he had considered setting up in Brighton, but had some strong reservations, 'Brighton was just not right for that client group. There are a lot of lifestyle businesses which are set up there which really never make enough money to survive, so there is a high turnover of businesses, but they drive the cost of shops up,' he explained.

Not only is "location, location, location" the retailing mantra - but renting a shop on the wrong side of the street can be the difference between healthy profits and commercial disaster. This is where the big multiples have the edge. They spend thousands of pounds analysing local retailing environments before deciding where to locate. In particular, they use software that enables them to compare their knowledge of their existing customers with the demographic profile of a new investment area.

Until recently, it has been very difficult - and very expensive - for a new, small independent trader to match this expertise. Consequently, a large proportion of independent retailers close in their first year of trading. And the mistake of many, perhaps most, is that good ideas are ruined by opening in the wrong place.

To help him with his decision about where to open a shop Soud employed the services of a business called Cartogen. They did an analysis of the areas where he had thought about opening a shop. As any business advisor will say, saving a firm from making a bad decision is just as important as helping one make a good choice. And retailers that understand much more about their potential locations are likely to make much better commercial decisions.

Cartogen gives clients a clear indication of the mix of customer types within a catchment area, their behaviour and purchasing habits. Demographic data such as age, ethnicity, family structure,

employment status and housing type in any location is held on the database, along with behavioural information indicating the local population's lifestyle and spending habits. The database also provides information on potential competitors.

The service is offered across commercial retailing sectors - including bars, cafés, restaurants, health clubs and salons. "It works for all sectors, especially for customer profiling information," says Kennedy. But what makes the service particularly attractive is its affordability - a basic survey costs just £95, rising to £450 or £750 for more comprehensive information. Cartogen is keeping its charges low in the hope that initial surveys will lead to continuing retail consultancy services.

In the end Matrix Mobiles decided not to open a shop in Brighton after receiving advice from Cartogen. Paul Jukes is managing director of Vivid Design & Print, one of Cartogen's first customers. "It's great," he says. "I moved into my premises two years ago." But he remained concerned about the quality of his local market analysis, which he admits was "amateurish". "Cartogen checked all the area for me to check that my research was correct," explains Jukes. As a result, Jukes is able to commit more strongly to his existing marketing strategy, knowing that he chose the correct location for his business.

Source: adapted from The *Independent* 3.7.2007.

(a) Identify the distribution channels:
    (i) currently used by Matrix Mobiles; (3 marks)
    (ii) under consideration by Matrix Mobiles. (3 marks)
(b) Explain TWO reasons why finding the most suitable method of distribution is so important for Matrix Mobiles (6 marks)
(c) Examine the factors influencing Matrix Mobile's decision to open a shop. (8 marks)
(d) Discuss whether Matrix Mobile should open its own shop. (10 marks)

48 | Marketing and competitiveness

Markets and competition

There are many different markets in the UK. Markets might be divided by geographical boundaries, for example:

- local markets, such as the market for housing in South London;
- regional markets, such as the market for entertainment in the North West of England;
- national markets, such as the market for national newspapers in the UK;
- international markets, such as foreign exchange markets.

On the other hand they could be markets differentiated by use such as:

- highly specialised markets, such as the market for water polo playing equipment;
- non-specialised markets, such as the market for carrots.

Assessing the level of COMPETITION faced by business in a market may not always be straightforward. For example, two businesses operating on a local bus route may seem to have little competition but each other. However, they may actually face competition from other forms of transport, such as taxis, cars and trains

The degree of competition in a market will affect the **marketing mix** of a business. It will influence the:

- **prices** charged by the business;
- nature of the **products** offered by the business for sale;
- **promotion** used by the business to make consumers aware of the product and influence their spending;
- **places** where the products are for sale.

Determinants of competitiveness

Not all markets are the same. Different markets have different features and characteristics. The features and characteristics of markets are known as MARKET STRUCTURES. It is these market structures that largely determine how competitive a market is.

The number and relative size of businesses in the market In some markets, such as farming, a large number of businesses compete with each other. None of these businesses is particularly large compared to other businesses in the market. So the market share of any single business is small.

In other markets, a few businesses dominate the market, even though there might be a large number of other small firms. For example, in the UK washing powder and liquid detergent market, two businesses (Unilever and Procter & Gamble) have over 80 per cent of the market between them.

In some markets, there is only one business, a monopolist. For example, on most railway routes in the UK, there is only one train company operating a service.

The extent of barriers to entry In some markets, it is easy for a new business to set up. Many people each year set up small shops selling everything from groceries to clothes to toys. This is because the BARRIERS TO ENTRY are low. It doesn't cost much to open a shop. The amount of knowledge of the industry required is fairly little. In most cases, there are no special licences or other legal obstacles in the way. In certain markets, barriers to entry are high. In the rail transport industry or mobile telephone industry, the government gives licences to a limited number of businesses to operate. In the drug industry, newer drugs are protected by patent. This prevents other businesses from copying them.

In other markets, the costs of starting up a business are large. Car manufacturing, aeroplane production or oil refining are examples. In the perfume industry, the main companies devote a large proportion of their costs to marketing. Any new entrant then has to be able to afford to spend millions of pounds launching its new product.

Where barriers to entry are high, competition tends to be lower. One consequence of this is that businesses often compete on issues other than price. This means that they tend to emphasise the non-price elements of the marketing mix, such as promotion and place.

Potato supplier

Bank

Small cafe

Water supplier

Question 1.

(a) **Explain the factors that may influence competition for the businesses in the photographs above.**

Question 2.

It isn't difficult to set up in the grocery industry. A few tens of thousands of pounds will give you a grocery store on a little parade of shops giving personal service to the local inhabitants. But don't expect to survive or make a large profit because the grocery industry today is dominated by just a few supermarket chains.

Supermarket chains are valued in the billions of pounds. They do change hands from time to time. Asda, for example, was bought by the US giant Wal-mart in the late 1990s. Safeway was the subject of a fierce takeover battle in 2003 and was eventually bought by Morrisons. Somerfield made a huge mistake when it took over the KwikSave chain in the mid-1990s. However, it would be almost impossible now for a new chain to set up from scratch because it is so difficult to acquire sites for large new supermarket stores.

There is no rocket science involved in running a supermarket. Success is about making a few key decisions. What mix of goods are you going to sell? How are your stores going to present the goods for sale? How much are you going to charge and how much will you make in profit on each item? How are you going to organise your supply chain? What price will you offer your suppliers? Different supermarkets offer different mixes. Asda, for example, combines groceries with other goods such as clothes. Its market share has increased in recent years due both to this and to its low price policy.

(a) What is the relative size of businesses in the grocery industry?
(b) What barriers to entry exist?
(c) How do supermarkets differ in what they offer?
(d) To what extent is knowledge about how to run a supermarket chain available to all grocery store and supermarket owners?
(e) If Tesco increases its sales, what could be the impact on Asda?

The extent to which products can be differentiated In some markets, products are homogeneous. This means that they are the same whichever business produces them. Typically, there are standards to which products conform. So nine carat gold is the same quality whatever business produces it. Homogeneous products are often found in raw materials markets and in basic manufacturing, such as steel. Where products are homogenous competition tends to be largely based upon price with this element of the marketing mix emphasised.

In other markets, products differ according to which business makes them. A McDonald's meal is different from a Burger King meal. Ford cars differ from Volkswagen cars. Heineken lager is different from Budweiser lager. Individual products or product ranges can then be branded. The stronger the perceived difference,

the stronger the brand. Where product differentiation is strong the non-price elements of the marketing mix such as promotion tend to be emphasised by businesses.

The knowledge that buyers and sellers possess In some markets, buyers and sellers have access to all the information they need to make rational decisions. Buyers, for instance, would be able to find out the best price in the market. Sellers would have open access to the most efficient methods of production. This is known as having perfect knowledge. Where knowledge is perfect, price is strongly emphasised in the marketing mix.

In other markets, knowledge is not available to all. One business might not be able to find out how much a rival business is charging for its products. A consumer might not know which of 20 cars will be most environmentally friendly. If there is imperfect information in the market, this can give a competitive advantage to some businesses over others. Where knowledge is imperfect businesses will tend to place a great deal of importance upon non-price elements of the marketing mix such as the product and promotion.

Degree of interrelationship In some markets, the actions of one business have no effect on another business. Businesses are independent of one another. In farming, the decision by one farmer to plant a field with carrots has no impact on a nearby farm in terms of the price it will receive or how much it produces.

In other markets, such as car production, increased sales by one business will mean reduced sales by another business if the size of the market remains the same. Businesses are then interdependent.

Legal factors Competition between businesses is generally seen as being in the best interests of customers. They can shop around between businesses offering the same or similar products for the best deal. This means that businesses have to offer what the customer wants or face closing down through lack of customers.

In contrast, monopoly is usually argued to be bad for customers. They are forced to buy from one supplier whatever the quality of the product and whatever the prices. The monopolist has enormous power over customers and acts to maximise the benefits to itself.

Monopolies, therefore, tend to be controlled by governments. In the USA, they are illegal. In the UK and the rest of the European Union they are **regulated**. A monopolist exists where there is only one firm in a market. However, firms in a market can act as if they were a monopoly by COLLUDING. This means they get together, usually to fix prices and output in a market. They then have formed a CARTEL. For example, a group of firms making vitamins may fix a high price between themselves at which they will sell vitamins to customers. Then they have to restrict output between themselves to sustain those high prices.

The degree of competition and the marketing mix

Markets may be classified into a number of different types according to their mix of characteristics. The market conditions in which a business operates and the degree of competition it faces will affect its market mix.

Perfect competition PERFECT COMPETITION is a situation where there is a large number of small businesses, producing almost exactly the same product. Consumers are aware of what is being offered by all businesses. There are no barriers to prevent businesses setting up. Businesses are **price-takers**. They have no influence over the price they charge. If a firm charged a higher price than others, customers would know exactly where to go to buy an alternative. An example of this type of competition is found in agricultural markets. There are often many small farmers, each with a relatively small market share, producing almost identical products.

Businesses operating under these conditions have little or no scope to determine their prices. Therefore, they may have to consider other elements of the marketing mix, such as promotion methods or how distribution channels can be used. For example, some farms have attempted to sell directly to customers through farm shops, but others through national supermarket chains. Some farms have promoted themselves as free range or organic producers.

Monopolistic competition MONOPOLISTIC COMPETITION is a situation where there is a large number of relatively small businesses in competition with each other and there are few entry barriers. Each business has a product that is differentiated from others through **branding**. But the brand identity of

Question 3.

In January 2004 TelePassport Telecommunications, the first private telephone operator in Cyprus, pledged to reduce call rates by 15 per cent after gaining approval from the Telecommunications Regulator. Previously the only telephone company had been CyTA, a government controlled company.

TelePassport's president, Socratis Hasikos, said 'Statistics show that in 1998 CyTA made a profit of £50 million which increased to £62 million in 1999 and in 2001 reached £91 million. According to CyTA they expected to reap a profit of £107 million from the period 1998-2002, yet they earned a profit of £218 million. How can this be possible if they are not over-charging their customers? Now, they must present their costs and expenses to the Telecommunications Regulator, who has given them 15 days to do so.' He believed that CyTA delayed presenting its expenses because 'they have been paying out too much money and need to earn it back by charging more, or they have simply been ripping off customers'.

It was suggested that the entry of Cyprus into the EU would open the door to healthy competition for CyTA. Hasikos argues 'Our aim is not to attack CyTA, but to offer customers a better service at cheaper rates. Competition need not be negative, but could push CyTA into also lowering their prices.'

Source: adapted from www.xak.com.

(a) Identify and explain the type of competition before the entry of TelePassport Telecommunications into the market in Cyprus.
(b) Examine how (i) businesses and (ii) consumers are likely to be affected by the change in competition that is taking place in Cyprus.

products is weak. A business will face competition from a wide range of other businesses in the market with similar, but differentiated, products. Businesses operating under these conditions are not price-takers. But they will only have a limited degree of control over the price they charge. Examples of this type of competition in the UK might include legal service providers and certain types of clothing retailing.

Given limited scope for price changes, businesses operating under monopolistic competition may stress other elements of their marketing mix, such as product, place and promotion. So a business might use promotional techniques that help to compete against other businesses. For example, a financial services advisor might promote its services aimed at business investors. A clothing retailer may stock clothes aimed at a particular market, such as young people, older people or taller men and women.

Oligopoly When there are many firms, but only a few dominate the market, OLIGOPOLY is said to exist. Examples include the markets for petrol, beer, detergents, paint and sweets. The majority of businesses in the UK operate under this type of competition.

Under oligopoly, each firm will have a differentiated product, often with a strong brand identity. Several brands may be competing in the same market. Brand loyalty amongst customers is encouraged by advertising and promotion. Firms in such markets are often said to compete in the form of non-price competition. Prices are often stable for long periods, disturbed only by short price wars.

Although brand loyalty does allow some price control, businesses often follow the price of the market leaders. This means that they tend to be interdependent.

Barriers to entry exist. If it was easy for new firms to enter the industry, they would set up and take the market share of the few large producers. Examples of barriers to entry might be:
- legal restrictions, such as patents which prevent other businesses copying products for a period of time;
- high start-up costs, such as the cost of manufacturing;
- the promotion or advertising required, for example, in the tobacco or soap powder industries;
- arrangements between businesses, for example in the 1990s newsagents could not stock ice creams by other producers in certain manufacturers' freezers (known as freezer exclusivity);
- collusion between businesses in cartels, which act together to prevent new entrants.

Businesses operating under oligopoly emphasise promotion in order to maintain their brand. They promote heavily in order to develop and maintain brand loyalty. However, pricing may also be an important feature of the marketing mix. A strong brand may enable a business to charge a relatively high price for a product if, for example, it has a market leading brand. Customers loyal to the brand will continue to buy the product rather than switching to another.

Monopoly MONOPOLY occurs when one business has total control over a market and is the only seller of the product. This

pure monopoly should not be confused with a **legal monopoly**, which occurs in the UK when a firm controls 25 per cent or more of a market.

Monopolists are likely to erect barriers to prevent others from entering their market. They will also exert a strong influence on the price which they charge for their product. However, because monopolists are the only supplier of a product, it does not mean that they can charge whatever they want. If they raise the price demand will fall to some extent. Because of the influence monopolists have on their price, they are often called **price-makers**.

In the past, in the UK, certain businesses have come close to exerting pure monopoly power. For example, British Gas used to enjoy a monopoly position in the gas market. It was the sole supplier of piped gas in the UK. On the other hand, it could be argued that British Gas was operating in the energy market and therefore faced competition from electricity and oil companies. One of the main reasons why one gas company no longer exerts control over the market for gas is that the government introduced **legislation** to increase competition in markets where monopolies previously existed.

Today, the markets for water, power, rail and communications are regulated by **regulatory bodies** such as Ofcom (communications), Ofgem (gas and electricity) and Ofwat (water). Former state monopolies have been PRIVATISED. Limits are placed on their price increases. So telecommunications businesses offer an ever-expanding range of services and water and power companies promote to home-owners to attract their custom. In the absence of regulation monopolies may stress pricing as part of their marketing mix. Being the only provider of a product, they may seek to set a price that will maximise sales revenue. So the only supplier of a boat repair service in a harbour area, which has a **local monopoly**, may be able to regularly increase prices and not lose customers as there is no alternative service.

Methods of improving competitiveness

The market structure a business is operating within does determine to a large extent the competition that a business faces. However, businesses also adopt a range of strategies intended to increase their own competitiveness. The intention of such strategies is that they can compete more effectively within this given market structure. What businesses generally seek is to gain a **competitive advantage** over competitors.

Methods of improving competitiveness may be **marketing methods**. This will involve adapting and developing the marketing mix. The marketing mix is fundamental to a business' ability to compete effectively within a given market. By amending and developing its marketing mix a business can become more competitive. For example, a business marketing a fast-moving consumer good in an oligopolistic market might develop a new national advertising campaign that captures the imagination of consumers. This would enable the business to boost sales in the short term and, if other aspects of the marketing mix were developed to support this campaign, it might form the basis for a

medium- and/or long-term increase in sales.

However, the methods used may be **non-marketing** methods.

Reducing costs Businesses use a range of strategies to reduce costs, including the setting of new budgets, changes in management processes and procedures, renegotiating contracts with suppliers, reducing staffing and employing a range of measures to improve efficiency and productivity.

Improving quality For manufacturing businesses this means producing a product that consumers recognise as being of higher quality. For service providers it means improving consumer perceptions of the quality of service that they receive. For businesses other than those operating under perfect competition improving quality enables a business to increase its competitiveness in a given market.

Staff training Staff training is a key component in a business' efforts to manage their competitiveness. A well trained and efficient staff responsive to the needs and wishes of customers can enhance competitiveness considerably. This is true in all

KEYTERMS

Barriers to entry – factors which make it difficult or impossible for businesses to enter a market and compete with existing producers.

Cartel – a group of businesses (or countries) which join together to agree on pricing and output in a market in an attempt to gain higher profits at the expense of customers.

Collusion – in business, where several businesses (or countries) make agreements among themselves which benefit them at the expense of either rival businesses or customers.

Competition – rivalry between businesses offering products in the same market; competition may take forms such as price competition, distinctive product offerings, advertising and distribution.

Market structures – the characteristics of a market, such as the size of the barriers to entry to the market, the number of businesses in the market or whether they produce identical products, which determine the behaviour of businesses within the market.

Monopolistic competition – a market structure where there is a large number of small businesses producing differentiated, branded products, where barriers to entry are low and businesses are price-setters.

Monopoly – a market structure where there is a single business in the market and there are barriers to entry.

Oligopoly – a market structure where a few large businesses dominate the market producing differentiated, branded, products, where barriers to entry are typically high and where businesses are price-setters.

Perfect competition – a market structure where there is a large number of small businesses producing identical products, where barriers to entry are low and where businesses are price-takers.

Privatisation – the sale of government-owned assets to the private sector.

business sectors but it is especially the case in those service industries, such as personal services like hairdressing, where

responding effectively to customers on a daily basis is at the heart of the business' activities.

KNOWLEDGE

1. How do businesses compete with each other?
2. Explain three possible barriers to entry into a market.
3. Explain two ways in which businesses can engage in unfair competition.

4. In what ways might the marketing mix of a business operating under perfect competition and a business operating under oligopoly differ?
5. State three non-monetary methods of improving competitiveness.

Case Study: **UK sandwich sales**

Are British workers losing their taste for the traditional sandwich as their favourite midday snack? New research suggests that this may be so. Office or manual workers are more likely to have a ready-chilled curry in their lunchbox, rather than a cheese sandwich. Almost three-quarters told researchers for Geest, an own-label manufacturer of convenience foods for supermarkets, that they were fed up with sandwiches and about half said they looked forward to something hot to give them a boost. Some 30 per cent of the 919 employees questioned said they bought ready-chilled supermarket soups or meals to take to work and heat up in a microwave, taking a bite out the sandwich market. The survey also found that 17 per cent thought lunch was the 'highlight' of their working day. But a quarter described colleagues with plastic lunch boxes as 'very sad'.

The market for sandwiches in the UK is shared between a range of operators of varying size. These range from the supermarkets such as Tescos and Sainsbury's and large specialist bakers such as Greggs through to small independent bakers' shops and specialist sandwich shops found mainly in town and city centres. Important arrivals on the UK sandwich market in recent years have included sandwich chains such as Pret a Manger which is largely focused in big cities such as London and Manchester.

Bakers' shops have seen their share of the sandwich market slip in the past year with competition from sandwich and snack bars and supermarkets increasing, according to a new report from market research company Key Note. The report says bakers' shops (a category that includes the Greggs chain) are still the dominant player in UK sandwich sales but their market share in terms of the value of sandwich sales value fell from 28.6 per cent in 2005/06 to 26.4 per cent over the year to May 2007. At the same time, supermarkets have increased value sales up from 12.2 per cent to 13.4 per cent over the same period. Sandwich chains had a 9.8 per cent value share of the market, with Subway the dominant player with a 7.2 per cent share of sandwich sales by value, up 4.2 per cent.

Figures on total sandwich sales don't entirely correspond with the research conducted for Geest. Total sandwich sales were £3.73 billion in the year ending May 2007, up from £3.61 billion the year before, although the 2.46 billion packs sold in 2007 was less than the 2.54 billion the previous year. The report also says that 51 per cent of sandwiches sold

are wedges, 17 per cent rolls and baps, 13 per cent baguettes and 5 per cent sub rolls. Other sandwich carriers, such as pittas and wraps, accounted for 10 per cent of volumes.

Retailers say there are no signs of customers turning their backs on the humble British sandwich. Marks & Spencer, which claims to be the leading retailer in this sector, says it is 'an extremely buoyant market'. Its most popular sandwiches include chicken salad, prawn and mayonnaise and chicken tikka. However, the retailer says it has noticed an upturn in sales of foods which can be heated up, such as stuffed naans. M&S is also expanding its range of lunch foods and as recently as six weeks ago launched a line of sushi in response to customer demand.

Upmarket sandwich chain Pret a Manger also denies the threat of the ready meal to its sandwich business, saying people always turn to hot food in winter. The company adds that it is planning to increase its total number of shops in England to 200 from its present 74 over the next two years.

Source adapted from www.bbcnews.co.uk and www.bakeryinfo.co.uk.

(a) Explain what is meant by the terms (i) competition (3 marks) and (ii) dominant player. (3 marks)
(b) How would you classify the UK sandwich market? Justify your answer. (6 marks)
(c) Examine TWO factors that might influence the competitiveness in the Uk sandwich market. (6 marks)
(d) Explain how a small retailer might improve its competitiveness in the sandwich market. (8 marks)
(e) Discuss whether a small business could grow to dominate over 50 per cent of sales in the UK sandwich market. (10 marks)

Presenting data

Businesses gather a variety of data. Some data are used **internally**, within the business. Some are available to people outside the business, such as customers, suppliers or the government. Data can be presented in a variety of ways.

In words Data can be presented in written form. For example, a report might state that 'first quarter sales in 2008 were £1.2 million, falling to £1.1 million in the second quarter and £0.8 million in the third quarter, whilst rising to £1.5 million in the fourth quarter'. A QUARTER here is a period of three months. If too much data is presented in a report it can be difficult to read and understand. It can also be difficult to tell at a glance what is happening. For these reasons, data is often presented in a table or chart.

Tables Table 1 shows the data from a report in the form of a table. When presenting a table, it is important to number the table clearly if it is to be referred to elsewhere. It must also be given a title, which explains what the table shows. If the data refer to a period of time, this should be shown clearly in the title or on the table. Units of measurement must also be included, usually as a label for the table. In Table 1, the unit of measurement is '£ million'. Tables have the advantage over graphs that exact figures can be read. For example, in the fourth quarter, sales were exactly £1.5 million. This is more difficult to read off the line graph or bar graph in Figures 1 and 2. When there is a great deal of data, though, it can often be difficult to identify trends or see relationships between different variables in a table.

Line graphs Line graphs show the relationship between two variables. Figure 1 is a graph showing the data in Table 1. The two variables are time and quarterly sales. On a line graph, time is usually shown on the horizontal axis. The number of times something occurs, the FREQUENCY, and the value or amount, such as sales, are usually shown on the vertical axis. Line graphs are good for showing trends which can be seen at a glance. On the other hand, values of variables can be difficult to read accurately from the scale on the vertical axes. There can also be problems constructing or reading line graphs where there are several lines showing more than two variables, with very different values. For example, it would be difficult to construct a readable line graph with 2008 quarterly sales figures for 10 companies with sales

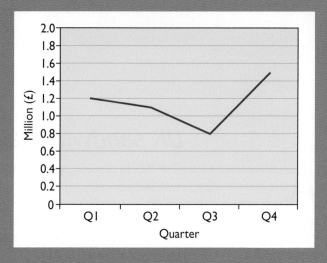

Figure 1: A line graph showing sales per quarter, 2008

ranging from £30,000 to £250 million. A table would be far more effective at showing this information.

Bar charts A BAR CHART shows information in the form of bars. Table 1 has been converted into two types of bar chart in Figure 2. The first is a vertical bar chart, the most often used of the two. As with line graphs, time is usually placed on the horizontal axis. The second is a horizontal bar chart. Here time

Table 1: Sales per quarter, 2008

Quarter	£ million Sales
Q1	1.2
Q2	1.1
Q3	0.8
Q4	1.5

Question 1.

John Menzies plc is a company which specialises in logistics - transporting products from one place to another for other businesses. Table 2 shows the value of its profit between 2002 and 2006.

(a) Describe in words the change in profit of the company.
(b) Construct a line graph showing profit between 2002 and 2006.
(c) Construct a bar chart showing the information in Table 2.

Table 2: John Menzies plc, profit before taxation 2002-2006

	2002	2003	2004	2005	2006
£ million	17.7	-0.10	37.6	36.7	35.6

Source: adapted from Menzies Group, *Annual Report 2006*.

Figure 2: A bar chart showing sales per quarter, 2008

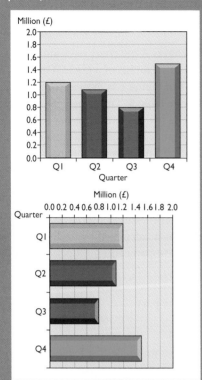

Table 3: Sales per quarter, 2007 and 2008

Quarter	£ million 2007	£ million 2008
Q1	1.5	1.2
Q2	1.3	1.1
Q3	0.9	0.8
Q4	1.7	1.5

Figure 3: A component bar chart showing sales per quarter, 2007 and 2008

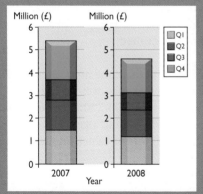

Table 4: Sales dispatched by cost of order, third quarter 2008

Cost of sales order, £	Number of orders
0-1,000	30
1,001-3,000	80
3,001-6,000	60
6,001-10,000	20

is shown on the vertical axis. A horizontal bar chart is simply a vertical bar chart turned clockwise through 90 degrees.

A **component bar chart** allows more complex data to be presented clearly on a bar chart. Table 3 shows the 2008 value of sales for the business in Table 1. But it also adds the 2007 figures. Figure 3 shows two bars, one for total sales in 2007 and the other for 2008. But each bar is broken up according to the sales for each quarter. These quarterly sales when added together make up the total yearly sales.

An advantage of using a bar chart is that it can be easier to read values from a bar chart than a line graph, but less so than from a table. As with a line graph, it is often easier to see trends from a bar chart than from a table. However, the more data displayed on a bar graph, the more difficult it is to read.

Histograms A HISTOGRAM looks similar to a bar chart. However, in a vertical bar chart the value of a variable (its frequency) is shown by the **height** of the bar. In a histogram, it is shown by the **area** of the bar.

Table 4 shows the number of orders dispatched in the third quarter of 2008 by the cost of the order. For example, there were 30 orders sent out costing between £0 and £1,000 and 20 orders costing £6,001-£10,000. If the data were drawn as a vertical bar chart, as in Figure 4, there would be four bars of equal width with values (i.e. frequencies) of 40, 80, 60 and 20. On the horizontal axis, the bars would be labelled '£0-£1,000, £1,001-£3,000, £3,001-6,000 and £6,001-10,000'.

If the data in Table 4 is drawn as a histogram, as in Figure 5, the unequal ranges of the cost of deliveries are now taken into account. The horizontal axis is divided up into equal **ranges**. From the data in Table 4, an easy division would be to mark every £1,000. Then the bars are drawn.

- There are 30 orders in the first £1,000 range. This is shown by a bar with a height of 30 orders.
- There are 80 orders in the range £1,001 to £3,000. This is made up of two £1,000 ranges, whose average value is 40 orders (80 ÷ 2). So the height of the bar is 40 orders and its horizontal length is two £1,000 ranges (i.e. from £1, 001 to £3,000). The area of the bar is 2 x 40 orders, i.e the 80 orders shown in Table 3.
- There are three £1,000 ranges between £3,001 and £6,000. So, with a total of 60 orders over this range, the height of the bar will be 20 orders (60 orders ÷ 3).
- With four £1,000 ranges between £6,001 and £10,000, the height of the last bar will be 5 orders (20 orders ÷ 4).

Looking at a histogram compared to a bar chart, the visual difference is that the bars are of different horizontal length. Note too that there is never any gap between the bars. The bars form a continuous area. This is because the histogram records **continuous data** - data which covers a complete range of values.

Figure 4: A bar chart showing sales dispatched by cost of order, third quarter 2002

Figure 5: A histogram showing sales dispatched by cost of order, third quarter 2002

in Figure 5. The area bounded by the frequency curve and the horizontal and vertical axes is called a **frequency polygon**.

Pie charts A pie chart represents data as segments of a circle. The pie chart in Figure 6 is drawn from the data in Table 5. This shows the value of sales for the four largest companies in a market, and sales for all other businesses in the market. The pie chart has five **segments**, representing the value of sales for each company together with the 'all other businesses' component. The number of degrees of each segment is calculated by finding the proportion of total sales for each company and multiplying it by 360°. As a formula:

$$\frac{\text{Value of the part}}{\text{Total}} \times 360°$$

For example, the segment representing sales for Reading's would be equal to:

$$\frac{£0.9m}{£4.2m} \times 360° = 77°$$

Pie charts are useful for getting an idea of the relative values of the various parts of a total. However, unless clearly labelled with the absolute quantities of the parts, it can be difficult to read an accurate value off the chart. Pie charts are unsuitable for displaying complex data with many components. They are also not particularly suited for showing changes over time.

Mean, medium and mode

Frequently, businesses want to calculate an average. There are three types of average commonly measured.

The mean The arithmetic MEAN is perhaps the most often used average measure. Say that a business had sales over the last five years of £0.9 million, £1.2 million, £1.7 million, £1.7 million and £1.5 million. The mean is calculated by adding together the value of sales and dividing by the number of values. So the mean is:

$$\frac{£0.9m + £1.2m + £1.7m + £1.7m + £1.5m}{5} = £1.4m$$

The median The MEDIAN is the 'middle value'. It is found by placing values in rank order, from the least to the most. Placing sales values in rank order would be:

£0.9m, £1.2m, £1.5m, £1.7m, £1.7m

The middle value or median is the third number of the

Figure 6: A pie chart showing market share, 3rd quarter, 2008

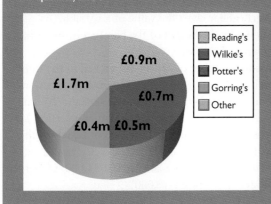

£0.9m
£1.7m
£0.7m
£0.4m £0.5m

Reading's
Wilkie's
Potter's
Gorring's
Other

Table 5: Sales of four largest companies and all other businesses, 3rd quarter 2008

	£ million
	Sales
Reading's	0.9
Wilkie's	0.7
Potter's	0.5
Gorring's	0.4
Other	1.7
Total	4.2

Sometimes, a **frequency curve** is added to a histogram. This is a line which connects the horizontal mid points of the vertical value of each histogram bar. This is shown

Question 2.

Table 6 shows the number of customers visiting a supermarket chain in four age ranges.

(a) Draw a histogram showing the number of customers in each age range. Note that there will be four blocks. Put age on the horizontal axis and frequency of customers on the vertical axis.

(b) On your histogram, draw a frequency curve.

(c) Explain in words where the frequency polygon is located on your diagram.

(d) Draw and label a pie chart to show the data in Table 6. Note that each segment of your pie chart will represent the number of customers in a particular age range.

Table 6: Number of customers visiting a supermarket chain

Age range of customers	Number of customers (millions)
10-19	0.6
20-39	1.4
40-69	2.4
70-79	0.3
Total	4.7

sequence of five numbers which is £1.5 million.

If there had been six numbers, the median would have been found by taking the mean of the third and fourth values, the middle two values. Assume that sales in the sixth year were £0.8 million. Then the rank order would be:

£0.8m, £0.9m, £1.2m, £1.5m, £1.7m, £1.7m

The middle two values are £1.2 million and £1.5 million. So the median would be:

$$\frac{£1.2\ million + £1.5\ million}{2} = £1.35\ million$$

The mode The MODE is the most frequently occurring number. In the sales figures only one number occurs more than once. This is 1.7. So 1.7 is the mode.

These three methods of calculating an average are useful in different circumstances. The mean uses all the data available. However, one untypical value can lead to a distorted picture. For example, assume that sales in one of the five years was not £1.7 million but £12 million due to a one-off special order. The mean for the five years would then be £3.46 million (£0.9m + £1.2m + £1.7m + £12m + £1.5m ÷ 5) and not £1.4 million. This is over twice as high as the values in the other four years. One advantage of the median and the mode is that a £12 million order would not influence the average because it would be an extreme figure. On the other hand, if there is relatively little data, the mode can produce unhelpful results. For example, can it really be said that the two years when sales were £1.7 million were typical simply because the mode is £1.7 million?

Moving averages

Sometimes, data can be subject to fluctuations. For example, most clothes retailers are faced with large changes in sales over the year. In the run-up to Christmas, sales peak and may be four

times greater than those in August. It can be difficult to spot a trend from such figures. One way around this is to calculate a MOVING AVERAGE. This smooths out fluctuations, allowing a trend to become clearer.

Table 7 shows quarterly sales figures for a business over three years. There are great fluctuations in sales between quarters. So it is not immediately obvious whether the business is performing better at the end of the period than at the beginning. Calculating a moving average should help make the trend clearer.

Moving averages can be calculated using any period of time. In Tables 7 and 8, they are calculated for three quarters or four quarters. The longer the period chosen, the more fluctuations from period to period will tend to be smoothed out.

A three period moving average Look at Table 7. Using a period of three quarters for averaging, the moving average for Q2 in 2006 is £3.3 million. This is calculated by adding together sales in the two quarters either side of Q2, i.e. Q1 and Q3, to Q2 itself and dividing the total by 3:

$$\frac{£5m + £3m + £2m}{3} = £3.3m$$

Table 8: A 4 period moving average: quarterly sales figures for a clothing retailer

Year	Quarter	Actual sales	4 period moving average	Centered 4 period moving average
				£million
2006	Q1	5		
	Q2	3		
			4.5	
	Q3	2		4.625
			4.75	
	Q4	8		4.75
			4.75	
2007	Q1	6		4.75
			4.75	
	Q2	3		4.625
			4.5	
	Q3	2		4.25
			4.0	
	Q4	7		3.875
			3.75	
2008	Q1	4		3.75
			3.75	
	Q2	2		3.75
			3.75	
	Q3	2		
	Q4	7		

Table 7: A 3 period moving average: quarterly sales figures for a clothing retailer

Year	Quarter	Actual sales	3 period moving average
			£ million
2006	Q1	5	
	Q2	3	3.3
	Q3	2	4.3
	Q4	8	5.3
2007	Q1	6	5.7
	Q2	3	3.7
	Q3	2	4.0
	Q4	7	4.3
2008	Q1	4	4.3
	Q2	2	2.7
	Q3	2	3.7
	Q4	7	

Similarly for Q3, the moving average is:

$$\frac{£3m + £2m + £8m}{3} = £4.3m$$

No moving average can be calculated for the Q1 2006 because there are no sales figures for Q4 2005. Similarly, the moving average for Q4 2006 cannot be calculated because there is no figure for Q1 2007.

Odd number moving averages are easier to calculate. This is because there is a **mid-point** in the series. The mid-point of a seven period moving average, for example, would be the fourth period, as there are three periods either side.

A four period moving average Even number moving averages are more complex. No single period provides a mid-point around which an average can be calculated. For example, the mid-point of Q1, Q2, Q3 and Q4 of 2006 in Table 8 lies **in-between** Q2 and Q3. Calculating a four period moving average for this in-between point would be:

$$\frac{£5m + £3m + £2m + £8m}{4} = £4.5m$$

Calculating a four period moving average for the mid-point of Q2, Q3, Q4 of 2006 and Q1 of 2007 would be:

$$\frac{£3m + £2m + £8m + £6m}{4} = £4.75m$$

To resolve this problem, a process called CENTRING is used. This allows an average to be plotted against a central figure. Look at Table 8. How can a four period moving average for Q3 2006 be calculated? One method is to take an average of the two figures above. This gives a centred average of:

$$\frac{£4.5m + £4.75m}{2} = £4.625$$

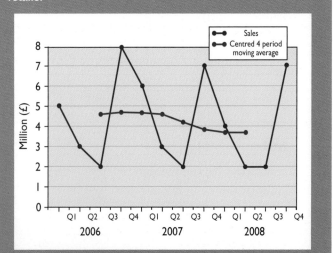

Figure 7: Moving averages: quarterly sales figures for a clothing retailer

Question 3.

Eco-Gaveda is a business which specialises in selling eco-friendly products by mail order. New customers are sent a catalogue with their first order. Table 9 shows the number of catalogues sent.

Table 9: Numbers of catalogues sent to customers

Year	Quarter	Actual catalogues
2006	Q1	500
	Q2	300
	Q3	100
	Q4	10,400
2007	Q1	540
	Q2	340
	Q3	170
	Q4	11,100
2008	Q1	580
	Q2	350
	Q3	210
	Q4	11,200

(a) Calculate (i) a three period moving average; (ii) a four period moving average; (iii) a centred four period moving average from the data in Table 9.

(b) Plot (i) the actual number of catalogues; (ii) the three period moving average data; (iii) the centred four period moving average data onto a graph.

(c) Discuss what the data indicate about the sales of Eco-Gaveda.

Mathematically, it is often quicker to add together the eight numbers which form the four period moving averages and divide by 8 rather than calculating the two averages and dividing by 2. For example, to calculate the centred average of Q3 in 2006:

$$\frac{(5+3+2+8) + (3+2+8+6)}{8} = 4.625$$

To calculate the centred average for Q4 of 2006 would be:

$$\frac{(3+2+8+6) + (2+8+6+3)}{8} = 4.75$$

It is possible to plot the data from Table 8 on a graph, as shown in Figure 7. Looking at Figure 7, a clearer trend picture can be seen from the centred 4 period moving average than from the sales data. Trading conditions deteriorated in 2007, but may have stabilised towards the end of 2008.

Index numbers

Table 10 shows sales figures for two companies over a five year

Table 10 Heart's and Tyler's, value of sales, £ million, 2004-2008

	£ million	
	Heart's	**Tyler's**
2004	742.3	487.4
2005	769.6	521.5
2006	801.5	560.5
2007	802.6	587.8
2008	826.5	599.0

Table 11 Heart's and Tyler's, index of the value of sales, 2004-2008, 2004 = 100

	2004 = 100	
	Heart's	**Tyler's**
2004	100.0	100.0
2005	103.7	107.0
2006	108.0	115.0
2007	108.1	120.6
2008	111.3	122.9

£769.6 million in 2005. If £742.3 million is 'called' 100, then the index value of £769.6 million is 103.7. This is calculated as:

$$\frac{2005 \text{ value}}{2006 \text{ value}} \times 100$$

i.e. 769.6 ÷ 742.3 x 100 = 103.7. The same process is used to calculate the index numbers for sales in 2006-2008, shown in Table 11.

One advantage of using index numbers is clear from Table 11. It is much easier to see at a glance how Heart's has performed. Instead of the large numbers used before, it can be seen that over the five period sales rose by 11.3 per cent. It is also possible to compare the performance of Tyler's with Heart's. The 1998 value of sales for Tyler's is also 'called' 100, since 1998 is the BASE PERIOD. This is the year around which all other values are compared. In relative terms, Tyler's has outperformed Heart's. Its sales over the five year period increased by 22.9 per cent, compared to 11.3 per cent for Heart's.

The disadvantage of using index numbers is that they do not give absolute values. For example, just using the data in Table 11, it is not possible to say how much in £ million were the sales of

period. It is not obvious which company has performed better. One way to make comparisons easier is to present the data in INDEX NUMBER form. This converts one value into the number 100. The rest of the values are then changed so that their proportions remain the same. For example, Heart's sales in 2004 were £742.3 million. They increased to

Heart's in 2008. Nor is it possible to say which of the two companies had the largest sales turnover.

Index numbers can be used to simplify the presentation of a single set of data, as in Tables 10 and 11. They are also used when the results of complex averages are presented. Indexes often mentioned in the news are the **Retail Price Index (RPI)** and the **Consumer Price Index (CPI)**. The RPI is an average of the prices of a typical basket of goods and services bought in the UK by the average household. It is calculated monthly from thousands of different prices which are averaged out using a complex formula based on the relative amounts spent on different items. Rather than saying that the average household spent £1,263.98 last month on this typical basket of goods, the value is converted into index number form. This makes it much easier to see the relative **change** in prices from month to month and year to year. This relative change in prices is called the **rate of inflation**. It is easier to see that the rate of inflation was approximately 2 per cent when the index of prices rose from 106 to 108 than if the price of the average basket went up from £1,263.98 to £1,289.26.

KNOWLEDGE

1. What is the difference between a line graph and a bar chart?
2. What is a component bar chart?
3. What is the difference between a bar chart and a histogram?
4. Total sales for a company are £300 million. Of this, £200 million comes from the UK and £100 million from the USA. If you were drawing a pie chart to show this, how many degrees would you measure to draw the segment for (a) UK sales and (b) US sales?
5. Using an example, explain the difference between the mean, the median and the mode of a set of sales figures.
6. Using an example, explain the difference between the way that a three period moving average would be calculated and the way a four period moving average would be calculated.
7. Sales for company A increased by 10 per cent between 2008 and 2009. Over the same period company B saw its sales increase by 20 per cent. Using 2008 as the base year, explain how this data could be expressed in index number form.

Question 4.

Severn Trent Water and Bristol Water are two UK water companies. Table 12 shows the value of sales turnover of the two companies between 2003 and 2007.

(a) (i) Convert the sales turnover figures for Severn Trent Water into index number form using 2003 as the base year. (ii) Do the same for Bristol Water.

(b) Compare the sales performance of the two companies between 2003 and 2007.

Table 12: Sales turnover: Severn Trent Water and Bristol Water

	£ million	
	Severn Trent Water	**Bristol Water**
2003	1,852	70.0
2004	2,015	70.6
2005	1,252	70.6
2006	1,455	81.9
2007	1,480	86.3

Source: adapted from Severn Trent Water, Bristol Water, *Annual Report and Accounts*.

KEYTERMS

Bar chart – a graphical presentation of data where the value of a variable (its frequency) is shown by the height of a block on a vertical bar chart, or the length of a block on a horizontal bar chart.

Base period – the period, such as a year or a month, with which all other values in a series are compared.

Centring – a method used in the calculation of a moving average where an average can be calculated for a particular period rather than in between periods. It is used where there is an even number of periods, such as two periods or four periods, to be averaged.

Frequency – the total number of times a variable occurs; on a graph or vertical bar chart, it would be shown as a value on the vertical axis.

Histogram – a graphical presentation of data where the value

of a variable (its frequency) is shown by an area on the chart rather than, as with a vertical bar chart, the height of a block.

Index number – an indicator showing the relative value of one number to another from a base of 100.

Mean – often called the average, it is a method of representing a set of numbers by adding up the value of the numbers and dividing by the quantity of numbers.

Median – the middle value of a set of numbers when the data is put in rank order.

Mode – the value which occurs most frequently in a set of data.

Moving average – a method of smoothing out fluctuations in data by calculating an average for several periods around a single period and recording it as the average for that period.

Quarter – a period of a quarter of a year, i.e. three months.

Case Study: Littway

Littway plc

Littway is a UK based company which specialises in creating and producing high quality freshly prepared foods. It sells its 1,500 different products to retailers who in turn sell them on to consumers. Freshly prepared food is a fast growing segment of the UK market. Last year, it grew by 10 per cent compared to just 2 per cent for all food.

Although the freshly prepared foods sector continues to grow strongly, it still represents only 9 per cent of total food purchases by value. Less than one-third of consumers buy freshly prepared foods in any month, and for most product categories it is less than 10 per cent of consumers. In addition, the average purchase is two items per month or less. These statistics suggest that there is considerable scope for further growth.

Table 13: Real[1] household spending, UK 1971-2007, index numbers

| | | 1971=100 |
	Food	All household spending
1971	100	100
1981	105	121
1991	117	167
2001	137	227
2007	153	267

1 i.e. after inflation has been taken out of the figures.
Source: adapted from *Economic & Labour Market Review*, Office for National Statistics.

Table 14: UK market for freshly prepared food

	Total UK market £m	% UK market growth year on year
Sectors into which Littway sells products		
Ready meals	954	15
Prepared salads	289	2
Prepared leaf	249	22
Pizza (incl. in-store delicatessen)	259	5
Prepared vegetables	125	38
Fresh pasta	96	9
Chilled breads	70	7
Fresh sauce	71	9
Fresh soup	75	1
Dips	65	3
Stir fry	55	12
Prepared fruit	57	18
Other major fresh prepared food sectors into which Littway does not sell		
Yoghurt/Fromage frais	742	0
Sandwiches (multiple retailers & stores)	525	11
Hot eating pastry products	428	2
Dairy desserts	355	16
Chilled cake	247	16
Cold eating pastry products	215	4
Quiche and flan	162	12
Hot eating desserts	89	30
Party food	63	9

(a) Explain what is meant by an 'index number' (Table 13). (3 marks)

(b) Using Table 14, calculate (i) the mean growth rate of those UK markets in which Littway is active; (ii) the mean growth rate of those UK markets into which does not sell; (iii) the name and size of the median sector of the freshly prepared food market; (iv) the name and size of the mode of the sectors of the freshly prepared food market. (8 marks)

(c) Examine and compare the growth rate of total UK household spending with that of the UK food sector, freshly prepared food, and the sectors within it. (8 marks)

(d) Comment on whether Littway is pursuing a strategy which will optimise its growth and profit. (12 marks)

50 Study skills

Studying and assessment

Study skills are the skills that a student needs to plan, organise and carry out their work effectively. They also help a student to answer questions and carry out tasks which are designed to test their abilities. This unit and the next are set out like a manual. They provide guidance and examples to help students when working in term time or when taking examinations. Examples are shown in italics. The units could be used:

- at the start of the course to get ideas on the best way to study;
- constantly throughout the course when studying;
- before examinations during revision preparation.

Action planning

Studying is more effective if there is a plan or strategy. An action plan can be formally written out, but it does not have to be. For any piece of work, it is important for a student to plan:

- how long it will take, bearing in mind any deadline;
- where the student will work;
- when the student will work;
- in what order tasks will be carried out;
- factors likely to affect the work, such as unforeseen occurrences.

A plan can be made for an individual piece of work, work over a term, coursework or project work, revision or an entire scheme

Title and nature of work	What needs to be done? What is the focus? How will it be judged?
Start and finish date	What is the deadline? How long will it take?
Collecting information	Where from? How can it be obtained? What help is needed? How long will it take? How will it be used?
Carrying out the work	Where? When? How long? Who with? What order? Continuous or broken down? Help needed? What factors might affect the work? Possible changes?
Review	Did the plan work? Was the outcome successful? How could it have been done better? Was everything covered?

of work. It is important for a student to develop a **routine** of work that is effective. It is also important for students to be **committed** to complete the plan. The table below shows a possible action plan that may be used for study, work or revision.

Time management

An important part of the action plan is planning how long to study or work. Certain factors must be considered when deciding how much time to take when studying.

When to start and when to finish There is a deadline for most pieces of work. This is the date by which they have to be completed. It is important to start early enough and to leave enough time to finish the work. Some people work faster than others. This will affect the time they allocate.

How long the work will take Some pieces of work will take longer than others. Short answer questions will perhaps take less time than an essay. A piece of coursework or project work may take months. So will revision. Some people work more quickly than others, which may reduce the time taken.

How long to work The length of time spent on work can affect its quality.

- Spending a greater amount of time preparing and planning may improve a piece of work.
- The time spent writing may also improve work.
- Working for too long can be tiring and work may suffer. Sometimes it is better to take a short break.
- Some work, such as coursework and revision, cannot be done all at once and must be broken up.
- It is useful to try to break up revision, by learning as you go along. There is likely to be too much to learn in one session at the end. Spreading the work also allows practice.

When to study This will depend on the time available. Some people have a free choice of time. They could work in free time in the day, at lunchtime, in the evening or at weekends. People with part-time jobs or with great commitments may find it more difficult. They may have to work when they can. Sometimes there may be free time which could be usefully used, such as travelling to school or college on a bus or train. Students should also consider that it may not be useful to work:

- late at night because they are tired;
- after strenuous exercise because it may be difficult to concentrate;
- when they are doing lots of other things.

Where to study

It is important to consider where to work. Some students will work better in certain environments than others. Should you work at home or in a different place such as school, a library or another person's house? Issues to consider might be:

- the availability of materials. A library will have books you can use. It may also have a facility to find book titles, newspapers and magazines, perhaps on CD Rom, and access to the Internet. If you keep all your materials at home, it may be better to work there;
- ease of access. Working at home allows easy access to drinks and food. Some people may also want to take a break to watch television or do something else;
- comfortable or not? Working in a familiar environment, such as home, can make work easier. Other people prefer to work in a more 'academic' atmosphere;
- alone or in a group? Some people prefer to work alone. Others like to work with someone else, even if they are doing their own work. Sometimes group activities demand that people work together;
- silent or not? Some people prefer to work in silence as they concentrate better. Working in a library would allow this. Others prefer things to be happening around them.

Other learning considerations

There are other factors that students may want to take into consideration when working.

- Some people prefer to sit on a hard chair. Some prefer to be more comfortable and sit on a soft or relaxing chair.
- Some people like to listen to music whilst they are working. Others prefer silence.
- Some people prefer bright lighting so that everything is clear. Others work better in dimmed lighting.
- Some people prefer to carry out several tasks or activities at once. Others prefer to do one task and then move on to another.
- Some people prefer to eat or chew while they are working as it helps them to concentrate. Others don't.
- Some people learn better by moving around from time to time and some by standing up.

Learning and memory strategies

Different people learn in different ways. Some people learn and remember more easily when they hear something. Others prefer to see it written down and to read it. Some prefer a diagram or picture. Each of these styles of learning may be useful in different circumstances. If a student finds learning something difficult in one way, he or she might try another.

Written methods In many cases students will have to read information and take notes. This is often the most common form of learning on a course at advanced level.

A possible technique used to read information is to:

- choose a section of written material that you will read and quickly scan through it to get the overall idea;
- read the material more slowly;

- put the written material aside and recite the key ideas or points that you have read;
- check that you have covered the main points;
- if you have missed anything, re-read the information.

Often in work or for revision students have to condense large amounts of information into shorter note form. This makes it easier to remember. Steps to note taking may involve the following:

- reading the information and making sure that you understand it first;
- dividing up the information into topic headings and subheadings;
- making suitable notes that are clear and easy to read, and are in a logical order;
- underlining or highlighting important words or key phrases that will trigger memory of the point;
- using page references to the written material;
- leaving space for additions;
- creating an index for your notes, either using a card system or a computer package and updating the order.

Once you have a set of notes you can use the reading technique above to make sure you understand them or for revision.

Example – Business failure

In January 2008, Martha Williams walked out of her farm office for the last time. Her market garden business had ceased trading that day – it had run out of cash. In four weeks' time the assets would be auctioned off and the proceeds used to pay creditors. Heath Farm Food Supplies had become another victim of the 'credit crunch'. Martha needed to borrow around £40,000 to keep the business running until the spring when produce such as lettuces, spinach, watercress, rocket and other salad leaves would be ready to sell and generate much needed cash. Unfortunately, Martha could not find a single bank, or any other financial institution, that would lend her the money.

It all started to go wrong for Martha in early 2007. Against the advice of her accountant, Martha decided to purchase some new harvesting equipment rather than lease it. Martha believed that the long-term cost of leasing was far too high and would eat savagely into profits. However, the £45,000 cost of the equipment left the business very short of working capital. Martha argued that a good harvest would pay for it and the loan of £30,000 was easily affordable at current interest rates.

Unfortunately, during March and April a very dry spell of weather had an adverse affect on yields. In a six week period not a single drop of rain fell. This reduced yields by 40 per cent and put back the beginning of the harvest by five weeks. As a result Martha had to extend the bank overdraft by about £10,000. At about the same time interest rates started to rise. The Monetary Policy Committee increased rates three times in 2007. This raised costs for Heath Farm Food Supplies and the business was beginning to struggle. Martha realised that a problem existed and took some appropriate action. She decreased drawings, laid off a member of staff, cancelled all but essential spending and chased up a few long standing debts. This helped for a while but later in the year things got very tight. 'The problem is the yields' said Martha. 'They were 40 per cent down in the spring and since then they haven't recovered enough'.

In January 2008, the business received another very serious setback. One of its main customers, a local supermarket chain, had gone into receivership. The supermarket owed Heath Farm £24,000. This had been due in December 2007 and Martha had been waiting tentatively for the cheque to arrive. She knew that the customer had been struggling and in some ways was half expecting the news. However, it wasn't the end of the world. Provided some long-term funding could be raised Heath Farm Food Supplies would soon begin to flourish, Martha thought. However, she hadn't counted on the 2008 'credit crunch'.

Notes – Business failure (Heath Farm Food Supplies)

- *Heath Farm Food Supplies closes down in 2008 due to the 'credit crunch' – it couldn't raise £40,000 to boost cash flow.*
- *Early 2007, £45,000 equipment purchased with £30,000 loan – tight working capital.*
- *Poor weather reduces yields – bank overdraft extended to £10,000.*
- *Interest rates rise – business starts to struggle and action is taken to help improve cash flow.*
- *January 2008 - bad debt of £24,000 – can't raise cash – business collapses.*

Oral methods It is sometimes easier to remember or understand something if you hear it. When you meet people do you remember their name? If so you may have a strong oral memory. Strategies for learning might include:

- answering questions asked by another person;
- making oral notes onto a tape recorder and playing them back regularly;

- constantly repeating phrases or key words, perhaps in an order;
- make up a **mnemonic**, rhyme or phrase which can be repeated. For example, PESTLE analysis considers the Political, Economic, Sociological, Technological, Legal and Environmental factors that can affect a business.

Pictorial/visual When you meet people do you remember their face? If so you may have a strong visual memory. Visual material can provide an instant 'picture' of information. Sometimes it is easier to see relationships by means of visual representation. Visual information may make use of some of the note taking techniques explained above. It may also make use of photographs. Examples of visual presentation include the following.

(a) Mind maps. *Promotion methods.*
(b) Family trees. *The sources of funds.*
(c) Flow diagrams. *The stages in the design process.*
(d) Horizontal family trees. *Herzberg's two-factor theory.*
(e) Block diagrams. *Calculating profit and loss.*
(f) Method of loci. This involves taking a room you know and imagining certain key words in parts of the room. *Types of integration.*

Learning by doing You may think that you know something or know how to do it. But you might only find out if you test yourself by doing something. It may be possible to test yourself by using:

- classroom or homework activities you have already completed earlier in the course;
- activities in textbooks or workbooks;
- applying ideas in a project or a piece of coursework;
- past examination questions;
- your own activities.

(a) Mind maps

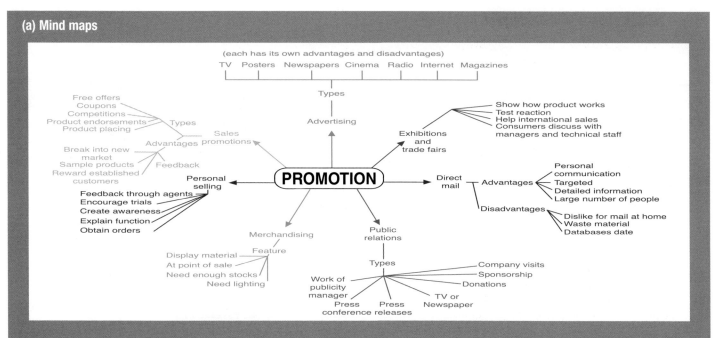

(b) Family trees

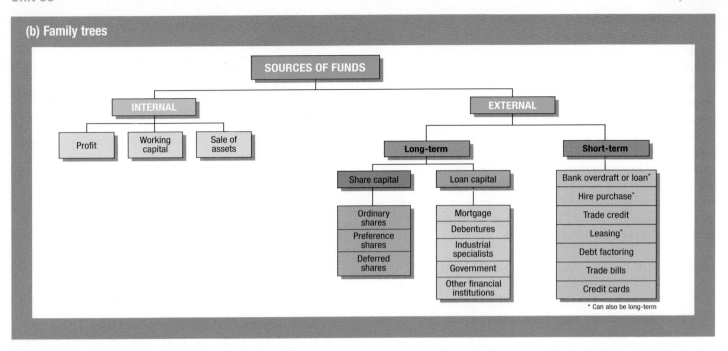

(c) Flow diagrams

(d) Horizontal family trees

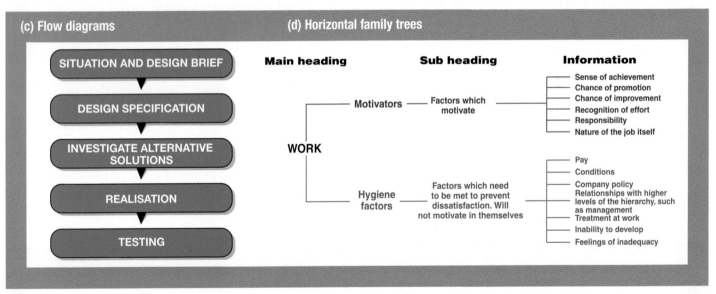

(e) Block diagrams

(f) Method of loci

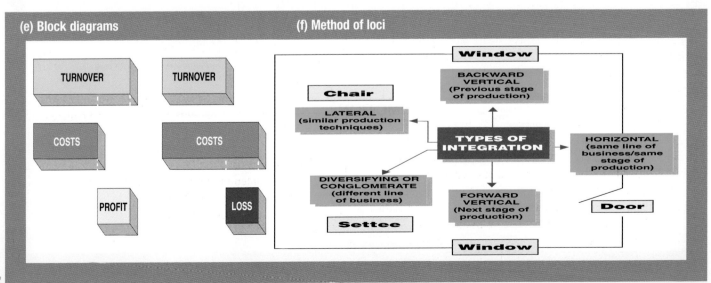

51 | Assessment

Assessment criteria/objectives

It is possible to use a range of criteria when assessing the performance of students. This means that examiners or assessors want students to demonstrate a range of different skills. In order to be successful students must:
- understand the skills required by examiners or assessors;
- recognise the skill that is being assessed in a particular question;
- demonstrate all of the skills assessed by the examiner;
- practice skills before the examination.

The criteria used by examiners may fall into the following categories.

Knowledge Students have to demonstrate that they:
- understand business theories and concepts;
- recognise and understand business terms;
- interpret information given in a business context.

Students can recognise questions which test knowledge by looking at the command words in the question. Such words are explained in the next section. An example of a question assessing knowledge might be: *What is meant by best practice benchmarking?*

Application and understanding This assessment criterion requires students to apply theories and concepts in both familiar and unfamiliar situations. This might involve:
- using a business formula in appropriate circumstances, for example, calculating the current ratio for a business;
- using a theory to explain why a business has chosen a particular course of action, for example, using McGregor's Theory Y to explain why a business has introduced quality circles;
- using a business theory to suggest a suitable course of action for a business, for example, suggesting that a chainstore uses loyalty cards to increase repeat sales.

Questions requiring application can again be recognised by looking at the command word. An example of a question requiring application might be: *Explain why the business has cut its research and development budget.*

Analysis Students have to demonstrate that they can break down information and understand the implications of what they have been presented with. Students will encounter both qualitative and quantitative information and will need to:
- identify causes and effects and interrelationships, for example, recognise from a graph that sales are falling and could be a result of new competition in the market;
- break down information to identify specific causes or problems, for example, realise that a business is suffering from inefficiency because according to the information

staff motivation has fallen, equipment is worn and working practices are outdated;
- use appropriate techniques to analyse data, for example, use ratio analysis to assess the solvency of a business;
- use appropriate theories, business cases/practices to investigate the question, for example, use elasticity theory to show that raising price may be ineffective.

Questions requiring analysis can be recognised by looking at the command word. An example of a question requiring analysis might be: *Examine the factors which have influenced the firm's decision to close its Cardiff factory.*

Evaluation Evaluation involves making a judgment. Evaluation questions are often used to award the highest grades in examinations. Students might be expected to:
- show judgment in weighing up the relative importance of different points or sides of an argument, in order to reach a conclusion;
- comment on the reliability of information or evidence;
- distinguish between fact and opinion;
- distinguish between relevant and irrelevant information;
- draw conclusions from the evidence presented;
- show judgment on the wider issues and implications.

Questions requiring evaluation can be identified by looking at the command word. For example, *To what extent has the decision to delayer the business been successful?*

When evaluating it is often possible for a student to draw a number of different conclusions. Examiners may be less concerned with the particular conclusion drawn. Very often in business studies there is no 'right' answer. They are more interested in whether students have actually made a judgment and also the quality of their argument in support of the judgment.

Synthesis Opportunities to demonstrate this particular skill may be limited. Synthesis is required in long written answers such as essays, project work or report writing. It involves bringing together a wide range of information in a clear and meaningful way. In particular, students must:
- develop points and themes in a way which builds on previous material and ends with a rounded conclusion;
- produce an argument in a logical sequence;
- provide a clear summarised argument which draws on all the individual elements.

Examiners will tend to look for evidence of synthesis in essays and report writing questions. The sections below on essay writing and report writing will explain how students can demonstrate synthesis.

Quality of language Codes of Practice may require the

assessment of candidates' quality of language wherever they are required to write in continuous prose. In these circumstances students are required to:

- avoid errors in grammar, punctuation and spelling;
- provide well structured arguments which are consistently relevant;
- write in sentences and paragraphs which follow on from one another smoothly and logically;
- express complex ideas clearly and fluently.

Command, directive or key words

When presented with a task or question as part of internally assessed work or externally assessed examinations:

- how do you know what the question is asking?
- how do you know what the assessor or examiner wants you to do?

In many forms of assessment certain **command, directive or key words** in a question will tell the student what is expected of them. Sometimes two or more words appear together in a question. They must all be taken into account when giving the answer.

Information and knowledge Certain command words are designed to find out what a student knows about the subject.

- Define - to state the exact meaning of a term or a phrase. *Define what is meant by marketing research.*
- Describe - to give an account or a portrayal of something. *Describe the hierarchy and span of control of the business.*
- Give - to write down or say something. Sometimes followed by 'an example' or 'an account of'. *Give an example of a private limited company.* May also be followed by 'reasons for' which may involve greater analysis.
- How - to present an account of something. *How has the business raised funds to buy new machinery?*
- Identify - to pick from a variety of information. *Identify three reasons for the merger.*
- Illustrate - to show clearly, often with the use of an example. *Illustrate the main methods used to promote the product.*
- Outline - to give a short description of the main aspects or features. *Outline the view of workers by management.*
- State - to write down or say something. Sometimes followed by what that 'something' should be. *State three features of an effective leader.*
- Summarise - to provide a brief account covering the main points. *Summarise the approach to quality at the business.*
- What - to clarify something. *What is meant by a stakeholder?*
- Which - to select from certain options or to indicate a choice. *Which location did the business find most suitable?*

Application and explanation Certain command words are designed to allow the student to apply knowledge to a given situation, to work out why something has happened and to give

reasons for something that has happened.

- Account for - to give reasons for. *Account for the growth in part time workers over the period.*
- Analyse - to examine the importance of certain things in detail, show relationships and make criticisms if applicable. *Analyse the approach to lean production of the organisation.*
- Apply - to bring knowledge to bear on a situation. Note that sometimes the word does not appear in the question. For example, 'Using examples from the article, explain how the business might promote its product' requires an application of knowledge to a particular situation. *Apply the Boston Matrix to the product mix of the company.*
- Calculate - to work out mathematically, usually numerically, but sometimes from a graph for example. *Calculate the return on net assets for the business.*
- Compare and contrast - to show the similarities and differences between two or more things. *Compare and contrast the approaches to recruitment of the two companies.*
- Distinguish - to show the differences between two or more things. *Distinguish between job and batch production.*
- Examine - to investigate closely to find out the 'truth' of the situation as if carrying out an inquiry. *Examine the factors that may have led to cash flow problems.*
- Explain - to make clear a concept, idea or viewpoint. It may involve giving an illustration of the meaning or examples. Note that it is sometimes followed by the word 'why' (see below). *Explain the pricing strategies used by the business.*
- Explore - to investigate or examine in detail, as explained above. *Explore the ways in which a business is affected by changes in interest rates.*
- Investigate - to carry out a detailed examination. *Investigate the factors that may have led the business to go into liquidation.*
- Suggest or give reasons for - to explain why, giving a justification. *Suggest reasons why the business chose to reduce its workforce.*
- Why - to present reasons for something. *Explain why labour turnover has increased.*

Evaluation Certain command words are designed to allow students to make a judgment or to evaluate a judgment that has taken place.

- Assess - an invitation to measure or place a value on the importance of something. *Assess whether the change to just-in-time manufacturing is likely to be successful.*
- Comment on - to give an opinion about the extent to which something has occurred. *Comment on the environmental policy of the organisation.*
- Criticise or critically analyse - to pass judgment on a debatable area. *Critically analyse the growing globalisation of business.*
- Determine - to settle, decide, or find out the nature of. *Determine the most suitable new location for the business.*
- Do you think - to comment on or give an opinion on the

basis of evidence. *Do you think the decision of the business to expand was a suitable strategy in the circumstances?*

- Discuss - to consider a contentious statement or to review an area which might have two or more views. *Discuss whether the business should have introduced group decision making.*
- Evaluate - to make an appraisal of something and to find out how important it is. *Evaluate the strategy used by the business over the period.*
- To what extent (does/do) - to make a judgment or to measure. *To what extent has the change in corporate culture been successful?*

Structured questions

The main features of structured questions are as follows.
- They contain several parts.
- The parts normally follow a sequence or pattern.
- Some of the parts may be linked in some way.
- They are generally accompanied by some data to provide students with a stimulus.
- The whole question may require students to demonstrate all skills covered by the assessment criteria, but only one part may be testing a particular skill.
- The parts of the question generally get more demanding as students work through it.
- Different parts may be assessed by different levels of response.
  Structured questions are broken down into 'parts'.

First part The first part of the structured question is usually the easiest. This may help students to 'settle' into a question and perhaps give them some confidence. The first part of a structured question:
- is usually designed to test knowledge of a business concept or business term;
- may require a student to perform a simple skill, e.g. a calculation;
- may require a student to give a straightforward explanation or definition;
- usually requires students to provide a basic level response.
- would carry only a few marks.

Examples
(a) *Explain the term 'working capital'.*
(a) *Distinguish between job analysis and job evaluation.*

Middle part The middle part of structured questions may vary. There is no set pattern and this gives examiners and assessors some flexibility when setting structured questions. However, the middle part of structured questions:
- may contain two or more parts;
- usually test knowledge, application, analysis and sometimes evaluation;

- may require students to perform simple or more difficult calculations;
- may require a mixture of straightforward explanation and more complex analysis;
- may carry more marks than the first part.

Examples
(b)(i) *Calculate the gross profit margin and the net profit margin for the business.*
　(ii) *Comment on your findings in (i).*
(b)(i) *Explain the meaning of the term price inelastic.*
　(ii) *To what extent is the concept of price elasticity helpful to a business?*
(c) *Analyse the possible reasons why increasing numbers of companies are introducing flexible working practices.*
(c) *Examine the possible implications of the data for:*
　(i) *employees;*
　(ii) *a large manufacturer planning to export for the first time.*

Final part This part of the question is usually the most demanding part. The final part of the structured question:
- will nearly always require a higher level response;
- will usually test knowledge, application, analysis and evaluation;
- will usually carry a higher mark allocation;
- may not be broken down into smaller parts.

Examples
(d) *Assess the view that business advertising practices should be more heavily regulated.*
(d) *Evaluate the non-financial factors which might influence the firm's decision to relocate its operations.*
(d) *Discuss the factors that have influenced the business to change its marketing strategy.*

Data response questions

Data response or case study questions are used to test student skills in unfamiliar circumstances. The key features of data response questions include:
- the provision of qualitative or quantitative data, or both, to provide a stimulus for students;
- hypothetical or real case study data;
- the use of structured questions;
- opportunities for students to demonstrate knowledge, application, analysis and evaluation.

Hints
- Always read the data at least twice.
- Use a felt pen to highlight important words, sentences or key numerical information.
- Read the structured questions very carefully, perhaps highlighting command words and other key terms.
- Some of your answers must be related to the data

provided.
- Some of your answers must use ideas, concepts and theories not mentioned in the data.
- Answer the parts of the question in order.
- Allocate your time according to the number of marks offered for each part.
- Show all your working out when performing calculations.
- Always attempt all parts of the questions.
- Do not use bullet points when writing your answers.

Answering the first part The information below contains data from a case study question. The data is just a small extract from the question.

The directors are recommending a final dividend of 18p, making a full year dividend of 27p, an increase of 8 per cent over the previous year. The Directors will consider further limited reductions of dividend cover in the medium-term, allowing real dividend growth to be maintained.

(a) Explain the term 'dividend cover'

- To begin with it is helpful to highlight the key words in the question and the key words in the data as shown above. This might help students to focus.
- To pick up all marks in this case it would be necessary to use a couple of sentences to explain the term and then give the formula which is used to calculate the dividend cover.
- The explanation needs to be crisp, clear and uncomplicated. Students need to demonstrate in their answer that they understand the term. The formula can be added at the end.
- A student could give a numerical illustration here. *For example, if a business made a total dividend payment of £300 million and net profit for the year was £500 million, dividend cover would be given by:*

$$\frac{Net\ profit}{Dividends} = \frac{£500m}{£300m} = 1.67\ times$$

Answering the middle part The data below is from another case study.

One of the things troubling Renton's is the accumulation of stock. Both stocks of raw materials and stocks of finished goods have been building up over recent years. The build up of finished goods is linked to poor sales performance. However, there seems no real reason why stocks of raw materials should have grown. The suggestion made by the production manager to introduce just-in-time methods may be worth considering.

Renton's current assets and current liabilities 2005 - 2008				
				(£)
	2005	2006	2007	2008
Raw materials	21,000	22,900	26,600	34,200
Finished goods	31,300	36,800	42,300	49,600
Other current assets	42,300	41,200	44,900	43,800
Current liabilities	109,900	113,500	119,400	138,600

(b) (i) Use ratio analysis to show how the build up of stocks is causing liquidity problems for Renton's.
    (ii) Analyse the advantages and disadvantages to Renton's of introducing just-in-time methods.

- Again the first step is to highlight the key words in the question as shown above.
- The question cannot be answered without reference to the data. The first part of the question requires students to analyse the data using a quantitative technique (ratio analysis)
- Students need to calculate the current ratio and/or the acid test ratio to comment on Renton's liquidity position.
- To earn all the marks in this question the student would need to perform the calculations correctly, interpret the results appropriately and draw a meaningful conclusion.
- In this case both the current ratios and the acid test ratios are below the 'ideal' range of 1.5:2 and 1:1 respectively. The acid test ratio is particularly low. This suggests that Renton's has liquidity problems.

The second part of this question requires more analysis.
- Again, begin by highlighting the key words in the question and data as above.
- Before writing the answer it is helpful to jot down a few key points for analysis, such as two advantages and two disadvantages of JIT. Advantages could be less money tied up in stock, more space for other activities or less waste stock. Disadvantages might be vulnerability to a break in supply, loss of flexibility in production or increased ordering and administration costs. These points are not likely to be in the case material. Students will have to bring in outside knowledge. There is nothing to be gained from identifying lots of advantages and disadvantages. The quality of application and analysis will generate marks for this question.
- Marks will be awarded for knowledge, application and analysis. Evaluation marks might also be awarded at this stage.

Answering the final part It is important that students leave enough time to answer this part properly as it usually carries high marks. The data below contains an extract from another case study.

It has been suggested that the economy will grow at a slower rate next year – around 2 per cent. Currently interest rates are historically higher than they have been in the recent past, for example in 2002-03. However, they are predicted to come down in future. The use of credit cards to finance spending is likely to continue and the amount spent using this method of payment may fall due to the higher interest rates.

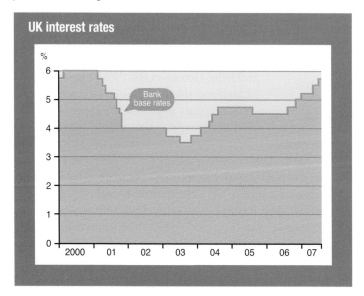

UK interest rates

(d) To what extent do external factors, such as those mentioned in the case, influence the performance of a business?

- Students will need to introduce a lot of their own material into their answers.
- Before writing, students should jot down a plan. A plan for this question might appear as follows.
  1. *Explain how external factors, e.g. interest rates, affect businesses.*
  2. *Identify two other factors which might affect businesses, e.g. consumer confidence, borrowing.*
  3. *Analyse the two factors.*
  4. *Evaluate, for example, by saying that external factors have a great influence because they are beyond the control of businesses. However, a good business will include their effect in its forecasting.*
- If the above plan is executed effectively the student will demonstrate all the skills required.
- Students should remember that it is not necessary to identify and list lots of factors. Listing is a low order skill and more marks are awarded for application, analysis and evaluation.

Decision making and problem solving case studies (unseen)

These are often in the form of extended case studies. They can be demanding and require a slightly different approach to answering than shorter data response questions.

- The case material tends to be hypothetical but is usually based on a real life situation.
- The case material tends to focus on a single business.
- The volume of material given is much greater.
- There tends to be some financial information in the case material.
- The case often emphasises analysis and evaluation skills.
- Many of the case questions require an integrated approach when answering. This means that students will need to embrace the full range of the specification in their answers. A single answer may need to address issues such as marketing, production, human resources, finance and external factors all at the same time.
- Questions set usually require students to make decisions or solve problems. For example, a question may require students to suggest a suitable future strategy for a business.
- One question will often require students to use a quantitative technique when answering.
- Examiners often want students to be critical.

Hints
- Skim read the case material to get a feel for the business, its people, its circumstances and its objectives (see section below on things to think about).
- Read again thoroughly, highlighting key information.
- Look at the numerical information and analyse it briefly, without performing any calculations.
- Make brief notes on the key objectives and key themes.
- Read the questions, highlighting command words and other key terms.
- Identify some business theories you might consider discussing in your answers. Questions will probably not request specific theories. The onus is on students to introduce relevant theories.
- Re-read the hints on answering data response questions above.

Issues to think about when planning answers
- People. Business is about people and your answers need to reflect this. Consider the age, family circumstances, the attitudes and personal interests of the people involved in the case material. What motivates them? What is their background? What are their objectives? What are their strengths and weaknesses? These are some of the people issues which students need to consider when shaping their answers.
- Situation. It is important to think about the context in which the business is set. Examples of issues to consider include the type of business organisation (Ltd, plc or sole trader), the prevailing culture, the type of industry, the nature of competition, the size, its financial position, its age, history and potential. It is often helpful to liken the case material to a business which actually exists in a similar context. However, this may not always be possible.

- Objectives. Answers to questions are bound to be linked to what the business is trying to achieve in its given context. A business may be trying to survive following a recession, it may be trying to break into new markets, it may be trying to raise finance for a big investment project, it may be trying to change its culture or take over another business. It is often useful to consider, and distinguish between, short-term and long-term objectives.
- Theories. Students should introduce business theories into their answers. There may be little or no guidance as to what theories are required. Students need to be on the lookout for opportunities to introduce some business theory into every answer they write. For example, if a business is considering a price change, price elasticity theory could be introduced. If a business is merging with another, economies of scale may be discussed. If a business is downsizing the effect on staff might be discussed, in which case motivational theories such as Herzberg or Maslow might be applied.
- Be critical. Be prepared to challenge statements or claims made in a case study if relevant and applicable. Students with an enquiring and critical approach will be rewarded.

Example 1

Most of the structured questions in decision making/problem solving case studies usually require lengthy answers with analysis and evaluation. Therefore it is important to plan before writing an answer. Below is an extract from part of an extended case study. The case study is about Henshaws Ltd, a components manufacturer for the computer industry. It has faced difficulties in recent years due to escalating costs. It is considering ways of improving efficiency and reducing costs.

> *One option currently being considered by Henshaws Ltd is to outsource its marketing activities. The directors of the company have not been impressed with the performance of this department. Their expenditure has consistently exceeded their budget and they seem to get new business and then lose it. In addition, communications between the department and others in the organisation have not been good. Two of the four company directors have long claimed that the company's strength is in manufacturing high quality components, although the other two directors argue that the company must avoid clinging to 'past glories' and move forward with the times. A number of marketing agencies have given presentations to the board of directors and a decision about whether to outsource marketing is imminent.*

(b) *Assess the likely advantages and disadvantages to Henshaws Ltd of outsourcing its marketing function.*

- To answer this question it is necessary to identify and analyse two or three advantages, identify and analyse two or three disadvantages and then evaluate by making a judgment about whether Henshaws should outsource

marketing or not.
- Although the question does not specifically ask for a judgment examiners are probably expecting one. This is because the mark allocation may be quite high.
- A plan should be drafted which might look like this:

Adv.	1. Costs fall.
	2. More focus on manufacturing.
	3. More effective marketing by specialists.
Disadv.	1. Redundancies.
	2. Loss of control of a vital function.
	3. Long-term marketing costs might rise.
Eval.	Yes - outsource because current marketing is expensive, ineffective and is causing problems. Henshaws will then be more focused and able to exploit its strengths.

- In the answer it is necessary to analyse the above advantages and disadvantages in detail explaining their relevance.
- In the evaluation some students may suggest that Henshaws should not outsource its marketing function. This does not matter. Examiners just want students to make a judgment and support it with a coherent and plausible argument. Remember that these case studies are decision making case studies and therefore a decision must be made!

Example 2

Some quantitative analysis is usually required in extended case studies. It may be quite complex and students often make the mistake of spending too long on this section. The data below contains an extract from an extended case study about a business which is considering a new investment. Arpan Shrinath & Co manufactures training shoes and Arpan is deciding which investment project to go ahead with.

Project 1. *Arpan has considered buying a large delivery van and undertaking his own distribution. At the moment he pays a local company to distribute training shoes to his customers. This has proved expensive and often ineffective.*

Project 2. *A new moulding machine has just been launched on the market by a German machine manufacturer. It is computer numerically controlled and would help to improve the quality of Arpan's products. It would also be more productive than his existing machine.*

				Expected returns				
	Cost	Year 1	Year 2	Year 3	Year 4	Year 5	Year 6	Total
Project 1	£15,000	£4,000	£4,000	£4,000	£4,000	£4,000	£4,000	£24,000
Project 2	£40,000	£12,000	£10,000	£10,000	£9,000	£9,000	£9,000	£59,000
Project 3	£30,000	£7,000	£7,000	£7,000	£7,000	£7,000	£7,000	£42,000

Project 3. *Arpan is becoming increasingly concerned that his office staff are working in conditions which are too cramped. Staff frequently complain and he is aware of inefficiencies due to a lack of space. He is considering the construction of a purpose built annex to the factory where office staff can work more effectively.*

The table on the previous page shows the costs and expected returns for each of these projects over a 6 year period.

(c) *Calculate the (i)payback; (ii)average rate of return for the three investment projects and decide which project is the most attractive. Take into account your results from the calculations and any other information you feel is appropriate.*

- This question requires knowledge and understanding of investment appraisal techniques. Provided students have revised the quantitative techniques required they just need to apply the appropriate formulae.
- It is often helpful to produce calculations (or the results of calculations) in tables. One way in which the answers to the above question might be presented is:

	Project 1	Project 2	Project 3
Cost	£15,000	£40,000	£30,000
Total return	£24,000	£59,000	£42,000
Total profit	£9,000	£19,000	£12,000
Profit p.a.	£1,500	£3,167	£2,000
ARR	10%	7.9%	6.6%
Payback	3.75 years	3.88 years	4.29 years

- According to the calculations above project 1 appears the most attractive. It has the highest ARR and also the shortest payback period.
- There is likely to be other information in the case which will influence the decision here. For example, if customers are complaining about the quality of products, Arpan might decide to buy the new machine to improve quality, even though the projected financial returns are slightly lower.
- This question is likely to offer a high mark allocation. The calculations alone would not generate all the marks. Students must bring in other information from the case, use their own ideas and also evaluate.
- Some thought must be given to the setting out of numerical answers. Good presentation is important. Avoid deletions and sprawling calculations. Space answers generously and underline final answers.

Example 3

The final question in an extended case study often requires

students to suggest a strategy or give an overall view. The question might also carry higher marks. A possible question might be:

(d) *Taking the whole case into account, do you consider that the board of directors should discontinue production at the Newport factory?*

- Again, planning is very important here. A lengthy answer is required with relevant points being identified, thorough analysis and evaluation. Students need to bring together a range of relevant points and make a decision.
- Timing is also crucial. Students must ensure that they leave sufficient time to plan and write the answer to this final, and important, question properly.
- Students may use some of the material generated in other answers in the case. But obviously repetition must be avoided.
- Again, it probably does not matter in this question whether students suggest that production is discontinued or not. Examiners want to see a well structured, logical argument with a meaningful conclusion drawn.
- Remember to consider the people, the situation, the objectives and to introduce theories.

Pre-seen case studies

A pre-seen case study is a method of assessment which involves giving students case study material before the day of the examination. This allows students to prepare more thoroughly for the examination by analysing the information and forming ideas in advance.

- Case study material may be issued a number of weeks before the day of the examination.
- The structured questions relating to the case study will not be known until the day of the examination.
- Additional information regarding the case may also be supplied within the question structure.
- The nature of the material provided in the case is likely to be the same as any other case study, but perhaps in more detail. Students should read the previous sections on data response and decision making questions.

Hints
- The general approach to pre-seen case studies is little different from those which are not pre-seen. The only important difference is that students have a great deal of time to study the data. Again, the hints in previous sections on answering data questions should be read.
- There is much more time to read the material so more time can be spent highlighting key words and terms. Students could also note theories, issues or themes which are relevant.
- Any words, terms or theories which are unfamiliar or forgotten can be looked up in the text book. For example, if the case contains an extract from a balance sheet, it

might be helpful to consult the balance sheet unit to reinforce understanding of balance sheet terms and structure.

- It is helpful to try and predict possible questions which the examiner might set. This will allow students to prepare answers.
- Try to identify trends, patterns and links in the data and account for them.
- Get help from friends and parents.
- When answering the questions in the examination it is very important to answer the ones set. Students should not try to reproduce their own 'model answers'.

Essay writing

An essay is an assessment method used to find out how students can respond in depth to an open question. It involves writing in continuous prose and provides an opportunity to explain something in detail.

- The quality of grammar, vocabulary, sentence construction and spelling is particularly important.
- A strong emphasis is usually placed on analysis, evaluation and synthesis.
- Essay questions may be integrated and synoptic. This means that students must consider the full range of the specification areas when writing answers. Essays based on one section of a specification or syllabus, such as marketing, may draw on all areas within it.
- The length will vary depending on the time allocated.
- They require a great deal of thought and planning before writing begins.
- The use of real world examples to illustrate points is essential.
- The use of diagrams, such as the Boston Matrix, is encouraged.
- There is rarely a 'right' answer. It is possible for two students to put forward opposing arguments and for both to be awarded high marks. It is the quality of the argument which is important, not the nature of it.

Planning

- Read the question very carefully.
- Highlight the command words and other key words to help provide focus.
- Planning could be in two stages. Stage one might involve a two or three minute session where students jot down an explosion of points and issues they think might be relevant.
- Stage two would then involve sorting points into an appropriate order and planning out a structure which will accommodate an argument.

Introduction

- It is common to begin with a short introduction where key terms are defined and the question is put into context.

Some general information may also be given. An introduction should be no more than a third of a side long, for example.

The main body

- When writing the main body of an answer it is important to follow the plan and write in detail, ensuring that evidence of analysis and evaluation is provided.
- It is vital to answer the question. It is better to write one side of relevant material than five sides of 'waffle'.
- Never use bullet points in essays.
- Never use subheadings in essays.
- Never write lists in essays. Extra marks are not awarded for identifying a large number of relevant points.
- Remember to include real world examples where appropriate.
- It is inadvisable to switch emphasis during the essay. It is best to stick to the plan.
- Diagrams, graphs and other illustrative material may be used but make sure they are clearly labelled and explained in the text.

Conclusion

- It is important to write a conclusion. It may be a statement which answers the question 'in a nutshell', drawing on the points analysed in the main body.
- Conclusions should not repeat material used elsewhere.
- The best conclusions are those which demonstrate evaluation and synthesis.
- Students are often required to make a judgment or give an opinion. Do not 'sit on the fence'.

Example

It has been argued that the productivity of UK businesses falls well behind that of its overseas rivals. Suggest possible reasons why this might be the case and examine the measures which might be taken by UK businesses to improve productivity?

- Essay questions can carry a relatively high number of marks.
- The words highlighted in the title are productivity, UK businesses, overseas rivals, suggest possible reasons, examine, measures and improve productivity.
- The following ideas may be suggested for the essay.
  Define productivity, labour, capital, Rover productivity poor, Nissan good, lack of investment, lack of funds, lack of R&D, dividends too high, too short-termist. Standardisation, re-engineering, kaizen, JIT, outsourcing, virtual companies, TQM, benchmarking, work study, culture, trade unions, weak management, quality circles, technology, training, labour flexibility, delayering, downsizing.
- The ideas generated may not be in any particular order.

The focus in the above responses appears to be on production and ways of improving efficiency.

- Another two or three minutes spent planning might deliver the following essay structure.

Introduction

▶ *Define productivity - output in relation to inputs.*

▶ *An example of evidence which might support the statement is the low productivity of Rover compared with, say, Japanese car makers.*

▶ *Suggest that there is a number of approaches to improving productivity, some specific and some strategic.*

Main body

▶ *Analyse three possible reasons why productivity is lower in UK.*

▶ *Low investment, therefore inadequate and dated technology.*

▶ *Lack of R&D because the City wants higher dividends NOW.*

▶ *Trade unions may have resisted changes which might improve productivity.*

▶ *Explain that measures designed to improve efficiency might be specific or strategic.*

▶ *Analyse three specific measures - JIT, benchmarking and new technology.*

▶ *Analyse three strategic measures - kaizen, re-engineering and TQM.*

Conclusion

▶ *Argue that the statement is probably right for the reasons given. Evaluate by saying that one particular reason may be more important, e.g. lack of investment.*

▶ *Argue that the methods employed to improve efficiency depend on the individual firms and their needs.*

▶ *Evaluate by suggesting that particular methods may be more suitable, if, for example, a business has dated machinery new technology may have a very significant impact on productivity.*

▶ *Argue that all measures will require co-operation of staff if they are to be successful.*

- When the essay is finished it is important to read through it and check for errors such as spelling, grammar and punctuation. However, avoid frantic crossing out at the last minute because this tends to have a negative effect on presentation.

Index

Index

Index

Index